SPLIT VISION

THE PORTRAYAL OF ARABS IN THE AMERICAN MEDIA

Edited by EDMUND GHAREEB

blished by the AMERICAN-ARAB AFFAIRS COUNCIL

SPLIT VISION: THE PORTRAYAL OF ARABS
IN THE AMERICAN MEDIA
Edited by Edmund Ghareeb
Copyright © 1983
by the American-Arab Affairs Council, Washington, D. C.

Printed in the United States of America

The American-Arab Affairs Council is a nonprofit organization whose goal is to promote a better understanding between the United States and the Arab countries through publications and other educational programs.

American-Arab Affairs Council
1730 M Street, N.W., Suite 411
Washington, D.C. 20036
Tel: (202) 296-6767
Tlx: 440506 AMARA UI

Revised and expanded edition

First printing, June 1983
Second printing, November 1983

Library of Congress Catalogue Card Number: 83-071909

ISBN 0-943182-00-X
ISBN 0-943182-01-8 (pbk.)

For Shirin and Faris

CONTENTS

FOREWORD

When I was first assigned to the Middle East by *The Chicago Daily News* in 1969, in journalistic terms it was a world as different from today's as the world of the early telephone from the world of video tapes and cable television.

Let us be honest and perhaps even painfully so. The Arab world was set up—largely subconsciously, to be sure—in the minds of the American people and even of the American press as a kind of "outcast" world. The unspoken expectation of editors, friends and even of oneself was that the Arabs were a decadent and backward people, left behind by history and even slightly abhorrent in their ancient and odd habits of past times. Part of this was due to the overwhelming emotional and originally idealistic American commitment to Israel; part of it was due to one of those epic time lags between peoples and cultures; and part of it was due to deliberate Israeli and organized American-Jewish community influence and information.

It was at first quite a shock to many of us who thought of ourselves as honest and well-meaning to find that the Arab world was not at all made up of those stereotypes of lascivious sheikhs, doe-eyed women in flowing black robes with unrequited passions, and corrupt and/or revolutionary leaders (not to speak of whirling dervishes and riddle-bound sufis).

It then came as quite a shock to many of us, who genuinely believed ourselves to be fair-minded and uncorrupted, to see what had been done. What a surprise it was, for the first time, to find the great social purposes of oil wealth among the Gulf sheikhdoms! What a surprise to find that the Palestinians, whom we had thought of as only poor, sunken-eyed refugees in endless UNRWA-supported camps, had as many college graduates in the last quarter century as the Israelis! What a surprise to find in some quarters an energetic women's movement!

Then all of these original and dangerous misperceptions began to change, and I would go so far as to say that they changed because of the journalists, diplomats and scholars on the spot. It was not easy for them either. Indeed, it was often very painful. For the rewards—from the American public, from the editors, from the Israelis and from the American-Jewish community—all went to those who embraced the old concepts, the original but flawed perceptions. It is never easy to be different anywhere, although, as the great writer Vladimir Nabokov wrote, if one is to be fully and intelligently human, one must "avoid the cliche of your time."

Cliches, of course, make life comfortable, if they do not imbue it with truth.

Today, thanks to this brilliant and now representative array of American journalists and thinkers, the coverage of and thinking about the Middle East, the Arab world and the Arab-Israeli conflict have changed enormously. It is still a struggle, but both sides today are far more fairly and justly represented. Editors no longer look for the easy story; the search for the little relative truth about the area—the people and conflict that make up journalism and upon which everything from public perceptions to diplomatic policy is based—today is growing in soundness.

Still, those men and women who cover the Middle East take on extraordinary and often fatal risks. The war in Lebanon was far more dangerous—and with not many thanks from either side—for the correspondents than the war in Vietnam. Yet, without them, no one would ever have known what happened.

The Arab governments can still do more, much more. There remains a tendency to complain about anything that is not considered overwhelmingly "pro-Arab." Access to leaders and to news sources and information in many Arab countries is still difficult or even more difficult than before, although in other countries the situation has improved markedly. The tendency in war situations to make journalists into "new targets" for attack and arrest, particularly from irregular, guerrilla and terrorist groups, sometimes approaches a new insanity.

Yet, things have improved beyond what anyone would have believed in the early days. The old idea of "dishonesty" in American journalism, which was characterized by the acceptance of a bottle of whiskey at Christmas time, has now been broadened to include much more of the dishonesty and prejudice against, or disdainful coverage of, an entire people.

The brilliant and respected scholar and journalist, Edmund Ghareeb, has carefully brought together in these pages the most representative and revealing series of essays on this problem published anywhere. It is a story of much more than just journalism and scholarship in one part of the world, however. It is, finally, the story of man's mind and how information initially can misshape it and then, through the honest efforts and struggles of many individual people, finally come to shape it honestly.

Georgie Anne Geyer

viii

PREFACE

The Middle East is one of the most sensitive areas in the world today. It is a powder keg, ready to explode into war at the touch of any spark. The United States, like other responsible nations, is trying to act as a damper for such an explosion. There is much that we can do to influence all sides in the conflict, but we must be able to see the situation clearly before we can deal with it effectively.

Even if a settlement of current hostilities is achieved between Israel and the Arab nations, the problems of communication that have plagued U.S. relations with Arab nations will persist. If we are to see today's situation in the Mideast clearly, the misleading stereotypes and incorrect ideas about recent Mideast history must be cleared up.

The unfortunate fact is that the vision most Americans hold of the Mideast situation has been badly blurred since 1948 by the imbalanced presentation of the American media. This book is an attempt to describe this imbalance and document its existence, to trace its origins, and to follow its ramifications through American public opinion and public policy.

The American public today generally sees Israel as "little," "brave," "beleaguered," "heroic," while the Arab nations are seen as "backward," "ignorant," and "bloodthirsty." It would be virtually impossible to catalog all of the mechanisms by which the images of a "good" Israel and an "evil" Arab world have been formed. But it is useful to explore some of the more visible ones.

From long before the creation of Israel, the Arab image had been formed by stories of Crusades against the "murdering infidel," by the sultan of the Arabian Nights, and by films of Rudolph Valentino.

Leon Uris' fictional account of the beginnings of the Middle East war, *Exodus*, more than any other single expression, set the tone for the mass market. Uris ignored the years of history and the chicanery of Zionist politicians. He glossed over how the Palestinian Arabs were driven out of their lands to allow the creation of a Jewish majority, and thereby an exclusive Jewish State. The entire affair was boiled down by *Exodus* to a simple struggle for freedom by an indigent people against British colonialists and Arab aggressors.

ix

Perhaps the most fundamental lie told by Israeli propagandists is the claim that the establishment of Israel was justified because it was the original homeland of the Jews. Even if one totally accepted this statement, it is the most doubtful interpretation of laws of property I have ever heard. In addition, evidence documented by Arthur Koestler in his book *The Thirteenth Tribe* strongly suggests that European Jews, who dominate Israel and its government, are descendants of the Khazar tribe—a tribe of Turkic origin—whose only connection to Palestine was their adoption of Judaism as a religion. It would seem that the 2000-year old claim to Palestine of those demanding the right to return is apparently without basis, a fact that lays waste to whatever moral argument Zionist intellectuals have provided as a justification for displacing the Palestinians.

Descriptions by the media of terrorism committed by both Arabs and Jews are discussed in many chapters of this book. Boiled down to public perceptions, an act of terrorism committed by an Arab is labeled for what it is, "terrorism," but an act of terrorism committed by an Israeli is usually applauded as a "daring raid" or "retaliation" or as "seeking out terrorists."

The Irgun and Stern Gang had pretty much done it all by the time Israel declared itself a state in 1948. Among other things, they had massacred an entire village in Palestine, blown up the King David Hotel in Jerusalem, and sent letter bombs to British politicians, killing and injuring a great many people in the process.

In early 1973, the Israelis landed agents on a Beirut tourist beach and succeeded in assassinating three Palestinian intellectuals. Golda Meir declared that it was a "wonderful raid," a declaration duly carried in the American press without any words of reproach from editorial writers.

Israel has saved its best shots for the people of southern Lebanon, however. The five-year campaign of terror bombing southern Lebanon from Israel fits the classical definition of terrorism—indiscriminate violence designed to strike fear into the heart of civilian population. While the headlines in the United States screamed with the deeds of Palestinians at Quryat Shemona and Maalot, the incessant pounding of the Lebanese peasant population and Palestinian refugee camps barely was accorded honorable mention in the American press. According to news stories of this institutionalized terrorism, which were really nothing more than reprints of official Israeli military communiques, Israel was "searching out terrorists." Never did I see a news story or an editorial pointing out the lie contained in this propaganda line. Dropping phosphorous bombs, napalm and cluster bomb units on civilian villages and refugee camps full of women and children hardly qualifies as a gallant search for terrorists.

The same disparity appears when Arab threats to withhold oil are labeled "blackmail," although "diplomacy" is the word applied when the United States does the same thing.

Most of the coverage of Yasser Arafat's 1974 visit to the United States concerned whether the holster under his jacket contained a pistol, yet it passed lightly over the press conference of Rabbi Meir Kahane of the Jewish Defense League (JDL), who placed his pistol on the table in front of him and announced that he would kill Arafat when he came to New York.

The news media fail to carry on a regular basis the activities of the JDL in New York. I was totally unaware of some of their activities against the United Nations until I was so informed by U.S. diplomats there. While news editors did not think it newsworthy, I thought the JDL's attempt to bomb the Soviets' U.N. Mission with a radio-controlled drone airplane merited some kind of attention—including the fact that the JDL conducted a dry run in a New York park before aiming it at the Soviets. The plane was blown up by the FBI before it reached the mission.

The overall effect of the kind of coverage to which we have been subjected is to preserve the image of Arabs as terrorist murderers, and of Israelis merely as patriots defending themselves from belligerent neighbors. It is amazing that this public perception exists when you stop to think that most of Israel sits on Arab lands it forcibly acquired.

Jews, who have been primary targets of racism throughout history, would be shocked to be told that some Jews are committing racist acts on a continuous basis in their efforts to discredit the Arabs. We have all seen newspaper advertising by various Jewish groups of the most racist nature, seeking to inflame American audiences against the Arabs. The portrayal of all Arabs as either greedy, rich spendthrifts, or as murderous bandits is the primary thrust of this campaign.

Some people are so used to the situation that they fail to realize its insidiousness—just as for generations no one questioned the "fact" that Blacks or women are naturally inferior. But substitute "Jew" for "Arab" in many of these situations, and the racism of such statements is immediately obvious. Noam Chomsky summarized this situation well when he said, "The American press is regularly disgraced by racist caricatures of 'Arab sheikhs' who are bent on destroying Western civilization by raising the price of oil. Comparable references to Jews would be denounced as a reversion to Goebbels and Streicher. We read learned discussions of the 'the Arab mind,' the 'sham culture' that prevents Arabs from coming to terms with reality, Arab trickery and deceit and violence, the corruption of the Arab language, in which, we are informed, one can barely tell the truth. It is inconceivable that Jews or Israelis could be discussed in similar terms outside the literature of the Ku Klux Klan."

Numerous stories have appeared recently about some sort of powerful "Arab lobby" in the United States under whose auspices a massive grand propaganda plan has supposedly been designed to brainwash the American public. A recent rundown also appeared in newspapers identifying several lawyers who were lobbying for the Arabs, listing their salaries. I asked the reporter why no corresponding story appeared about the Israeli lobby, and his response was that he had written the piece based on who had been registered as a foreign agent. He could not respond to my statement that nearly every Jewish organization in the United States, such as B'nai B'rith, lobbied directly for Israel without registering as a foreign agent.

I find it strange that stories continually pop up in the press that Arabs are buying all the banks or property in the United States. In the first place, I've noticed that only Arab business acquisitions, which have been relatively few in number, appear prominently in the general news sections of newspapers. Normally, such transactions appear in the financial sections, if at all. Secondly, if newspapers were to report on their front pages that "Jews Buy a Bank," the outcry would be deafening, and rightly so. But stories of Arab purchases do appear, and the upshot of this kind of reporting is to further encourage a highly unfavorable image of the Arab.

Yet another deficiency of this one-sided view is the stereotyping of the Arab states into one whole. Average annual per capita incomes vary from $15,500 in the U.A.E. to $177 in Yemen. Population varies from close to 40 million persons in Egypt to only about 170,000 in Qatar. Yet all this is submerged in the label "Arab." With all this working against them, it is no wonder that the Arab nations have been unable to be fairly presented in the media.

Lopsided American support for Israel's objectives will continue, I am afraid, until the public's perceptions of the Middle East somehow change. It is axiomatic that most people in the U.S. electorate have little interest in Middle East affairs. Because of this, Members of Congress are relatively free to vote however they see fit, without much concern for constituent backlash. The propensity of politicians to cause the least trouble for themselves makes natural a vote in favor of the Israeli position. There is great pressure from the Israeli lobby for such a vote, there is no public sentiment against it, and thus there is no counter pressure to offset the pressure of the Israeli lobby.

The one-sided media coverage and attitudes toward the Middle East not only affect the public's perception of it and so their lobbying; it also directly influences the government—for the President and Congress all read *The Washington Post* and *The New York Times* each morning, and none of us have access to another, counterbalancing side of the story.

The rude awakening experienced by a great many members of the American press corps as a result of the 1982 Israeli blitzkrieg of Lebanon represents a new development. All of the events surrounding the invasion—the official lies by Israeli government spokesmen, the murderous invasion of the militiamen into the Shatila and Sabra refugee camps—marked a time when American journalists lost their innocence vis-a-vis their Middle East coverage.

But while they began to see—and to report—Israel in a different light, they have yet to view Arabs as anything more than ciphers, or chattels, who exist solely for the purpose of ridicule or as objects of Israeli and U.S. actions. The best and most recent examples of this kind of human neglect came immediately following the Shatila and Sabra massacre. *The Washington Post* devoted several days and dozens of column-inches recording Jewish American reaction to the massacre, but never thought to probe the feelings of even one Palestinian American.

Similarly, the *Post*, on Sunday, November 7, 1982, published an article by Joyce Wadler that attached a heroic coloration to Jewish Americans who are emigrating to Israel to settle the West Bank. We knew from the sympathetic article how Jewish Americans felt about settling in the occupied Arab territories (in violation of international law), but again the *Post* failed to consider, or to print, how West Bank Palestinians might feel about settlers coming from Manhattan to wrest away from them their land, their water and even their freedom.

It is this aspect of the de-humanization of people of Arab descent, this subtle (and at times not so subtle) racism that must be overcome in order that Arabs may be made safe from massacre, from occupation, from imprisonment. How does one teach the American press that Arabs die, and bleed, and cry for their loved ones just as everyone else? People in the Arab world cannot afford the horrible human cost which comes with slight changes in attitudes of the press. Their awareness must come in some way other than by massacres and invasions. Hopefully, this book will be a contribution to a needed change.

James Abourezk

INTRODUCTION

The role of the media in shaping a nation's policy and attitudes toward other peoples and cultures is a subject that has generated a great deal of controversy. To what extent does imbalanced and biased news reporting, editorializing and drawing of cartoons encourage the people of one country to support political hostility against another group? And even if reporters make an effort to present a balanced coverage, do their editors assign them to cover only certain events, or censor or edit the reporter's work according to their own perceptions of what is needed or what the public should read?

One area where accusations of bias in news media coverage have been made concerns the Arabs and the Arab-Israeli conflict. Charges are frequently made in the Arab world and by Middle East experts in the United States that the American media have been biased against the Arabs.

Stereotypes and caricatures provide a convenient shorthand in the identification of a particular group. Limits of time and space pressure journalists to use such a shorthand in identifying individuals, groups or causes. This means of identification, however, usually does not reflect the reality of the situation or the qualities of the individuals and groups being covered. Blacks, women and each of the immigrant groups have been stereotyped in the American media, and unfortunately the attitudes created toward these groups have not been completely erased. In many cases, though, recognition of the stereotype was the first step in changing it. But while the media have, through an evolutionary process, sought to discontinue pejorative characterizations of ethnic groups, Arabs, and as a result Arab-Americans, still suffer from malevolent and inaccurate characterization. Consequently, this book seeks to generate similar analysis of the stereotyping of Arabs. It is hoped that it will lead to further discussion of this subject by those within the American media and by others interested in the formation of American public attitudes toward the Arab countries.

The issues raised in this book will lead the reader to judge whether there has been a slant in the presentation by the American media of Arabs and their views. Because American popular attitudes are largely fashioned by the media's news and commentary, any change in those attitudes will be difficult to accomplish if the media continue to provide a distorted picture of the people, cultures and politics of the Arab countries. Yet given the commitment to fairness that has marked the American media throughout their history, it is possible that the challenge of accurate reporting of the Arab countries and peoples can be met. It is hoped that readers of this book will consider carefully the views expressed in the following pages, and will examine their own opinions in light of those views.

Each issue of the *Columbia Journalism Review* contains a quotation from its 1961 founding editorial. Just as it restates the mission of that esteemed publication, it also serves as a goal for this book. The quotation reads: "To assess the performance of journalism in all its forms, to call attention to its shortcomings and strengths, and to help define—or redefine—standards of honest, responsible service. . . , to help stimulate continuing improvement in the profession and to speak out for what is right, fair and decent." It is to be hoped that all U.S. journalists and media analysts who read this book will reflect on the characterization of the Arab peoples with the *Review* credo in mind.

All this book and other analyses can do is provoke fresh thinking on the subject. Any change obviously must come from the journalists in whose professional absence of bias is a public trust older than the United States itself. Few journalists today are proud of past stereotypes of minorities and ethnic groups, and I hope that this publication will mark the beginning of a period in which Arab stereotypes will be replaced by a more fair and equitable depiction.

This work does not contain a detailed content analysis of American media coverage of the Arabs; nor does it offer an extensive scientific study on the subject. Rather, the chapters in this book simply present the individual viewpoints of many prominent journalists and scholars who are directly involved or interested in reporting of the Arab countries in the United States.

The following interviews and essays were done during two different periods: 1975-77 and 1981-83. Part I was originally published in 1977 by the Institute of Middle Eastern and North African Affairs, Inc. All the interviews in that section were conducted by the Editor in 1975-76, with the exception of the one with Nick Thimmesch, which was done in 1977. Part II contains further interviews conducted from 1981-83 by the Editor, except for the one with Hodding Carter, which was done by Erik R. Peterson during the same period. Jack Shaheen's essay, which appeared in the first edition under the title, "The Image of the Arab on American

Television," has been updated and appears in Part II as "The Arab Image in the American Media."

The analysis of these two time frames will allow the reader to measure the evolution of attitudes in the United States toward the Arabs. Although it is arguable that changes of attitude are in evidence, and that as a result of recent events there is now a greater awareness of the Arabs in this country, it is equally arguable that many of the seemingly organic biases toward the Arabs continue to persist. The old adage goes, "The more things change, the more they stay the same." The following proves the aptness of that phrase.

The opinions and ideas expressed in the subsequent chapters represent solely the views of their authors.

I would like to thank the Editor of the *Journal of Palestine Studies* for permission to reprint interviews contained in Part I. I also wish to thank Helen Hage, Patricia Hleihel, Jim McCartney, William Ringle, Mara Gonzalez, Joe Malone, Rafic Maloof, Samir Nader, Walt Evans, and Lucinda Shastid for their pertinent observations on Part I, and Carol Anders, Claud Morris, Ann Luppi and Erik R. Peterson for their valuable suggestions on Part II.

Finally, for making it possible to expand and refine this work, I would like to express my appreciation to George A. Naifeh, President of the American-Arab Affairs Council.

Edmund Ghareeb

PART I: 1975-77

1

IMBALANCE IN THE AMERICAN MEDIA

Edmund Ghareeb

During the last decade the American media have witnessed the best and the worst of times and are now more powerful and more criticized than ever before. It is demonstrable that they have aroused the public awareness of injustice and the misuse of power. Their authority can also mold and channel public opinion according to their own biases and misconceptions.

The media survived the cynicism of the late 1960s. However, they have not been untouched by it. In unprecedented numbers and with incisiveness Americans have begun to question their public information services, and accuse them of elitism, superficiality in dealing with complex issues and deliberate distortion.

Coverage of Watergate, Capitol Hill sex scandals and the Bert Lance affair not only aroused interest but also brought forth a barrage of criticism. Many objected to what was regarded as a media vendetta against President Nixon, carried out with as much vigor as was given to the fulfillment of their public duty. Some compared the media's reporting on the Bert Lance affair to a wolf pack "gone mad" with a post-Watergate blood lust. Whatever the truth of these charges, incidents such as these highlight the all-pervasive influence of the press.

The media's role is no longer limited to news gathering and disseminating or to the molding of public opinion, but has also moved into the realm of news making as well. An eloquent example of this trend was manifested during President Anwar al-Sadat's historic visit to Israel when a number of TV news "personalities" served as conduits for Sadat and Begin. This situation led the news director of one TV network to say: "It certainly looks as though the media was the main arena of negotiation. There is no question we were the conduit. But where journalism ends and message carrying begins is hard to tell."

The American media are by far the most free and powerful in the world. Today the channels of communication in the United States are technologically far advanced beyond those available to other countries' media institutions. The American print and broadcast organs are mighty instruments in shaping American attitudes and public opinion on foreign policy.

Foreign policy issues are particularly susceptible to journalistic whims. The average American is less interested in foreign than in domestic issues. A high level of susceptibility to interpretive reporting on foreign affairs therefore exists. Often such reporting critically affects U.S. policy, especially on strategic issues about which minority views are infrequently published.

The Middle East is the most obvious area in which imbalance has been prevalent. It is an area about which the American public understands little, yet there is no shortage of opinions. This irony relates directly to the shaping of U.S. Middle East policy. However, in recent years there have been improvements in the coverage and accuracy of reporting on Middle East issues.

A dramatic example of the improvement in coverage was evidenced by the manner in which the media handled the Israeli air attacks on southern Lebanese villages on November 9, 1977. These attacks were declared by Israeli Chief of Staff Mordechai Gur to be "retaliation" against "purely terrorist bases" for the Palestinian guerrilla rocket attacks on Nahariyya. The immediacy of the on-the-scene coverage by the media revealed that there was no evidence of guerrilla positions at the sites of the attack, and that the majority of the dead and wounded were noncombatant men, women, and children. Only a handful of Palestinian guerrillas were among the victims. The media also pointed out that the Israeli "reprisal" was out of proportion to the initial attack. Only one Israeli woman was killed and two children were wounded, while over 120 people were killed and scores wounded by the Israeli attack. The prominence the story was given in the media and the balanced manner in which it was carried revealed a greater awareness of the dimensions of the Middle East conflict.

This trend was also manifested over the past two years in the number of balanced and perceptive reports about the Arabs and the Middle East problem and its origins in newspapers including *The Washington Post* and *The New York Times*. It is also noteworthy that a significant number of these articles were written by Jewish journalists. And while these articles remain small in number, they nevertheless represent a step in the right direction.

American newsmen are better informed about the area than ever before. They are making serious efforts to present balanced and accurate coverage of the complex issues of this volatile area. The presence of these new professionals augments the handful of editors, correspondents and writers who since 1948 have attempted to deal with issues fairly and objectively, at times risking their own careers and/or reputations. Ironically, the catalyst for improvement came from the military and political implications of the October 1973 War and the Arab oil embargo. It may be hoped—if not assumed—that the growing importance of Arab markets for American goods and the greater understanding which comes with increased contacts will perpetuate this trend.

Nonetheless, coverage of the Arabs and of the Arab-Israeli conflict remains inadequate. Part of the problem is ignorance—most Americans have had only the most fleeting and superficial exposure to Middle East history and culture in their educational experience. And too often this brief glimpse is distorted and confirms inaccurate stereotypes of the Arabs.

Even during the November 1977 visit of President Sadat to Israel, a time when the American media bombarded the public, and legitimately so, with news about this historic event, there still were many Americans who remained unaware of the event and of who Begin and Sadat were. A number of football fans were interviewed by a TV network about their reaction to the Sadat-Begin meeting. Several responded by saying "Sadat-Begin who?" or "Sadat-Begin? What is that?"

Programs in Middle East studies, languages, culture and economics are offered in a few of the larger American institutions and less than five percent of all four-year colleges. The Middle East is not usually covered in general history or cultural studies courses. A few books dealing with the Arab world are published annually and too often they reinforce existing prejudices.

Such purportedly unbiased publications as almanacs frequently contain subtle (and less than subtle) pro-Israeli propaganda masquerading as facts.

Middle East Perspective, a monthly newsletter dealing with Arab-Israeli issues, recently highlighted such problems with an analysis of the "Nations of the World" section of the *Readers Digest Almanac*. The *Almanac* offers blatantly propagandistic essays in the guise of country profiles.

The discrepancy in space allotted to the Arab states of Syria and Egypt, as compared to Israel, and the nature of the information supplied, create and perpetuate misunderstanding and bias. To quote directly from the introduction to each section:

5

> *ISRAEL TODAY—About the size of New Jersey, Israel is a small Middle Eastern nation on the east coast of the Mediterranean Sea. It is the only nation in the world in which Judaism is the official religion. Most of the people are the families of Jewish immigrants who came to their biblical homeland in the past 50 years from Europe, Africa, Asia and America.*
>
> *Surrounded by Arab nations that wish to destroy the Jewish state, Israel has fought four wars for its existence since declaring its independence in 1948. Its troops occupy over 25,000 sq. mi. claimed by Palestinian Arabs. The nation remains continually on the alert against attack from its neighbors and spends two thirds of its national budget for military preparedness.*
>
> *EGYPT TODAY—Egypt is the largest and most powerful of the Arab countries of the Middle East. But it has lost four wars in the past three decades with neighboring Israel, a Jewish state with a population only one-ninth the size of Egypt's.*
>
> *SYRIA TODAY—A militant Arab state, Syria has joined in four wars in three decades against its neighbor Israel.*

Israel is portrayed as the fledgling state surrounded by incompetent but threatening neighbors who outnumber the tiny state ten-fold. And while the *Almanac* alludes to the existence of Palestinian Arabs, it provides no information on the nature of Palestinian claims to the Jewish "biblical homeland" or their situation as refugees. In succeeding paragraphs, the authors misinform their readers on the true background of what they call the Third Arab-Israeli War (1967). Here one is informed that Israel, fearful of an Arab attack, "launched air and land strikes at Egypt, Jordan and Syria on June 5."

The popular media's portrayal of the Arab has been so pervasive as to lead Alfred Lilienthal, a Jewish scholar and writer who publishes *Middle East Perspective*, to comment that ". . .it is doubtful whether Zionism would ever have succeeded in the United States had public opinion been adequately and impartially informed. But, instead, Zionism has been made to appear as a force for progress and liberation in a backward Arab World. The Arabs were thought of in terms of pyramids, camels, dancing girls and, perhaps, oil."

Similarly, an editorial in *The National Observer*, November 10, 1973, declared:

> *There has been a tendency in recent years to portray the Arabs in two guises. They are either incompetent boobs, forever fumbling with their fezzes, or bloodthirsty primitives not far removed from Attila the Hun. But such amusements have their cost. These obviously contradictory stereotypes not only dehumanize a considerable slice of this planet's humanity; they also develop a pervasive, insidious, cultural blind spot that this nation can no longer afford to tolerate.*

6

Most Americans picture Arabs as backward, scheming, fanatic terrorists who are dirty, dishonest, oversexed and corrupt. On the other hand the Israelis are seen as tough, energetic, hard-working, persecuted and courageous people. They are modern pioneers who have made the desert bloom and democracy a reality in the midst of the backward Middle East.

Following the 1967 War another dimension was added to the Arab image, that of the "bumbling, cowardly Arab." When the Palestinian commando movement came to prominence, this image was replaced by that of an "Arab terrorist." The 1973 War and the ensuing oil embargo gave rise to yet another image: that of the super-rich Arab sheikh controlling world oil, squeezing the jugular vein of the Western world by threatening its oil supply. Editorials and feature articles in leading papers charged the Arab oil embargo was "blackmail." Little was said as to why the Arabs would use oil as a weapon. This attitude led *Washington Post* columnist William Raspberry to write on November 23, 1973:

> *Why is it "diplomacy" when the United States uses national resources as a leverage in its foreign policy and "blackmail" when the Arabs do the same thing? We hear the Arab oil embargo described so frequently and so matter of factly as blackmail that we start to take it as undisputed fact. But when American wheat or American technology or even American military strength is proffered or withheld in order to influence the diplomatic postures of other countries, it seems the most reasonable thing in the world. Why the inconsistency? Is it simply a question of whose ox is gored? Or is it frustration over the obvious dilemma in U.S. policy formulation? How to side with Israel against the Arabs without making the Arabs angry?*

Full-page newspaper advertisements appeared throughout the country to reinforce the assertion that the Arabs were attacking the West through oil price hikes. Yet an examination of hard facts, divorced from rhetoric, makes it apparent that the Arab nations were divided on the size of the oil price increase at the Vienna OPEC meeting. Non-Arab producers were more insistent than Arabs on a price rise. Yet it is the Arab who is singled out as the villain in the oil melodrama.

Commenting on this situation, Joseph C. Harsch of *The Christian Science Monitor* wrote (December 30, 1976):

> *The latest rise in the price of imported oil has generated in the United States another round of headlines and cartoons presenting Arabs in a wide range of unattractive images. The implication is that they are malicious, sinister bandits stealing from good Americans who become the innocent victims of Arab greed.*

7

Despite major differences among the Arab states, the press usually classifies all Arabs as part of one great mass. More often than not, the Persians are thrown in for good measure, particularly in articles dealing with the increase in oil prices or the squandering of wealth. The nationally circulated Sunday magazine *Parade* will frequently publish stories with "Arab" in headlines, although the text contains accounts of both Arab and Persian extravagance. Negative and inaccurate portrayal of the Arabs in the media has led columnist Nicholas Von Hoffman to write: "No religious, national or cultural group has been so massively or consistently vilified."

In the spring of 1971, Peggy Alexander, a history teacher in the Sacramento, California area, asked her eighth grade students, "What is your image of an Arab?" These are some of the answers: "Arabs don't wear underclothes." "They are all hippy-type nomads." "Most of the men wear beards." "All Arabs have many wives." "All Arabs are Mohammedans." "The camel is the only means of transportation."

Such distortions and misconceptions are not limited to 12-year olds. Dr. Ayad al-Qazzaz, a professor of sociology at California State University at Sacramento, reported on a group of adults going to Saudi Arabia to work for ARAMCO. While attending a company orientation school on Long Island, they were asked several questions on the Middle East and the Arabs. The questions, "What is Islam?" and "Who is the Prophet Mohammad?" brought some interesting answers. Islam was defined as "a game of chance similar to bridge," "a mysterious sect founded in the south by the Ku Klux Klan," "an organization of American Masons who dress in strange costumes." The Prophet Mohammad was said to be "the man who wrote the Arabian Nights," "an American Negro Minister who was in competition with Father Divine in New York City," and someone who had "something to do with a mountain."

One wonders how stereotyping of the Arabs is so pervasive in the most highly educated, most elaborately informed nation in the world, possessing the most effective media apparatus anywhere. With so much power in the hands of so few, the responsibility of the media is awesome. *The Washington Post* recently published an article on "The Press and its Myths," excerpted from a speech by John Siegenthaler, publisher of *The Nashville Tennessean*:

> *Except in rare, occasional news stories, it is misrepresentation to assert that we are the press of the people. We speak for our own interests. And sometimes—hopefully often—they serve the interests of some in the society*

8

who need a voice. When we boast of our "objectivity," we deal in semantics.
There is little pure objectivity in the American press.

Siegenthaler criticized the "overcommitment to personal coverage," asserting that the press fails ". . .as an institution to use what resources we have to meet responsibilities for broader coverage."

Siegenthaler raised the issue of public access to the pages of a newspaper. "We say, 'write us a letter' or 'do us a guest column' or 'we have an ombudsman, call him' or 'we have a press council.' That isn't the sort of access special interest groups want; it isn't the access and we are going to give them damned little, because we don't think they are entitled to it—and maybe just because we don't want to."

When it comes to attempts to present a pro-Arab or neutral point of view, the situation is even worse. Many Americans, Arab-Americans and Middle East experts complain that major newspapers often fail to publish their responses to pro-Israeli articles or other items, including letters to the editor as well as "guest columns." In most areas of domestic and foreign policy the media attempt to represent all viewpoints; however, where the Middle East is concerned, this policy has not been followed with any rigor. The result is lopsided coverage and little understanding of the conflict between Arabs and Israel, its essence or its roots. It is argued that important news has become far too complex for the reader to comprehend on his own. Many in the media contend that there is no such thing as an objective story: It is better to be honest and admit this fact and allow the reader the benefit of experienced conclusions than to allow the individual to decide for himself or herself.

This reasoning has created a plethora of problems, some due to the very nature of American journalism, and others attributable to the inordinate trust the American public has placed in its media. Most readers will not question the media on issues with which they are unfamiliar, nor will they attempt to find other sources of information on the subject. More often than not, an editor's or writer's bias or interpretation may be taken as fact by an unsuspecting audience.

But, critics say, the American press is free and diverse, which makes for good, fair journalism and a well-informed public. Surely the bias of the foreign editor of one newspaper will be countered by the editor of a competing daily. This assumption is not justified.

Recently, in *The Washington Post*, Charles Seib discussed developments in the nation's system of newspaper ownership. He reported that all the buying and selling of the past few years has resulted in chain ownership of three out of five of the country's 1,750 dailies. The 12 largest chains publish 40 percent of the 61 million newspapers sold daily. The communications industry, said Mr. Seib, is becoming a big business—as big as any in America. So big that a former U.S. Secretary of the Treasury, John Connally, suggested including it as the fourth member of America's institutional giants—big government, big business, big labor and big media. This situation, warns Mr. Seib, may well result in an American newspaper system which resembles the slick superficial harmonies of a barbershop quartet. What is at stake is diversity, the diversity which has to an extent insured that the American press lived up to its responsibilities despite opinionated journalism.

Connally and Seib are supported in their arguments by Kevin Phillips, a lawyer, publisher and syndicated columnist. In an article appearing in the July 1977 issue of *Harper's* magazine, Phillips stated that the media are increasingly playing a "quasi-governmental role in American politics and society," that network anchormen may be more powerful than the top leaders of Congress. Therefore, he argues, the media should be held more fully responsible for the great power they wield.

In support of his argument, Phillips quotes the findings of a study conducted by Notre Dame psychology professor Lloyd Sloan on the media's effect on audience reactions to the second Ford-Carter presidential debate. The study reveals that press commentaries following the debate influenced the opinions of one out of every five viewers. That is, network news analyses "by themselves produced overall net changes of 27 percent (CBS) and 22 percent (ABC) in the direction of Carter. Those who viewed the post-debate news analyses saw both as being biased in favor of Carter."

The implications of Sloan's study are astounding. If this theory is correct, and from all indications it appears to be so, television has the power to electronically stuff the ballot boxes not only of American elections but other issues as well. This, combined with the concentration of several influential media organs in the hands of a few major news companies, led Phillips to raise the question of government regulation of the media to offset the concentration of power in the hands of the few. Phillips gives The Washington Post Company as an example of a news company that has a "quasi-governmental role" in Washington since it helps determine how the government communicates with the American people through its five-level presence in Washington—a newspaper (*The Washington Post*), a radio station (WTOP), a television station (WTOP-TV), a news magazine (*Newsweek*), and a major news service (Los Angeles Times-Washington Post). There are a small number of other giants in the news business which wield national influence, including The New York Times Company, CBS, NBC, ABC, Time Inc., RCA, Gannett and Knight-Ridder. One must ponder the implications of this trend on matters not so near at hand, nor so urgent in American priorities as presidential elections, matters with which most Americans are unfamiliar.

The problem in areas such as the Middle East is greater, not only because American knowledge of the area is limited to what is published in the most popular media (and which is often erroneous), but because of the lack of publicized minority opinion on the Middle East. The Arab is virtually without a spokesman in the United States, while Israel benefits from the support of many articulate Americans, both Jews and Gentiles. Also, most of what is published in the American press is true, which creates a special problem when we come to Middle East coverage. Rather than ignore the truth, some journalists take it into consideration, adapt it to their own purposes, play hide and seek with it, specializing in pseudo-truth and half-truths. Often the results are astounding. The recent war in Lebanon offers an excellent example. It was presented in most media organs as simply Christian versus Muslim, or as Christian rightist against Muslim leftist. While there was a sectarian dimension to the Lebanon conflict, it was but one of many factors behind the conflict.

Israel's image as a fledgling nation besieged on all sides by antagonists has persisted in the thinking of the American press and the American people because the media tend to write, publish and broadcast those stories which support this view. At the same time, there is a hesitancy to balance this with uncomplimentary stories on Israel, or favorable stories on the Arabs. Instead, stories about Arab extravagances are often highlighted and rarely do stories appear about positive Arab achievements in education, in development or in raising their living standards.

It is therefore understandable why there has been much more reporting on the Israeli point of view of the Middle East situation. More often than not, only the Israeli view is presented. During the 1967 War, headlines in many U.S. newspapers reflected sympathy and support for Israel. A *Chicago Sun-Times* headline read, "Israel Reports a Victory Sweep: What a Great Day." The *Sun-Times'* bias went even further when an editorial feature declared that Israel's "smashing and quick victory" offered the world "another chance for peace, not only for the Middle East but globally."

A study prepared by the American Institute for Political Communication, a non-profit, non-partisan organization interested in improving the flow of communication to the American people, found that of 18

Washington-based syndicated columnists writing during the 1967 War, only one writer did a column which set out the difficulties, problems and needs of the Arabs.

Dr. Michael Suleiman, chairman of Kansas State University's Department of Political Science and an Arab-American, using a content analysis technique, did a study of the coverage of the 1967 War by *Newsweek, Time, Life, The Nation, The New Republic, U.S. News and World Report* and *The New York Times'* "The Week in Review" to detect any change in attitudes since the 1956 invasion of Egypt. Suleiman found that all of the magazines covered were anti-Arab and anti-Nasser with the exception of *The Nation.* As for editorials, all the magazines were anti-Nasser except *Time,* anti-Arab except *The Nation,* and pro-Israel except *Life* and *The Nation.* Nasser was seen as the cause of all the trouble, and his dictatorial attitudes and "associations with communism" were stressed. All the magazines except *The Nation* described the Arabs as dishonest, unreliable and inefficient, and all depicted the Israelis as efficient, heroic and self-reliant. Crude jokes about Arabs flourished. Cartoons, particularly those of Bill Mauldin, were seen as part of an anti-Arab hate campaign.

A study by Dr. Ali Zaghal of the University of Utah found that the thrust was not simply against Nasser and the Arabs, but even tended to distort the causes and nature of the 1967 Arab-Israeli conflict. Many muddled the issue of who attacked first. A *Life* reporter wrote that according to U.S. sources, "The UAR has launched an attack on Israel." Further, the war was portrayed erroneously as an Arab-Jewish or Jewish-Muslim conflict, and Israel was shown as the little David fighting against the big Goliath. Israel was also depicted as an "oasis of democracy which made the unpopulated desert of Palestine bloom."

Dr. Janice Terry, a historian at Eastern Michigan University, in collaboration with Don Mendanhall, a graduate student at the university, assessed coverage by *The Washington Post, The New York Times* and *The Detroit Free Press* over a period of nine months before and after the 1973 War. They declared that the results of their study revealed "a rather consistent pro-Israeli and anti-Arab bias in the three newspapers studied; this bias is particularly evident in editorials and, to a lesser extent, in feature stories. It is also important to note that much of the bias is purely anti-Arab in nature." Terry, nevertheless, found that coverage became more balanced in spite of bias. A small number of pro-Arab and pro-Palestinian articles were published—such articles were absent before 1973. More recently this bias reappeared in the coverage of the Arab boycott against Israel. The press, quick to repeat Israeli charges of discrimination and anti-Semitism, failed to present the boycott for what it is, an economic sanction against a military enemy modeled after the U.S. boycotts during World Wars I and II. Administration testimony that in fact only 25 instances of discrimination were discovered in almost 50,000 boycott transactions was for the most part ignored.

It is also interesting to study the substance of the information circulated. Whenever there is accurate reporting on an item such as the overwhelming amount of government, public and private support and assistance to Israel, or on the nature of Israeli society and the internal issues confronting Israel, such as the role of the political party the Black Panthers and the discrimination against Palestinian Arabs and Sephardic Jews, it is often limited and buried on the inside pages. Coverage by many newspaper reporters and television commentators is colored by their personal political attitudes. Methods include false historical comparisons, insinuating headlines and stylistic hints which become apparent to the critical reader. A recent example of the inaccurate analogies appeared in an article by columnist Rev. Lester Kinsolving (in the Globe newspaper's June 2, 1977 weekly supplement, published by the Panax Corporation). The author takes issue with President Carter's call for Israeli withdrawal from occupied Arab territories in accordance with U.N. resolutions. He concludes his article as follows:

> President Carter is perfectly reasonable in asking Israel to return to such perilous boundaries—if he would have no objections to a Soviet missile battery in Arlington, with two Russian divisions bivouacked between Falls Church and Manassas.

An excellent example of the sin of omission is the coverage of Israel's violation of human rights and its torture of Arab detainees. On June 19, 1977, the London *Sunday Times* published an exhaustive report resulting from a five-month investigation by its "Insight Team," in which it was concluded that Israel's violations of human rights have occurred through the use of "primitive" as well as "sophisticated" methods of torture. An accompanying editorial of the three-page report concluded that Israel routinely used torture in the occupied Arab territories. The report was generally ignored in the American media. The lack of coverage in the American media led syndicated columnist Nicholas Von Hoffman to write (July 1, 1977 in *The Washington Post*):

> Most Americans will never know any of this. As of this writing, only one newspaper, The Boston Globe, has seen fit to run the report. The indifference isn't owing to doubt about the caliber of the journalism. The Sunday Times

13

Insight Team which did the story is universally respected in the business and has been copied by papers like The Washington Post. *The lack of interest on this occasion may be explained by* The New York Times *covering the torture investigation with an 86-word article, if you can call a piece that short and appearing on page 13 an article.*

To some extent all news in America is what The New York Times *calls news, but even more so with foreign news. In part this is because the* Times *spends money that other papers, the magazines and the networks won't spend on foreign correspondents, but it is also because so few print or broadcast editors are able to make independent judgments on the news. They simply lack the character and stature to have an opinion of their own and prefer the safety of letting the nation's most prestigious paper do their decision-making for them.*

This is particularly easy with an issue like Israel, where any adverse publicity is likely to win an editor vociferous abuse from one of the nation's best-organized lobbies. It doesn't work that way abroad, however, where the mass media are giving the publics in the other democracies far less-biased accounts.

How have the overwhelming majority of newspapers and television stations defined what is news? Obviously, the media cannot report everything. Editors must select those 'happenings' which they see as "fit to print." But the media also have the obligation to print those things that have relevance in today's world, things that might provide insight into or more understanding of major issues that demand our attention. Certainly the media have no right to bury or suppress news which does not agree with a preconceived idea of the world and how it should be. But how does this pertain to the Middle East? Let us look at an example. Certainly a Palestinian commando raid resulting in the deaths of Israelis deserves front-page coverage by every major network. Editorials and commentaries express revulsion and condemnation of the act. The victims and their families are made real to the American public. U.S. satellite coverage in Israel makes possible direct and immediate American involvement with the family at its time of sorrow.

A few days or weeks later, Israeli forces attack a Lebanese village and Palestinian camps. Hundreds of people are killed or wounded and many left homeless. The act is often wanton, but the press merely reiterates Israeli official communiques which refer to "reprisals against terrorists." This is "official terrorism," but when it is presented as a retaliation, the act is mitigated and the aggressor emerges as a hero. But for the press these raids do not constitute news. The innocent men, women and children killed during the raid are given brief mention, buried someplace on the back pages of the newspapers. Arab deaths are accepted as necessary to maintain Israeli security and as punishment for "terrorist acts." With very few exceptions no newspaper, journal or news station has had the courage to question the acts and the Israeli communiques or to honestly deal with the actual effects of these so-called "clean-up jobs."

Many in the American media are guilty of the practice of accepting terminology coined by the Israelis. This is a highly effective device for influencing opinions. Thus, the Palestinian guerrilla becomes the "Arab terrorist," the October War becomes the "Yom Kippur War" (although with equal justification it could be called the "Ramadan War"), the June War becomes the "Six-Day War," and Haram al Sharif (The Noble Sanctuary) becomes the "Temple Mount." The occupied Arab territories become the "captured territories" to the ABC correspondent and the "captured" or "administered territories" to the NBC correspondent. Israeli occupation has been referred to in *The New York Times* as "one of the mildest military occupations in history." Following the election of Prime Minister Begin, some American correspondents in Israel have begun to use his description of the West Bank of the Jordan River as "Judea and Samaria," which leads one to wonder if correspondents will go all the way with Begin's definitions and describe it as "liberated Judea and Samaria."

Minority opinions are lacking at a time when the media are admittedly becoming more opinionated, and editorial or self censorship is rampant in the coverage of the Arab-Israeli issue. Many times a reporter may consciously cable only that information which he knows is acceptable. Sometimes stories sent by reporters are not printed.

A correspondent for *The National Observer* wrote a story in which he referred to the Palestinian people. His editor wanted him to drop the term, asking him to whom "Palestinian people" referred.

Another writer who contributed to one of America's leading dailies asked, "Why is it that stories on torture of Arabs are not published in the paper?" The foreign editor told him that torture occurs all over the world and therefore is not news. This same paper plays up torture stories in many parts of the world.

Following the 1973 Israeli raid on Beirut, during which three leading Palestinian intellectuals were murdered at their homes and a number of innocent bystanders killed, *The Washington Post* expressed the opinion that the Israeli action was condonable as the "best" kind of violence since it struck at the Palestinian "menace." The newspaper based its argument on an at best highly controversial opinion that the Palestinian cause was morally bankrupt, that the Lebanese would be grateful to be rid of the

15

radicals and that the Israeli aggression was a step toward peace, since only a handful of radicals stood in the way of peaceful coexistence between Israelis and Palestinians. On the other hand, commented the *Post*, Palestinian raids are the worst kind of violence. Thus the editorial position of one of America's two most influential newspapers: that raids on southern Lebanon are acceptable and necessary.

Former Senator J. William Fulbright objected to this "moralizing" by the press, stating that he had been "disturbed by what has often seemed to me an arbitrary and prejudiced standard of 'newsworthiness' in the national press, especially as applied to the Middle East. I have noted repeatedly, for example, the quantitative disparity between press coverage of Palestinian guerrilla attacks within Israel and of Israeli attacks on South Lebanon, although the loss of civilian life in the latter has almost certainly been greater. I have even made a statement on the subject in the Senate in August 1974, but the statement itself was ignored."

Let us turn again to Senator Fulbright for another instance of press "censorship." On October 3, 1975, Senator Fulbright delivered an address at the opening session of a conference held by the Middle East Institute in Washington, D.C., in which he analyzed the Middle East conflict. In particular he dealt with the Sinai Agreement, its implications for the concerned parties and the potential pitfalls. The media, both electronic and print, were informed and copies of the Senator's speech were sent to foreign news editors of all the major papers. Yet with the exception of *The Christian Science Monitor*, none of the papers saw fit to cover a major address of this kind. It is important to note that while this was taking place, Congress was in the process of debating the Sinai Agreement. In the opinion of many Middle East experts at the conference, the former chairman of the Senate Foreign Relations Committee was making a significant contribution to the debate on the issue. The public was thus deprived of access to the Senator's views. A foreign editor of a Washington daily was sent a copy of the speech. When asked if he intended to use the story, he said he had lost it. He was provided with another copy. When contacted two weeks later, he replied that he did not get a chance to read it.

The Washington Post and *The New York Times* furnish still another example of the sins of conscious omission. These two leading U.S. dailies covered the Congressional hearings on the sale of Hawk Missiles to Jordan; both papers listed the names of witnesses opposed to the sale and their statements, while neither mentioned the witnesses in favor of the sale. Those in favor included two former U.S. Ambassadors to Jordan and the

Director of the Middle East Institute. In fairness to the *Post*, however, one must admit that attempts at presenting a more balanced coverage have been made over the past two years. In a small number of editorials and columns, Palestinian and Arab grievances have been taken into account, and Israel has been criticized because of its intransigent position on the establishment of settlements in the occupied Arab territories.

The New York Times led the press coverage of the Zionist travel boycott imposed against Mexico and Brazil in retaliation for their votes during the U. N. General Assembly debate equating Zionism with racism. The *Times* focused a great deal of attention on the matter. But when a *Times* correspondent covered a press conference called by 200 American clergymen to release a statement calling on Israel to "recognize the rights of displaced Palestinians, Christians and Moslems, to return to their homeland" in keeping with the Universal Declaration of Human Rights, the importance the *Times* placed on this statement was displayed by its coverage—the story appeared on page 20.

Concern, a magazine for Canadian journalists, directed the attention of its correspondents to how well the Israelis fought on Yom Kippur while fasting. The reporters on the Israeli front were quite right in extracting a human interest story out of this. At the same time, editors remained oblivious to the equally interesting fact that the Arab soldiers were observing Ramadan, a month-long period during which Muslims neither eat nor drink from sunrise to sunset. The Arab armies fought the entire war under conditions the Israelis had to contend with for only one day.

Senator Fulbright provides yet another example of inadequate coverage. In April 1971 the Senator delivered a speech critical of Israeli policy. While some newspapers provided fair and adequate coverage, *The Washington Post* ignored the speech. On the following day the *Post* carried an article on the Israeli reaction to the speech they did not see fit to carry, headlined, "Israeli Press Lashes Out at Fulbright." Still later, one of the *Post's* columnists devoted an entire column of criticism to the Senator's unreported speech.

Headlines present yet another problem. If a reporter writes an objective story, his editor may, for reasons of his own, choose to give the story a one-sided slant through the headline. Thus, a Dallas paper headlined a story on PLO participation in the U. N. debates with, "PLO Invited to Raid Debates." In September 1975, Drew Middleton of *The New York Times* wrote a fair and analytical piece on the impact of the potential sale to Israel of Pershing missiles, which are capable of carrying nuclear warheads, which ran under the banner, "New Missiles for the Mid East, a Destabilizing Factor."

There are instances of outright prejudice and inaccurate reporting. Earlier this year, *The Manchester Union Leader*, the powerful New Hampshire daily published by William Loeb, ran an interesting commentary by Ray Saidel entitled, "Arabs Continuing in Slave Trade." The article urged Americans who saw "Roots" to take note that the slave trade is not dead. According to Mr. Saidel, who bases his arguments on "authoritative sources," including ex-Black Panther leader Elridge Cleaver, the black slave trade is "flourishing" in Saudi Arabia and the rich Persian Gulf oil emirates. He quotes his British sources who claim that there has been "a substantial increase in the slave trade due to the growth of oil income in Aden, Kuwait, Yemen, Muscat, Oman, Qatar, Sudan and Saudi Arabia." Aside from the falsity of the content, Mr. Saidel and his sources have obviously not bothered to check either their geography or their history. Aden is the capital city of South Yemen, and Muscat is the capital of Oman; neither is a separate state. South and North Yemen, Oman and the Sudan are not oil-rich—quite the contrary. The two Yemens rank among the poorest countries in the world today. The Sudan is not in the Persian Gulf: it is a black, Arab, African nation.

During an attack on the Egyptian embassy in Madrid, NBC showed film of scenes with PLO signs in the background, even though the PLO had condemned the operation. In an ABC-TV Evening News commentary, Harry Reasoner justified the actions of Israeli demonstrators against the Kissinger mission on the grounds that the Arabs had started all the Mideast wars, "including 1948, 1956, and 1967." One wonders if this was a restatement of Israel's communiques. Syndicated columnist George Will is another journalist who has blamed the Arabs for starting the four Arab-Israeli wars. He has also described Arab nationalism as a "romantic theory" and as a "myth" that is void of any real meaning.

During a CBS-TV special, which was hurriedly put together following the assassination of King Faisal of Saudi Arabia, correspondent Bill McClaughlin responded to a question about the motive for the assassination by saying, "God knows the Middle East is filled with plotters." CBS's State Department correspondent Marvin Kalb elaborated on this theme: when asked if he was surprised by the act, Mr. Kalb replied, "Well, as a new Middle East hand, I would say I was not really surprised by the assassination, because every time we would go to Riyadh with Kissinger, you would have the feeling, looking, feeling that environment is for

18

plotters. People were walking around and there was a constant shifting of eyes."

But the misleading headline, the composition technique that magnifies or underplays a story, and the deadly weapon of neglect or burial of a story—all are petty techniques of oppression when compared to the new trend in news reporting of sending out writers and broadcasters with only superficial knowledge of their topic to cover serious, important events. Since only major metropolitan-area newspapers give much space to international news, the writings of a very few journalists reporting for major established newspapers become the source for overall U.S. coverage of foreign news. Another problem is the reliance on wire service correspondents or the dispatching of a correspondent to an area only during times of crisis—the result is superficial coverage. Yet this is an improvement over the more common practice of sending reporters only to the Israeli side—even in times of crisis. One newspaper chain editor justified this practice on the grounds that what constituted news for his paper was determined by the large pro-Israeli and ethnic Jewish population in the cities served by that chain.

There are five major reasons for the media's failure to cover the Middle East fairly and objectively: (1) cultural bias; (2) the think-alike atmosphere within the impact media; (3) the Arab-Israeli conflict; (4) media ignorance of the origins and history of the conflict; and (5) the determined, sophisticated Israeli lobby. Arab failure to understand the American media and how they operate, plus the lack of interest and identification with the Arab world by the Arab-American community compound the problem. Arab-American apathy contrasts sharply with the close identification by many American Jews with Israel. The inordinate influence of the many pro-Israeli reporters (Jews and Gentiles alike) in media positions as editors, correspondents or reporters has been a significant factor in American coverage of the Arab world. Furthermore, few American-Arabs or Arabs cover the Arab nations for U.S. media; yet there are many Israelis and American Jews who cover Israel for U.S. newspapers.

Many American journalists carry into their work a strong subconscious tendency to ascribe virtue to Israel and malevolence to the Arabs, as if the conflict were a simplistic western movie scenario with "good guys" and "bad guys." This support is bolstered by the ever-watchful Israeli lobby, which is a very well-organized and powerful guardian of Israel and its interests in the United States. The lobby acts immediately on any issue it sees as a threat to Israeli interests. Letters to the editor immediately go out whenever articles critical of Israel's policies are published. Any criticism of

19

Israel or its actions is quickly stifled by charges of anti-Semitism, a powerful weapon in a country still guiltridden by the plight of Jews in Europe during World War II. As Edwin Roberts, one of the editors of *The National Observer*, writes: "Most people would rather keep silent than be charged with anti-Semitism." Thus a number of prominent journalists who were critical of Israel were subjected to intense pressure, and pressure was put on their employers to control their pens. Some observers believe the activity of the pro-Israel lobby is closely synchronized with the Israeli Embassy in Washington.

So powerful is the Israeli lobby that *Haolam Hazeh*, an independent liberal Israeli newsweekly, asked the following questions in an article published on December 25, 1974:

> *Has the United States become a branch office of Israel? Funny question. But not so funny to the attentive listener and reader of the American mass media, which rides currently on the Israeli wave. The name of the state of Israel, its personalities and the events that take place there make up the headlines practically every day; every whisper worth being mentioned enjoys disproportionate coverage.*
>
> *The picture depicted to American citizens is colored with all the shades of pink, but no black or even grey is to be found. Any hint of the economic scandals, for instance, which have agitated the whole of Israel in the last months has not yet reached the United States. . . .*
>
> The New York Times, *American television,* The Washington Post, *and hundreds of other newspapers which consecrate their front pages to every whistle of Yigal Allon, Golda Meir, or Yitzhak Rabin, do not publish a single word about the affair of the 'Israel Company' of Tibor Rosenbaum, of Soleh Boneh and the refineries (some of the companies involved in the financial scandals).*

This of course does not justify the notion advanced by a number of people that "the Jews control the American media." Such a statement is as inaccurate and racist as saying the WASPs control the secret mechanisms of Wall Street. It is true that some leading American newspapers are owned by Jewish families. It is true that many of the presidents, news directors and correspondents of the television networks are Jewish. It is true that many of the leading journals are edited by Jews. It is true that there are many Jews in leading positions in the American media. But it is not true that Jews own or control the majority of the newspapers in the United States. A study done by *More* magazine shows that Jews own only about 3.5 percent of American newspapers, although these include some important ones.

Arab-American writer Djelloul Marbrook dealt succinctly with this issue in a recent article in the National Association of Arab-Americans' 1977 Yearbook, by stating, "The point is that the media conspiracy theory simply will not wash. There is bias among the media, there are willful omissions and sometimes distortions; but there is no national conspiracy."

The fact that many American Jews hold important positions in the media does not mean that they are Zionist. Some of these journalists or editors tend, for historical reasons, to support the Israeli policies which they identify as correct and just and allow this support, consciously or unconsciously, to influence their writing on Middle East issues. But it remains also true that there are many non-Zionist Jewish reporters, commentators and editors who, more often than not, are fair and objective in their coverage. There are a few who are anti-Zionists. It is also important to note that some of the more balanced articles or TV reports have been authored by Jewish-American correspondents. Furthermore, there are non-Jewish reporters, commentators and editors whose anti-Arab bias exceeds that of most of the pro-Israeli Jewish reporters. It was a Gentile journalist who advised Israeli Prime Minister Begin to "keep his powder—and his uranium—dry, and his troops firmly planted along the Jordan." This was the conclusion of an article by Lester Kinsolving, on July 14, 1977. However, like other special interest groups, pro-Israeli Jewish organizations have, according to Dr. Zaghal's study, helped bring about "media socialization to pro-Israeli orientations." But this has come about as a result of long years of dedicated effort. Dr. Zaghal quotes Elasar, a leading American Zionist and scholar of the American Jewish community as follows:

> Jewish influence on the American press, to the extent that it exists, comes from slow and patient educational efforts over many years to make the men who determine the editorial position of newspapers, radio or television stations aware of the justice of the Israeli cause. In fact, this work has been undertaken by a variety of Jewish groups over the years, with editors and editorial writers being invited to visit Israel, and being provided with relevant information, and the like. At least partly as a result of this, the overwhelming majority of the American press that took a stand was favorable to Israel, and only a few papers, of which only The Christian Science Monitor has a respectable professional reputation, took stands in opposition. These criticisms of the press stem, not from resentment over the ethnic or religious character of publishers, editors, owners, managers or reporters, but from disappointment over the lack of courage in reporting on unpopular issues.

Journalists will write what is fashionable more often than not. They are somewhat like bureaucrats, fearful of overstepping the bounds of accepted

21

wisdom. Senator Eugene McCarthy likened the American press to blackbirds sitting on a telephone wire—when one flies away the rest follow. It is fashionable in America today to portray Israel as the tiny bastion of democracy and freedom in the midst of dictators, demagogues, fanatics and terrorists bent on destroying a refuge of the persecuted. This image, entrenched in the minds of the American public, is all the more astounding when one reflects that it is the Israelis who control Arab land. This fact, however, is often overlooked by American journalists, and the public, unaware of the history of the area, accept popular opinions on the Middle East without question.

Israel capitalizes on its Western image. Its leaders, the vast majority of whom have their origins in Europe or America, consciously exploit the similarities between Americans and Israelis. Both our peoples, they say, are pioneers who have created new and better worlds from backward regions; both our peoples are working toward bringing democracy and freedom to the world. Israelis, like Americans, they say, are efficient, well organized and have achieved great things in short periods of time. In addition, much is made of the common origins of Christianity and Judaism. In this atmosphere the Arab, his culture, traditions, history and religion appear alien and backward. There is little knowledge of Arab contributions to Western culture in art, architecture, science and literature. Nor is there any comprehension of the commonality of Judaism, Christianity and Islam.

The Arab countries are made to seem backward and almost comical when contrasted to the Israelis with their Western-oriented, middle-class life style. Arabs are portrayed as either desert-dwelling Bedouins or millionaires; little attention is paid to the strong urban and rural origins of the vast majority of the Arab people.

Yet not all of Israel's success with the U.S. media should be attributed to the pro-Israeli lobby or "friends" in the media. At times, the Arabs are their own worst enemies and can take credit for some of Israel's success. Restrictions, suspicions, bureaucratic red tape, lack of access to news sources or news makers, the cultural and linguistic gaps—all of these have helped make it difficult for the American journalist to accurately assess the Arab viewpoint. Apprehensions of Western journalists, at times justified, have had a tragic effect on the presentation of the Arab position throughout the Western world. The Israelis have astutely recognized the importance of the journalist, and accordingly the American correspondent in Israel has access to all important news sources; he is well treated by a government which has on the whole benefited from media coverage. In the

Arab countries, Western journalists are often resented and mistrusted, and their coverage of the issues often helps to perpetuate the already existing suspicion.

Confident of the righteousness of their cause, the Arabs often refuse to explain themselves to an outsider. Senator James Abourezk tells the story of an Arab cabinet minister who indignantly refused the Senator's request to explain the Arab position to the American people because, "We have the truth," and so there is no need to explain it to anyone. Not only do the Arabs refuse to recognize that the United States is an important battleground of the Middle East conflict, but when they do make an effort they mistakenly identify the center of power. They as yet do not understand the mechanisms of the American political system. The Arab governments concentrate their public relations efforts on the Administration, ignoring Congress and the American people. They present their arguments to the Administration without realizing that the Administration can achieve little without Congressional approval and, ultimately, a mandate from the American people. With rare exceptions, they have not taken the time or effort to educate the American people on the facts of the Middle East conflict.

Arab embassies and diplomatic missions to this country are often the only representatives of the Arab world to the West. Until recently they have not been able to transcend the weaknesses of their governments and effectively communicate the Arab position. Arab efforts were handicapped since diplomatic posts were—and to some extent are today—often awarded as political favors or as punishment, with little regard for necessary qualifications for office. Furthermore, most diplomats are given few responsibilities and are often kept in the dark on their government's position on critical issues. The embassies are not given the vital information and statistics necessary to function and consequently are unable to respond to public inquiries of the most basic kind. Most Arab diplomats are not functioning in the manner in which their American or Israeli counterparts are. Arab governments often go over the heads of their ambassadors by dealing directly with American officials, leaving the Arab diplomat in a position of frustration and helplessness that reduces his effectiveness. For this reason one sees many able Arab diplomats isolated and unable to communicate with their official counterparts or with the media and through them to the American people. It is often not because they do not want to do this, but because they lack the information or authority to act effectively.

Another problem leading to disrupted communications is the lack of

23

awareness on the part of some diplomats and representatives of how the American media function. Many diplomats avoid the press. This is due to suspicion of the press, timidity and/or inexperience in such matters. Fearful of rocking the boat or disrupting Arab diplomatic consensus, Arab diplomats at times fail to take any action at all. The Arabs also suffer from a lack of a central organization with the power to coordinate a united Arab public relations offensive. Arab public information efforts, reflecting intra-Arab politics, are often disunited, disorganized and contradictory. But ultimately the Arabs can be blamed for their inability to correctly gauge the American mentality. Unlike the Israeli propaganda effort, which has been successful primarily because of its ability to tell the Americans what they want to hear in a language they can understand, the Arabs have at times alienated even those people sympathetic to their cause.

All this does not, however, justify U.S. media treatment of the Arab world. Like an incompetent lawyer who unsuccessfully defends an innocent client, Arab failure to present their case before the world community is not a reflection of any weakness of the Arab argument. Surely the American media, which pride themselves on their ability to uncover and present the facts to the public, have an obligation to cover the Arabs and the Middle East situation in a fair and balanced manner.

2

Interview with
RICHARD VALERIANI

Mr. Valeriani is the State Department correspondent for NBC Television News.

Ghareeb: Many Arabs believe that the American media have been biased against them in favor of Israel. Do you see this as accurate?

Valeriani: It is hard to prove a negative. My answer to you is, why do they believe there is an anti-Arab bias?

Ghareeb: Because of the way the Arab has been depicted in the United States media. The image of the Arab is either that of a terrorist, a Bedouin riding a camel, a murderer, or someone who is totally incompetent in the modern world. Is this an accurate picture?

Valeriani: I do think it's an inaccurate picture from the diplomatic beat. There may be a public image formed through a whole series of outlets, however, that comes to that conclusion. You would have to show me how American reporters, reporting in responsible journals from the State Department, the White House, or the Hill, have given that impression. I don't have that impression. I will grant you, after the 1967 War, there was an image of military incompetence that has been projected not only from the United States but around the world. For example, I'm of Italian ancestry and the Italian Army has an incompetent military image. No matter how well the persons were fighting, there is that image. There is a long standing impression of the Italian Army since World War I. There might be that image of the Arabs militarily, based on the 1967 War.

Ghareeb: Each time there is a Palestinian commando attack against Israeli targets, either inside or outside Israel, NBC refers to the Palestinians as "terrorists." Yet they justify Israel attacks by calling them "retaliation." You do this on your program, not once or twice, but regularly. Why are the Palestinians called "terrorists," while the Israeli attacks are "retaliation?" Why don't you call the Palestinian attacks "retaliation?"

Valeriani: I describe them as terrorists or guerrillas. If you conduct an unorthodox kind of warfare, and there is no state of war, you have to find a way to describe it. When we were involved in Vietnam, we referred to the Viet Cong who used those methods as terrorists. If military forces strike across the border—for example, when the Lebanese Army fights—they don't describe the resistance to the Israeli attacks as Lebanese terrorists.

Ghareeb: You're aware that the word terrorism creates certain negative reactions. Since Israel conducts state terrorism, why not refer to it as that? Meanwhile, anything against Israel is characterized as terrorist. Why do you present it that way?

Valeriani: That is precisely why they are called terrorists. They're using terror as an instrument of political persuasion.

Ghareeb: Have you ever called the Israelis terrorists?

Valeriani: If you go back to 1948, the answer is yes.

Ghareeb: Israel bombs Lebanon and Palestinian camps daily.

Valeriani: We do not call them terrorists.

Ghareeb: Why not?

Valeriani: They're not referred to as terrorists. That is described as retaliation. There would be no Israeli retaliation if there were not an initial attack.

Ghareeb: So what is news? Israel has attacked Lebanon daily for the past two weeks, yet this does not seem to come across. Many people have been killed, and this is not presented on television. Why not? You know that if a Palestinian attacks Israel you see it flashed on every TV news show; it is on the front pages of every newspaper throughout the United States.

Valeriani: First of all, I don't know the situation you're talking about. If there is access to the area, which is frequently a problem within the Arab countries, our man in Beirut goes and films the reports. If you film an attack on the first day, by the nature of the news, it is reported. If you have it the second day, it is used. By the third day, you ask, "What are the pictures?" They are the same two pictures of the last day, and it is used copy.

26

Ghareeb: I don't think reporting from Lebanon is a problem because there are many reporters there and they have never complained.

Valeriani: Our man in Beirut and our man in Damascus have complained about it. There are restrictions on both sides, and they complain in Israel when there are restrictions. You might recall that one of our men broke the censorship in Israel a couple of years ago and was almost thrown out of the country. It works both ways.

Ghareeb: There is a certain racism in this type of reporting; Arab lives are less important than Jewish lives . . . Jews are more human than Arabs. When Arabs are killed it is not mentioned at all. For example, two days before the attack at Maalot, the Israelis attacked the village of K'fier in the south of Lebanon. Four Lebanese civilians were killed; they included three children and one woman. NBC said the Israelis attacked terrorist targets when in fact they were not terrorist targets. Following that came Maalot, which was the top news item for three nights in a row. Isn't there a disparity here?

Valeriani: I can't answer in terms of the decisions that were made about the coverage of that previous case. In Lebanon I agree with the general impression that the problem is caused by guerrilla groups engaging in terrorist tactics. There would be no action initiated by the Israelis if it were not for that. This is the way they feel; they have to cope with the problem. That may be why they can't cope with it.

Ghareeb: On December 25, 1974, the Israeli news magazine, *Haolam Hazeh*, published the following. I would like you to comment on it.

> *Has the United States become a branch office of Israel? Funny question. But not so funny to the attentive listener and reader of the American mass media, which rides currently on the Israeli wave. The name of the state of Israel, its personalities and the events that take place there make up the headlines, practically every day; every whisper worth being mentioned enjoys disproportionate coverage.*
>
> *The picture depicted to American citizens is colored with all nuances of pink, but no black, not even gray is to be found. Any hint of the economic scandals, for instance, which have agitated the whole of Israel in the course of the last months, has not yet reached the United States . . .*

Haolam Hazeh adds the report from its correspondent in the United States, who draws attention to the emphasis on Israeli "social" news in *The New York Times* and other media. He then refers to General George

27

Brown's statement about the "Jewish Connection" in the U.S. press. The article continues:

> It may well be that General Brown is an anti-Semite. Nevertheless, no doubt exists that he was right; indeed, the "Jewish conspiracy" exists in the United States.
>
> The New York Times, American television, The Washington Post, and hundreds of other newspapers which consecrate their front pages to every whistle of Yigal Allon, Golda Meir or Yitzhak Rabin, do not publish a single word about the affair of the "Israel Company" of Tibor Rosenbaum, of Solel Boneh and the refineries (some of the companies involved in recent scandals). This proves that the conspiracy exists.

Valeriani: That's not true; *The New York Times* ran front page articles on it. They did major coverage on the scandals in Israel.

Ghareeb: Much later, however. After this article was printed.

Valeriani: I admit, I have read the pieces but I haven't read them in detail. I saw the coverage and I thought the story wasn't worth as much coverage as it got. But economic difficulties, military censorship, and the problem of the minorities were discussed. We did a story about [the Israeli political party] the Black Panthers.

Ghareeb: That's just one minute part of it, a political group. What about the discrimination that takes place? Why is this not covered in the same way that you cover stories on the discrimination in the South, here?

Valeriani: You'd have to ask the people who put together the show, because I don't see it all the time.

Ghareeb: What about the human rights of Palestinians inside Israel? The denial of legal process to the Palestinians? The blowing up of homes of the Palestinians and expelling them without any legal process whatsoever. This has rarely been covered, particularly by NBC.

Valeriani: I'm not sure you can document that.

Ghareeb: I've watched NBC, and have not once seen anything about the blowing up or destruction of homes.

Valeriani: Suppose they did a story last year, would you have them do it every six weeks? Every month?

Ghareeb: When it happens; isn't that what determines news?

28

Valeriani: When it happens, it is reported. When you deal with television, you have to talk about where it happens, and whether there was a film of it. The wires run it, the wires are picked up and used on the evening news shows. They get a lot of their news straight off the wire.

Ghareeb: For example, torture and inhuman treatment of Vietnamese civilians was almost a regular feature during the Vietnam War. You have reporters in Israel and in the occupied territories. Yet nothing has been reported or printed about the torture of Palestinians inside Israel.

Valeriani: If there is, I don't know about it.

Ghareeb: Why is it that other Western media have done something about it while American television has not?

Valeriani: I can't answer that.

Ghareeb: Some people believe there has been a slight shift, or at least more objectivity on the presentation of the Arab side of the news. Do you believe that to be correct?

Valeriani: Let me get back to your original premise. If I accept your original premise, the answer would be yes. But if I don't accept your original premise, the answer is how did you mean that the Arabs are portrayed in a different light?

Ghareeb: There is less negative coverage of the Arabs.

Valeriani: There is more coverage because during the last X number of years the Arab-Israeli conflict has been seen as a news story with occasional numbers of feature stories elsewhere. Oil made the Arab world more newsworthy, because oil became a major energy source and a major issue. So more attention was paid to oil centers. In that sense, when you say more objective, there is certainly broader coverage for what are obvious news reasons.

Ghareeb: There were restrictions in the Arab world against correspondents. What have been some of these problems you have faced as an American correspondent?

Valeriani: We see it less than anybody else, because we travel with Mr. Kissinger, and certain doors are open. But finding people to talk to, getting to see people, especially for cameras—we went to Syria maybe 30 times before we were allowed to ask President Assad questions. Filming was very restricted in Saudi Arabia, and we see it in the best of circumstances because we travel with Kissinger.

Ghareeb: What about Jordan and Lebanon?

Valeriani: King Hussein and President Sadat would answer questions. It changed as they became accustomed to having American correspondents there. It was a different style of coverage, a different style of journalism, and they weren't used to it. I think it became more and more open as they became exposed to that kind of thing. But in the beginning, it was all very tight. We were almost treated with hostility, as though we were somehow from the enemy camp. It's not easy to go to Iraq and film, or to get a film crew in Saudi Arabia. If you want to send a film crew with a Jewish member to Saudi Arabia, you can't even get him in the country.

Ghareeb: One criticism is that there are many Jewish correspondents in television and a number of people suspect their objectivity. How many of the State Department correspondents who went with Kissinger were Jewish?

Valeriani: At least 6 out of 14.

Ghareeb: I heard it was 8 out of 15.

Valeriani: On a particular trip it might have been. I know some of the people who go regularly.

Ghareeb: Isn't that a high percentage? Jews are less than three percent of the American population.

Valeriani: That's right. You say unusual. In what terms? In terms of a flat statistic. But they're here as State Department correspondents.

Ghareeb: How many Arabs or Arab-Americans were there on the trip?

Valeriani: I don't think we had any. Then you tell me how many Arab-Americans are in journalism?

Ghareeb: There are some. How do you, as a correspondent, think Arabs could get their side of the story across? What would you say is the best way to deal with the American media?

Valeriani: Well, the first thing, and this is essential, is that people have to know what's going on, what's happening. To be perfectly frank with you, I've discussed this with ambassadors here. They are not told what's going on by their own governments, and if they are told, they don't tell their own staff. I would suggest that they first have information so that they are able to disseminate it. Forget about the rhetoric and the propaganda, and deal with the issues on their merits. The essential part of it is simply to know what's going on, and to be able to talk about it to some degree.

Ghareeb: Why have the Israeli lobby and pro-Israeli groups been so effective in presenting their case?

Valeriani: First of all, they're working in a vacuum; Arabs have made no effort to present their case. For example, in Washington there are 20 Arab embassies, and one Israeli embassy. The Israeli embassy has been much more active in dealing with the press, Congressmen and opinion leaders than the Arabs. I have discussed this with Arab ambassadors. Maybe they felt before that they didn't want to spend the money; maybe now, through oil, they are willing to spend more money; maybe techniques for public relations weren't available or they didn't approve of it. In terms of activity and public relations, it's a question of organizing a case.

Ghareeb: A number of columnists and reporters have said that when they criticize Israel, or say anything that could be construed as such, they get into hot water. One even said, "I'm in enough trouble without adding to that." James Reston once wrote: "You may put it down as a matter of fact: any criticism of Israel will be met as a cry of anti-Semitism."

Valeriani: That is overstated. If your reporting is fair, you can't be faulted. You can be critical of Israel. Israelis have complained to me privately about Israel and we have talked about it on the substance, the merits. We have argued it, but they never raised any question about me professionally, because they know I'm regarded as a fair, honest, objective reporter. Anybody who does a job well can be accused of taking both sides. I've been through that in the Middle East and in the South.

Ghareeb: I'm not sure you were there when Mr. Kissinger made the statement that Abba Eban thinks if he is only 98 percent pro-Israel, that's the same as being against Israel.

Valeriani: This was said in jest, but there may be a lot of truth in it.

Ghareeb: A criticism about people like Barbara Walters of the "Today Show" is that when Israelis appear on the show, they are given easy questions. They're almost begging by being so nice and sweet. If they ask a negative, critical question, they are almost apologetic for it. When an Arab

31

comes, they attack him constantly. I've watched many of these programs, and I feel this is a legitimate criticism. Why do you think this is done?

Valeriani: I don't feel it is a legitimate criticism, as I see it from my own perspective. Questions are asked basically to get information and not to make points. You may have that impression, starting from a point of view.

Ghareeb: One example, out of many, is Byron McClaughlin, the Canadian who wrote a song about Americans and America complaining about the sale of Israeli bonds. When he appeared on the "Today Show," that part was not aired, and the words on Israeli bonds were not mentioned. What do you call this?

Valeriani: I have no idea.

Ghareeb: It is this type of thing that we are talking about.

Valeriani: That's the kind of thing I don't know about. In terms of the news side, you have got to make a case that goes beyond simply saying, "It is my impression."

Ghareeb: It seems while there is this restriction, the media in Europe and other places and certain correspondents from the United States manage to present fair and objective coverage. For example, *The Christian Science Monitor* has had reporters on both sides for years.

Valeriani: That's like comparing apples and oranges. You're not going to keep a three-man crew in Cairo if you can't get any film or if you can't get radio reports out. It doesn't do them any good to write press copy that you can't use on the air. We are a different kind of media.

Ghareeb: True, but the BBC [British Broadcasting Company] and other European stations are the same type as you.

Valeriani: No, the BBC is traditionally different, if you compare it to the VOA [Voice of America], and the VOA has correspondents in all those countries.

Ghareeb: How many Arabs are employed by NBC?

Valeriani: NBC has lots of Arabs.

Ghareeb: Are any of the reporters Arabs?

Valeriani: No.

Ghareeb: How about in Israel? How many correspondents do you have, and what percentage of them is Jewish?

Valeriani: We only have one full-time correspondent. He's an American. All of the principal personnel are Americans. My understanding is that NBC has never had a Jew in Israel. No, I'm sorry, we had Rosenfield. The local people are Israelis, the cameraman and the crew, just as in Beirut, the cameraman is British and the soundman is a Palestinian. In Egypt, all are Arabs.

Ghareeb: So you have two correspondents in the Arab world, and one in Israel?

Valeriani: Plus the roving correspondent in Rome. But we have one correspondent in Latin America. We have another problem when you talk about restrictions. Even now, you can't get a plane and fly from Tel Aviv to Cairo. Why? The Arabs don't want it. Until very recently, I couldn't even go anywhere directly with a stamp from Israel on my passport. In terms of coverage, it doesn't make any sense to me, as a journalist.

Ghareeb: You mean the policy of a state has to be changed to suit journalists?

Valeriani: No, but when you complain about the coverage, if you put those obstacles, those restrictions . . .

Ghareeb: That's correct, but you're implying a state has to change its policy to facilitate the work of American journalists.

Valeriani: From the point of view of an American journalist, I would say yes, it should. The government here should change a lot of things. No question about that.

Ghareeb: I agree there has been some difficulty, but I don't think it justifies the type of coverage that has taken place.

Valeriani: I think if you want to be persuasive, you have to document the cases.

Ghareeb: Well, I cited three incidents and you said you knew nothing about them.

Valeriani: Out of a persistent mass, you don't create impressions about what you have told me.

Ghareeb: This was not an impression. These were facts that happened. One can only draw certain conclusions.

Valeriani: Do you think there was a persistent pattern of bias?

Ghareeb: I think it has improved recently; there are some reporters who have tried to be objective. But generally, there has been a bias. The Palestinians aren't even characterized as "Palestinian terrorists," they're called "Arab terrorists." Your correspondents from Israel call the occupied territories the "captured territories." This is bias, and you are guilty of perpetrating it.

Valeriani: Are they terrorists?

Ghareeb: That is my question. What did you call those Israelis who broke into the house in Beirut and killed civilians while they were asleep? NBC called them "commandos," and you called them commandos. Why didn't you call them terrorists, as you do the Palestinians?

Valeriani: I'm not familiar with the report that you're talking about.

Ghareeb: Almost everybody knows what happened to the PLO leaders in Lebanon, about what happened to Kamal Nassar, Abu Yussuf, and Kamal Adwan. This made the news all over the world.

Valeriani: That was three years ago. But to get back to the point, if you start with terrorism, what you get in response would not happen if it weren't for the original act of terrorism.

Ghareeb: What do you mean, it would not have happened? This is another example of the distortion. Why don't you say that it would not have happened had not the Israelis overrun the Palestinians and occupied the Palestinian lands? Why don't you ask this question instead of asking the other one? This is the tilt I am speaking about!

Valeriani: Go back to 1948. Where's your starting point? I have heard Kissinger say that the reason the Middle East is so complicated is that you are not dealing with a right or wrong, you're dealing with two rights.

Ghareeb: Except there is one right that is constantly ignored. One group is identified as faceless Arab terrorists, the other as Israeli commandos who are the defenders of democracy and a Western outpost in the Middle East. If that isn't bias and a one-sided point of view, I don't know what is.

34

Valeriani: The Palestinians who have attacked from Lebanon are terrorists. I don't know who attacked in Munich, but they were terrorists.

Ghareeb: How about the Israelis who attacked in K'fier? How about the Israelis who have been attacking inside Lebanese territory in the last two weeks killing Lebanese civilians, villagers and peasants? What do you call them?

Valeriani: That kind of retaliation is . . .

Ghareeb: You say "retaliation." That incident I cited in K'fier happened before Maalot and was not in retaliation for anything.

Valeriani: Let's assume it stops today, no more attacks. Do you think the Israelis would bomb in Lebanon next week? I think not.

Ghareeb: Exactly. If you think that the Palestinians are allowed to return to their territory, do you think there would be any attacks?

Valeriani: I don't know.

Ghareeb: If they are given what they believe is justly theirs, do you think they would attack?

Valeriani: I don't know. When I talk to people who are militant in the movement, they are interested in destroying Israel, as well as getting back what is rightfully theirs, or what is seen as rightfully theirs. I think there is an obvious conflict. I think that's part of the problem in the coverage. When the extremists talk about wiping out the State of Israel, you can conjure up the image that goes beyond freedom fighters trying to return to their homeland. I recall Barbara Walters asking Rabin and some other Israeli visitors, "Why don't you deal with the Palestinians more justly? Of all the people who should understand the yearning for a homeland, it should be you." That's not what you would call a "patsy" kind of question.

Ghareeb: That happens once in a while.

Valeriani: You have a different starting point. If it is framed in terms of a homeland, that's a different approach. If you expect any kind of sympathetic treatment for the kind of terrorism that has been exercised . . .

Ghareeb: I am not asking for sympathetic treatment. I'm asking for accurate reporting, for objectivity in reporting. Why don't you call them

35

Palestinians instead of calling them Arabs? Why do you call them terrorists while you call the Israelis commandos?

Valeriani: On the first point, as far as I know, when they know or assume they are Palestinian, they are called Palestinians. But then the second, third or fourth time around, you don't say Palestinians; for the sake of variety, you switch.

Ghareeb: At the expense of objectivity and truth?

Valeriani: The distinction is, if you say, "Palestinians, Palestinians, Palestinians," you've reported it's a Palestinian terrorist.

Ghareeb: What about the cry in the media about Soviet discrimination against Jews? The Jackson Amendment is based on the right of people to leave a country, as contained in the U.N. Charter. Why isn't that position taken by the media on behalf of the Palestinians and their right to return to their land?

Valeriani: Maybe you need someone like Jackson, in Congress, who can publicize and make those cases known. If they become an issue it's because someone makes them an issue. The discrimination against Jews in the Soviet Union was not a flaming issue ten years ago. The discrimination issue arose with detente and as Soviet society opened up. It's been there a long time.

3

Interview with **LEE EGGERSTROM**

Mr. Eggerstrom was a Washington correspondent for the Knight-Ridder newspaper chain at the time of the interview. He is currently with The St. Paul Pioneer.

Ghareeb: Arabs believe that the U.S. news media have been, generally, pro-Israeli and anti-Arab. To what extent do you believe this to be true?

Eggerstrom: The Arab world is correct in assuming that the U.S. media have been generally pro-Israeli and anti-Arab. Until the October 1973 War and the resultant Arab oil embargo, the U.S. citizen and the media paid little attention to the Arab states. The 1960s marked an era where attention was focused on the newly created African states in the Third World, and relations continued with the polarized European states. But the Middle East was a unique area, and the creation of Israel was watched with great interest fostered by an effective "interest group" within the United States. The religious fervor of the Arab states, which makes a vast majority of Middle East nations anti-Communist, was perhaps taken for granted. The Arab oil embargo in 1973 made many changes in the United States. One significant result was a "new discovery" of the Arab nations by the American news media. It is safe to assume that the news media stories about the Arab nations since the October 1973 War equal the total news coverage of those countries from 1948 to that time.

Ghareeb: When Palestinian commandos attack Israeli targets, stories about "Arab terrorists" are splashed across the front pages of the newspapers and on American TV screens, but when Israel attacks civilians and refugee camps and inflicts heavy casualties in south Lebanon, the U.S. media report it as "retaliation" against "terrorist bases" or bury it in the back pages, if it is reported at all. Are the Israelis perceived to be more humane than Arabs? How is what is news determined by the media?

Eggerstrom: The treatment of Palestinian commandos or guerrillas represents, in my opinion, the best example of the American news media's lack of understanding about what is really happening in the Middle East. Good reporters, like the correspondents from Reuters' wire services, have a long record of experience in the Middle East. Jim Hoagland of *The Washington Post* can write provocative and informative articles about the Middle East, its altercations and developments. The headline over their stories, however, will end up stating "Arab Terrorists Strike Again." It is unfortunate that the desk editors and news room personnel do not know the differences among the various Arabic ethnic and national groups, but more so for the American people who must rely on the news media to inform them of wars of liberation for homelands and what the real issues are abroad.

The question, "What is news?" is determined by news personnel in charge at the time of a breaking news story. That means nations of the world receive the attention of the U.S. news media when the editor-in-chief in charge at the time of the occurrence determines the extent of its importance and newsworthiness. If an editor doesn't understand a development in the Middle East, he is likely to ignore or "bury" the story. It is my opinion that lack of understanding about the Arab nations affects news treatment more than any intentional effort.

Ghareeb: Some think that there is a conformity of views resulting from the importance of New York as a news center for the Eastern press and from the disproportionate numbers of Jewish and Gentile editors and reporters who happen to think alike on issues relating to the Middle East. What is your opinion on this?

Eggerstrom: To what extent New York influences news media in the United States is a question that I cannot answer. The organization I write for has 19 newspapers in the Midwestern and Western states of the United States. The small number of intelligentsia in those areas, primarily college professors, do read *The New York Times*, *The Washington Post* and other so-called "Eastern" press. I do not believe the newspapers I write for base judgments of foreign policy matters against any "Eastern" U.S. model. It is my opinion, however, that if the news media share opinions about any area of the world, it is because that is the conventional wisdom in the country at that time. If the assumptions and opinions are inaccurate, then other forces must show the people and the news media new realities. There is a post- and a pre-Arab oil embargo attitude; prior to the October War and to the embargo, the American media paid little attention to the Arabs, partly because of the Cold War mentality that prevailed in the United States from World War II until the Nixon-Kissinger-Brezhnev breakthrough of "detente." The world was split under this line of thinking, and everything fell into a "good" or "bad" sphere. The presidents and secretaries of state who came and went during this period attempted the "evenhanded" policy sought by non-aligned nations, and met with both success and failure. But an evenhanded policy is not easy to explain during a divisive period in a nation's history. At the same time it was not politically astute for a U.S. Administration to try to explain what its objectives were amidst the rhetoric of the Cold War if it meant an evenhanded approach to quarreling nations; everything becomes black and white. The oil embargo created a new era. Now the United States thirsts for knowledge about the Arab nations and their people; and for the first time, the American people are learning that Israel is divided internally over questions of peace and that serious domestic problems exist in that country, as they do to some extent in all nations. As for the stereotypes, they don't disappear overnight.

Ghareeb: Some observers of the U.S. media believe that a slight shift toward objectivity has been made since the October War. Do you believe this is the case, and if so, to what do you attribute this shift?

Eggerstrom: I would disagree with the description of a *slight* shift. The shift toward objectivity is dramatic. Before the October War, most Americans assigned to the Middle East were in Tel Aviv and Jerusalem. Reporters on the "other side" were stationed in Cairo, because of its historic role in Arab relations, and in Beirut, where the only free press similar to the U.S. media can be found in all the Middle East. The staffing of bureaus in the Arab states has multiplied dramatically, although Beirut remains the media center because of its free and uncensored access to U.S. and European offices.

Ghareeb: What has been your experience with the Zionist lobby? What is its impact? How does it go about getting its desired objectives? What impact has it had on the media in general?

Eggerstrom: Your question about the Zionist lobby's effect on the media is difficult to answer. I have seen it work effectively in Congress, and we in the media report Congressional actions, if not necessarily uncovering the actions' origin. But whatever effect it has had, it is also changing.

Ghareeb: One argument given by some media persons for not covering Arab issues while covering Israel is that the Israeli news sources are more accessible and easier to get to than Arab sources. Do you feel this is an important factor?

Eggerstrom: The Arabs have been their own worst enemies in trying to reach the American media. The Israelis, on the other hand, have been the most effective spokesmen of a foreign nation with whom I have ever dealt. King Hussein has been the exception, especially when addressing the American people through major forums such as the National Press Club in Washington, D.C. Recently, a special envoy of the League of Arab States, Clovis Maksoud, had successful missions in explaining the Arab side to the American people. But all these efforts are minuscule in comparison to the steady stream of Israeli spokesmen and sophisticated media relations programs conducted in the United States by pro-Israeli organizations. The League of Arab States is contributing the most to raising the news media's and the American public's sensitivity to Arab countries. All of a sudden, Americans, including news reporters, are discovering that their next door neighbor with that unusual name is a Lebanese, a Syrian or an Egyptian American. The shocked reaction is usually, "But they are nice people." Yet the League of Arab States is underfinanced, and understaffed Arab Information Offices in New York, Washington, and Chicago cannot match the Israeli information operations. This access to information assists the news media in explaining Israeli positions, but it leaves the Palestinians as a collective group of "terrorists" led by Yasser Arafat, who is identified as a hijacker or bomber instead of a leader of a liberation movement.

Ghareeb: How can Arabs get better coverage for their side of the story in the news media in this country?

Eggerstrom: It was my observation in Beirut, Baghdad, Cairo, Amman, Damascus, Kuwait, Doha, Bahrain, Jeddah, Jerusalem and Tel Aviv that the businessmen, whether private entrepreneurs or state-owned manufacturers, had one thing in common. If you wanted to sell more merchandise than the competition, you advertised your product. Businessmen made information about their products available to the consuming public. Israel applies the same principles to international relations and the news media. The Arab states, however, are only beginning. If the Arab people want the U.S. media and the American people to understand their problems, access to information is the key. Censorship in several Arab countries creates some problems for journalists, and this does not help understanding. A more professional effort in the American information system—that is, making Arab positions known to the news media—is needed before headlines start showing Egyptians as Egyptians, and Palestinians as Palestinians.

4

Interview with
MARILYN ROBINSON

Ms. Robinson is an NBC correspondent who often covers minority groups in the United States.

Ghareeb: Do you believe that there has been a pro-Israeli and anti-Arab bias in the media?

Robinson: Yes, without question. For instance, on the first day of the October 1973 War the nightly news show of NBC, the big network show with John Chancellor, devoted an entire half-hour to the Arab-Israeli war. Only one or two stories dealt with American news. The entire cast adopted a pro-Israeli stance. After the program was over, half the Arabs in the United States must have called the network to complain about what it did that day. And I went down to the guys on the desk and I said, "Well, you just aired a whole half-hour show on almost Israel alone. You should expect this reaction." They said nothing. I don't even think they knew the Arabs existed too much before the oil question came up.

Ghareeb: Why do you think that this pro-Israeli tilt exists?

Robinson: It exists because the Jewish lobby here is so intense. There is Jewish influence over a lot of the Congressmen and Senators. A whole lot of people who are pro-Israeli are so simply because they know that Jewish money will not be coming in for the next electoral campaign if they don't take a stand that is pro-Israeli. On the other hand, the Arab community here has never been unified; it has always been spread out either here in Washington or across the United States. The Arab community has never been wise about the media.

Ghareeb: How is news determined on this issue, in your experience?

Robinson: It's determined by the reporters. There are a lot of reporters who are Jewish, and they want their stories done and they go and ask that they be done. You can get things done if you really ask to do them.

43

Whereas there are not so many reporters who are pro-Arab, or pro-minority groups, or pro-other groups.

Ghareeb: Do you feel that it's not just a pro-Israeli but also an anti-Arab bias?

Robinson: Yes, I think there's a great deal of anti-Arab bias, especially in the magazines, where you have caricatures. They have to be a bit more careful on television. I'll never forget when *Newsweek* magazine came out with an Arab on the cover who had a gasoline tank in his hand and he was grinning in such a way as to scare the public. You know, there are Irish White guys who pick this up and think, "Oh, my God, I don't think I can stand this."

Ghareeb: I have heard it said often that anyone who criticizes Israel comes under heavy pressure and is at times labeled anti-Semitic. Do you feel that this is generally true from your own experience?

Robinson: Now that you mention that, I used to do "cut-ins" on the "Today Show," from 7 to 9 a.m. It is one of the biggest shows on TV in America. At 7:25 and at 8:25 every morning, the local stations cut in and do their own local news for five minutes and then go back to the "Today Show" in New York. Well, I was in charge of the local cut-ins for Washington during the time when Yasser Arafat was supposed to come over to the United States. I was doing the cut-ins and I led with Arafat every day. When I began to introduce my copy about Arafat, I would never refer to the Palestinians as terrorists; I'd say Palestinian fighters and Israeli fighters. Or I'd say Israeli terrorists and Palestinian terrorists. I'd even-up the copy. When Arafat went to the United Nations I was evening-up the copy and I was using a lot of tape on Arafat, letting him have a chance to talk. But when we cut back to New York at 7:35, the guy who did the national news was doing the same story and he didn't even-up the copy. He would repeat the same story that I had read locally, using words like "terrorist," which means that everyone who was listening to the local cut-in and listening to the national news right after heard me even-up the copy and heard him leave the copy as it came straight over the wire. It graphically portrayed this difference in copy because there I was reading my news evenly and then they cut back to the national news and there he was calling the Palestinians dogs. I got a lot of phone calls from Jewish people saying that I had no business reading national news on a local cut-in. That is, they knew that I was supposed to be doing local news, but I was doing national news. But they also knew I was evening-up the copy,

44

and they didn't like it. And they wrote to the news director. Within a week I was told never to do national news on the local cut-ins again. Not one Arab between here and the Mississippi River called in to say, "Thank you, Miss Robinson, for being fair." Not objective, but just fair. Now nobody can do national news on the local cut-ins.

Ghareeb: Do you know of any other recent incident?

Robinson: Mike Wallace did a rather positive piece on Syria and the word from the grapevine is that they really tried to pressure him to retract many things in that story. But he refused to do it and CBS backed him. And I imagine there are others who have the same kinds of tales. For me, it was always hard to do Arab news because they didn't think there were enough Arabs here who were interested. You have a silent community that is backing you, not writing in or calling in and requesting. You're fighting alone. It is hard to do.

Ghareeb: Is there such a thing as Black media in the United States?

Robinson: Yes.

Ghareeb: What is their attitude?

Robinson: The Black media is pro-Arab because it views the Arab people as Black people, which is hard for a lot of people to understand. Most people outside the United States do not really understand the United States. They don't understand that you're either on one side of the fence or the other. That's partially after what the White people say: "If you have an iota of Black blood, you are a Black," which means that anybody who is halfway dark is Black. So, basically, the Black media and the Black people support Arab people because all you have to do is take one look at Anwar Sadat: He is one of us.

Ghareeb: Many reporters have criticized Arab performance in that it is much easier to get to news sources or news makers who are Israeli or pro-Israeli than to get to Arab news. Is this a serious problem?

Robinson: Yes, it is serious, and it is true. The Jewish people know how to manage the press. They're at home with media and communications, and they are very good.

The Arabs, on the other hand, are not at home with communications. They are afraid when a reporter comes up to them. They don't know that if there is something anti-Arab on the air and enough Arabs call and say, "We're not going to take this," it will stop. The Arabs are so scared of voicing their opinions that they lose out every time. The Arab diplomats are too busy running around being diplomats. I asked a number of the diplomats at a memorial service for King Faisal to comment on what kind of a man King Faisal was. Only the Syrian Ambassador agreed. Every one of the others turned me down.

Ghareeb: Can you cite any other examples?

Robinson: Yes. I wanted to do a piece on another Arab diplomat. It was requested of me by an Arab-American friend, because the Arab countries needed the publicity. It was a new Arab country, making its way into the Arab world. So I went to see the ambassador to explain what I wanted to do, and that we should get together on doing something. I said to him, "Trust me, I won't harm you. I am one of the folks you can work with, and I wouldn't nail you to the wall." But he was afraid that I was going to ask him about his personal life. In the same way, I have asked others to comment on what they think and they won't comment.

Ghareeb: What do you think Arabs can do to get their side of the story across?

Robinson: I have suggested they start with the Black press, but they shy away from it. I don't know why. They don't think that the Johnson publications are anything near to *The New York Times*.

I remember one time the three major news directors of the three largest Black radio stations in town said that they wanted to do more Arab news because they had recognized that the Arabs were getting wiped out by the White media. So, I said, "Well, what do you want to do?" And they said, "Why don't you go to some Arab ambassadors and diplomats and see if we can get tapes from the presidents of their countries?"

I got in to see some ambassadors as a representative of the Black press. I got nothing. They could have set up a feed line between Egypt and every Black station in Washington, between Libya and every Black station in Washington, between Syria and every Black station in Washington, just regularly feeding them stuff which would have been run on the national Black network. They were not interested in the Black press.

The interesting thing about Washington is that our Black stations are listened to by as many White people as the White stations because we carry jazz and new Black music, the kind of music that the White people like too.

Also, they could make use of the minority colleges in this town.

Ghareeb: How?

Robinson: They could call the Black educational institutions and ask what programs they might have for the Ambassador of Iraq, for example. If they would just make an effort to reach out!

I can't charge only the Arabs with that. Very few African and Arab diplomats really try to get into the minority community that is here. They stay in Diplomatic Row and they segregate themselves. The Arabs party with the Arabs and the Africans party with the Africans and the Spanish party with the Spanish. None of them will even come into the Black community where the people of Washington really are.

Ghareeb: Do you feel that there has been a shift in general media coverage in the last year or two?

Robinson: Yes, because when I started with this it was really hard to get the news through. But then I noticed that my station became very proud that I was doing Arab features. My argument was that if local reporters cannot do national news, they should do local features on Arab families— highlight the Arab holidays like Ramadan, Id al-Adha, and all the holidays that mean so much to them. So I'd do features about family gatherings in times of celebration, about students studying here, which had nothing to do with the Arab-Israeli conflict, but nevertheless showed the Arabs to be honest-to-God human beings, contrary to popular belief. And all of a sudden I noticed my news director was very happy that we had paved the way in that area.

What happened was that when the Arabs stood together and were undivided, Americans began to look at them as a force. A house divided cannot stand. Anytime you present a united front they will respect you. And that's the key. This power comes about as a result of a unified Arab front, in particular with Black Africa backing them for the first time. As soon as we saw Black Africa recognize that Egyptians were African people and when we saw Kenya, Zaire and Ghana move and back the Arab world, we backed them too.

Ghareeb: Do you have any comments on the way the Palestinians are presented in the U.S. media?

Robinson: The way they present the Palestinians is not to present the Palestinians. Anyone who tells the story of these millions of refugees stashed away in some desert or something is going to have to cause some kind of feeling about these people. You'll hear a lot about Arafat and

47

Palestinian raids, but what Palestinians are feeling, what they're thinking about, how they're working out in the refugee camps—no chance.

5

Interview with JIM McCARTNEY

Mr. McCartney is the military and national security affairs correspondent in Washington for the Knight-Ridder newspaper chain.

Ghareeb: Walter Lippmann once wrote, "The theory of a free press is that the truth will emerge from free reporting and free discussion." Do you think that the truth emerges and that there is free reporting and free discussion on the Middle East conflict in the American media?

McCartney: That is an extremely complicated question. There's free reporting in the sense that there aren't any restrictions being placed, at least that I'm aware of, on the reporters by the newspapers that they work for in the United States. I don't think there's particularly free reporting or accurate reporting out of the Middle East, or about the Middle East in the American press, not so much because of a lack of desire, but perhaps because of traditions and almost ingrained apprehensive attitudes—that kind of problem.

Ghareeb: But Arabs believe that the American media are biased, that, in a sense, there is no free discussion of the Middle East issue. One side is presented while the other is not. Do you agree that there is a bias?

McCartney: Yes. I think there is a serious problem and that the Arab concern is legitimate. They are accurately perceiving a problem that has existed for a long time in American journalism, which exists today and will probably exist for a considerable period in the future. It's demonstrable that there's been a great deal more reporting on the Israeli side of the Middle East situation, an attempt to present what is conceived as the Israeli position and Israeli views, than there has been to present the Arab side and Arab views. The American public as a whole has been very poorly informed about the Arab position or Arab culture and very frequently simply not presented with adequate information to make intelligent judgments.

49

Ghareeb: Is it just because there is ignorance of the facts on the Middle East? For example, even though there was ignorance on Vietnam, there was good coverage in the American media of the Vietnamese question. Coverage was often superb. The media tried to be fair and you heard all sides. But when it comes to the Middle East, you do not get the views of all sides.

McCartney: This is a built-in bias that grows basically from the underlying sociological fact that there are a great many more Jews in the United States, particularly in the big urban population centers, than there are Arabs. They make themselves felt, not just in the media, but in the culture. They have economic resources, they represent economic power and influence in the culture, and they have very strong views about Israel and the Israeli position. They sell those views, try to implement programs, and support pro-Israeli intentions.

Ghareeb: Many Jews are influential in many parts of the media. Do you think this contributes to the bias? Is there a general agreement between them? Some people even speak of a conspiracy. Do you believe this to be the case?

McCartney: Not to my knowledge, but it is a lot more complicated than that. I do not pretend to know exactly what the Jewish influence or power is in the Eastern press, in *The New York Times* and *The Washington Post*. I do know that there is an immensely large Jewish community in New York City and there isn't any question about the fact that *The New York Times* was and is owned by a Jewish family. Whether you can draw the possible inference that that leads to slanted reports on the Middle East—I am not willing to make that judgment and impugn the integrity of *The New York Times*. However, there are certain questions any newspaper ought to ask itself in the reporting of any controversial situation in which there are known divergent views. In my own mind, there are questions about the *Times* and its reporting of the Middle East. If the *Times* wishes to present a credible position it could, perhaps, increase its own credibility by not assigning Jews to play major roles in covering Middle East issues. That problem exists in many newspapers where those with the greatest interest in the Middle East on the staffs are Jews, and because of their interest in Israel they do have, in some cases, a certain degree of bias.

Ghareeb: In addition to the pro-Israeli bias there seems to be an anti-Arab bias. Most people don't seem to be aware that there is an Arab side. Does this happen in your newspaper?

McCartney: What you ask is a very complex question because only a few newspapers have their own staffs covering the Middle East, and thus the information presented in many newspapers comes from a relatively small number of reporters on the scene in the Middle East; the wire services, *The New York Times*, *The Washington Post*, and so forth. It would be difficult to make a case on hard day-to-day news reporting. The reporters there are trying to do an honest day's work. However, those covering the situation from Israel tend to take on, or their reporting tends to reflect the point of view of, the Israeli position. It is a phenomenon that is always true everywhere. I don't think that there has been an adequate effort within the media to counterbalance the stationing of reporters in Israel with the stationing of good and informed reporters in the Arab world. The obvious illustration of the problem in today's Middle East situation, the situation that has developed over the past eight years, is the development of the Palestinian "terrorist" campaign. Essentially, I very much believe that the Palestinian resort to terrorist activities has been a public relations effort, an effort to bring attention to an undeniably serious problem and to dramatize a real problem that exists for many, many hundreds of thousands of people.

It is my personal belief, and it may seem simplistic, that if the press (meaning the writers as well as the television people) in the Western world had done an adequate job in reporting from the Middle East, it would not have been necessary for the Palestinians to resort to violence in order to draw attention to their case.

Ghareeb: I have heard from some Western reporters who report from the area on the Arab side that the stories they file either end up edited beyond recognition, buried on the back page, or not printed at all.

McCartney: I have never had this problem with the papers that I work for. I want to add that it is the nature of the media, and perhaps the weakness of the media, to dramatize and report fully on violence and to underreport social problems. Therefore, when a reporter writes about a complex social problem, it is a harder story to get into the paper. I think you can make a comparison between the American peace movement on Vietnam and the Palestinian liberation movement in the Middle East. The peace movement domestically resorted eventually to techniques of either borderline violence or, in some cases, deliberate violence to get attention, because it couldn't get attention by the normal political means. Now that is a problem which is very serious and very complex.

51

Cutting stories that should be printed, or putting them on the back pages of the papers happens to all reporters all the time. It would be hard to assign motivations, and I'd be in a weak position to do that. I don't want to attack my editors, because they have been essentially fair, I believe, in handling my material.

Ghareeb: What is news, and how is it determined? During the 1973 War, your newspaper sent a reporter to cover it from the Israeli side, but no one was sent to the Arab side of the battle. Was the Israeli side the only one worth reporting? How was this determined?

McCartney: As a matter of fact, what you say is true. Because of the large Jewish populations in major cities, there is a kind of built-in audience for what's happening in Israel. The automatic reaction of some of our editors was to view the situation in terms of what those readers would want to know, and they wanted to know what Israel was doing. I did not participate in the decision at the time. It was my opinion at the time, and it is my opinion now, that it would have been a wiser decision to send reporters to cover each side. But I was talking to a reporter who covered the war for another newspaper who said that as a practical matter, it was a lot easier to cover the war if you only had one reporter from Israel because of the many restrictions in the Arab countries. However, I don't think that is any excuse for not making an effort to balance your coverage. You should be trying to retain your credibility, and to do that you should balance your coverage of any controversial event to the greatest extent possible.

Ghareeb: To many Americans the image of the Arab is either a dirty Bedouin, a wealthy oil sheikh or a terrorist. This image has come across in the media. Why are such negative aspects emphasized in articles, editorials and cartoons? Is this responsible journalism?

McCartney: You certainly see this in cartoons. It is an unfortunate fact and due, I think, to the cultural differences between the essentially European culture of Israel and the Eastern Arab culture. For the most part, Arabs have not really been understood very well, reported on in the American press or explained to American school children. One of the things that has happened since the 1973 War and the oil embargo is that there has been a growing realization of the Arabs by many Americans and by some of the media. Up to this point, however, I do not think the problem of stereotyping has been solved. If you ask any reporter who has been there and has begun to see the problems, he will usually say that the Arab cultures are very different from one another. The culture of Saudi Arabia is tremendously different from the culture of Egypt. I don't say this as criticism but as an observation.

Ghareeb: Do you think there has been a change in the media coverage recently?

McCartney: I think there has been some.

Ghareeb: To what would you attribute the change?

McCartney: Mostly to the demonstration of Arab economic power, as a result of the oil boycott.

Ghareeb: You hinted earlier that one of the problems for the Arabs was their inability to get their point of view across to the Western media. What are these problems, as you see them, and how can they be remedied?

McCartney: It seems to me that you have to consider all the sources of information about the Middle East that typical readers are subjected to in a typical American community. Because of the active role Jews play in civic life, a lot of information and background and many points of view are presented in American newspapers as a result of an extremely active effort by Jewish people who are interested in Israel. They have been extremely active in major American cities where there are large Jewish populations. Now the Arabs, for all practical purposes, have been unrepresented. I think this is quite important. If there had been any way to measure the amount of information available to the mass media in the mid 1950s about the Israelis and the Arabs, you would have found a tremendous amount of information on the side of Israel. This situation still persists. I don't think any chief editorial writer for a paper in Philadelphia or Detroit goes for many months without a visit from someone representing the Jewish community and with a pro-Israeli view for a luncheon or something of that sort. The Arabs, for all practical purposes, have not entered this whole area, but are getting into it now. I started to get *The Arab Report* in my mail a few months ago, I don't know who put me on its mailing list, but it is new and it seems to be reasonably well produced. I have been getting, also without any effort on my part, a number of Jewish publications. Do I read the *Report*? Yes, I do. Do I learn anything? Sometimes. Unfortunately, for any group in this country trying to explain its position, it takes time, effort and money, and it is competing for people's attention. I think the Arabs are working at it a little harder now and are doing better.

Ghareeb: What about the restrictions?

McCartney: I am not experienced enough to answer that. I spent six weeks in the Middle East last summer and I was welcomed on both sides. I found more problems on the Arab side, in the bureaucracy and red tape, in getting things done. Also, a more serious problem in the Arab world is the language. In Israel everyone speaks English, or at least it seemed so. You don't run into very many people who don't, especially on an official level. I remember my astonishment as a reporter in 1970 when I was unable to find any in-depth reporting on the Palestinian problem in the Washington newspapers that I read and in the clippings I could find. I was trying to learn about the Palestinian problem and its history and I found extremely shallow reporting, which itself was difficult to find. There is still very little reporting about the problem, and I think it is still true that the actual Palestinian situation is poorly understood in this country. It is a very complex issue that is difficult to write about. Yet most of what you read about the Palestinian problem has to do with terrorism—what is described in the American press as "terrorist raids." I was surprised when I encountered the fact that this was an objectionable term to many Arabs. Once you learn why it is an objectionable term to Arabs, you have moved a little step forward. But in order to learn or discover that, you have to have some communication with Arabs.

Ghareeb: One of the things the media in this country seem to do is portray the Arab countries as backward.

McCartney: Reporters encounter many things like that which grow out of the State Department's choice of words and phrases to characterize a situation. For example, I remember when the State Department people tried to explain to me their stereotyping of the various Arab countries, they called the Jordanians and the Saudis "Arab moderates." I would begin to say to myself, "Well, what does moderate mean?" It is a term which is very frequently used in the American press. Very clearly, it is actually a Cold War term derived solely from a hypothetical notion about the Soviet Union as the "enemy." Anybody who is anti-Soviet is moderate, as defined by the State Department's invented term. I don't know that I agree with "moderate" as a good term for what is essentially a very dictatorial regime in Saudi Arabia. If you wanted to measure it against traditional American political standards, I would have to call it a dictatorship, a right-wing dictatorship.

54

Ghareeb: How about Israel? In this country, Israel is presented as a democracy, yet there is discrimination against Oriental Jews. There is a denial of the human rights of the Palestinians.

McCartney: I think that to a great extent the press has fallen for the stereotypes that various "pressure groups" have tried to peddle off from both sides of the Middle East. There is a very grave question in my mind as to whether the degree of militarism in Israel has not become a very serious problem, threatening any kind of a democratic society. I was very surprised when I discovered personally on the West Bank the number of homes that the Israelis had destroyed with bulldozers, without trial, under military occupation conditions. I don't think there has been very good reporting about that serious situation. I think there are very serious problems in that kind of reporting.

6

Interview with
LAWRENCE MOSHER

Mr. Mosher is a staff correspondent for the National Journal. *He previously covered the Middle East for Copley News Service and* The National Observer.

Ghareeb: Many Arabs believe that the U.S. media are generally pro-Israeli and anti-Arab. To what extent do you believe this is true?

Mosher: I think it's still true to a large extent. To give you a recent example, last Monday night ABC-TV news was reporting the seizure of the Egyptian Ambassador in Madrid by "Arab terrorists." In the coverage they had a picture showing some persons, whom I assume to be "Arab terrorists," with a sign proclaiming the PLO in the background. This was despite statements from the PLO in Beirut that they neither had any involvement in the incident nor did they approve of it.

The question, I suppose, is to what extent this is an example of bias, of carelessness and unprofessionalism? I think there is a combination of both but it becomes very difficult sometimes to distinguish between the two. This country is culturally prejudiced in favor of the Israelis and against the Arabs simply because they know a lot about Western Jewish culture and not very much about Eastern Arab culture.

Ghareeb: How did this come about?

Mosher: I think it is due to exposure.

Ghareeb: Why was there so much exposure?

Mosher: In other words, we're in the West and the Arabs are in the East.

Ghareeb: But is there really a Jewish culture, as such?

Mosher: No, but I think that the Western Jews who founded Israel and the Zionists from western Europe, central Europe, and western Russia by and large represent the European culture that transplanted itself to the North American continent. Therefore, it is easier for us to connect with an Abba

57

Eban, who is part of an identifiable culture, than with an Anwar Sadat, even though Sadat has had experience in the United States. The same applies to President Hafiz al-Assad of Syria, for instance.

Ghareeb: I am wondering whether there is a conscious effort to give one-sided exposure of this situation?

Mosher: I think there is. It's easier for Americans to understand and to get on the same wave length with an Abba Eban than it is with a Hafiz al-Assad. The only reason that King Hussein of Jordan has traditionally been thought to be the most effective spokesman for the Arabs in the United States is because he is, to some extent, Anglicized. He was educated briefly at Sandhurst and therefore is Westernized to a degree that makes it easier for him to be accepted and understood than someone who hasn't gone through that process, a truer Arab.

I think there is a cultural gap between the Arab world and the United States, perhaps more so than between the Arab world and Great Britain. Great Britain has devoted a far greater amount of energy to understanding the Arab world through its diplomats, scholars, journalists and colonial bureaucrats. This has had an input into the British mind. In the United States there has been no particular interest in the Arab world until very recently.

Ghareeb: What about the ignorance? How about the other side of conscious bias?

Mosher: There are people with a vested interest in having the United States think a certain thing about a certain issue. The Zionists have propagandized this country for years to make Americans sympathetic with the Zionist political ideology and to make them unsympathetic with Arabs in general.

Ghareeb: Can you give me an example?

Mosher: I can give you a perfect example and it is very close to me. It has to do with the senior editor of *The National Observer*. In November 1967, early on, I wrote a story on the Middle East in which I used the term "Palestinian." This particular senior editor caught me on that term, struck it out of my copy and said that there is "no such thing." I looked at him incredulously and said, "What do you mean, this doesn't mean anything? The term refers to roughly three million persons who consider themselves and call themselves Palestinians. This is in essence what the whole Arab-

58

Israeli dispute is all about and you are telling me this doesn't mean anything?"

What this illustrates is that he had been brainwashed over so many years by a carefully orchestrated Zionist propaganda point of view that said, "The Palestinians don't exist." Hence, the term did not exist for the editor, and he struck it out of my copy. I was barely able to overcome his built-in and developed prejudice because of the power of my three years' experience. I forced him to accept that, but it was a near defeat for me. I think this example illustrates better than anything else the extent to which the propaganda has gone to absolutely obliterate the very essence of the issue through language.

Ghareeb: How effective do you feel this Zionist propaganda has been in the media generally?

Mosher: This particular editor demonstrates the effectiveness of it, and it is going to take years to turn it around. That was in 1967, just after the June 1967 War, and now eight years later this has already started to turn around through a number of processes that are unavoidable. But it will take another eight years, or longer, to get back to an evenhandedness.

Ghareeb: How do the Zionists go about getting their message across, and why do you think they were so effective?

Mosher: It goes to their organizational structure. The Zionists, as a group of people dedicated to the creation of a Jewish state, were always considered in American Jewry as a somewhat unpopular minority. The Sulzburger family, who own *The New York Times*, were known at one time to be anti-Zionist. The events of Europe during the Nazi period and into and through World War II in a sense helped turn around this situation and gave the Zionist point of view greater effectiveness, a greater appeal. Events brought about mainly by the Nazis gave the militant Zionist leaders greater leverage, which helped the Zionists in this country take over the structure of American Jewish organizations and of community life to the extent that they have.

Ghareeb: How does that translate into influence within the media?

Mosher: The newspapers in America are traditionally owned by conservatives and executed by liberals. That is, reporters and editors tend to be more liberal politically while owners tend to be rather conservative. What gets printed often is liberal reporting with conservative editorials. I think that the connection between the media and Jewish liberal thought

59

developed that way and when the Zionist point of view took over Jewish liberal thought, it was then able to take over non-Jewish liberal thought easily. This senior editor at the *Observer* was a person who considered himself an old-fashioned political liberal, and that's one reason why, to this day, he is still pro-Israeli. He has been so imbued with the goodness of the cause, the rightness of that cause, that he cannot and does not choose to re-educate himself with new facts and refocus his point of view.

Ghareeb: What about the old line about Jewish reporters, editors, etc? Many say that Jews have an inordinate influence in the media. What about the role of pro-Zionist reporters, editors and correspondents?

Mosher: I think that has been on the ascendancy in some areas. Traditionally, American Jews entered into reporting and journalism in inordinate amounts to their numbers in the general population. This is also true concerning American Jews in politics and voting. They are, in general, a very aware and a very involved group of citizens, more than their numbers would suggest. As Zionism took over Jewish organizational structure—community organizations, synagogues, groups like the American Jewish Committee (which was never pro-Zionist originally and now is very much pro-Zionist)—people just changed and adopted the Zionist point of view because that was appealing to them. They were not subverted or anything—this is what they wanted to do. The Zionist viewpoint came to dominate the American Jewish focus away from other Jewish interests, and then focused it more clearly and more determinedly on the welfare of Israel.

Ghareeb: How is this sympathy for Israel reflected in the copy of Jewish and non-Jewish liberals in news writing and editorials? How was the pro-Israeli bias reflected in the coverage of the Middle East?

Mosher: I am not sure I can answer that very accurately. I don't know how news was reflected during the 1940s when Israel was created, but I can speak about the coverage leading up to and after the 1967 June War. In this instance, I have the impression, but I am not able to document it without further work, that an American Jewish reporter would be inclined to carry into his professional work a blind prejudice that he might not even be aware of, which equated the Israeli scene as deserving and the Arab reaction to the scene as being inordinately unreasonable. Now this kind of cultural bias is in a sense blind because one is not aware of it. I think there are many (I would say the majority of American Jewish editors and reporters) who are well meaning, professionally conscientious reporters who, if they once came to terms with the bias, would attempt to deal with that as honestly as anybody else. I think a lot of American Jewish reporters and editors have been victims of this culturally blind bias even unbeknownst to themselves, and therefore would not think that they were doing anything non-professional.

Ghareeb: Does this also apply to non-Jewish editors and reporters?

Mosher: Of course. In other words, it's the same kind of cultural perspective that has been adopted largely by this country, regardless of whether you're Jewish, Christian or whatever.

Ghareeb: Specifically, there was a great deal more U.S. media coverage of the 1973 War from Israel than from the Arab side. Coverage of the Arab side, for example, was more negative than the coverage of Israel. You have a rosy picture painted of Israel as the democracy in a sea of barbarians in the Middle East. At the same time, you don't see anything about the denial of human rights to Palestinian Arabs, about the economic scandals, or about the persecution of Oriental Jews. On the other hand, the Palestinians are often referred to as "Arab terrorists," the Arab is portrayed as a camel driver, somebody who is a murderer, or something of this sort. Do you feel this picture is generally accurate of the American press?

Mosher: Without question. I agree totally with that generalization of how the American press has dealt with the Middle East and the various peoples there. They have stereotyped the Arab as an unsavory character with dark tendencies, and they have ennobled the Israeli as a hero. I think that these have been unfortunate excesses that are not particularly doing anybody any service, either Arab or Israeli, or the American public. The Israelis will eventually suffer for being thought of as ten feet tall when they are not; the Arabs will eventually suffer for being pictured as all bad, which they are not; and the readers in America are being disserviced by simplistic and over-generalized, stereotypic reporting.

Ghareeb: Reporters or columnists who try to present the facts of the situation or try to appear evenhanded are often attacked or criticized as anti-Semitic by the Zionist movement, and there is, in a sense, an attempt to silence them. Do you feel that this is generally correct?

Mosher: I don't know how common the practice is, because I haven't done any exhaustive study, but I can speak from my own experience, and the experiences of others I know of. From these experiences I would make a tentative conclusion that whenever journalists or writers have attempted to write objectively, they have been attacked vehemently, doggedly and persistently by Zionist groups in this country. I am one who has suffered that fate too. I recall even such lesser examples as having a story datelined from "occupied" Jordan. I got letters saying that I was an anti-Semite, that I was misreporting, that this was not occupied Jordan (I'm referring to the West Bank), that this was part of Eretz Israel. Therefore, I was against all Jews because I wouldn't acknowledge that the occupied West Bank of Jordan in fact belonged to Jews and to the state of Israel in particular. Now, as to the pressure in silence; yes, pressure was brought to bear to silence me at *The National Observer*. Pressure was also brought against top executive people of Dow Jones by very eminent persons from New York who have important positions in the financial community of Wall Street, to pressure me into silence because of a particular story I wrote in 1965 dealing with how Zionist organizations operate in America, the implications they hold for all Americans and America's relations with the Middle East. Dow Jones did not succumb to this pressure, and I am still with them.

Ghareeb: How do the Zionist organizations in America operate, especially inside the media, to influence the media?

Mosher: For one thing, they're very hard working. They have a very effective network of communications, a seemingly indefatigable army of workers who will generate hundreds or thousands of letters to Congressmen, to newspaper editors, etc., whenever the occasion seems to warrant it. You have at the top of this American structure a conference of major American Jewish organizations with offices at 515 Park Avenue, Manhattan—a building owned by a Zionist organization called the United Israel Agency which receives donations gathered by the United Jewish Appeal, or the United Israeli Appeal. UIA is the corporate receiver of funds donated to the United Jewish Appeal and slated for The Jewish Agency for Israel. About 65 to 70 percent of all monies gathered by the UIA is turned over to the Jewish Agency, which then spends the money on a variety of activities in Israel.

Now, the UIA is the umbrella group for all the various Jewish organizations, such as Hadassah, the American Zionist Organization, B'nai B'rith and so on. This structure wields considerable amounts of money and manpower. When a particular issue comes up, the Zionist organization holds a meeting and decides what to do about it. The word goes out and the people act. This can then result in people going to see the State Department, the President of the United States, Congress or whoever. Letters are written, telegrams are sent, people are alerted all over the country, demonstrations are put on, etc. It's an enormously successful, potent and legal operation.

Ghareeb: Is there anything similar to this in any way, by Arabs or by groups sympathetic to the Arabs?

Mosher: Nothing that measures up to or comes near the effectiveness of it. I don't think there is an Arab lobby yet, but there are groups of Americans—the National Association of Arab-Americans and the Association of Arab-American University Graduates. There are also groups that are not Arab in origin that may or may not have Americans of Arab origin as their members, such as the Americans for Middle East Understanding, American Friends of the Middle East, and Near East Refugee Aid (which is in the business of trying to help Palestinian refugees and also gets involved in a little public relations). All these groups help Arabs with scholarships and connections to enable them to come to the United States for their university education. They are, however, relatively powerless in the United States since they don't wield any weight. Nobody listens to them on Capitol Hill, at least insofar as I can tell.

Ghareeb: I often hear one of the problems is that the Arabs have not made themselves available to news makers or newspersons. I don't think it has been easy for a reporter or a correspondent to work with them. From your experience in the Middle East, is this generally accurate? What are the problems of an American correspondent working with them?

Mosher: I don't know what they are right now. I was in the Arab world from 1964 through 1967 and I've been back to the Middle East on two extensive trips, one in 1971 for three or four months and again in 1974 for two months, at which times I visited Arab countries as well as Israel. From all of these experiences, I would say that Western journalists, particularly American journalists, have a very difficult time operating in the Arab world for a number of reasons. One is that an American journalist and a typical Arab bureaucrat in the government don't make the same assumptions about the role of journalism, the flow of information, or how they ought to act toward one another. Because of this, tremendous misunderstandings arise and the American journalist finds himself increasingly frustrated in the pursuit of information; the Arab bureaucrat finds himself frequently annoyed and angered by the American journalists who are considered not to be knowledgeable and understanding of his situation. There's a real gap that works to interfere with the flow of information, which is the problem. To be specific, the bureaucrat will serve his interest best in the long-run by making information available, by assuring that the information is desired, that the journalist comes from an independent perspective, and that he is beholden to no particular vested interest. This is the cultural bias.

On the other hand, from what I have been able to perceive of the Arab world, most of these assumptions are not shared. Information in the Middle East is considered to be a commodity to be dealt with like other commodities; to be swapped, traded, distorted or used to achieve certain ends. That the journalist is not an independent operator but generally represents a vested interest is assumed. It would be very unusual to them if that were not the case. Therefore, in general, the journalist is not held in as high esteem as he is in his own country. The Arab journalist is looked down upon much more than the American journalist. He's on a lower level and therefore the whole basis for news sources and news gathering is entirely different there than it is in the United States. Bureaucrats assume that journalists can be bought off or dealt with in a certain way, so that they would accept whatever information is provided, or no information, with grace—and there would be no argument.

When it comes to the Arab-Israeli conflict issue and the American reporter's attempt to go to the Arab world and to represent it to the American readership, blocks are thrown up to interfere with this job being performed. In the American perspective these blocks are unnecessary, and I think that this is tragic in terms of serving the Arab interest in the United States.

Ghareeb: Do you feel that there has been a recent change in the general coverage of the Middle East in stories in the American media?

Mosher: Yes, I think there has been a gradual change, but I don't see any dramatic changes if you would compare, for instance, the time before the 1967 Arab-Israeli War with today. I think that the direction of the change is toward better, more accurate, more realistic and more perceptive reporting.

The reasons for this change are three: First, more Americans are becoming involved in the Middle East one way or another. More American journalists are going to and are being stationed in the Middle East since 1967. Hence, you have a volume buildup that is simply a growing journalistic expertise that will assist the whole process in better coverage as time goes on. Second, there is a growing national interest in the Middle East for very obvious reasons. The acuteness of the Arab-

Israeli problem continues to build, getting worse rather than better. In a sense, we are more involved with it now than we were ten years ago, and the public awareness of it has grown because of the dangers that it creates in U.S.-Soviet confrontation.

Then, finally, there is the oil interest. Clearly since the 1967 War, and more particularly since the October War of 1973, you have had that exacerbated severely by the price increase, in which the Arab oil embargo, in my view, was not the prime Arab interest. I'm talking about the members of OPEC and the Arab members of OPEC. I don't think there was conscious thinking of using the Arab-Israeli political problem as a further reason for raising the price, keeping the price up, and limiting production.

Ghareeb: What can the Arabs do to get their part of the story across to the American people?

Mosher: I think one thing they could do is to establish an organization here, or utilize an organization that's already established, to monitor the American mass media assiduously, just as carefully as the Israeli lobby monitors it. To look for the bad reporting, the unfair reporting, the inaccurate reporting, the stereotypic reporting, as well as the stereotypic cartoonists' portrayal. The cartoon makers of America are the most reprehensible lot of them all in terms of how they picture Arabs; always in the burnoose, always with a sulking, dirty face, always with a dagger in hand, and always on a camel. These stereotyped cartoons keep appearing.

It is necessary to have this monitoring function so that whenever there is an act that can be reacted to with cause and data, you then react respectively, whether it be toward the television stations, a network television company, the newspapers, or whatever. You say, "You have said this, and you have done that, and we feel that this is unfair, inaccurate and wrong, and this is why."

Now the Israeli lobby and the American Jewish groups do this all the time with a telling effect. They have been doing it for years and, in fact, I think the psychological impact of these expected Jewish reactions to whatever gets put in print, put on the television tube, is cumulative—so much so that editors are almost sometimes weighed down by it in advance and inhibited from doing things they would normally do if they didn't know that an onslaught of letters, cables and telephone calls would follow if they write or show such and such. It wears them out.

Of course, it doesn't wear them all out, and some editors, publishers and television producers get their backs up even more. But I don't know how many times something isn't published or portrayed simply because some executive somewhere just didn't want to take on the Israeli lobby again.

7

Interview with
GEORGIE ANNE GEYER

Ms. Geyer is a syndicated columnist and a former correspondent for The Chicago Daily News.

Ghareeb: Many Arabs believe the American press has been pro-Israeli and anti-Arab. Do you believe this to be true?

Geyer: Yes. When I first went to the Middle East in 1969 there was no question that this was true. I was stunned to find the one-sidedness of the coverage. At that time, there was real racism in much of the coverage.

Ghareeb: How did it manifest itself at that time?

Geyer: In what I had been reading in the United States and probably what I saw. Most of all, in my own reactions. Having read material that was anti-Arab and that made the Arabs out to be brutes, uncultured and uncivilized, when I arrived in the Middle East I was surprised to find this was *not* true. The press and other communications media were leading the public to unconsciously believe these things. Because I had been in that part of the world, I saw for myself what was real and true.

Ghareeb: Why do you think this was happening?

Geyer: The common impression is that this is a Zionist or Jewish conspiracy by American Jews who own the newspapers or the television stations, or who have tremendous influence. I think this is overdone. One instance occurred in 1971 when I was the first foreigner to interview Mrs. Sadat after she became the First Lady. I interviewed Mrs. Sadat first for my own paper, and then CBS asked me for an interview with her because they couldn't get one. I asked Mrs. Sadat, she agreed and we spent hours doing this for CBS. CBS paid me for the interview but never used it. I heard from intermediaries at CBS that the reason was that some of the editors who were Jewish did not want an Arab First Lady who was that attractive and that well-spoken being presented to the American people.

However, what seems to be involved are feelings about Israel, an idealistic feeling that this was indeed the promised land, backed by feelings of guilt on the part of the Americans about World War II. This is curious, because the United States did not take part in the Hitler nightmare. It is more of a tendency to oversentimentalize.

Ghareeb: There are two theories for this manner of presentation. You mentioned one, the influence of pro-Israelis in the media. The other theory takes into account cultural biases as well. What is your opinion on that?

Geyer: I lean much more toward the latter, toward the cultural bias. I see things dramatically changed today because it was a cultural bias. There was some control of the media and there was certainly a tremendous amount of money and lobbying put in by Israeli and American Zionist groups. However, this couldn't have been effective had there not been the cultural bias. Another factor was the terrible absence of information and learning in American universities about the Arab world and about the Islamic culture. I suspect that it will now become very fashionable to study the Arab world. Americans will probably go the other way, which is the American tendency when they find there is an emptiness; they even go too much the other way.

Ghareeb: I was told by the foreign editor of a prominent U.S. daily that his predecessor had ordered the reporters not to publish anything favorable to the Arab side, and to publish anything that would give a good image to Israel. Do you think this was more than an isolated incident?

Geyer: I really don't. I can tell you what I know from other correspondents and from my own experience with *The Chicago Daily News*. We are one of the six major newspapers with foreign staffs. The man I replaced in the Middle East was widely thought of as pro-Arab. I think he was just trying to be fair; but if you tried to be fair, you were considered to be pro-Arab, an "Arab lover," and all kinds of stupid things. I went over and wrote as honestly as I could. I did a long series on the Palestinians in a way they were never covered before. I covered not only the poor people in the camps, but the Palestinian intellectuals, and told what fantastic business-men they were and how they were running the bureaucracies. These things had not been reported about the Middle East before. I was stunned that no one had put this picture together; who the Palestinians were and how they operated in the Middle East. The series was printed in papers with large Jewish constituencies, such as *The New York Post,* and received a lot of negative response from the Jewish community in America. However, I never heard one word about the response to the series from an editor. I began to write columns in the *Daily News* and took some very strong stands, in fact, blaming Israel for the fate of last March's disengagement agreement. I asked the editor-in-chief if the paper had received letters about this and he said yes, a tremendous amount, but he never saw any reason to say anything to me. It was just never brought up to me.

Ghareeb: Isn't it unusual for a press as free as that in the United States to, first, fail to understand the Middle East situation and, second, to use slanted terms in the press; Palestinian terrorists but Israeli commandos, Yom Kippur War rather than the 1973 War?

Geyer: In 1969 there was a tendency in the American press to see things in black and white, in moral terms. There was a tendency to sentimentalize— and I can't stress this enough—to make one party the hero. Very early Israel became the hero. By 1971-72, the majority of the American press was giving a very fair picture and beginning to cover the Palestinian problem—beginning to give credit to the Arabs for the kind of people they are, for trying to bring development to their countries, and for their excellent minds. Things have changed so that today you can hardly notice the bias. The fact that it has changed is one of the factors that have made the Israeli and the American Jewish communities feel uneasy, feel that they are being sold out. I've been told by numerous Israeli officials that there isn't one American correspondent in the Middle East who isn't pro-Arab. Today they feel that because the Arabs are getting honest coverage, these correspondents are pro-Arab. I don't believe that. I think they're just trying to do a job. Then there is the other problem that can't be overstressed, and this has recently changed too: the unwillingness of the Arabs to tell their own story. You would go to the Ministry of Information in Egypt, for example, and they just did not do anything for you (there were a few that were different; Jordan and Saudi Arabia had very good and efficient Ministries of Information). What they would say to you was, "Well, you're not going to write anything good about us anyhow, so why should we help you?" And you'd say, "But I'm new, and I want to learn things; I'm perfectly honest." They just would not do anything. And it wasn't just that, it was also the tremendous bureaucratic mix-ups.

Ghareeb: I've been told by many correspondents that they write stories about Israeli raids on south Lebanon, for example, that are buried on the back pages or not printed at all. The reporters may send back balanced stories, but the problem still remains here. Do you feel the situation has also changed in this respect?

Geyer: Yes, the situation has changed. My own experience is that I did not have a single problem. My stories were used by a hundred papers in the United States, so it was not just my own paper. However, I am sure this continues to exist in other papers. I think it is more in terms of the mind-set of the editors. They have become used to seeing Israel as the little superpower that will be destroyed by all its gigantic neighbors who have no reason to do it. It becomes an internal refrain that has to be changed by shocks and real changes in the area. I think President Sadat has done more than anyone to change this because he suddenly acted differently and people had to respond.

Ghareeb: One New York reporter suggested that since New York is the center of news media, and it's a fact that there are a lot of Jews in New York City, that what's important to the people there becomes news. This means the influence of New York on the news in the rest of the country is part of the problem. Do you agree?

Geyer: Yes, I think it is a part of it.

Ghareeb: What about the role of pro-Israeli Jews in the communications media? Do you think this contributes to the problem?

Geyer: Yes, I do. But I don't think it is, as the Arabs believe, in terms of direct control. Instead, it is much more subtle; it is a result of the tremendous cultural influence that the Jews have in this country. Some 80 percent of the most popular novels about young people, about problems in this country, for instance, are written by American Jews, and many of them are not typical of what's going on in this country at all.

I think cartoonists have been a much more insidious influence. I talked to two cartoonists who work for my paper in Chicago about this, and there is no way to convince them that they are portraying the Arabs in a totally unreal, racist way and that they are doing harm. One cartoonist said, "Well, I don't care, I like the Israelis." He had covered one of the wars in Israel from the Israeli side and he liked the people he knew. There is an immediate affinity with people they know. The Jews are very active, very innovative, very outspoken and creative people. Most people in the United States have Jewish friends; whereas, until recently, not many Americans had Arab friends. This is another thing that is changing because suddenly the Arab population in the United States is becoming visible and vocal.

There is a lot that can be done by the Arab community in terms of presenting themselves and presenting what is Arab and what is Islamic.

Ghareeb: One problem that you mentioned is the restrictions imposed by the Arab bureaucracy compared with the Israelis, who help newsmen. How much does this contribute to the problem?

Geyer: Enormously, but I now think 1969, just before Nasser died, was a turning point. He had accepted the Rogers Plan, which in effect was the first time that Egypt would implicitly recognize Israel. Everything started to change in the Arab world and in the whole Middle East at just about the time when I went over. Reporters who had the best of intentions would find themselves absolutely frustrated by the bureaucracy. A lot of it, I now understand, is due to the fact that the Ministry of Information in Egypt, for instance, doesn't have much influence at the top levels. Most reporters are afraid to ask the different ministries for interviews, and if they do ask, they do not get any response. After about a week of going every day and really expecting help, which they do not give, you become very disillusioned and tend to react against these people. I went out and made my own contacts, which takes time, and it worked for me. I conducted interviews with many Arab leaders, and I have done it greatly on my own through my own personal contacts. The ministries, for instance, never had lists of the major newspapers in the United States, how many of them have foreign staffs or what their coverage of the Middle East has been. They had nothing to relate to at all. You would arrive at the ministry, and you could be the greatest writer on the Middle East in the world, or you could be a complete fraud, and they wouldn't know. It's very easy for people to misrepresent themselves as journalists. This was very disturbing. When I went to Iraq in 1973, however, they wanted to show that they were turning their program around for foreign journalists. I saw everybody from Saddam Hussein to the heads of all the ministries. By this time they had investigated me, and I was very thankful because they did a great job and it saved me a lot of time that might have been wasted.

In many ways the Palestinians were the most efficient. Their information office—even in Amman before 1970—would always give you something or take you to a training camp. By the time the Palestinians had investigated, you had already done a number of things. I still do not go to the Ministry of Information in Egypt, but once in a while I'll give in and say, "Well, I'll ask them to arrange for me to see a school teacher, or something really simple, because it will just save me time." It doesn't because they just never do it, and this is a great fault of the Arab

71

governments. They have not made efforts to put their point across. They could take advantage of the opportunity to deal with correspondents who are on their doorsteps and who come to them, but they haven't.

Ghareeb: Could you compare the treatment of correspondents in the Arab world to their treatment in Israel?

Geyer: Yes, but also in terms of different times. After being in the Arab world in 1969 for about three months, I went to Israel and there things were very businesslike and efficient. I registered the first or second day with the press center in Tel Aviv, and they would call me every day and say, "You have an interview with so and so, or such and such, or how would you like to talk to this person?" There was always something. They would carefully rate people, and according to how you were rated you'd get something, an interview or exposure. They were taking people out to the Suez Canal or the Golan Heights, but that eventually gravitated against them because it was too promotional. I think the Israelis eventually gravitated against it too. I have seen a change, however, in the last five or six years. The Israelis are becoming less friendly toward foreign correspondents and the Arabs are becoming more friendly.

Ghareeb: What can the Arabs do to change or improve their image?

Geyer: There is a lot they can do in this country. Let me tell you a couple of my own experiences. As I have told you before, the editors never told me when we had a lot of negative letters concerning the article I wrote. Of course the letters to the editors would appear in the paper, which is perfectly natural. The editors would ask me, "Why don't you get any letters from Arabs?" I was angered about this myself, and I said, "Well, I just don't get any." And one of the editors said, "Can't you go out and get us some Arab letters?" I said, "No, damn it, I won't go out and have anybody make up any letters. If they want to send them, fine, if they don't. . . ." This was the problem. In the six years I've been writing about the Middle East (and I've been spending at least half of my time there, interviewing all the Arab leaders—Khadafi, Sadat, Saddam Hussein, King Hussein, and Palestinian leaders), I have never gotten one single letter from an Arab and the paper has not gotten one! This could have helped immensely in balancing the treatment, but there was no Arab presence. Those of us who are trying to do a fair job, not to be pro either side, find it hard when all the pressure is coming from the pro-Israeli side. After the 1973 War, the editors called me and said, "We want to get some Arab response in Chicago. Who are some Arab names we can call for a response?" I gave them the names of six or seven Arab Americans or Arabs I knew of in Chicago. When I opened the paper the next day there was a long column with Jewish responses. There was no Arab response.

Ghareeb: Do you feel that the Arab embassies do their job in dealing with reporters?

Geyer: There has been a tremendous improvement over the past two or three years. In the past, Arab embassies were few and it was difficult to get very much done. You usually had to go to Egypt and get your visa at the airport and work through embassies in Cairo. However, in the last two years the number has increased and now there are embassies for almost all the countries and they are very helpful. The Syrian Embassy here is an example. Syria used to be a very difficult country for American journalists to enter, and if you did get in you couldn't see anyone. Recently I talked to the proper person at the Syrian Embassy, who was very helpful and efficient. He forwarded my name and my request to Damascus. When I arrived in Syria, I didn't get everything I wanted, but I got something, which is all that you really expect. If you can't see the minister, you see the deputy, and any journalist is happy with that. You're not happy when you are just left with nothing, or when they don't know you are coming, or when they have never heard of you, and so on. I wrote a number of articles about Syria, and a lot of it was critical. I sent them to this gentleman at the Syrian Embassy, because I wanted people to know what I've written, even if they don't like it. He wrote me back immediately and said how pleased he was with the articles and that he hoped he could help me again if I ever wanted to go back to Syria. I can't imagine this happening four years ago. The situation is much better because he didn't expect me to write everything 500 percent pro-Syria, and because he could take these articles that were critical, but shed favorable light too, and tell me that he liked them. That was such an improvement that I could hardly believe it.

Ghareeb: How important do you think the Israeli lobby is in influencing the media?

Geyer: This is not my best area. I wish I could tell you, but I've been overseas for 12 years and, thus, I'm better equipped to talk about my personal experiences overseas. I have not seen it myself, except in terms of massive letter writing campaigns to the paper. Of course, I am from a Midwest paper which is different from the East Coast papers. I know our editors were getting angry about calls from Zionist groups that were complaining or demanding too much. I think there was an editorial reaction against it, and I've seen that in our own paper.

Ghareeb: Have you been criticized for any of your writings by a pro-Israeli group?

Geyer: Yes, and I got a lot of letters which seemed to be form letters. In fact, I received leaflets telling people to write letters against me. That used to be an effective weapon but it isn't any more. If letters obviously look alike, editors don't pay any attention to them, but they do pay attention to individual letters that make good points.

Ghareeb: Many times if one criticizes Israel, he or she is accused of being anti-Semitic.

Geyer: I am familiar with this and I've seen it occur. However, I think it is rapidly losing its effectiveness, if it hasn't already, and becoming counterproductive. People don't like to be made to feel guilty when they are not. I think journalists and editors are beginning to react very negatively toward this kind of effort. I have seen instances which lead me to believe that Jewish groups and Zionist groups recognize this and are not applying these tactics anymore. But, these are just impressions. I have no examples.

Ghareeb: You said there has been improvement in the coverage since 1969. What do you think caused the change?

Geyer: There is no question that there has been a change. In television, for example, the equal, unbiased coverage now being given to the Arabs is done more honestly. There are several reasons for it. One is the consistent work of overseas correspondents who really tried to show the Arab side better. You must remember the change in position in the Arab countries. It was the summer of 1970, when Nasser accepted the Rogers Report and Sadat came in and carried it through. Implicitly the Rogers Plan aimed at procuring the recognition of the borders of Israel. That was a major political change because Israel could no longer say that the Arabs only wanted to destroy Israel. The more subtle changes came to a head with the October War. In August 1973, I spoke to Hisham Nazer, the Minister of Development in Saudi Arabia, who was educated in the United States and knows this country well. As a result, he has a great understanding of how things work here. During our conversation we spoke of the possibility of an oil embargo and of a war. I was convinced that it was going to happen and I predicted it. I said to him, "How do you think things will change in the United States if there is an oil embargo or something dramatic happens?" I asked if this would cause the American people to go against the Arabs, and he said, "No, I don't think so. The way the American body politic works is first it will get the shock, then it will ask, 'Why is this happening?' Once it really hits them personally, they will begin to look at the situation and analyze it because the whole thing in the Middle East really didn't cost the Americans anything before." I think Hisham Nazer's analysis was accurate. A lot of people thought if there were an oil embargo, the American people would react against the Arabs. They didn't, but what they did do was start to think, "What is this situation that we just took for granted because it really hasn't cost us anything that we know of?" And you see it really didn't, since we weren't directly involved in any wars in the Middle East. The money that was going out of the United States was through Israeli bonds and such things and it wasn't noticeable. Suddenly people did feel it and at the same time they were seeing the Arab world in a more realistic manner. Therefore, the entire situation began to fit together for the American public. That, in short, is the way I see that things have changed, and changed dramatically since the 1973 War. There is little change and upheaval right now, because the situation is stalemated. However, if another crisis happens again, it could dramatically change again. For instance, the Israelis, according to many that I have talked to, are very aware of this change in perception. To make a preemptive strike now with the change of feelings in this country would be a real disaster for Israel's public relations with the United States. I don't think that option is a realistic possibility on their part if they want to continue to have their favored place. The fact that the situation in the Middle East is quiet now doesn't mean anything because it's all happened beneath the surface and everyone is waiting for what is going to happen next.

Ghareeb: Go back to what you were saying about the problems of a reporter working in the Arab world.

Geyer: To show the difficulties of working in the Arab world, there are a couple of cases that I will cite. One was the fact that for many years I wanted to cover Saudi Arabia. But as a journalist who is a Western woman and single, I couldn't get into Saudi Arabia until 1973. Once I got in, the Saudis were marvelous. In fact, they were fantastic. It was the kind of arrangement where every day the Ministry of Information had a car waiting for me in the morning. We had the mornings completely arranged, things that I had asked for. If they couldn't manage that, they would arrange something else. However, the fact remains that it took me a long time to get in to do that coverage.

I have a speciality of interviewing leaders. Therefore, I wanted to interview Muammar Khadafi to write about Libya and the cultural revolution of 1973. I was trying to get to Libya from Cairo. Americans at that time, in particular American women, couldn't even get into Libya, much less see Khadafi. I was talking to a very good friend of mine, an Egyptian woman who is very important in the government, and she said, "If you want to send me to Libya, I would go and I would talk to Khadafi for you, and explain to him what you have written about the Arab world, and I think we could get you in." So I decided I could send her on my expense account. To my delight, she came back and said that Khadafi would see me as a state guest. That was August 1973. I finally got to Tripoli. I went to the office of the Minister of Information because he was the one who was supposedly inviting me. Libya was in the midst of the cultural revolution and the ministers, the secretaries and the receptionists had all left their offices in order to go out and work among the people. Finally, I found the Minister of Information going down the back steps one day and said to him, "I'm your state guest." And he said, "Well, that's wonderful, have a good time." It was difficult but gradually I got to know people. I was there about two and a half weeks, and I began to know the meaning of the cultural revolution. But there was hardly an apparatus that would help you get into the things you should be seeing. Then, quite by accident, I did get an interview with Khadafi, and it was excellent. I know the Libyans would agree that my articles showed them in a very honest light, but it wasn't because of any help from them. It was because I just kept persisting and insisting that I had to do this, often being somewhat obnoxious. However, it could have been done quite easily had they had a good working ministry. Everything you arrange you have to arrange yourself. You have to do it through your own personal friends, through pull, or through whatever influence you have. It shouldn't be done in this way. It should be done on the basis of who is deserving of an interview at that point, who represents the most important newspaper, and who has written most objectively about the Arab world.

8

Interview with
BERNARD GWERTZMAN

Mr. Gwertzman is the State Department correspondent for The New York Times.

Ghareeb: Do you believe that the American media since the creation of Israel, and even before that, in general, have been anti-Arab and pro-Israel?

Gwertzman: I think you have to distinguish between opinion and news articles. It is true that the overwhelming majority of American newspapers have tended to be sympathetic to the Israeli cause. I wouldn't say anti-Arab so much. I think there has been more published the past two or three years on Israel's views than on the Arab views largely due too often to the mechanics of it. The Arab spokesmen have not had as high a degree of credibility in America. Perhaps this is due to cultural differences. For example, often the rhetoric in the speeches in the Arab world is translated literally into Western languages, where it has a much more sensational, irrational, sound that is perhaps meant or that is perhaps a misunderstanding. This was particularly true when Nasser harangued his audiences for effect. When this was translated, it didn't have a positive impact on people in the West.

Ghareeb: Granted that rhetoric plays a part in Arabic language, but I think here it points to something important. On one hand, ignorance of the Arabic language, culture and society sometimes leads to misinterpretation of what is said. On the other hand, the reporters or the correspondents coming to the Arab world often do not know Arab culture. This may be a failure on the part of the Arabs, but could it be that the reporters know when they distort and slant?

Gwertzman: I can only speak from my own knowledge. I know there is no effort to deliberately distort events in any part of the world. Countries feel that the positive aspects of their societies are not reported accurately or in enough detail in the West. That's unfortunate, but it does happen. I would think, for instance, the fact that the Arab world suffered a setback in the 1967 War with Israel caused a loss, or for a better word, a sense of paranoia in the Arab world that was reflected in a supersensitivity to everything published in the West. I think the feeling since 1973 has been that the Arab countries have regained some of their prestige, which has also caused them to relax a bit in their supersensitivity. I don't think that there has been any deliberate anti-Arab campaign, as such. I think that often is the perception in the Arab world.

Ghareeb: Let me cite some specific examples. In *The New York Times*, when Palestinians conduct a raid inside Israel or attack an Israeli target, it is splashed on the front page in bold headlines. When Israel attacks Palestinian refugee camps and Lebanese villages and commando targets, it is buried in the back.

Gwertzman: This I do know: as far as the play the story gets in a newspaper, if it is a major attack it gets front page treatment, because of its unusual character. I think the Arab attacks against Israel, in which many people were killed, tended to get front page coverage as did also several of the Israeli airplane attacks against Lebanon. Now, there are daily intrusions in both countries that do not get much publicity, not because of any attempt to favor one or the other, but because they happen so often that they are no longer news.

Ghareeb: Except in the case of Israel, where it is often reported. But the same coverage doesn't exist on the Arab side. There are many incidents that have been cited.

Gwertzman: I don't agree with your premise at all. But I know as a fact, and quite angrily deny this premise, that there is no attempt to place stories because they are about Israel or about the Arab world. I was in the Middle East in May 1974 when there was an attack of terrorists against the Israeli school house, and that was all over the front page. I use the word terrorist because there were children held hostage. The next day the Israelis bombed the Palestinian camps in Lebanon, and that was also on the front page. The editors do not sit around in their room and say, "Ah, this will get the Arabs, we'll put this on the front page," or vice versa. That articles are selectively placed because of a slanted bias is totally inaccurate.

Ghareeb: Sometimes there seems to be a general pattern. You cited Maalot. Two days before Maalot happened, the Israelis raided a village in Lebanon, and several people were killed. This did not get coverage on the front page or anywhere else. The attack was not in reprisal, as it is often written in the *Times* or other American papers. That was neither a "reprisal" nor a "retaliation."

Gwertzman: I am only telling my view and you don't have to agree. I'm saying it tends to be a theory that there is some kind of a plot. Often the news is not published in much detail because it is not available in much detail.

Ghareeb: Many people such as Alfred Lilienthal describe the role of *The New York Times* in the following manner: "Day in and day out, with free news coverage and advertising space the New York press propagates Jewish Nationalism. Historical, anthropological, sociological, psychological and philanthropic factors generate this nationalism, of which Zionism is the political arm. Suppositions and hypotheses, emanating from sources interested in using fear to keep Jews conscious of the fact that they are Jews, are given excessive coverage as facts."

Gwertzman: I don't want to get into what are, in a sense, domestic quarrels between Mr. Lilienthal and other Jewish leaders over who is anti-Zionist, who is anti-Israel. Other Jewish leaders have other views, and that is of no importance to me.

Ghareeb: Do you feel that he has isolated a problem of any sort?

Gwertzman: No, but I think I would say this: what gets into newspapers tends to be sometimes a mixture of the routine and the unusual. Mr. Lilienthal has gotten a lot of publicity in newspapers because he takes an unusual point of view. You have to look very far to find Jews opposed to Israel. Although many Jews don't care about Israel and many are very pro-Israel, there are very few Jews in the world who are anti-Israel. So, he is, in a sense, very unique. He gets publicity, because he is unique, not because he represents a strong view. I think there is a lot of publicity in the American media about all religions. The Jewish religion becomes publicized now because of trends toward assimilation, or loss of Jewishness, which is just the opposite of what he is saying.

Ghareeb: There are some who attribute the pro-Israel stance in the media to influence by Jews in important media organs, either through outright ownership, as is the case with *The New York Times*, or through the predominant number of Jewish correspondents, editors, etc. who have a certain feeling, either conscious or unconscious, of sympathy toward

Israel, and think alike on this issue. Do you think there is any truth in this?

Gwertzman: My own impression, as a reporter and as a reader of newspapers, is that these are very simplistic views. The fact of ownership in the American context really doesn't say much. For example, Mr. Sulzburger's predecessor as publisher, his father, came under constant attack for being anti-Zionist. Many books have covered this subject. In the newspaper world, you never please all of the people all of the time. Again, I think that the record of the *Times* in covering the Middle East is very good. I think *The New York Times* has tried to lean over backwards to get all sides of the dispute, and has always had correspondents in the Arab world, wherever possible. We were kicked out of Egypt for a while and we have had people in Beirut. We had as an expert Dana Adams Schmidt, who covered the Middle East for a long time, and who probably knew the Persian Gulf area better than most people. There is an effort to cover the news fairly and without reference to people's background or ownership. I think it is insulting to suggest that because of a person's background, that background will influence his news judgment. I know in the Arab world people are generally free of prejudices, and this view is particularly distasteful to hear from Arab sources that are repeating a kind of modern day racism that has come out of Europe.

Ghareeb: Again the emphasis is on Israel. Israel seems to get a great deal of coverage in *The New York Times*. Even one Israeli newspaper, *Haolam Hazeh*, has this to say: "The name of the state of Israel, its personalities, and the events that take place here make up the headlines practically every day. Every whisper worth being mentioned enjoys a disproportionate coverage" and they give examples of *The New York Times* and other media organs consecrating their front pages to every whistle of Yigal Allon, Golda Meir, or Yitzhak Rabin. The articles tell of how "Golda Meir was photographed in the yard of her house with a dog; Avraham Yaff, with a picture of a tiger that was hunted in the Dead Sea. Those who were the State of Israel's photographic heroes were pictured on the first and second pages of *The New York Times* last week."

Gwertzman: Who said this?

Ghareeb: *Haolam Hazeh*, Israel's largest circulation weekly.

Gwertzman: I never heard of it.

80

Ghareeb: What is interesting is that it is an Israeli newspaper and it is saying that *The New York Times*, in particular, presents all of the positive sides of Israel and not the negative ones.

Gwertzman: That's absolutely untrue. I am going to tell you what I think and you'll make me repeat the same thing over again. If anything, we try our best to be balanced—not only balanced, but we try to tell a story accurately. The *Times* is criticized constantly by Israel for emphasizing the negative, particularly after the October War. We do what we do as our duty. We run nice pictures of President Sadat if we have anything to do with him. We do the same with any of the leaders. We are, by no means, flooding the paper with Israeli news. It is easier for a correspondent in Israel to have contact with high officials than it is for a correspondent in many other countries. It happens that in the Israeli political system the leaders are very accessible to not just Americans, but any journalist. In Egypt or in Beirut, or in Syria, it's much tougher. You have to make appointments and it's not that easy, but we do our best. We are not by any means an Israeli paper. We do have stories about the religious aspects of Israel, both for Christians and for Jews but not very much for Muslims. There are very few Muslim readers. It is true that there is great interest about Israel by many people who read *The New York Times* because New York is a large Jewish area. It is true that there are perhaps some articles of some interest to them that might not appear in some other papers, but this is just a minor aspect. I think if you went through the *Times* in recent years, you would find heavy coverage of Egypt that is almost balanced. Again, it's not deliberate, it's just that Sadat gets almost as much, if not more, play in the American press than Rabin.

Ghareeb: A *Times* employee recently said that sometimes there were certain articles written by correspondents in the Middle East about certain news events, and they either did not get printed or were edited. Do you feel this is true? Do you know of any?

Gwertzman: Editors always have the privilege of not using an article and they have the final word. I personally don't know of examples to cite. Obviously, articles often get edited since no correspondent is perfect. My own experience in covering both sides of this war is that I have not had any problems of a serious nature. Occasionally there is disagreement on what the important news would be on a certain story, but I think the editor's only criterion really is to be fair.

Ghareeb: Sometimes it seems that the positive side of Israel and the negative side of the Arabs are stressed. At least this is the impression that many people get. Another employee of *The New York Times* told me that the question of torture of Israeli-Arabs in Israel was not mentioned in *The New York Times*, and when he asked the editor about it, he was told that this happens all over the world and therefore this story is not news.

Gwertzman: I don't understand that. I have read articles about it in *The New York Times*.

Ghareeb: From your own experience as a reporter in the Middle East, can you give me an idea of some of the basic problems that you, as a reporter, face in the Arab world, and perhaps compare it with the problems in Israel?

Gwertzman: For one thing, I have to say that I have not been stationed in the Middle East. My only experience in the Middle East has been accompanying Mr. Kissinger. So it's a unique kind of reporting. The easiest place to report is Israel. The second easiest is Egypt, and the third is Syria, and those are the major ones. Israel is easier for several reasons. The Israeli press itself is much more aggressive than the press in Egypt and certainly more so than in Syria. So that often stories leak out in the Israeli press. Beirut often has stories also, but I have not worked in Beirut. The example I am talking about deals with negotiations. It's easier to get access to Israeli negotiators to find out their views on what's happening than it is, for instance, with the Egyptians. I'm not saying one is better than the other. In Egypt we had access to spokesmen, and Sadat often has press conferences. In some ways, journalistically, I think Sadat does make better news copy than Rabin. Sadat always has a press conference when we arrive, which always guarantees publicity on his views. The Israelis don't have press conferences as such. In Syria, during the entire shuttle in May 1974, which lasted a month, we never saw Assad. The news policy is much more tightly controlled there. Again, I'm not saying that's good or bad, it's just easier for newsmen if they have someone who will speak to them than if someone doesn't. Also, there has been a great deal of improvement in communication. When we first went to the Middle East at the end of 1973, the Israeli communication policy was more advanced since they had better facilities. Obviously, a story can't get into a newspaper unless it can be sent. Today there is a satellite in Egypt which makes it easier, and the facilities have been improved immensely in Saudi Arabia where there were not any before. So, the oil price has improved the telecommunications facilities in the Arab countries. I don't think it's as bad as some people feel. The Egyptian officials have been quite helpful and this is reflected by their change in policy. There used to be a very tight censorship in Egypt, but now there is virtually none. Without censorship, of course, you can send your story much quicker. I think the fact that Egypt now gets positive coverage in the newspapers, in part, is a reflection of the fact that Sadat has a much more open news policy.

Ghareeb: How do you think it can be improved further?

Gwertzman: The easiest way to improve is to simply create a reputation that the facts a spokesman or a high official is giving are accurate. That takes time because only history will tell whether what a person said at one time is entirely true. I think this is improving and there is more consciousness of this in the Arab world. In our stories, there is much more accurate information involved. And this, in part, is reflected by better coverage.

Ghareeb: How do you think the American media itself can improve its coverage?

Gwertzman: The easiest way is to have more people covering the area, which is a gradual process. In the United States, in my newspaper, we are putting more resources in the Middle East. Don't forget, we have had for ten years very heavy demands on us from Southeast Asia. Now that that conflict is over with, we are able to reallocate resources to the Middle East. I think it is useful to have people who, for instance, in the Arab world, speak Arabic. This is a problem.

Ghareeb: Do you have any Arab-Americans working for the *Times*, that you know of?

Gwertzman: We don't have any Arab-Americans as far as I know and I don't know of any, in fact, who report anywhere in the media. I don't know the reasons for that. However, we have people who are now studying Arabic. Our man in Beirut speaks Arabic and is studying to improve. It's tough because in most of the Arab countries, as in Israel, the people that the newsman normally deals with usually speak English, or at times French. So, there isn't much incentive to study the language. Our correspondent in Israel, for instance, doesn't speak much Hebrew, for similar reasons.

83

Ghareeb: *The New York Times* is one of the leading newspapers in the United States and is considered very important, at least when dealing with the Arab-Israeli conflict. Yet in many places it is viewed with suspicion because, while there are some stories that are objective, you get some that seem to distort the facts. For example, during the recent hearings on the Hawk missile sale to Jordan, I believe it was on July 22, 1975, witnesses testified both in favor of and against the sale to Jordan. The *Times* reported on all of the witnesses that were opposed to the sale of Hawks, but not on any one of the people who were in favor of the sale.

Gwertzman: I am not sure we covered the hearing. Is there a story about it?

Ghareeb: Yes. That's why I am referring to it. I believe it was by Finney.

Gwertzman: I'll tell you my honest impression of the story. But ask Finney to give his answer. I don't think there is any secret that he made a judgment earlier that the Hawks would be approved very easily and that Jordan would have no trouble. So, he recommended against coverage, that it wasn't necessary. He turned out to be wrong. We tried to give the Jordanian viewpoint on this.

Ghareeb: This certainly didn't come through, at least here.

Gwertzman: No, not here. If that was the case, we should have done more. I think the feeling was it wasn't worth covering the hearing. I think he only had about three paragraphs on that story.

Ghareeb: That was a long article, an interesting one. Those witnesses appeared, both on the same day.

Gwertzman: Who are the witnesses for this side?

Ghareeb: They were two former U.S. Ambassadors to Jordan. One of them is the head of the Middle East Institute, Dean Brown, and one is from New York.

Gwertzman: I would say if that were the case, it was a mistake. No one in New York said not to cover it. Certainly, John Finney is not pro-Israeli by any means. He probably thought more news was in those opposed to the sale because up until then, the sale of equipment went through routinely. If he highlighted the views opposed to the sale, it was simply what was the newsworthy aspect. This is a tough decision.

84

Ghareeb: Today there is a good article by Drew Middleton. The headline says, "New Missiles for the Mid East, a Destabilizing Factor." The article focuses on, specifically, the Pershing missiles sold to Israel that can carry nuclear weapons. Yet the headline says, "New Missiles for the Mid East" while the missiles are for Israel.

Gwertzman: I think this article says, if I'm not mistaken, that the question of missiles to Israel raises the question of the Soviets giving new missiles to Arab countries. So, the article is about missiles in both Israel and the Arab countries.

Ghareeb: Yes, but what has triggered it is the idea of the Pershing going to Israel, which would be the destabilizing factor, because the other one would be a response, a reaction.

Gwertzman: You might have a point. I won't argue with that.

Ghareeb: Are attempts made to silence or criticize people who try to criticize Zionism in Israel or criticize U.S. policies in Israel? Even one of your own people, James Reston, has said that "You may put it down as a matter of fact that any criticism of Israel's policies will be attacked as anti-Semitism." How important or wide ranging is this?

Gwertzman: I'm afraid that sounds like one of those quotes that he may never have said but got repeated. You might check with Mr. Reston. In any event, it is true to a certain extent in this country. We have very activist Jewish people who resent any article printed against Israel and make their views known. They criticize *The New York Times* often, and probably that's what Mr. Reston is talking about. There are other people who have other views. This is an open society of people in the sense that people are free to sound off. There is a very big Jewish press in this country that circulates mostly among Jews. There is also an Arab press with a smaller number of people. What they say, you know, often reflects their very strongly held positions. The newspapers have to try to seek the truth as they see it and often they get criticized, but that's part of the American way.

Ghareeb: The Zionist lobby itself is perhaps one of the most powerful lobbies in the United States today. How does it go about trying to influence the media?

Gwertzman: Well, I would say pro-Israeli lobby. I don't like the word Zionist. In a sense it's not exact enough for me. I would like to say pro-

Israeli lobby because Zionism is something like Islam in the sense of one having an emotional attachment to it that often has nothing to do with politics. But I would say it's a very effective lobby because it has a lot of support on Capitol Hill from Senators and Congressmen who support its basic aim, and who strongly believe, as does the Administration, in securing the survival of Israel. That's their basic policy. The lobby is very effective because it starts with basic support. It doesn't have to twist arms anywhere in the Administration or on Capitol Hill on that basic policy. I think it's also effective with the press, because the information it has tends to be accurate and nonrhetorical. It pays to be accurate. For instance, obviously the pro-Israeli lobby was opposed to this sale of the Hawk missiles to Jordan. However, if their information had been inaccurate, they would not have had much influence at all with the media. I think, too often, other lobbies come to the newspapers with a very emotional case but without news and as a result they get very little publicity. An Arab spokesman in this country does have statements to make but gets little publicity because what is said is no different from what has been said in Cairo, or Syria, or in Beirut two weeks ago and reported at that time. They are not getting publicity not because of any hostility to what is said but because it's not news. It would help the Arab cause to send more people to American journalism schools or to give them experience with an American newspaper to learn how the press operates. Too often, ideological meaning is put on things. During the recent (pre-summer 1975) negotiations, for example, the Israelis were always a better source of information than the Egyptians. The Egyptian Embassy in Washington had no information, and as a result a journalist would talk to the Israeli Embassy. The Israeli Ambassador was involved in the negotiations and was very current on the issue, whereas the Egyptian Ambassador was not even told by his foreign office what was happening.

Ghareeb: Would you say that this reflects the situation of the Israeli and Arab embassies?

Gwertzman: Generally, yes. I think the Arab embassies in Washington, and I may be wrong, are more goodwill embassies and don't involve themselves with negotiations on any issues. Most of the negotiating is done through American ambassadors in the Arab countries, and I think the home offices don't inform their ambassadors here of what's happening. I may be wrong about some of the embassies and I don't mean this critically, but it's a fact. There is no law that says the ambassador has to know everything.

Ghareeb: New York is a large place with a large Jewish population, many of whom support the State of Israel. Do you think this affects the news media in New York?

Gwertzman: It has been said that *The New York Times* is very interested in the Middle East, not only because it is a very important issue, but because the *Times* knows its readers are very interested in it, and not only because of the oil issue. It's also because, as I was saying earlier, there is more information available now concerning the Arab side and there is, as a result, a greater sensitivity. The *Times* feels it is important as a diplomatic, economic issue to give more men and resources to covering the Middle East than to Paris or other parts of the world.

Ghareeb: From what you have said, do you feel there has been a change recently in the coverage?

Gwertzman: No. What I am saying is that there are more articles about the Arab world in the media in general due in part to greater interest in the Arab world, partly to the oil embargo, and partly because of a greater need to know what is happening. I think the change in leadership in Egypt brought about a new policy there and now it's easier to get information with less rhetoric and more rational discussion. I think the intention of the American news media throughout has been to give as balanced a picture as possible. Often it has been very difficult to get a very good viewpoint from the Arab world. Now, for instance, you must know that *The New York Times* is criticized constantly for being too pro-Arab. There are Jewish leaders who think we favor Sadat, for instance, and there are many articles written criticizing the use of the word "moderate" when we refer to Arafat or Sadat.

Ghareeb: How important is New York as a center for the media?

Gwertzman: Very important, because it is essentially where the networks and the news magazines are located, as well as *The New York Times*. Obviously, *The New York Times* is very important to the other media because news magazines and networks read the *Times* in the morning and that influences what they program.

Ghareeb: The impression I get from you is that the problem is not the failure of the American media, but the failure of the Arabs.

Gwertzman: I don't think there is a failure anywhere. I think it is interrelated. I think the Arabs have been doing very well in getting their

87

message across. But I don't think anyone has a lasting knowledge of what the Arabs want at this point. There may be some confusion about the Palestinians, but this is due largely to the Palestinians, whose organizations are now so divided that it is very hard to say what the Palestinian position is.

Ghareeb: Except the PLO?

Gwertzman: Even the PLO. It is very hard to say, for instance, what the PLO wants. When it comes to the question of a national home, will the West Bank be sufficient? Some might say, "yes," and others would say, "no." That is an ambiguous point. So it is very hard to accurately report that issue or that position. It's inherent because the PLO is not a state with a capital and a regular foreign office.

Ghareeb: The issues are so very complex that they sometimes need a great deal of background.

Gwertzman: We try. There are many articles on this but I am afraid that, like Vietnam, not too many people read them all.

Ghareeb: Not always, but often you get the feeling that the editorials are pro-Israel and anti-Arab. Take the Arab boycott for instance.

Gwertzman: Often the *Times'* editorials have been critical of the boycott.

Ghareeb: Not in the beginning.

Gwertzman: Generally speaking, the fact that the *Times* was critical of that has not been powerfully written. We took a very strong position opposed to that kind of boycott, I think, in general. The *Times* is not anti-Arab. It's pro-Arab, it's pro-Israel, in the sense that the *Times* would like very much to see a Middle East settlement that's fair to all sides. It is opposed, I think, to anything that would lead to the destruction or dismemberment of Israel. The *Times* is generally supportive of various proposals leading to a final settlement which Israel would essentially avoid. I say essentially because I don't think the *Times* supports giving up every inch of territory. I think there is a need for negotiations, and some compromises here.

Ghareeb: To change the subject to a technical question: How do you determine what is news? What does it depend on?

Gwertzman: That's a very hard question. What is news? I would say if a dog bites a man, it is not news. If the man bites the dog, it is news. That expresses it. Obviously, my job as a diplomatic correspondent in the general aspect is to report new developments, to make sure the readers generally know the politics somewhat. From Washington, my emphasis is largely on American politics. I don't deal with other countries' politics or policies except as they affect the United States. I'd be very happy to have news on the Arab side. Obviously discussions go on all the time between American officials and Arab governments, but the Arab governments don't report them very well. There is nothing of any importance that I ever heard about the Arabs. There are many embassies here with very sophisticated press attaches, but there have never been any press releases. There is nothing to report.

Ghareeb: There are many reporters in the Arab world who know the area, but there are others who are sent there without knowing anything about the current developments or the historical background.

Gwertzman: I think every reporter that we have sent to the Arab world may not have been an Arabist to begin with, but after he is there a year he certainly knows the country. Again you have to have serious feelings.

Ghareeb: Do you think this applies to the other media organs as well?

Gwertzman: Yes, my impressions are that most of the media are making serious efforts to find out what's happening and to report it honestly. Unfortunately, it's hard to get solid information.

Ghareeb: Another item is the American people's perception of the Arab world. They often see the Arab as a terrorist, as a murderer, or someone greedily stopping the oil at the pump. Do you think this image reflects the Arabs currently?

Gwertzman: No, finite images are tough. It's true that you have one image of what Arabs want to create here. It is sort of "Fedayeen-guerrilla."

Ghareeb: I wouldn't say Arabs. I would say Palestinians.

Gwertzman: All right, Palestinians. One image of the Palestinians is that they are militant. You also have the image of the rich oil sheikh, the image of an arrogant cartel. The Americans are not very fond of the higher price of oil. It would be unusual for the Americans to applaud the high rise in the price of oil in the last few years. The image of the Arab world in the United States—the interviews with people complaining about the high price of oil—is that people basically think they're being gypped.

Ghareeb: Yet nothing was said about the price of oil, for example, when the prices were kept very low. They even went down between 1951 and 1973.

Gwertzman: From your point of view you have a case. The Arabs are trying to justify their oil rise, but the Americans who have to pay it don't see it that way.

Ghareeb: Many people in the Arab world have been incensed by the stereotyped coverage in the U.S. press, which is in a way similar to the treatment of Jews in the Nazi media. You get the caricatures.

Gwertzman: I think part of it was the humiliation suffered by the Arabs in the 1967 War. I think it was a very important thing because they were defeated so quickly. This led to a lot of jokes not only in the United States but everywhere in the world. It inflated the prestige of Israel and deflated the prestige of the Arab world. I think the 1973 War had the effect of bringing things back to normal. I don't think you find as much stereotyping now as you did after 1967. My feeling is that the press is seriously trying to do a good job. Any story can be criticized, but the overall approach is to try to be honest.

9

Interview with ROBERT REGULY

Mr. Reguly is a producer of news documentary programs for Canadian television and the former Europe and Middle East correspondent for The Toronto Daily Star, *Canada's largest circulation daily.*

Ghareeb: Do you think the Canadian press is anti-Arab and pro-Israeli?

Reguly: I don't think the Canadian press is so much anti-Arab as it is pro-Israeli. Because of the tremendous Jewish lobby in Canada, only the Israeli point of view gets carried across. Although there are only 300,000 Jews in a population of over 22 million, they carry an inordinate amount of influence, and as is usually the case, those people who are farthest from the scene of battle are much more militant than the people doing the fighting. From my experiences, I find that the Canadian Zionists are much more militant about Israel than the Israelis are, and they get almost paranoiac.

The newspaper scene in Canada is dominated by three chains that control, overwhelmingly, most of the newspapers in the country. They do not send their correspondents to see for themselves, but take the news from wire service copy. The Canadian Wire Service copy is called "The Canadian Press" and it has no correspondents in the Middle East. They rely, in turn, on rewriting either Reuters, or much more important, the Associated Press. It is generally this laziness and cheapness that leads to ignorance. On the big newspapers, I think it is almost a deliberate policy to have a very heavy pro-Jewish slant because of the Jewish influence in Canada.

Ghareeb: How does this "slant" manifest itself?

Reguly: The U.N. Conference on Crime, for example, was scheduled to be held in Toronto in September. Now there was a tremendous Jewish lobby led by, among others, Philip Givvons, the former mayor of Toronto, and the Rabbi Gunther Plout. They prevailed upon the Canadian government to ask the United Nations not to cancel the Conference but to postpone the Conference on the grounds that the PLO was to be invited as an observer.

91

The major efforts of Zionists and Israelis are to deny any credibility to the Palestinian movement, to characterize them as assassins, terrorists, bullies, and outlaws; that is the theme that they carry. The word guerrilla is never mentioned with reference to the Palestinian. It's always terrorist. It's a perversion of the language. One man's freedom fighter is another man's terrorist, for instance, and the Israelis ignore their own history of terrorism!

Ghareeb: Isn't that part of the problem? Some cartoons that have appeared in the Canadian press have portrayed the Arabs in general as terrorists and untrustworthy. Doesn't this go beyond the pro-Israeli to an anti-Arab stance?

Reguly: As I said, I am making two distinctions here. Most of the papers are too cheap to find out for themselves what is going on, so they take what is called "hand-out news" and do reprints. Let us say that some local man out West, a Jewish-Zionist man, says the Arabs are all dirty and we shouldn't let the Arabs or PLO into this country for the Conference. Bang! They carry that, and don't bother to give the other side. It's a politics of lazy journalism. I don't think it's deliberate, but of course the influence is felt in the major papers, particularly in *The Toronto Star*, which is by far the largest newspaper in the country in terms of circulation and a paper for which I have worked for 14 years. As their Middle East correspondent, I can personally state that its bias is definitely heavy and deliberately pro-Israel, without any qualms.

Ghareeb: Can you cite for me examples of how you have experienced this?

Reguly: For instance, I was covering the Middle East from 1969 to 1972 from Rome. *The Toronto Star* had two correspondents in Israel who were stringers, one in Tel Aviv and one in Jerusalem; they were approximately an hour's ride apart. Yet we had none in the Arab world. Let's take a particular incident. I was sent to do some stories on the Palestinian movement, which took me six weeks of driving all over the country. They wanted these stories done, not because they were particularly interested in the Palestinian movement, but because Mr. Al Forrest had just written a book in which he came out heavily for the Palestinian point of view and probably rightly so. Mr. Forrest wanted to sell a series based on the book to *The Toronto Star*. As a means of stalling him, as an excuse for not coming out and saying, "we don't want to print your story," they said, "oh well, we will send our man to do this," as a subtle way of averting, or not running, the story. That was the only reason I was sent to cover the Palestinian side.

Ghareeb: I have been told by some American journalists that when they wrote an article that might have been construed as anti-Israeli, it was either edited or not printed at all. Have you experienced this at all?

Reguly: Yes, that has happened to me. In the case of some of the Arab stories I wrote, particularly the series of six stories I wrote on the Palestinians, the copy was edited out; the harsher judgment quotes, shall we say, were edited out. Specifically, I did an interview with one man in the occupied territories who was a former mayor, I think, of Ramallah. He said that the occupation by the Israelis was worse than what the Nazis did in France. That was edited out, a direct quote. The *Star* didn't particularly like what I sent back, but I must give them credit because eventually they did publish it. For a month they sat on it, not knowing what to do with it because they did not expect it. Finally they ran it, you know, in a slightly watered-down form. In essence that whole story ran except for some of the more violent quotes and specifics, which were deleted. The reaction was fairly heavy. My picture ran on the front page of *The Canadian Jewish News*, as being not anti-Semitic, because they didn't dare say that, but anti-Zionist and playing into the hands of the terrorists. There was quite a vigorous denunciation of me and a letter-writing campaign. Toronto, which has either the largest or the second largest number of Jews in Canada, after Montreal, has a very well organized pro-Israel lobby, so that when a story such as this appears, they will write hundreds of letters, form letters that are almost identical. It is as if a club operates and someone clicks it into operation by saying, "You must write a letter denouncing this." In my case, 400 letters to the publisher criticizing me were written. However, letters to the publisher are not printed as are letters to the editor. This is their own private influence. And of course I presume there were a lot of telephone calls and so on and so forth. The influence is very heavy and vicious, by the way, because I noticed the letters to the editor often contained straight lies. My reaction at that point was to engage in a debate over radio in Canada with one of the main critics, who was the head of the Zionist League in Ontario. I merely said, "You are a paid propagandist . . . paid or unpaid, but you are certainly a propagandist and you have no intention of presenting an unbiased point of view. I merely call your attention to the fact. Prove me wrong on one fact, never mind the interpretation . . . one fact." He couldn't. So I said, "Is it right, or is it wrong? I'm merely concerned with whether it is right or wrong."

Ghareeb: In the United States many journalists who have criticized Israel are labeled as anti-Semitic in an effort to discredit them. Is this common in Canada?

Reguly: Yes. The Israeli lobby or the Zionist lobby is very potent, particularly in the media. They are very well organized, and ready to jump on anything; they are the essence of anti-democratic action. That is strictly the Nazi-fascist reaction—to stifle any dissent. It's the tactics of the mob. Shout down any man who dissents from your point of view. In a democratic country, or an ostensibly democratic country, I don't know whether this sort of thing should be tolerated or even listened to by any thinking person.

Getting back to the subject of canceling the U.N. Conference, which I think is the classic case, the Canadian government requested that it be postponed. This finally put to rest the hypocritical policy of the Canadian government of pretending to be evenhanded in the Middle East. Finally and irrevocably, they were going to show their true policy in the Middle East, which is cowardly, certainly pro-Israeli and not evenhanded as they had been pretending.

Ghareeb: Is there much of an Arab lobby, or any groups which try to present the Arab point of view?

Reguly: They are present, but they are badly organized. They don't know how to propagandize or use influence. They should take a page out of the Zionist book on how to influence people, how to merely present their point of view. They don't organize on the simplest level, which is simply to write a letter to the editor when they are being slandered. Nobody seems to bother in that respect. Yet, cne of the main vehicles of the Zionist pressure is letters to the editor; some of it is open, some of it is subtle, but whatever, there are a lot of them.

Ghareeb: What about the Arab embassies? Are they active at all?

Reguly: From my limited contact with them, I would call them totally inept.

Ghareeb: Do you think it is because they don't make an effort, or is it because even if they try, they get nowhere?

Reguly: From my personal experience, I have never been contacted by any person from any Arab embassy, either before, during or subsequent to the time I was the Middle East correspondent for the *Star*. Nobody made the slightest effort. But, of course, the other side has made one hell of an effort.

Ghareeb: Another criticism leveled at the Arabs by correspondents is that correspondents are not given easy access to news sources or news makers. You have been in both Israel and the Arab countries; could you make a comparison?

Reguly: Yes. My first visit was to Israel in late 1969. I went to the Israeli press ministry and introduced myself as a new journalist in the country for the first time. The Israelis made a very determined effort to capture my thoughts; they provided me with a car and chauffeur, access to all sorts of government officials—immediately doors opened. It was a week-long courting effort, because they knew I was going to be around for some time. It was a very deliberate, conscious effort to do this over a week's period. They do this to everyone, of course. If you go to the Arab side, they just don't seem to give a damn. You fight your way through roadblocks, administrative and bureaucratic chaos, and as far as I can see, nobody really cares very much. It's either shyness or arrogance, but I'm not sure which. One side certainly cultivates the press, while the other side does not. The Israelis also do it by trying to capture political figures in Canada. For a former prime minister, they will name a forest after him in Israel, "replanting of a forest"; they give testimonial dinners, "Friends of Israel"; a little lowly town mayor is invited to Israel, his name put on a little shack called a medical clinic. The essence of flattery, all the way through. It is an incessant effort to capture influential political figures for their cause.

Ghareeb: In the American media, bias is often reflected by word usage. For instance, Palestinian commandos become "Arab terrorists," the June War becomes the "Six Day War," and the October War becomes the "Yom Kippur War." Do you feel Canadian journalists employ this tactic as well? You also see Israel portrayed as a lone democracy in a sea of backwardness. Is this common in the Canadian media?

Reguly: Yes, I think it generally applies. When I did my writing, I always referred to the Palestinians as guerrillas, because I think that's an accurate word. Guerrilla comes from the word war, "guerra" or "guerre," and it generally is taken to mean unconventional warfare, and I consistently used that word. I never used the word "terrorist" because that is a libelous word that was invented by the Israelis to characterize a whole people. It's an emotionally laden word and simply inaccurate.

95

If you read the Canadian media—I was set to believe this myself—you attribute all sorts of miracles to Israel. How they "made the desert bloom." People believe they replanted it; they have suddenly transformed barren Arab desert into orange groves in Haifa. People don't realize that there were orange groves in Haifa for the last 300 to 400 years. They didn't make the desert bloom. They were in one of the more fertile parts of the Middle East. People just don't realize that. There is tremendous propaganda about Israeli pioneers going into a nothing land and making it their own. This appeals to North Americans, because they still think of themselves as pioneers. Witness television laden with pioneering and cowboy shows; it's part of the ethos of America. So, you sympathize with this pioneer spirit.

Ghareeb: How did the Canadian press, including radio and television, deal with the Arab oil embargo?

Reguly: Well, for one thing, the Canadian government simply lied consistently throughout the Arab oil boycott by never once admitting that the boycott applied to Canada, which of course it did. There seemed to be at the time a concerted effort to blame the Arabs. I don't think it took in Canada because Canada is in a surplus oil position. Unlike the United States, we export more oil to the United States than we consume in Canada. So the boycott really didn't affect Canada that much. The effort to say "you're going to freeze in the dark at home because of those lousy Arabs," simply didn't take hold in Canada. People realized that it didn't matter.

Ghareeb: But did the media attempt to portray the Arab as the "bad guy" in relation to the oil question?

Reguly: Not too much. I think most people realized it didn't affect Canada that much. Canada got very little oil from the Middle East. However, in Canadian oil politics, there is a great amount of anti-Americanism, and people tend to blame the American oil companies, their manipulations and their shady practices, for any oil shortages they might feel. They wouldn't tend to blame the Arabs.

Ghareeb: Is there much difference in the Middle East coverage presented in Canadian radio, television or the printed media?

Reguly: If you read any story dealing with the Middle East, the odds are that the dateline will be Tel Aviv or Jerusalem rather than Beirut or Cairo, simply because they generally put more people there. Most of the networks are there. Even during the Kissinger negotiations, you would invariably see a by-line from Jerusalem rather than, say, Beirut. I must say I can sympathize with that because of the sheer practical difficulties that are placed in the hands of the foreign correspondents who try to operate out of places such as Cairo. There's total censorship and there's blind censorship.

Ghareeb: But this has recently changed.

Reguly: It was that way in my days there, and I think this raises the animosity of some of the reporters who go in there and try to be impartial. You have to write your way through to present a favorable story of the Arab side. It's just virtually impossible in Cairo. Now Beirut is an exception. But the rest of it is ridiculous.

Ghareeb: In the Canadian media, in coverage of the Middle East, what determines what is news? Specifically, what happens, for instance, when Israeli forces attack a Lebanese village? Is this type of story covered from Beirut or Tel Aviv? Does it receive front page coverage?

Reguly: News is determined, essentially anywhere, as the exception to the rule. If Palestinian guerrillas attack a school in Israel, that's front page news. If some Israeli planes drop Napalm on some refugee camp in the south of Lebanon, then it will be a paragraph on page 19. Placement, of course, determines order. News is what you say is news. Similarly, if a great big event, a cataclysmic event, is not recorded, no one is there to witness and report, then as far as news is concerned, it didn't happen. The Israelis know this and they try to beat the others to the punch, and being first at the news counts a lot. They usually make their announcements, and they have very good control over the news there. They have censorship too, but they call it "military censorship." But, of course, they have a very broad interpretation of what is military. Like the oil that goes into the pipeline from Eilat to Ashkalan; that has been placed under military censorship. You couldn't even write about the pipeline, because it would be censored. They also give tremendous breaks to foreign correspondents living in Israel. They pay no taxes. It's a coddling effort.

Ghareeb: What about the government-owned Canadian Broadcasting Corporation? Is its coverage of Middle East developments more evenhanded and objective?

Reguly: They pretend to be evenhanded. I know personally of one film producer who did go to the Middle East—he now works for us, by the way—he did a sympathetic story on the Palestinians and it did get aired.

After that, he was subjected to such intense pressure internally from other employees in senior positions that he eventually quit over that program. He was harassed. But there was nothing in writing—nothing you could put your finger on. You couldn't say what happened because it was subtle pressure.

Ghareeb: How should the Arabs present their side of the story to the Canadian people?

Reguly: For one thing, don't make it so difficult for correspondents to get stories in their country. Secondly, don't treat them with almost eternal suspicion of being an Israeli spy in disguise. In other words, take a leaf out of the Israeli notebook and try to court them into presenting the favorable point of view. And get their embassies and their press attaches off of their asses. Do some work on this; in effect, organize!

Ghareeb: Are there many people of Arab origin in Canada?

Reguly: More and more so in the past five years. There always has been a fairly large Lebanese colony in Canada, but very little else. The Lebanese are mainly in the Ottawa area, some in Toronto, and they have done exceedingly well, especially in the field of education. They are also in the lower echelon of the civil services. A number of Egyptians and a fair number of Palestinians have also recently settled in Montreal. Numerically, they are nowhere near as large a group as the Canadian Jews, and certainly they don't have anywhere near the same influence or control over money, banking and the media.

Ghareeb: Are they politically active at all?

Reguly: I only know of one in politics, Paul DeBane, who is now a member of the Parliament and the Liberal Party, which is the governing party. He is a Palestinian from Montreal.

Ghareeb: Has he taken any stands on the Palestinian issue at all?

Reguly: If he has, I haven't heard much on it, and if he has, the media hasn't reflected it, to my knowledge.

Ghareeb: Are there any groups of Canadians who are sympathetic to the Arab point of view? How is the Palestinian or the Arab in general perceived by the average Canadian?

Reguly: If groups of Canadians are sympathetic, they are not voicing it. Every time somebody voices it, he is harassed and shouted down. Most of the people who know anything about the situation are sympathetic, but I must stress, very few know anything about it. The average Canadian is taken in by the propaganda deliberately fostered by Israelis or the Zionists that all Arabs are identical, generally shoeless peasants, untrustworthy, carry a gun or a knife, and are furtive people. The whole propaganda effort is to fix them all as traitorous louts by lumping them all together as Arabs, deliberately avoiding the word Palestinian, as if it is a conscious effort. The Israeli policy is to deny there ever was such a thing as a Palestinian, or a nation of people called Palestinians. So they foster the image that Arabs are a bunch of people with guns who are going to blow up airplanes. But I think that recently there is a panic because with money comes respectability. In the North American ethos, people respect power, and power comes through money. I think you are seeing a subtle change. Now they are starting to pay attention to this, where they totally ignored it before. So, I think the Israeli propaganda, designed as a propaganda effort, is panicking in this regard.

Ghareeb: So you feel that there has been a change? To what would you attribute the change?

Reguly: I think there has been a great change in the last year and a half. Suddenly, the OPEC countries are making policy, and they have influenced the price of oil. Suddenly people awake and say, "Who are these people?" So there has been more of an effort and, as I say, there is a great respect for money.

Ghareeb: How is Israel perceived?

Reguly: A general comment on how Israel is paraded in the North American press, or the Canadian press: My conclusion of the country is that there is a greater discrepancy between the myth of the country (or the image as propagated abroad) and the reality of the country at home. It is a country which openly practices discrimination, prejudice and a system whereby even Israeli Arabs, who were given Israeli citizenship back in 1948 or after, are treated as second-class citizens. If this were to happen to Jews in North America, where they were subjected to one-tenth of the discrimination that the Arabs suffer in Israel, there would be a huge cry, an outcry of suppression of human rights, brutality. Yet it is tolerated there. I find it amazing, for instance, that it is against the Israeli constitution for a Jew to marry a non-Jew in Israel, and yet that is accepted here. And I think in North America that the advertisers do, indeed, have a lot of clout and influence. Particularly in the smaller papers, they are subjected to pressure from advertisers, seeing that there are many Jewish advertisers and very few, if any, Arab advertisers. They are playing to a constituency.

Ghareeb: When I raised the point with some American reporters, they denied that advertisers have any influence over the media's policy. I am talking about the general policy of the paper.

Reguly: On the reporters' level, they are completely unaware of it. It's just on the smaller papers because a little ad can make a big difference. On the larger papers, a lot of them are turning away from ads. I don't think *The Toronto Star*, for instance, is subject to advertising pressure. I know a reporter who wrote a critical review of a restaurant owned by one of the big American chains. The American chain pulled out almost half-a-million-dollars-worth of advertising annually, and all the paper merely said was, "go to hell." If *The Toronto Star* is influenced by the Israeli point of view, it is not done by advertising pressure. It is done through coddling, the board room influence. The personnel in charge, the higher echelon of the newspaper, is Jewish. I think there's a natural sympathy for them. They would be the first to deny that they are partial, but by the very nature of their upbringing, they would have to be. They consort, constantly, with the people who have the influence. They constantly put pressure on the Canadian government. For instance, in Israel, the Canadian Ambassador is subject to frequent but very subtle pressures. Prominent Jews come from Canada, are given the royal tour, and on their way back they will drop in on the ambassador just to say "hello" and to put their point of view across. Constantly, their point of view is given to them by the Israeli foreign office. This is the constant method of pressure. In some countries, the Socialist Party might represent the point of view of the underdog, but in Canada this just does not happen.

To my mind, there is only one major newspaper in Canada that tries to give, at least at times, a fair shake to the Arab side, and it has consistently done so over the years. That is *The Toronto Globe and Mail*, the second largest paper in Canada. I think they have been relatively uncowed by the lobby. I don't say they have been totally neutral, but they give the best and the fairest shake to the Arab side. They show some independence.

Ghareeb: Do they have any correspondents in the Arab world?

Reguly: No, they don't, but they do send them there on forays, in and out. They send their London man, but that is the only one that I can say makes a pretense of being fair.

Ghareeb: How does the Israeli lobby work?

Reguly: The way the Israeli media lobby works, partly in Toronto, is through organized letter-writing campaigns directed to newspapers which may project sympathetic but not necessarily pro-Israeli stories. In addition, they have a club dedicated against television and radio, but particularly television, called, I am told, the "Each One Phone Ten Times" club. For instance, if a television network like CBS, which is more susceptible to influence, puts on a story on which may not be 99 percent in favor of Israel, the club works very quickly. Each person telephones another member and then each of them will phone into the station or the network ten times in the evening, knowing that the station does not log or record who calls, just the number of calls pro and con. So the "Each One Phone Ten Times" club can log one hundred calls, and they do this just as a matter of course. By the way, this is a womens' club.

10

Interview with PETER JENNINGS

Mr. Jennings is a correspondent for ABC TV News. He formerly covered the Middle East for five years.

Ghareeb: I believe the U.S. media have been, generally, pro-Israeli and anti-Arab. To what extent do you believe this to be true?

Jennings: Traditionally, there has been more coverage given to the Israeli side, although that began to change, if not dramatically, substantially, after the October War in 1973, and particularly after the Arab oil embargo against the United States. The news media generally, if not always, has taken a much more productive and incisive look at the Arab world.

Ghareeb: Yet you continue to see word usage that is biased. For example, American network reporters and others refer to the June War as the "Six Day War," and Bill Seamans has referred to the occupied territories as "the captured territories" or the "administered territories."

Jennings: I always refer to them as the occupied territories. I refer to the June War as the June War, and the October War as the October War.

Ghareeb: Except that the October War is often referred to as the "Yom Kippur War" here by many reporters. It means that they use the Israeli point of view, the Israeli names for things, and I think this indicates a certain tilt.

Jennings: I disagree with the use of the phrase, "the Yom Kippur War," just as I would disagree with the phrase, "the Ramadan War." In 1967, the situation was somewhat different in that the war did last six days, and it's not inaccurate to say it was a six-day war. I still personally refer to it as the June 1967 War. Basically, it's something people don't precisely think of in the neutrality of our language in that respect.

Ghareeb: It goes even a bit further in editorial comment. In an editorial comment yesterday on the evening news, Harry Reasoner went beyond just naming names. He was trying to justify the actions of Israeli

103

demonstrators who are hostile to Kissinger and to the Kissinger mission. He said they are justified because the Arabs started all the wars. He blamed the Arabs for starting the 1948, the 1956, the 1967 and the 1973 wars. Whose history is he reading? And this is not just Reasoner; other commentators and editors do it.

Jennings: I personally have to disagree with Harry Reasoner's views on the Middle East. But you must similarly remember that Harry Reasoner is a commentator in this instance, and his comments are labeled as analysis. You have to differentiate very specifically between analysis, commentary and news reporting. So I simply repeat, I disagree in large measure with Mr. Reasoner's views of events in the Middle East and perceptions on the Middle East.

Ghareeb: What I am trying to get at is this: It seems the America media and the reporters either are ill-informed generally, with a few exceptions, about the Middle East conflict, or they follow the Israeli line, lock, stock and barrel, and this is what they feed to the American people.

Jennings: I wouldn't agree with the second part wholeheartedly, that American reporters swallow the Israeli line. I would agree that American reporters generally are very misinformed about the Middle East, particularly about the Arab world. But to suggest that we continuously swallow the Israeli line is, I don't think, particularly accurate.

Ghareeb: When Israel attacks Lebanese villages, or civilian Palestinian camps, it's not mentioned in the media, while a Palestinian commando attack against Israeli targets, either inside or outside Israel, is flashed all over the television screens and on the front pages of newspapers.

Jennings: Well, again, you are looking backwards too much. I can tell you for a fact that every time there was an Israeli attack against the south of Lebanon during the entire period I lived in Lebanon, ABC News was there, provided the military authorities in Lebanon allowed us to go; and on many occasions they did not allow us to go. I think if you go back some years, it is quite true that there was a greater preponderance of attention paid to Palestinian attacks on Israelis—or on Israeli occupied, Palestinian occupied territory. But I don't think that is any longer true. If you look at the news logs of, say, the last year or two, you will find that wherever possible—and I'm talking about censorship and about army prevention in Lebanon—the news media does now cover Israeli attacks on Lebanon as, of course, Palestinian attacks against Israel are covered.

Ghareeb: This is very true. I also have to give you credit for coverage of the recent raids on Lebanon. You reported that story but other networks did not, and many of the newspapers either did not report on them at all or had it on the back pages.

Jennings: I always reported them, very simply because from a news point of view, if you will, in terms of covering the Middle East and Israeli raids against south Lebanon—either against a Palestinian refugee camp or against a Lebanese village, or against Fedayeen encampments in the Arkoub—these raids are every bit as valid news as a Palestinian attack against Israeli settlements.

Ghareeb: I'm glad to hear you say this because many other reporters and editors I have talked to say when this happens, often it's not news. So I ask them what news is. Why, for example, are the Palestinians called "Arab terrorists"? Many times they are not even said to be Palestinian terrorists, but are called Arab terrorists. And when Israel raids, it is reported as retaliation.

Jennings: I agree with you that that's a very difficult perception for people to deal with. What is basic here is that nobody has satisfactorily arrived at a definition for the word "terrorist." You can have terrorism, you can have government terrorism, you can have individual terrorism, you can have terrorism on the ground, and you can have terrorism by aircraft. Again, and I don't mean to be defensive here, but we are moving away quite rapidly from simply saying all the time that Israeli attacks against south Lebanon were simply retaliation. A number of observers of the Middle East have realized that in some instances Israeli attacks against south Lebanon have been designed to alarm the government in south Lebanon about security for the Lebanese in the south. Therefore, an Israeli attack on south Lebanon brings pressure to bear on Beirut, and in return, the Lebanese may be expected to move against Palestinians, either in the south or elsewhere in Lebanon. We report that now and not simply as an Israeli retaliation for Palestinian commando action.

Ghareeb: What if I told you that Arabs believe, for example, that there is not just pro-Israeli bias in the media, but there is also an anti-Arab bias, partly because of the way Arabs are portrayed, often as dirty, as terrorists, or as rich sheikhs?

Jennings: There is definitely anti-Arab bias in America. Americans for years have been largely ignorant of the Arab world. I don't think it's a deliberate bias. I regret it, but there is, unfortunately, stereotyping in the media. It is unfortunate, for example, that we say Arabs rather than Palestinians, Iraqis, Libyans or Saudis. Again I don't mean to be defensive, but it is a slow process, and I think we are beginning to move away from that.

Ghareeb: There are basically two views. Some say that it is due to ignorance, others that it reflects pro-Israeli influence in the media.

Jennings: I can only really speak from my own experience of five years, off and on, in the Middle East, three of them full time. I probably did more reporting in the Arab world than any other television correspondent, and I was never edited, no matter what kind of story I covered, no matter what I had to say, and no matter what other people said on ABC camera. Now I've returned to do this broadcast of "AM America." Once again—you know, I haven't counted it up in terms of minutes or hours, or numbers of interviews—I've seen no sign whatsoever that anyone has resisted my presenting an Arab point of view when it was justifiable, just as I've not been prevented from presenting an Israeli view when it was justifiable.

Ghareeb: I have been told by a number of Arab officials that you interviewed them to appear on "AM America" and yet the program was never aired.

Jennings: That's only true in one instance, and it happened in the case of Hanna Nasser, who was expelled by the Israelis. He was the former headmaster of Bir Zeit College on the West Bank. We did interview Hanna, and it was due to air in a particular week, but it didn't go, and like so many things in the news business, it got lost in the shuffle. I regret it, because I thought it was an important story, but that is the only instance in which it has occurred.

Ghareeb: Then often there is a rosy picture of Israel painted, for example, as a democracy, as a bastion of democratic principles, with ideals and morality in the middle of a sea of barbarism. And yet the discrimination against Oriental Jews, the denial of basic human rights to the Palestinian Arabs are rarely, if ever, mentioned.

Jennings: Well, I'll give you two answers to that one. The first is, I don't know whether you'll recall an interview I had with Abba Eban some time ago, when he said that Israel was the only democracy in the Middle East. I challenged him on that. And the second thing is that I do agree that our coverage of Israel tends to treat the government view of Israel. I think

Americans essentially hear the government establishment view of what is going on in Israel. I don't think there's enough investigation into the kinds of social problems in Israel. Similarly, I must add, and this must be included, I don't think we do enough social investigation of what is happening in any country, whether it be in Egypt or Syria, where it is very difficult to do, or in Lebanon, where it is sometimes difficult to do, or in Israel. So I think we are guilty on all those counts, not just guilty on Israel.

Ghareeb: Yes. But this is the emphasis on Jewish issues. For example, you always hear about the discrimination against Jews in the Soviet Union. It makes one wonder, because the question of Palestinian human rights is rarely mentioned. One wonders if this is racist. One wonders if the Israelis are more important as human beings than the Arabs are.

Jennings: You are a journalist, and you are asking other journalists to be the total conscience of the world. Now that's a difficult thing to do because we're professionals in circumscribed ways, just like others. The issue of the Soviet Jews is a major issue in this country led by Senator Henry Jackson and, of course, Jewish groups in the United States. That issue became related to the trade agreement between the United States and the Soviet Union, and as a result Dr. Kissinger and others indicated quite strongly that the pressure by Senator Jackson and others on immigration for Soviet Jewry was the result of the Soviet refusal to agree to U.S. trade requirements or trade agreements. Similarly, I have to agree with you, you've got to separate them. Okay, that's one issue. Now take the issue of the Palestinians. It is true that we have mischaracterized the bulk of the Palestinians for many years. We've tended to look upon the Palestinians as only twofold—either people who reside in refugee camps or people who are Fedayeen. That's unfortunate. We don't do enough stories on the West Bank and we don't do enough stories on Palestinians who are non-refugees or who are non-Fedayeen. Again, I say that in 1969 I did the first program on Palestinians on ABC called "Palestine—New State of Mind," in which we never touched the Fedayeen or the refugees. So while we don't do enough, something has been done.

Ghareeb: Let's go to a slightly different area. How influential, do you think, is the Jewish community, which is basically sympathetic to the Israeli point of view and the Israeli government? Does it influence the media? How important is it in that area?

107

Jennings: That's a very difficult question to answer, and I don't mean that as an evasive answer. Someone asked the foreign editor of *The Washington Post* what would happen if Jewish Americans came to him and said they would withdraw advertising if he didn't write pro-Israeli articles. He said, first of all, they wouldn't do it because they wouldn't have any other place to advertise, and secondly, if they did he'd say goodbye to their advertising.

Ghareeb: Yet many correspondents and reporters have presented negative articles, or criticized Israel, and were attacked, and some even labeled anti-Semitic. James Reston once said, "You may put it down as a matter of fact, that any criticism of Israel will be met with a cry of anti-Semitism."

Jennings: That's quite true. The editor of an article in *Commentary* magazine labeled me, along with Reston and others, as being notably pro-Arab or notably anti-Semitic. It is extremely unfortunate and misguided to suggest that because someone happens to disagree with some or even all of the policies of Israel they should necessarily be regarded as anti-Semitic; the two are not necessarily synonymous.

Ghareeb: What are the problems encountered by American journalists in the Arab world?

Jennings: Historically, if only going back to 1967 or slightly before, there was easier access in Israel than there was in the Arab world. Again, I think that has changed. The October War made a very significant difference—the decision of Syria to allow correspondents to cover the October War from that side; the openness and ease with which one can now work in Saudi Arabia; the abolishment of censorship in Egypt. Jordan has always been an extremely easy country to work in, and the Palestinians, in my own experience, have always been easy to work with. It is my own view that, while it is still sometimes difficult in the Arab world, while Arab officialdom in particular is still sometimes extremely suspicious or skeptical of American journalists, an American journalist who says it is impossible to work in the Arab world now is simply not working hard enough.

Ghareeb: How can Arabs really get their side of the story better presented in the American media?

Jennings: The answer to that has always been the same—complete openness to American journalists. Heikal, when he was very briefly Minister of Information in Egypt, in his first address to foreign correspondents in Cairo was asked why he did not allow full and total access to Egyptian affairs to foreign correspondents. His answer at the time was, "Well, many Egyptians feel that we are damned if we don't allow journalists full access, and we are damned if we do. So we might as well not." Very simply, the Arabs have come a considerable distance in this respect. That is to say that although journalists are given complete and free access, they will perhaps still bring negative stories in some instances. But access and freedom invariably lead to honesty, and if honesty is positive, the story will be positive; and if honesty is negative, it will be negative.

Ghareeb: Is objectivity being served by appointing an Israeli or a Jewish correspondent to cover Israel and by not appointing an Arab or Arab American to cover the Arab countries?

Jennings: I personally think it is unfortunate that we do assign Jews to work in Israel. I think that the inference or the suspicion, whatever it is, would be the same by having an Egyptian correspondent serving ABC in Egypt; I am against having a Jewish or Israeli correspondent serving ABC in Israel. I don't think that one can automatically challenge objectivity, but I think it is safer to choose the most neutral route possible.

Ghareeb: You said there has been a slight shift in the coverage, a slight change. To what do you attribute this?

Jennings: A couple of things, really. The shift is more than slight in our case and it occurred four and a half to five years ago. First, the shift came with a very strong realization that we were not covering the Arab side of the Middle East story, or the crisis. In terms of coverage, it is much more than a slight shift. Second, if you take the October War as a turning point, the war and the oil embargo brought home to Americans the realization that their lives were much more intertwined (in particular economically) with those people in the Arab world, especially in the Gulf. This realization has led to increased coverage.

Ghareeb: Do you have anything to add?

Jennings: Your questions were reasonably perceptive. I would think it unfortunate if you wrote a story which simply said, Americans are racist, Americans are biased, without a really conscientious examination of it, because I think the American media is trying a good deal harder now. If you pick up any newspaper, look at any television network, you can see that both sides of the story are represented. There's no doubt that it is going to take a very long time for Americans to understand, or for Americans to escape or abandon the general stereotypes that they have of Arabs. The onus is very much on the Arab states in particular to allow Western journalists the kind of full and free access which leads, one would hope, to objective, open and continuous reporting of the Arab world. It is a fascinating, interesting part of the world which must be reported on; particularly in view of the economic relationship that Americans feel with the Arab world. But even more particularly because there is justice on the Arab side, and there is justice on the Israeli side. There is no such thing as one truth in a crisis like this. There have got to be at least two, maybe more, truths.

11

Interview with NICK THIMMESCH

Mr. Thimmesch is a columnist with The Los Angeles Times Syndicate and resident journalist at the American Enterprise Institute for Policy Planning, Washington, D.C.

Ghareeb: What is your assessment of the media's portrayal of the Arabs and their issues? Do you feel that the coverage of Arab societies and their problems has been a fair and balanced one?

Thimmesch: The media's portrayal of Arabs and Arab issues is increasingly balanced, following a period of little understanding and a lack of information. If by "issues" you mean the Arab-Israeli conflict, it must be understood that the United States helped form Israel, that there are several million Jewish Americans who amount to a political bloc on this issue, and that talented, earnest supporters have been highly successful in advancing the Israeli cause. Since Arab Americans are only recently—and partially—organized, their bloc's effort has had only a small impact, if any.

Since the 1973 War and the 1974 boycott, the press has been required by events to dig deeper into the Middle East situation, and the result has been a more balanced treatment of the news. It is not yet as balanced as it should be, but it is getting there.

Ghareeb: How have they been portrayed?

Thimmesch: Arabs have been portrayed in many ways. They have been stereotyped as Bedouins coming from the desert, tending camels and sheep, and wearing the traditional garb. They have been portrayed as fat, rich, bearded, swarthy Semites, grinning at the world as they gorge themselves on the fruits of oil wealth. They have been shown as pathetic soldiers, unable to contend with the smarter, braver Israelis. But the stereotypes are dying too, as newsmen come to know better. The cartoonist Herblock is part of the old order.

Ghareeb: What are the reasons behind the stereotyping of the Arabs? Is it attributable to ignorance, bias, or the think-alike attitude that has permeated much of the impact media? Or is it due to other factors?

Thimmesch: Ignorance is one reason behind all stereotyping, whether it be of Arabs, Jews, Asians or Eskimos. Additionally, in the past Arabs have had a bad image in the United States, even if undeserved, and images create stereotypes. There's no question that bias is a factor in some stereotyping of Arabs.

Ghareeb: Could you give me any examples of biased or unbalanced coverage in the media?

Thimmesch: Herblock, who is a casual friend of mine, admits that he stereotypes Arabs as rich oilmen, but only as rich oilmen. If cartoons are news coverage, then there are many examples of bias against Arabs. As for the media, I think that a better job could have been done in the Lebanese Civil War, to show that some Lebanese Christians were leftists and that some Lebanese Muslims were rightists, the point being that it was wrong to identify it as Christians against Muslims. I also think that Israeli jet-bomber raids on Palestinian camps could get more coverage, since the American press seems sensitive to any sort of bombing events. But I must add that the situation is improving in terms of fairness and balance.

Ghareeb: What has been the impact of the negative portrayal of the Arabs?

Thimmesch: The impact is obvious. The Arabs are only now being understood by the press and, therefore, by the U.S. public.

Ghareeb: How much of the imbalance is due to the influence of the pro-Israeli lobby or to pro-Israeli journalists in the media?

Thimmesch: The pro-Israeli lobby serves more as an alert protector of Israeli and Jewish interests than it does as a feeder of stories to the press. If a newsman is perceived by this lobby to have been inaccurate or unfair, he will surely hear from them. As for pro-Israeli journalists, there are some like George Will and Bill Safire—if they are indeed journalists and not essayists. But many columnists are evenhanded, although I really can't think of one with an out-and-out bias for Arabs. Affinity is a better word to use in terms of journalists writing about Israel, a nation which has been part of American thinking for 30 years.

Ghareeb: Have you come under pressure from pro-Arabs or pro-Israeli groups for writing articles on the Middle East that they do not find to their liking?

Thimmesch: Yes, I have, and some of this pressure is disgusting. But it can be resisted, met and even put down if it becomes extreme. It is part of the

American system to howl when something bothers a person, so when they howl at the press and the howling gets too loud, just howl back.

Ghareeb: Some reporters say the Arabs have failed to present their case effectively to the U.S. media. Do you feel this is so? What percentage of the blame would you place on the Arabs themselves?

Thimmesch: In general, Arabs have failed to present their case to the U.S. media. It is difficult for a newsman in Washington, D.C., for example, to get through to someone in any Arab embassy for information, although it isn't as difficult as it once was. Again, there are changes. The Egyptians are quite helpful and are probably the most savvy in dealing with the American press. There is nothing unique about Arabs on this score. Since many Arab nations "emerged" in the past ten years, it is more a case of "emerging" nations learning the ins and outs of American journalism.

Ghareeb: In your opinion, what are the responsibilities of the American media in this area?

Thimmesch: The American media, in their news presentation, should always try to be fair and balanced. When newsmen claim they are "objective," I wince a little, because none of us is "objective." Besides, you can objectively describe certain aspects of a story, ignore others, and come up with an unbalanced article. Therefore I always stress fairness and balance. Beyond that, a newsman or newsperson has an obligation to offer what people will receive. In other words, esoteric material which won't be received, in print or broadcast, is the surest way to turn people off a topic. It does no good to harvest good food and botch the cooking, thus causing people not to eat it. Finally, it is best in the long run to offer something of substance, even though the temptation these days is to do "people" stories.

Ghareeb: What could be done to correct the negative images of the Arabs in the public mind and to present them in a fair and balanced manner?

Thimmesch: Arab nations and Arabs in general could correct the negative images by making themselves available to the American press, by attempting to explain how they are developing their countries, by not starting off with suspicions of Zionist conspiracies, and by firmly presenting the Arab point of view on controversial areas, but without rancor. Inviting newspersons to Arab nations is another good method. Three U.S. Senators of Jewish background all have urged other Senators to visit Arab nations, as they did in 1977. Why? Because that's how people get to know each other. There's nothing like personal contact to break down communication barriers.

12

Interview with RONALD KOVEN

Mr. Koven was the Foreign Editor of The Washington Post *at the time he was interviewed.*

Ghareeb: Many people believe that there has been a bias against the Arabs in the coverage of the Middle East conflict. Do you believe this to be true? If so, to what extent?

Koven: I think it was true. I'm not qualified to say whether it is still true, generally, throughout the U.S. press. Among the best press that I read—a reputable, quality press such as my own newspaper, *The Washington Post, The New York Times, The Wall Street Journal, The Baltimore Sun* and so forth, I think it is much less true, if not completely untrue. I have a slight reservation—I don't want to go to the point of saying that there is absolutely no longer any pro-Israeli bias. That's the key, that if there is still a bias it is not an anti-Arab bias but a pro-Israeli bias.

Ghareeb: Many newspapers, including your own paper, print cartoons that portray Arabs as the Jews were portrayed in Europe by the Nazis; as people with long noses, either terrorists or dirty old sheikhs holding a gas pump in their hands and dripping with oil dollars. Now isn't that a reflection of an anti-Arab bias, and not just a pro-Israeli bias?

Koven: The cartoons are a special problem that should be treated separately from the question of press coverage. Realistically, I suppose, the cartoons must be included in the creation of public attitudes. But there is a practical problem in that cartoonists find it very hard to find images that are easy to put across. Fortunately or unfortunately, an Arab is very identifiable in a cartoon, so a cartoonist will automatically put somebody in an Arab headdress with a flowing robe or riding on a camel, and right away the reader knows he is looking at an Arab. It's a lot harder to depict someone in Western dress as being of a distinctive nationality, because there aren't enough differences in dress. I would like to treat that as separate, however, from the question of press coverage since cartooning is not a general expression of the condition of the press.

Ghareeb: But people rely on the media for their information. The cartoons are a big part of the media, as they shape public images.

Koven: I agree. The reader doesn't make a distinction between the cartoon that may or may not be outrageous, but in many cases does show a stereotype; cartoons deal with stereotypes. There can be a very good and balanced editorial next to a cartoon and the effects of the balanced editorial may be more than nullified by the cartoon. I don't want to be put in the position of defending American cartoonists. There is a special problem that you have to recognize; the difficulty of the cartoonist in getting his message across without caricaturing, without exaggerating, which is the whole point of cartooning.

Ghareeb: Why is it that when Palestinian commandos attack Israeli targets they are called Arab "terrorists" and the story is splashed all over the front pages of any newspaper, including your paper, but when the Israelis attack and inflict greater casualties on Lebanese civilian villages, or refugee camps, this either is not mentioned at all or put somewhere in the back pages in a small paragraph?

Koven: That's a fair question. First of all, terminology; Arab terrorists are called terrorists because they knowingly and consciously use terror as a tactic. A person who uses terror tactics in the pursuit of his cause is by definition a terrorist. Designating him so does not necessarily indicate an attitude one way or the other about his cause. I have a suspicion that in Ireland, for instance, there are many people who deal with news stories who are sympathetic to the IRA. Yet, we call them Irish terrorists because they use terror as a weapon, rightly or wrongly.

Ghareeb: Why is it, then, when terrorism is used as an instrument of the state, as it is in the case of Israel, they are called commandos, and this state "terrorism" is not even mentioned?

Koven: We also refer to the Palestinian guerrillas as commandos, not only as terrorists, but ordinarily the expression "commandos" is and should be used to designate the certain form of military force used by a constituted recognized state. When the PLO sends people in, since the PLO is recognized by the Arab governments as the authority of the Palestinians, I see no problem in describing them as commandos. If, however, they represent renegade organizations that are not under the umbrella of the

PLO, that are acting against PLO policies, then the term or expression "commando" would be a misnomer. Of course, these are people who are working as mavericks, they are not working in conjunction with the established policy of a recognized international authority.

Ghareeb: In the past two weeks Israel has waged a number of attacks on Lebanese villages. Why aren't these attacks put on the front page when so many people are killed and wounded? This happened on August 7 and 15, 1974, when the *Post* stories were buried in the back pages. One was put at the end of an article on an entirely different subject.

Koven: Unfortunately, I think you might ask the same question about the coverage of Ulster. Day in and day out, far worse horrors are committed in Ulster, but they have become routine. I think the editors and the readers are tired of them, and they have lost their impact. If and when Israeli actions are taken that have implications for the general Middle East situation that could tip it one way or the other, then we pay attention. If they are simply routine actions that even Egypt doesn't pay much attention to any more, then they lose their impact, they lose the quality of being news. After all, we are a newspaper.

Ghareeb: Two days before Maalot, Israel attacked south Lebanon and four people were killed, three children and one woman. The *Post* ran this story on the back pages. Yet the Maalot attack was carried on the front page, not just one day, but for two or three days.

Koven: Maybe it is unfair. Maybe we are wrong to have this presumption, but there is a presumption that when regular military engages in retaliatory raids and innocent civilians suffer, it is not the main objective, but simply a by-product of the main objective—the military action—however blameworthy that may be. But in the case of Maalot, the objective, as far as can be determined, of the raiders was an effort to inflict damage, pain and ultimately death on innocents and children.

Ghareeb: Many people seem to think that when Arabs are getting killed, it doesn't merit attention, while when Jews are getting killed, it should become front page news, even though the goal is political. I asked this question of a number of people, some of them correspondents and some of them editors, and they said that perhaps there is another reason: that for the large Jewish community in New York, for instance, the killing of Jews is news.

117

Koven: Let me talk about the coverage of the news in a more general way. Our coverage of the Middle East or the Arab-Israeli conflict specifically at *The Washington Post* is different in some regards from that of *The New York Times* for the reason that you mentioned. New York is probably the world's largest Jewish city, and everything that happens in Israel is of local interest for a large number of readers of *The New York Times*. It's almost like a hometown story. We don't cover Israel that way. We don't have a lot of stories about the mood in the kibbutz and social and current trends in Israel. We tend to cover Israeli politics primarily as a way of explaining their foreign policy and its implications for the Middle East generally, not as a story that has a great deal of interest to our readers in and of itself. And, by extension, it can be said of the major quality newspapers of the distinction of the *Times*—*The Baltimore Sun, The Wall Street Journal, The Los Angeles Times*—that they don't cover internal Israeli affairs with the same kind of loving detail that *The New York Times* does.

Historically, the American press is a reflection of its society. The press was a way for immigrant groups to be upwardly mobile. Up until about 1950 or earlier, news rooms of major quality newspapers, of major metropolitan areas on the East Coast, had large numbers of people of Irish origin in dominant positions. At about that period the Irish were accepted into our society in a different way, so newspapers apparently didn't seem to be so desirable as a profession. The Irish went on to places where they made more money, had more prestige. In the same way, the next wave in American journalism was the Jews. For that reason there were and are a disproportion of Jews in American media in proportion to the entire population. I think the next wave after the Jews—you can see the thin edge of the wedge—are the Blacks. There was a time when Jews were considered discriminated against, and if someone wanted to prove he was liberal he could do so by hiring a Jew. Now you don't hire Jews to prove you're a liberal because that's considered hiring another white by a newspaper. You have to hire Blacks. I want to explain the question of the presence of Jews in its historical perspective. It's not a Zionist plot.

Ghareeb: Some people feel that the U.S. media is tilted toward Israel because of the preponderance of Jewish editors, reporters, etc. in the Eastern U.S. media.

Koven: Preponderance is the wrong word. I accept the idea that the Jewish community is represented out of proportion to its population and perhaps represented in leading positions even more out of proportion to its population, but I think this is for historical reasons. The way to be upwardly mobile for a smart Jewish kid, just as for a smart Irish kid, just as it is now for a smart Black kid, was to become a newspaperman. That is, if the kid wasn't smart enough to be a doctor or a lawyer.

Ghareeb: Israel is painted in the media as a bastion of Western democracy. What do you think about this?

Koven: Israel has succeeded in its public relations in depicting itself as an outpost of Western democracy in a sea of dictatorships and backward countries, as a barrier to communism. That is an aspect of natural sympathy by Jews in the American press that can't be denied. You might have expected that there would be a corrective to that sympathy coming from somewhere inside American society. The fact is that, because of the "barrier to communism" label that is attached to Israel, this label has only served to reinforce that natural sympathy. It is a great irony that Israel, which was founded on socialism with origins in the European socialist movements, is now finding its natural support in the American and European Right. To the extent that Israel has adversaries, they are on the Left.

Ghareeb: Why does the *Post* not carry more about the discrimination against Oriental Jews inside of Israel or the expulsion of Arabs without trials and the blowing up of their houses without any legal procedure whatsoever?

Koven: We have and it is an old story.

Ghareeb: Has this been happening recently? Because it has rarely been brought to the attention of the people in the past five or ten years.

Koven: This kind of behavior is no longer news. If the Israeli police, the Israeli military, day in and day out are arresting suspects in Gaza and blowing up their houses each time, what they keep doing no longer becomes news.

Ghareeb: But isn't the militarism in a supposedly democratic society, which some segments of Israelis are manifesting, newsworthy?

Koven: That's not news, but something you cannot put your finger on. That's a judgment. The press has carried stories, even by Israelis, labeling Israel a latter-day Sparta, but there are other points of view on that question. That is in the category of commentary analysis and it's certainly open to question.

119

Ghareeb: During a recent hearing before the Senate Foreign Relations Committee on arms sales to Jordan the *Post* reported the testimony of all the people who testified against the sale, while at the same time two former U.S. Ambassadors supported the sale of arms to Jordan, and not one word was mentioned about those two.

Koven: I cannot speak to that at all because I don't know anything about it. I was not involved in that story. The reporter who did that story is answerable for it.

Ghareeb: How important is the fact that there are some Jewish reporters and editors, some of whom are sympathetic to the Israeli viewpoint?

Koven: I think for most Jewish reporters and editors, the question doesn't even arise because they don't deal with the question of the Middle East.

Ghareeb: But how about the atmosphere, this uniformity of viewpoints?

Koven: Okay, you might argue that a certain kind of atmosphere is created in a city room, but the people I know who deal with these questions and are Jewish are very conscious of the fact that they have a responsibility to be fair. If anything, most of them probably lean over backwards not to let any sympathy or bias affect what appears in the newspaper. In fact, if you were trying to get an honest answer from the Israeli Embassy, the press room, or a professional pro-Israeli lobbyist about their attitudes toward our writers who happen to deal with the question, you would find that they are not very happy with them, that they cannot be counted on to be mouthpieces. I think you would also find that the editorial writers judge on a case-by-case basis, and those who are in the business of reporting news do try to be fair, despite the case you just cited.

Ghareeb: When reporters who have been critical of Israel are asked about this, they say they don't want to get into hot water by answering questions of this type. Why is that so?

Koven: It's a sense of vision. You have to be careful what you say. I am not really aware of this situation because I speak quite freely about this question. I know what I think the ideal news coverage should be on this subject, and I can't say that every single piece that we have ever written was balanced in an anti-Israeli way. Our overall general coverage in the few years that I have been involved is very fair, very balanced. We make an effort to have it be, and it is an effort.

Ghareeb: Why do you think that the pro-Israeli lobbyists are so effective in getting their story across?

Koven: I'm not aware that they are effective as the Israeli lobby. I think there is a cultural problem in that the Israelis are of European origin, and they have an advanced public relations sense. They are effective because they have been in the game, because they know how to play it and they understand how we reason. The Arabs, as a group, have not even played the public relations game and are not very experienced at it. There is a cultural barrier. It is a fact that the cultural difference is such that people of European origins and the Arabs think differently, have different kinds of reactions. Israelis, for example, have been able to use to very good effect statements by Arabs that are intemperate. It has taken a long time for the American and the European press to realize that in the Arab culture rhetoric is often just rhetoric, that it is a thing that exists by itself and does not necessarily imply action. The Israelis have been more careful. Those who are the rulers of the state have been very effective in their public relations, in pointing to the temperateness of their own statements and the intemperateness of some past Arab statements. This is changing both because the American press is finally beginning to pay better attention to the Arab world and because the Arab world is beginning to understand public relations. That's the key element. There again is no conspiracy but just a historical background to the situation.

Also, there is the simple fact that maybe there are two million people of Arab origin in the United States who for the most part tend to be low on the economic scale and not to be opinion leaders, whereas the Jewish population in the United States is three times as large and twice as rich because they have been here longer, for all sorts of historical reasons. Having worked with the political system, they know how it works and are in positions of influence, once again out of proportion to their numbers in the political system, especially on the Democratic side.

Ghareeb: How do you think the Arabs can better get their point across to the reporters who go to the Arab countries?

Koven: You know, that's a problem. When an American reporter goes to Israel, he finds it easier to communicate because the people are less afraid to talk openly and he can detect the crosscurrents and the politics practically by going to a cafe and talking to the people. Also, Israeli public relations are very well outlined and very well oiled. They calculate the relative importance of this journalist and of his newspaper or magazine and accordingly they decide to grant him easy access to very moderate leaders. From a purely professional viewpoint, it's a lot easier to operate in Israel, whereas when a journalist goes to Syria or Iraq, if they decide to open all the doors for him, that's fine, then he'll see the leadership. If they have not made up their minds or are uncertain, or didn't know he was coming, then the simple process of getting to speak to people (and people who are not afraid to talk) becomes overwhelming from a purely technical viewpoint.

Obviously in Lebanon this isn't true. You can speak to and see anybody. You can sense all the crosscurrents in much the same way as in Israel. We have talked about the Arab countries as a totality—there are countries where it is hard and there are countries where it is easy.

Ghareeb: Some people say that the American media have not sent people to the Arab countries, or if they have, they are only skeleton staffs. How many people do you have in Israel, and how many in the Arab world?

Koven: We have nobody in Israel but we do have a stringer in Israel who is Israeli. One of our best reporters, Jim Hoagland, is stationed in Beirut. Our coverage in the Middle East is about to expand and we are sending Tom Lippman as a replacement for Mr. Hoagland. Tom will be studying at the University of Cairo starting in September to get a sense of the Arabic language and the Arab world before he starts working. At the same time, he will be teaching American-style journalism at the university. In addition, we now have the services for six months out of the year of another correspondent who has spent a lot of time in the Arab world.

A third person is being sent to the Middle East, but we have not decided who that person will be or where to locate his bureau. The choice seems to be, among the options we have, a second man in Beirut, or establishing a bureau in Cairo or in Jerusalem. Because we do not want to be restricted to covering Israeli affairs alone, there is discussion about putting him on the Arab side and letting him see if he can travel to Israel. That's an unresolved issue.

Ghareeb: Have you thought about hiring an Arab or an Arab American as you have an Israeli stringer?

Koven: An Arab American might be a possibility, but we use Americans if possible.

Ghareeb: Why is it that *The Christian Science Monitor* has managed to have both sides fairly represented while many others have failed to do so?

Koven: I don't think it's true that a quality press would represent only one side. Even *The New York Times*, which I think must have to make a tremendous conscious effort to be fair, has done a good job covering both sides. I think we have too.

Ghareeb: Reporters used to say that one of their problems was that if they did write the articles, they were not published or were heavily edited. From your own experience, does this happen often?

Koven: Not any more.

Ghareeb: Since when?

Koven: Since I've had anything to do with it.

Ghareeb: Could you compare some of the Arab embassies and their spokesmen with the Israelis'?

Koven: The embassies here are a mixed bag. There are people who are very sophisticated and effective spokesmen. There are also people who assume that one is hostile and are therefore reluctant, and then there are those who may be very hostile themselves. The twenty-odd Arab embassies in Washington represent the diversities of the Arab world and there is no reason why their spokesmen or representatives shouldn't also reflect this diversity.

The American reading public should understand that the Arab world is not a monolith, that it is not, as you started by pointing out, an Arab in a flowing robe on a camel with a magic carpet full of oil dollars. The Arab world is many things with many kinds of people. It has very sophisticated people with superb university educations who are steeped in French culture in Alexandria, and it has poor fishermen barely making a living in Oman. There are wide cultural differences among all the rest. The greatest change since the 1973 war, the great watershed in American coverage of the Arab world, has been the recognition that the Arab world is not simply the expression of one side of the Arab-Israeli conflict, but also is an overwhelmingly important area of the world, economically and strategically.

Ghareeb: Why are so many correspondents afraid to present an anti-Israeli article or an article which might be considered hostile to Israel? They are harassed by the Zionist community, and sometimes accused of anti-Semitism. A number of reporters have come under attack and some of them are very much aware of this.

Koven: This is a very delicate and sensitive issue that arouses a lot of passion. It's like Harry Truman used to say, "If you can't stand the heat, get out of the kitchen." There are reporters who don't want to present things as they see them objectively, or as they think they see them objectively, because they are afraid of somebody's reaction.

13

BIAS ON AMERICAN EDITORIAL PAGES

Harold R. Piety

Mr. Piety is associate editor and chief editorial writer of The Journal Herald, *Dayton, Ohio, one of the Cox Enterprises, Inc., newpapers.*

Newspaper editors and publishers, pointing to the diversity of ownership of American daily newspapers, deny that Jewish Americans exert influence on the press out of proportion to their numbers in the general population, and dismiss as unfounded—or bigoted—claims that Jewish and Zionist groups exercise unreasonable influence over editorial comment. There was outrage voiced when the charge of excess Jewish control of the American press was expressed by the Chairman of the U.S. Joint Chiefs of Staff, General George S. Brown (*The Washington Post*, November 14, 1974). President Ford forced General Brown to apologize. The remarks were "regarded as anti-Semitic," according to *Facts on File* (November 15, 1974).

The heated denial by editors and publishers of excessive Jewish control or influence, and the charge of anti-Semitism hurled at General Brown, do have the sound of overreaction. This should alert the skeptic. The critic of the American press might err in applying the European or Middle Eastern model to the American press, expecting to see news columns reflecting the political, ethnic or religious bias of the owners. But there does appear to be perceptible bias in favor of Israel on the editorial pages, without regard to ownership. Indeed, the Zionist bias in the American press is probably due much less to Jewish ownership than it is to the other factors, chief among them being a sizable Jewish readership for most large American newspapers. The Zionist bias that seems to be apparent on the editorial page of *The New York Times* may be principally due to the fact that New York City has the largest population of Jews in the world, having almost as many as all of Israel. A newspaper is shaped in part by its readership, and by the exceptionally able and indefatigable public relations efforts of Jewish and Zionist organizations all over the nation.

Finally, the Zionist-Jewish bias that seems apparent might be traceable in part to the Judeo-Christian culture in which the press operates, and which inevitably shapes the perceptions of journalists and editorial writers. A sizable number of American fundamentalist Christians (many Baptists, Assemblies of God, Nazarenes and Pentecostals) regard the creation of Israel and the ingathering of the exiles as the fulfillment of Biblical prophecy. A great many others, not surprisingly, look on a Jewish state in Palestine as "morally correct." Jews are familiar, Arabs are alien.

While this takes on the appearance of tautology, it is doubtlessly fair to say as well that editorial writers on newspapers all over the United States are also strongly influenced by the major metropolitan dailies, who are in turn influenced by the uniformity of opinion throughout America.

Despite the diversity of ownership of daily newspapers in America, very few newspapers exercise a strong degree of influence on the news columns and opinion pages of all the rest. *The New York Times* is by far the most important of the major dailies in its general influence, and the *Times* takes pride in the fact that newspaper editors across the land regard it as vital. The *Times* is the only truly national newspaper in the United States, and it is generally available in most American cities of 100,000 or more persons on a daily basis. *The Sunday Times* is available even more widely. It is the most comprehensive in its international coverage. *The Washington Post*, because it is published in the nation's capital, is also influential in special areas. *The Wall Street Journal*, a national business-oriented daily, has strong influence on some segments of the daily press, as does *The Christian Science Monitor*, also a national paper, with a somewhat different segment of the press. Several major regional newspapers—*The Chicago Tribune, The Los Angeles Times, The St. Louis Post-Dispatch* and *The Baltimore Sun*, for example—also have national influence, but less by several orders of magnitude than *The New York Times* and *The Washington Post*. And none of the major dailies has quite the Zionist bias occasionally exhibited in *The New York Times*.

The editor or editorial writer in Little Rock, Arkansas, say, or in Dayton, Ohio will read *The New York Times* daily for the completeness of its national and international news, and for the editorial comment offered by the *Times* on these events. What James "Scotty" Reston or C. L.

Sulzberger have to say about events in the world have impact on editorial writers who do not have Reston's access to the president or the secretary of state, or Sulzberger's access to foreign leaders. Provincial editors and editorial writers may write with confidence on local and regional issues, and out of their prejudice on political and social concerns, but they have a tendency to lean on the experts in the *Times* or *The Chicago Tribune* to interpret and make judgments of more exotic news.

While the *Times* has long influenced much of the American press, it has not always had a measurable Zionist bias. Adolph S. Ochs, grandfather of the present publisher, Arthur Ochs Sulzberger, was a strong anti-Zionist. He was a signatory to the petition sent to President Wilson in 1919 by a number of prominent American Jews in protest against the plan to incorporate the Balfour Declaration into the League of Nations mandate for Palestine. Arthur Hayes Sulzberger, son-in-law of Ochs and father of the present publisher, was also anti-Zionist, but he was less willing to be publicly identified as an opponent of Zionism, an attitude that may have helped to weaken the nascent anti-Zionist movement in the United States during the 1940s.

Elmer Berger, former long-time executive vice president of the American Council for Judaism, a once strongly anti-Zionist organization of mainly Reform Jews, recently wrote about his efforts to enlist the help of Sulzberger in the council's campaign against Zionism:

> *"The* Times' *editorial position in those days was rather consistently anti-Zionist. Its editorials were a favorite target of the big-wheel Zionists, particularly Abba Hillel Silver. We therefore hoped for good news coverage from the* Times *and also for editorial support. We even hoped Sulzberger would personally affiliate with the council."*

But after a meeting with Sulzberger, Rabbi Berger received a reply that said, "'as publishers of the *Times* the family thought it would not be wise to be so closely associated with a partisan view in such a controversial issue.' But the paper, we were assured, would give fair and even sympathetic coverage to our views."[1]

The forces that tend to pull the *Times'* editorial page into a position of partiality for Israel and Zionism are essentially the same—but much

---

[1] Elmer Berger, "Memoirs of an Anti-Zionist Jew," *Journal of Palestine Studies*, Vol. V, Nos. 1 & 2 (Autumn 1975/Winter 1976): p. 13, 14.

greater because of the larger New York Jewish population—as those which influence the rest of the American press: an articulate, importunate, resourceful, relentless and untiring Jewish constituency. Though relatively small as a percentage of the total population, the American Jewish population is concentrated in urban centers. Because it is affluent, highly educated and professional, it is a vocal and influential population. The Jewish community's fears are easily stirred. Its memories of the Holocaust are too fresh to permit an official or unofficial remark hostile to Israel, Zionism or Judaism to pass without swift rebuttal. Any careless word, any ambiguity, an incautious generalization is seized upon and demanded to be retracted. Reston, perhaps the most eminent news columnist in the United States, felt compelled to apologize for using the word "aggression" in describing Israel's occupation of Arab territory in the 1967 War. In the spring of 1977 the *Times* felt the need to apologize for using the expression "Jewish leaders" in a news analysis describing Jewish ambivalence about holding discussions with representatives of the Palestine Liberation Organization (PLO). The Conference of Presidents of Major American Jewish Organizations represented America's recognized Jewish leadership, the *Times* explained, and the news analysis should have said "some Jews" instead of "Jewish leaders." It laid the "error" to careless editing.

A former editorial writer for the *Times*, James Brown, related in a conversation with the author the difficulties and the pressure felt by an editorial writer on a newspaper in New York City in dealing with the delicate subject of the Middle East. Brown said he was always conscious that on this issue there were limits to permissible editorial comment. It was not a case of his being pressured to write something that he did not believe, but rather a case of not being able in every case to say quite as much as he might wish to say about the issue.

The *Times* could not be called a knee-jerk defender of Israel and Zionism. It has criticized Israel's reluctance to negotiate the opposed Israeli settlements on the West Bank and the Golan Heights. But the *Times'* editorial page can be singularly strident when it comes to Israel's defense. One of the more astonishing expressions of this tone can be found in the March 28, 1976 editorial in which the *Times* commended William Scranton, then U.S. Ambassador to the United Nations, for his veto of the U.N. Security Council resolution on March 25 assailing Israeli occupation policies in the Old City of Jerusalem and on the West Bank.

"It is a lie," the *Times'* editorial stated with uncharacteristic bluntness, "not just incorrect and unbalanced, as Ambassador Scranton diplomatically put it—that the Israeli authorities have been taking measures 'aimed at changing the physical, cultural, demographic and religious character of the occupied territories' of the West Bank. Endless repetition of this lie will not make it truth. . . ." This remarkable statement appeared in the same edition with an article discussing some of the changes. Moreover, the *Times* has printed a number of articles in recent years detailing some of the actions taken by the Israeli government that fit the description in the U.N. resolution. For example, new Israeli housing developments in East Jerusalem (condemned by some on aesthetic, as well as on political, grounds) and the Jewish settlements are physical, cultural and demographic changes. Archeological excavations in the Old City are changes. The demolition of Arab housing in the Old City in the vicinity of the Wailing Wall are changes. The creation of a synagogue at the Cave of the Patriarchs, which had for many years been only a mosque, is a religious change that has actually led to disturbances, although the disturbances came after the veto of the U.N. resolution. The archeological excavations in the Old City had been criticized by the United Nations Educational, Social and Cultural Organization (UNESCO) in resolutions dating back to 1969.[2] UNESCO repeatedly called upon Israel to cease excavations and to preserve cultural and religious properties in the Old City. Israel was subsequently expelled from the European section of UNESCO, but was readmitted in November 1976, even though the organization still condemned Israel's cultural and educational policies in the occupied territories. The general American editorial reaction was that Israel was treated unfairly, and an editorial in *The Journal Herald* (Dayton, Ohio) on November 25, 1976, on the occasion of Israel's readmission to the European section of UNESCO doubtless reflected popular opinion in America: "(UNESCO) has rectified an old wrong by readmitting Israel. . .," the editorial stated.

No individual issue better illustrates the general Zionist bias on American editorial pages than the votes in the United Nations on resolutions equating Zionism with racism. The U.N. General Assembly's Social, Humanitarian and Cultural Committee adopted a resolution on October 17, 1975, calling Zionism "a form of racism and racial discrimination." The same resolution was subsequently adopted by the

---

[2] *United Nations Resolutions on Palestine and the Arab-Israeli Conflict* 1947-1974, ed. George J. Tomeh, Beirut: The Institute for Palestine Studies, 1975, p. 195.

General Assembly on November 10, 1975. Most American newspapers commented on both votes, and the comments in November were largely echoes of the October remarks.

Editorial comment in the American press was almost universally negative toward the U.N. action. The Anti-Defamation League of B'nai B'rith conducted a survey of the 50 largest circulation newspapers in the United States and revealed in a report dated December 2, 1975 that all had condemned the U.N. action. Leading public figures in the United States— President Ford, Secretary of State Henry A. Kissinger, Congressional leaders, spokesmen of organized labor and religious leaders—were also vocal and seemingly united in their condemnation of the resolutions. The U.S. Senate unanimously adopted on November 11, the day after the U.N. vote, a resolution condemning the vote and calling for immediate hearings to "reassess the United States' further participation in the United Nations." The U.S. House of Representatives adopted a similar resolution, but deleted a call for a reappraisal of U.S. participation in the United Nations. (*Facts on File* 1975, p. 838.)

Not content with condemning the resolution, 34 of the major newspapers surveyed by the Anti-Defamation League interpreted the U.N. resolution as "tantamount to anti-Semitism." Fourteen of the papers surveyed, echoing the U.S. Congress, called for a reassessment of U.S. participation in the United Nations. The comments in *The Philadelphia Inquirer* (October 21, 1975) were not unusual in the aftermath of the two U.N. votes: In an editorial entitled, "Anti-Zionist vote is obscene," the *Inquirer* stated, "The Social, Humanitarian and Cultural Committee of the United Nations General Assembly has disgraced the U.N. . . ."

Yet, the facts clearly support the U.N. votes. Zionism stands self-condemned of the charge in the U.N. resolution. Zionists assert that Judaism is a nationality, and make this claim on behalf of all the Jews in the world, whether they be citizens of Israel, the United States, the Soviet Union, Egypt, France, Bulgaria or wherever they may reside. The Law of Return, enacted by the Knesset on July 7, 1950, invites Jews of the Diaspora to return to Israel and confers citizenship on Jews who come to Israel. Moreover, the definition of who is Jewish is left not to governmental authority, but rather to the Orthodox rabbinate. Thus, a Jewish Agency spokesman in Jerusalem explained in a July 28, 1964 issue of the *London Jewish Chronicle*, "the government [of Israel] and the [Jewish] Agency accept as a Jew one who is Jewish according to the Halacha—that is, has a Jewish mother or has been converted to Judaism in a ceremony which satisfies the requirements of the Halacha and who has not adopted another faith." The Orthodox rabbinate, through the Rabbinical Courts Jurisdiction Law of 1953, has exclusive control over all personal status laws (marriage, divorce, burial, inheritance, etc.). The law eliminates civil marriage entirely and excludes marriage between Jews and non-Jews.

Zionism certainly falls within the definition of racial discrimination established by the United Nations in its 1963 Declaration on the Elimination of All Forms of Racial Discrimination, to wit: "discrimination between human beings on the ground of race, color or ethnic origin." In 1965, in the International Convention on the Elimination of All Forms of Racial Discrimination, adopted by the General Assembly, racial discrimination was defined in Article 1 as "any distinction, exclusion, restriction or preference based on race, color, descent, or national or ethnic origin." Both the 1963 declaration and the 1965 convention were adopted without dissenting votes. Certainly the Zionist insistence that Judaism is a nationality, a people, not just a religion, and its creation of a state primarily for this "people," along with a steadfast refusal to permit the return of the Palestinian refugees who fled from the land in the first Arab-Israeli war, constitutes "distinction, exclusion, restriction or preference," as set forth in the 1965 convention.

Zionism is further condemned of the U.N. charge in the words of Israel's principal leaders. David Ben-Gurion, Israel's first prime minister, was quoted by Max Dimont in *The Indestructible Jew* as follows: "I believe in our (Jewish) moral and intellectual superiority and our capacity to serve as a model of redemption of the human race." Golda Meir, foreign minister under Ben-Gurion and later prime minister, repeatedly expresssed a discriminatory attitude toward Arabs, the most famous one coming in an interview with *The Sunday Times* of London (June 15, 1969), when she said in response to a question about the Fedayeen, the Palestinian guerrilla force, "There was no such thing as Palestinians. When was there an independent Palestinian people with a Palestinian State?. . .It was not as though there was a Palestinian people in Palestine considering itself as a Palestinian people. . ." Another time, in defending her rejection of pleas to permit the Christian Arabs of the villages of Berem and Iqrit to return to the homes from which they were removed in 1948, she said such an action to allow Arabs to return where Jews had been settled would be an erosion of Zionist values.

Finally, Zionism stands most eloquently condemned of the charge of racism by citizens of Israel, Jews, who have documented examples of discriminatory conduct, the most notorious of which was the fact that until the mid 1960s, more than 15 years after the creation of the State of

Israel, proclaimed by the Israelis and most Americans as the only democracy in the Middle East, Israel's sizable Arab population—citizens of Israel—lived under military rule. Even today the Arab population of Israel is subject to certain restrictions on where it can live and work. And land owned by Arabs is subject to expropriation by the government of Israel under a series of laws adopted by the Knesset for this purpose. Sabri Jiryis, a Palestinian lawyer and writer, has explained the land laws in detail and demonstrated how they work in his book *The Arabs in Israel.*

Professor Israel Shahak, chairman of the Israeli League for Human and Civil Rights, has written and spoken widely on the subject of racism and discrimination in Israel and has testified before the U.S. House Committee on International Relations. Professor Shahak, a biochemist at Hebrew University, has decried the destruction of Arab villages by the Israeli government, the discrimination against Arab farm laborers and the torture of Palestinian military prisoners.[3] The Israeli Law of Nationality, passed in 1952 and amended in 1968, makes it very difficult for Arabs to obtain Israeli citizenship, even if they were born in the nation. Other laws, and rules of the Jewish National Fund, which purchases and owns land and thereby regulates under what conditions the land is cultivated and under what conditions industries supported by the fund operate, make the movement of Arabs difficult, limit their employment and where they may live. These facts are not denied by Israeli officials, although the information is not widely publicized.

The overwhelming fact of Zionism, which obscures every other consideration, is that it must, perforce, discriminate against a non-Jew. A Jewish state must necessarily be less pleasant for a non-Jew than for a Jew. As Israeli historian Aharon Cohen put it in his book, *Israel and the Arab World*: "From the point of view of the law, the Arab citizens are equal to all citizens of the state; they participate in parliamentary elections and enjoy many rights of a democratic state. However, no such statement can obscure the fact that the Arab minority in Israel lives in conditions of painful discrimination."

A number of the editorials in the American press after the U.N. vote on Zionism sought to provide a thumbnail definition of Zionism even as they

---

[3] *Documents from Israel 1967-1973,* eds. Uri Davis and Norton Mezvinsky, London: Ithaca Press, 1975, p. 43.

denounced the vote. *The Philadelphia Inquirer* stated (October 21, 1975): "Zionism is, in plain fact, the oldest national liberation movement in the world, the yearning of the Jewish people through 2,000 years of exile and persecution for a national homeland of their own." *The Washington Post* stated: "Zionism in its most fundamental sense is Jewish nationalism, the doctrine that holds that Jews, like a hundred and more other groups—including 20 or more Arab groups—have a right to political self-determination.

A minimal regard for objectivity—and accuracy—would have obliged the editorialists to point out that not nearly all Jews are Zionists. Many do not regard Zionism as a national liberation movement. Even some who support the State of Israel have misgivings about the nature of Zionism. A number of Orthodox groups regard political Zionism as an abomination and the State of Israel as blasphemy, corruption and perversion of religious beliefs sacred to Judaism. A number of Reform Jews, including many in the United States, regard Zionism as an expression of the Eastern European ghetto mentality, as an incitement to anti-Semitism, and as a dangerous threat to the status of Jewish citizens in lands other than Israel.

There are individuals and organizations who, if contacted by reporters or editorial writers, might have persuaded some of the writers to moderate their strong denunciation of the U.N. vote. It is rare that such people are contacted; however, they are not silent. To the contrary, men like Rabbi Elmer Berger, Professor Norton Mezvinsky, Dr. Alfred M. Lilienthal, Edmund Hanauer and others, write and speak constantly on the subject. Berger is president of American Jewish Alternatives to Zionism as well as former executive vice president of the American Council for Judaism. Mezvinsky, unlike Berger, who is a Reform Jew, is of the Orthodox tradition. He was executive secretary of the American Council for Judaism for a time, and was co-editor of *Swasia*, a digest of news from the Middle East published until 1978 by the National Council of Churches. Hanauer, a political scientist, is executive director of Search for Justice and Equality in Palestine. Lilienthal is editor and publisher of *Middle East Perspective*, a monthly newsletter, and has written three excellent books on the Middle East.

Hanauer, in a statement prepared for the American Society of Newspaper Editors (May 5, 1973), described the attitude in the American press that produced the deluge of editorial denunication of the U.N. vote on Zionism. Pointing out that the American public was as ignorant of the Arab-Israeli issue as it was of the Southeast Asia conflict in the early 1960s, Hanauer said, "As newspaper editors you are presumably dedicated

133

to giving the reading public insights rather than mirroring and reinforcing the misinformation, narrow prejudices and fake assumptions that underlie and characterize much of the public's attitude towards the Arab world in general and the Arab-Israeli conflict in particular. . . for much of the media Israel is close to a sacred cow." Describing the steps that needed to be taken to correct American coverage of the Middle East, Hanauer went on to add, "We urge an end to simplistic, crude and often cruel caricatures of the Arab world and of the sentimentalization of Israel in the media."

The "simplistic, crude and often cruel caricatures of the Arab world" are most clearly found in editorial cartoons. Editorial cartoonists represent a special case, but they reflect in an exaggerated fashion the chief problem with American editorial treatment of the Middle East conflict. The problem is one of ignorance. Craig MacIntosh, editorial cartoonist for *The Minneapolis Star*, and a cartoonist who has drawn cartoons critical of Israel, acknowledges that both ignorance and an editorial cartoonist's habitual employment of exaggeration, caricature and stereotypes leads to a depiction of Arabs in editorial cartoons that can be described as racist.

"The Arabs are always in robes, the Palestinians always in 'terrorist' garb, with an AK 47 (Soviet-made automatic weapon)," Macintosh said. "When I draw the Saudis—someone like the late King Faisal—it was proper to put him in robes. That's what he wore. But not the Egyptians, not the Syrians."

While caricature is the cartoonist's stock in trade, most editorial cartoonists refrain from employing racial caricatures, or ethnic stereotypes, in depicting Blacks (except in the case of African dictators like Uganda's Idi Amin), Hispanics or Jews. The historic Jewish stereotype—the hooked nose, hooded eyes, skullcap, clasped hands—is fortunately not seen in cartoons. But the Arab stereotype, the derogatory stereotype, is seen.

"I could depict Arabs as murderers, liars and thieves," said Robert Englehart, the young editorial cartoonist on *The Journal Herald* (Dayton, Ohio). "No one would object. But I couldn't use Jewish stereotypes. I've always had the feeling that I'm treading on eggs when I try to do something on the Middle East, although most of the time I have been able to do what I pleased, as long as it is factual."

Englehart concedes that the depiction of Arabs generally in American editorial cartoons is racist, even though he is quick to add—as most editorial cartoonists do—that the caricature is always going to verge on racism when the subject is a racially or ethnically identifiable person.

134

MacIntosh says he has no trouble with his editors at the *Star* on this subject, although he encounters criticism from the local Jewish community. Englehart says cartoons on the Middle East "fall somewhere between local cartoons and national and international affairs." He has his biggest problems with local issues, where many readers have firm opinions. National and international issues present no problems (unless the subject is abortion).

Tom Engelhardt, the editorial cartoonist for *The St. Louis Post-Dispatch*, has also encountered serious criticism from the local Jewish community as a result of cartoons regarded as critical of Israel.

The ignorance cited by MacIntosh is not limited to cartoonists, who at least have some excuse. Their stock in trade is artistic skill, not knowledge of history and political science. But editorial writers are guilty of equal ignorance.

John Zakarian, an editoral writer for *The St. Louis Post-Dispatch*, conceding the fact of predominately Zionist bias on American editorial pages, says he's "afraid that the biggest reason is simply ignorance. The Arabs have just done a very poor job of telling their story to the American people."

Zakarian, who was born in the Old City of Jerusalem, is one of the few American editorial writers with a strong background in Middle East affairs. He is a Nieman Fellow, and was formerly the editorial page editor of Lindsay-Schaub Newspapers, an Illinois chain of small dailies that earned modest notoriety after the Israeli raid on the airport at Entebbe, Uganda by criticizing the raid. The editor of Lindsay-Schaub Newspapers, Robert E. Hartley, credits Zakarian's influence (by this time Zakarian was in St. Louis) for Lindsay-Schaub's unusual editorial position on the Middle East.

The American editorial writer is a generalist in most cases. He is usually a journalist who has spent several years as a reporter, although some newspapers are hiring young people for work on editorial pages even though they have had no prior journalistic experience. The editorial writer may or may not have any particular expertise. If he does, it is most likely to be in local or state government, sociology or education, or perhaps in economics. Only a few of the largest papers have experts in international affairs, and even then the "expertise" may be simply some years of experience as a foreign correspondent.

Americans do not know much about the Middle East, as Search's director Hanauer pointed out. They have little independent knowledge of Judaism or Zionism. On these subjects their knowledge is very likely to come from a local Jewish Community Council, rabbi or Jewish friend. Americans know even less about the Arab world or individual Middle Eastern nations. "Arab" is a word that conjures up a desert sheikh, the Arabian nights, a band of horsemen flying across a desert ridge. The history of the Middle East since the origin of the Zionist movement in the late 19th century and the breakup of the Ottoman Empire after World War I is only dimly perceived by Americans. It is not surprising, therefore, that Americans—including those who write editorials for the American press—are vulnerable to any well-organized, articulate and knowledgeable group that has a vested interest in advancing a particular point of view. The Zionists and much—but not all—of the rest of the American Jewish community has such an interest. And it works very carefully to promote a view of the Middle East, of Zionism, of the Arab and of the Arab-Israeli conflict that inclines Americans to sympathy for Israel and Zionism. A critical element in the sympathetic point of view is the blurring of the distinction between Judaism and Zionism.

Editorial writers have also blurred distinctions among the various Arab peoples and nations—and in this they have been aided by Zionist efforts, e.g., Golda Meir's statement about the Palestinians—with particularly unhappy consequences for both the Arab nations and the Palestinian people. It has only been since the 1973 October War that the word "Palestinian" began to be used with frequency and accuracy on editorial pages. There have been exceptions to this rule, of course, from the first. The Scripps-Howard newspapers ran a series of editorials in 1956 commenting on the plight of the Palestinian refugees. The late Dorothy Thompson, formerly a vigorous supporter of Zionism and Israel, became so sympathetic to the plight of the Palestinians that she became in the late 1940s and early 1950s a sharp critic of Israel. In the main, however, editorialists habitually referred to the "Arabs," meaning the several Arab nations and the Palestinians. And when guerrilla activity began in the mid 1950s, and escalated before and after the 1967 War, editorialists habitually referred to "Arab guerrillas," or "Arab terrorists." That still happens.

This careless usage—probably more the product of ignorance than of malice—has had two regrettable results: (1) Palestinians have been denied a sense of individual or national identity by only being counted among "the Arabs"; (2) the Arab governments of Egypt, Syria, Jordan and, to a degree, Lebanon, have been charged with responsibility for violence committed by Palestinian guerrillas. Unless and until the Palestinians are recognized as a legitimate national group, with aspirations for national self-determination, the violence committed by the Palestinians will not be regarded as legitimate. Jewish terrorism by the Irgun and the Stern Gang, as well as by units of the Haganah, during the mandate period and in the months between the U.N. vote on partition and the British exit, had an obvious political logic: the creation of a Jewish state. And the major self-proclaimed Jewish terrorist, Menachem Begin, is today prime minister of Israel.

But American editorial writers do not grant such legitimacy to Palestinian political terrorism, which for years was dismissed as "Arab" terrorism. It was regarded as senseless and diabolical, directed solely at the destruction of Israel and the murder of Jews. Over and over again on editorial pages there is reference to "Arab terrorism," to "wanton and senseless, mindless" acts. *The Journal Herald* (Dayton, Ohio), expressed a typical sentiment on May 16, 1974 in editorializing about Maalot, where Palestinians killed a number of high school students: "Arab guerrillas have managed to perpetuate all manner of irrational acts in recent years. The latest outrage should rouse Arab nations to quick and forceful action against those whose behavior threatens to undermine the positive steps taken toward peace in the Middle East." Some newspapers use the word "terrorist" almost as a prefix to the PLO.

The fact is that the PLO is a legitimate national movement. It was recognized as such in a profile published by the Israel Universities Study Group for Middle Eastern Affairs in 1974.[4] The author, A. Yaniv, said at one point, "Contemporary Palestinian nationalism, then, cannot claim a long history. At the same time it seems equally misleading to dismiss it as a fabrication. True, attempts by several Arab states to harness the Palestinian cause to their own ends are still made. But ever since the latter part of the 1950s, these attempts were accompanied by the emergence of a genuine and independent Palestinian national movement." This study also pointed out that Al-Fatah, the largest of the groups in the PLO, was first established in Kuwait in 1958. Gerard Chaliand, in a 1969 study of the Palestinian Resistance Movement published by *Le Monde Diplomatique*, said Al-Fatah, the group headed by Yasser Arafat, presently PLO leader, even "decided to bypass the heavy machinery of the PLO by entering the armed struggle as a Palestinian national movement, independent of the

---

[4] A. Yaniv, *P.L.O. (Palestine Liberation Organization)*, Israel: Israel Universities Study Group for Middle Eastern Affairs, 1974, p. 6.

Arab governments." Chaliand quotes from the list of principles drawn up by a Palestinian commission. The first point was that "revolutionary violence is the only way in which the fatherland can be liberated."

Nevertheless, there has been a notable unwillingness on the part of the bulk of the American press to undertake the kind of study of the Palestinian national movement that would produce definitive and constructive articles on the PLO, its various components and its methods. The Palestinian guerrillas, heroic figures to most of the Palestinian people and to many other Arabs, continue to be regarded on American editorial pages as mindless assassins.

It is obviously difficult for editorial writers conditioned to this view of the various Arab peoples, including the Palestinians, to give sufficient attention and consideration to occasional efforts by Arab sympathizers or Middle East academic experts to detail the efforts of the Arab governments to reach some accommodation with Israel. Moreover, Israeli raids into Lebanon, Jordan or Syria tend to assume the aspect of legitimate retaliation against these Arab nations for "Arab" terrorism against Israel. Similarly, condemnation of Israel's actions by the United Nations has been regularly denounced as unfair, as anti-Semitic, as "ganging up on Israel," when, as even a beginning student of international affairs would be able to point out, formal actions by a nation or group of nations cannot be taken against a stateless people. The Palestinians could not be condemned; no such thing as a Palestinian state exists.

It is a relatively simple matter for Zionist and Jewish public relations efforts to turn an audience, already inclined rather strongly toward a sympathetic view of Israel, into ardent partisans. And this is frequently done. The Zionist-Jewish public relations effort is pervasive. It is well financed, highly professional, and it is relentless and indefatigable. Much of it is also non-political in that it focuses on Jewish faith, culture or history, especially of the Holocaust. Local Jewish Community Councils become instruments for the government of Israel by sponsoring speakers from Israel and programs about Israeli culture and Middle East affairs. Jewish Community Councils become the instrument in many cases for registering collective Jewish opinion in the community about editorial topics. The Jewish press operating in most larger American cities generally employs material submitted by the Jewish Telegraph Agency, which is a news agency subsidized by the government of Israel. The Jewish Community Council in Dayton, Ohio receives in excess of $100,000 annually from the United Fund, an umbrella charitable group that funds most community activities. Every United Jewish Appeal campaign is a propaganda effort for Israel.

There is a steady flow of material, all of it very professional, coming across the desks of editorial writers. It comes from the Israeli embassy or consulate, from the Zionist Organization of America, from the American Jewish Congress—which is part of the World Jewish Congress and is to a degree controlled by the government of Israel—from the Anti-Defamation League of B'nai B'rith, from Hadassah and from local Jewish groups. One or more of these organizations, or local synagogues, will bring speakers to town from time to time, experts of one kind or another who will meet with editorial boards to provide background material on various aspects of the Middle East conflict. For those journalists with a casual concern about ethics there are junkets to Israel underwritten by the Zionists. For seven or eight years the American Zionist Federation has sponsored a media tour of Israel that costs the journalists about a third or half of what such a tour should cost. The price in 1976 was $439 from New York for a ten-day tour. A *Philadelphia Inquirer* editorial writer, Elsa Goss, took the 1976 tour and wrote a series of analytical pieces that were distributed by Knight News Service all over the United States.

There is no way of calculating the long-range impact on public opinion, including the opinion of editorial writers, of such cultural propaganda as Leon Uris' novel *Exodus*, which painted a heroic picture of the struggle to create the State of Israel, or of James Michener's novel, *The Source*. No less than three motion pictures were made based on the bold Israeli raid on Entebbe. In short, there are formidable forces, and a multitude of them, operating to shape public opinion in the United States favorably toward Israel. There is almost no Arab propaganda, and there are relatively few Arab experts who meet with editorial boards, relatively few Arab citizens who write letters to the editor.

If, despite the inundation of Israeli propaganda, an editorial writer or columnist has become reasonably well informed and offers opinions critical of Israel or Zionism, pressure is immediately brought to bear on the critic. Sometimes the pressure is no more than a flood of letters to the editor. Sometimes an offending editorial or column brings a delegation of Jewish leaders from the community to call upon the editor to discuss the matter. Or the Jewish community will bring in an outside expert to correct "misunderstandings" or "misapprehensions" on the part of the editorial writer. The hint of a charge of anti-Semitism is given. Criticism of Israel is regarded by many Jews as tantamount to criticism of Jews. *The New Anti-Semitism*, a book by Arnold Foster and Benjamin Epstein of the Anti-

139

Defamation League of B'nai B'rith, equates criticism of Israel with criticism of Jews and, therefore, with anti-Semitism. Forster and Epstein lay the charge at the feet of, among others, national columnists Rowland Evans and Robert Novak.

If the editor or editorial writer is not very well informed, he will be placed on the defensive by sharp critics who are very well informed indeed. It takes a special courage for a Gentile editorial writer to challenge a rabbi on the distinction between Zionism and Judaism, on Jewish history or on Jewish opinion. No editor or editorial writer will consistently advance ideas that are extremely unpopular with a large segment of his readers when many of those readers may know more about the subject than the writer. Either the editorial page begins to reflect conventional Zionist wisdom or it becomes silent on the subject, because the editorial writer cannot adequately defend his views in the face of criticism from Jews who know more about the subject than he does.

If the writer is, himself, an expert, or at least has sufficient knowledge to defend his views, the pressure can be ugly. The charge of anti-Semitism is leveled. There are veiled—and not so veiled—threats of economic sanctions, i.e., withdrawal of advertising. If the editor does not flinch, his publisher may, and the result is censorship.

There is no way of measuring self-imposed censorship, the kind of restraint that prevents an editorial writer from saying what he wants to say because of the storm of criticism that will be produced. Former New York Times' editorial writer James Brown's problems have their counterparts all over the country. The Times' Reston, replying to the author's inquiry about the famous retraction, and to a question about Jewish pressure, wrote, ". . . Of course, Israel has, outside of labor, the most powerful lobby in the United States, and I have no doubt that all columnists, including myself, are very careful about commenting on the topic." Zakarian says he feels obligated to remind readers of the Post-Dispatch that Israel has a right to exist and deserves guarantees of her security, etc. "It's like a litany that one has to go through. We believe it, of course, but we shouldn't have to repeat this every time we write something mildly critical."

To be sure, some commentators and editors do not bend before Zionist pressure. Dorothy Thompson did not, although major newspapers dropped her column, such as *The New York Post* in 1947, which cost her dearly financially.[5] *The Jewish Newsletter*, an anti-Zionist Jewish periodical published from 1948 until 1961, reported in its January 21, 1958 issue that "It is a great pity that, because of Zionist pressure, Miss Thompson's columns are not published in New York and in other cities with large Jewish populations."

William Ruggles, former editor of *The Dallas Morning News*, was another editor who spoke his mind and who tried to make clear that Arab discrimination against Jews was motivated by anti-Zionist, not anti-Semitic attitudes. The late Basil "Stuffy" Walters, executive editor of *The Chicago Daily News*, told Rabbi Berger that he threatened to publish a front page editorial listing the names of Jewish businessmen who threatened to withdraw advertising over objections to editorials critical of Israel.

Joseph C. Harsh, formerly a reporter, then chief editorial writer, and now a columnist for *The Christian Science Monitor*, has also consistently spoken his mind on the Middle East, and has incurred the wrath of Zionist pressure groups because of it. His resignation was demanded by Jews who threatened an economic boycott of the *Monitor*. Columnists Rowland Evans and Robert Novak have been fearless in criticizing what they regarded as U.S. Middle East policy that did not serve U.S. interests, but they felt obliged to write a column defending themselves against the charge of anti-Semitism. Syndicated columnists Nick Von Hoffman and Nick Thimmesch are two others whose remarks have drawn the wrath of the Zionist community upon them.

Unfortunately, these spokesmen are exceptions. The bulk of the opinion columnists seldom express criticism of Israel, if they take up the issue of the Middle East at all, and some of them express a strident (and uninformed) criticism of the Palestinians and the Arab nations. Criticism of Israel in editorial columns is seldom seen, and then is carefully muted. The result is that the opinion pages of the American daily press offer a depressing lack of thoughtful and useful guidance for the American people on one of the most critical foreign policy questions they face.

The average American knows for whom he plans to vote, whether for president or for county commissioner. He knows what he thinks about a

---

[5] Marion K. Sanders, *Dorothy Thompson, A Legend in Her Time*, Boston: Houghton Mifflin Co., 1973, p. 326.

local ward heeler or a national official who has been caught with his fingers in the public till. But he knows relatively little about major international events, and he knows next to nothing about the Middle East, or what policy the United States should be following in that part of the world. In fact, the situation may be worse than that. The average American has a grossly distorted, simplistic view of the Middle East, and this inclines him toward support for a dangerous and destructive national policy in that part of the world. The American press bears a major responsibility for this state of affairs.

14

A SURVEY OF POLITICAL CARTOONS DEALING WITH THE MIDDLE EAST

George H. Damon, Jr. (with the assistance of Laurence D. Michalak[1])

Dr. Damon is Assistant Professor of Media Communications at Framingham State College in Massachusetts.

The political cartoon is unique among editorial species and requires a different approach and standard of assessment than other editorial forms. Originating in caricature—distortion and exaggeration for fatuous effect—and in satire—sarcasm used to expose vice or folly—the political cartoon does not try to be balanced or positive. The cartoonists are concerned with blemishes, shortcomings and inconsistencies of a situation[2] and they best utilize their graphic shorthand to portray the essence of their topic.

In political caricature within political cartoons, the cartoonists will make a blunt assault on an individual's physiognomy including an unambiguous statement as to the mental and moral attributes he wishes his victim to carry.[3] Whereas the editorial writer may feel impelled to present

---

[1] Laurence D. Michalak did the research on *The San Francisco Chronicle* which has been integrated into this paper. The opinions and conclusions belong to the author.
[2] John Geipel, *The Cartoon, A Short History of Graphic Comedy and Satire*, A.S. Barnes and Company, 1972, p. 18.
[3] Ibid., p. 21.

all sides of an issue with the facts, the political cartoonist feels no such restrictions on going for the jugular. Some convey an extreme hatred for their subjects, refusing to meet them, considering it detrimental to their ability to criticize. Others ignore facts with no concern for whether they are right or wrong, priding themselves on being negative. Such practitioners call the political cartoons an underhanded or unfair art where "you're only going for the Achilles' heel."[4]

Political cartoonists like to be considered satirists but are often only propagandists, utilizing their skills to knowingly distort facts and reality for the promotion of a particular editorial posture. A few demand absolute independence for their work and it reflects a personal posture; Pat Oliphant, the current star of the negative art, and Paul Conrad at *The Denver Post* are among these. True consistent satirists are few, with Le Pelley of *The Christian Science Monitor* leading a group that joins him occasionally in equally poignant, if less flamboyant, statements than the pursuers of the negative art.

Concern with political cartoons stems from the knowledge that the editorial pages of the newspaper are the most widely read pages of a newspaper. People used to collect political cartoons and mull over their layers of meaning. Because this attitude no longer prevails, political cartoonists have evolved a compactness of meaning so that the average seven-second glance is adequate to absorb their meaning. The newspaper uses the political cartoon to grab attention and in many cases to signal a topic discussed in an adjacent editorial.

A good political cartoon is unmistakable in intent. It is an almost pure opinion expressed in graphic imagery and unencumbered by much fact. For these reasons, the study of the political cartoons of a particular period leads to a succinct outline of the opinion makers of that time. The cartoons analyzed here are from four newspapers, *The New York Times*, *The Boston Globe*, *The Christian Science Monitor* and *The San Francisco Chronicle*. They cover four periods corresponding to the four most intense periods of the Middle East conflict—May-June, 1948; November-December, 1956; June-July, 1967; and October-November, 1973. These periods were chosen

---

[4] Milton Bass, *People*, "BIO," August 1, 1977, p. 57.

because they seemed most likely to yield the highest numbers of political cartoons about Arabs—a total of 226 cartoons.

Each of the newspapers gives a different approach to the political cartoon. The *Chronicle*'s are generally propagandistic, occurring at the top center of its editorial page every day, except Saturday when there is no editorial. The cartoons are drawn by their staff cartoonist: in 1948, Sweigert; in 1956 and 1967, Bastiam; and in 1973, Graysmith. On Sunday, the staff cartoonist is not carried, and the *Chronicle* prints one or more cartoons by a well-known syndicated cartoonist such as Herblock or Conrad. The cartoon is frequently coordinated with the editorial next to it. A clear example of the propagandistic use of the cartoon occurred on June 25, 1967. An editorial by William Randolph Hearst, Jr., in the joint *Chronicle-Examiner* published on Sundays, attacks the U.N. debate and its reference to Israel as the aggressor in the Middle East war. Hearst takes a strong stand in defense of Israel in this editorial which is buttressed by two pro-Israeli, anti-U.N. cartoons.

In contrast to the *Chronicle, The Christian Science Monitor*'s cartoons are satirical in nature and occur at the top center of the last page. While the *Monitor* puts unique restrictions on its cartoonists to the extent that they may not have violence or bloodshed in their cartoons, the staff cartoonists, Carmack in 1948 and Le Pelley in 1967 and 1973, are just as poignant, if in a subtler fashion, than other cartoonists. A typical *Monitor* cartoon occurred on July 12, 1967, by Le Pelley, titled "One Good Turn. . . " The cartoon shows Kosygin and Johnson holding leaks in pipes labeled "Mideast Hot Water" and "Vietnam Hot Water" with each near the shut-off valve for the other.

The Boston Globe did not carry political cartoons in 1948, and in 1956 printed mostly syndicated cartoonists, predominantly Herblock, only during the week. By 1967 the *Globe* was still heavily dependent on syndicated cartoons, but it had diversified and increased the number, adding Haynie, Oliphant, Darcy, Mauldin, Shanks, Fischetti and Grant. As the paper grew, it acquired its own cartoonist, currently Paul Szep, who does little to mask his hatred for the Arabs or for anyone critical of Israel, and continued to print syndicated cartoons in a coordinated policy similar to the *Chronicle*'s.

The New York Times has had the most dramatic changes toward the use of political cartoons. In 1948 the staff cartoonist Marcus and representative cartoons from other papers were published in the "News of the Week in Review" every Sunday. By 1956 the pages of the "News of the Week in Review" dealing with international matters were saturated with cartoons

145

from other U.S. newspapers as well as foreign papers. The newspaper professed to be measuring opinion in other countries and parts of the United States. This flood of support for the cartoon had subsided by 1967 when only one or two cartoons appeared each Sunday. By 1973 the editorial staff of *The New York Times* had banned the political cartoon, purportedly due to its lack of seriousness.

The cartoons for the four periods fall into categories that are consistent across the four wars. The first group are cartoons that seek to summarize the situation in terms which do not include either an Arab or Israeli figure and may be called neutral. These cartoons take no sides and opt instead for doves of peace, figures representing war or other expressions of harmony or discord. Included in this group, for purposes here, are cartoons which attack a third party such as DeGaulle, Krushchev or Eden without implicating either Arabs or Israelis.

A second category are those which clearly attack an Arab leader, most notably Nasser. Third are those cartoons which are clearly anti-Arab by the presence of an Arab stereotype. A fourth group are those cartoons which are anti-Arab by implication, such as a cartoon in which U Thant is wearing blinders marked "Israel's fault." Since this cartoon represents U Thant as being blind, and since U Thant assigned most of the blame to Israel, a logical inference is that the cartoonist is expressing a pro-Israeli view that is by implication anti-Arab.

Groups five, six and seven are cartoons which attack Israel leaders, use an Israeli stereotype and are anti-Israeli by implication respectively. The paucity of cartoons in these last three areas is an early indication of editorial bias during these time periods. The *Chronicle* has only one cartoon which belongs among these three categories. That cartoon, by Graysmith of November 7, 1973, shows Sadat and Meir in shells, throwing matches at each other's fuses while Kissinger comes running with a watering can. As a paper noted for its pro-Israeli editorial stand, the lack of deviation in cartoons is no surprise. *The Boston Globe* is hardly a step removed from the *Chronicle*, with only one cartoon critical of an Israeli leader, Eban, for annexing Jerusalem in 1967 and two equally critical of Arabs and Israel, in 1973. The independent Oliphant is the creator of these poignant but non-pejorative statements. The depiction of the 1956 invasion is strangely absent of critical comment of Israel. During this same period, almost half of the cartoons dealing with the Middle East are critical of Arab figures.

The Christian Science Monitor is totally noncommittal in its cartoons under the pen of Carmack. There are no cartoons touching on Israel's role

"Fire two . . . any sign of the Israelis yet?"

"See what happens? And I ordered the same lunch!"

148

in 1948 or 1956, and only one about the Arabs which deals with Nasser's loss of revenue from the closed canal. The remaining cartoons fall into the first category. With Le Pelley during 1967 and 1973, three cartoons emerge depicting Israeli leaders: the first shows "Peace over Jerusalem" with a patch over one eye, and the others make the first direct jab at an Israeli leader, Golda Meir, for her policy of "Secure Boundaries on Conquered Territory" and her lack of cooperation with the United States due to the oil squeeze.

In *The New York Times*, the dearth of critical cartoons of Israel continues with only three of seventy-six recognizable as being critical. All three are in 1956, with the strongest by Jensen of *The Chicago Daily News*, December 30, 1956, titled "Staked Out Claim," showing Ben-Gurion standing next to the Gaza Strip cordoned off by guns and a rope. None of the other newspapers lay any blame on Israel for the 1956 invasion of Egypt in which its role is undisputed. This absence, and the *Times'* three cartoons of which one is from *Punch*, signify the lack of understanding of the cartoonist of both the evolution of events and Israeli intentions, as well as an editorial policy by the newspaper to look elsewhere for pictorial comment.

Whereas the other three newspapers took no definite stand on either side in the 1948 War, apparently being occupied with the Truman-Dewey election and other local issues, *The New York Times* did print three cartoons reflective of stereotypes persisting until now. The David and Goliath myth appears in a cartoon by Page of *The Louisville Courier Journal* in which Goliath is the "Arab Nations" and a small figure stands guarding Palestine. The role of the indigenous people is lost in Page's perception of the area as belonging to a determined minority of Jews or to all the Arab nations. A more defamatory connection occurs in Seaman's cartoon from the ILGWU newspaper, which shows a Western figure with a sword representing Palestine, implying that Palestine belongs to the West, talking to the Grand Mufti, who has a swastika on his back. The figure says, "Not Like Dachau, is it, Herr Mufti." This attempt to link various Arab individuals or organizations with the philosophy and actions of Hitler is erroneous but very effective in an America which has a Pavlovian response to any mention of a connection with the cruelty of Hitlerism.

The final pejorative myth which appears in *The New York Times* is present in the cartoon by Duffy of *The Baltimore Sun*. A misplaced GI in Arab dress with a cigarette hanging out of his mouth is being addressed by a doctor labeled the U.N. with a bird on its finger labeled PAX. Consistently, the Arabs are presented as the aggressors in the Middle East, a group of warmongers who desire conflict and who have to be cajoled into peace. No mention is made of Israeli intransigence, aggression, terrorism or military strength supported by the West in 1948.

In 1956, when who the invaders were was very clear, as mentioned earlier, Israel only received blame in *The New York Times*. The majority of the 60 cartoons printed are concerned with Soviet attempts, after crushing the revolt in Hungary, to become involved on the side of the Arabs, particularly Egypt, in the Middle East, or are concerned with the U.N. and U.S. search for peace in the Middle East. The cartoons depict Nasser or Syria as being duped by the Russians who later swallow them. Another misconception emerges as Nasser is depicted as handcuffing the U.N. No mention is made of Israel's refusal to allow U.N. observers on its side of the ceasefire line. The year 1956, which would be expected to bring the most evenhanded or anti-Israeli cartoons, produces only three, while 16 cartoons depict either the Arabs or their leaders as stubborn, aggressive, potentially Communist people.

With the weight of the response in 1956, no surprises occur in 39 anti-Arab cartoons in 1967. *The New York Times* had started to phase out cartoons; still, five of the seven printed include an Arab figure, usually Nasser, in a derogatory role. The strongest of these, by Cummings of *The Daily London Express*, also pokes at DeGaulle, who is shown shooting down British Common Market applications and the Swing Wing Aircraft while saying to Nasser, wearing old Arab clothes and surrounded by flies, holding a sign "Avenge the Battle of Sinai," "I understand you! I'm still avenging the Battle of Waterloo."

With their first definitive stand in 1967, the *Chronicle* and *The Boston Globe* through their cartoons make clear their pro-Israeli posture. For the one cartoon critical of Eban for annexing Jerusalem, there are 13 which attack Nasser and another 18 denoting the Arab through a visual stereotype while perpetuating the myths of 1948. Two of the country's best known cartoonists, Herblock and Mauldin, seem to have been effectively indoctrinated by Israel, as seen in their cartoons in *The Boston Globe*. In a cartoon of June 5, titled "Today the World—Tomorrow Ourselves" showing three figures entering the United Nations, one in African dress, labeled "Self-government Crises in New Nations," one in Arab dress, labeled "Dictatorships and Feudalism," and the last, mostly hidden, labeled "Military Coups," and in another of June 29, 1967, titled "Still the number one refugee," showing Nasser and other Arab leaders backed by Russia, pointing a gun at a battered female "Peace" and standing behind a sign "Keep Out of the Middle East," Herblock perpetuated the myths of the Arab as the only aggressor and a backward people. Herblock is matched by Mauldin in a cartoon sent from Israel titled "You don't need signs to tell the border" in which an Orthodox Jew is watering healthy trees while a barefoot degenerate Arab with a bone in his hand sits on a rock surrounded by wasteland.

The pejorative use of the Arab stereotype comes prominently to the fore in the *Chronicle* and the *Globe*. In the visual stereotype, the Arab is represented with a black mustache and/or beard, shadowy jowls, a hook nose, flowing robes and a kaffiyeh headdress; he goes barefoot or wears sandals, sometimes with pointed and curved toes. Dress alone is not pejorative, as can be seen in the cartoon of Jaheen of Egypt, Chalukov of Iraq, Rabah of Jordan and Sadek of Lebanon, all of whom use an Arab stereotype as a positive figure. As is readily apparent in their work, American cartoonists use the stereotype to vilify the Arab.

In contrast to the other newspapers, the *Monitor* in 1967 refrains from distortion of fact and, with satirist Le Pelley drawing, makes clear, non-pejorative statements. Among the most amusing is the cartoon of June 6 entitled "Oops, Sorry Chief." In this cartoon Nasser is shown cutting off the Soviet Union's pants as he steps into the Arab-Israeli war. Derogatory stereotypes are noticeably absent from *The Christian Science Monitor*. Additionally, Le Pelley's statement on the position of the refugees remains poignant today. The cartoon titled "Lost Tribe," shows a young boy and a young girl standing in a wasteland. This cartoon illustrates some understanding of the plight of the refugees. The *Globe* and the *Chronicle* refer to the refugees as a burden given to Israel for its victory. Noticeably absent still from their cartoons is any sense of the rights of the Palestinians.

By 1973, the number of cartoons has dropped significantly, but the *Globe* and the *Chronicle*'s posture on the Middle East remains steady. With one of the flamboyant stars of the negative art, Paul Szep, on its staff, the *Globe* found an active propagandist for its belief in Israel's innocence. On October 5, 1973, Szep displayed his bias in a cartoon titled "We mustn't be a party to anything so shocking," which shows a policeman labeled "U.N." watching as an Arab terrorist beats on an old Jew representing Israel. The hidden irony of his cartoon must escape Mr. Szep, as the State of Israel owes its existence to terrorism, political pressure and blackmail, culminating in the U.N. declaration of 1948. The major new aspect to appear in the cartoons of 1973 is the oil embargo, which allowed every cartoonist to represent the snickering Arab stereotype holding up the world for its own gain, never mind our economic blockade of Cuba for similar reasons.

151

The *Monitor* remains above the norm again in 1973, giving each side a good rap. Le Pelley in an October 10, 1973 cartoon, captioned "Borderline Case," shows two military men with guns pointed at each other, one Israeli and the other Arab, their guns labeled "Secure Boundary Demand" and "Return Arab Territory Demand," respectively. Whereas the *Monitor* still has not issued a cartoon which focuses on the essence of the problem—the implantation of an exclusive state dominated by Western ideas into a heterogenous area of distinctly Eastern culture, it does refrain from the crude pro-Israeli propaganda of the other newspapers.

The profile that emerges from these four periods is threefold. The first line designating those cartoons in our first category dominates editorial statements except in 1956, when Nasser, due to the completeness of the Israeli victory, is buffeted repeatedly. The cartoons are descriptive in nature or critical of the U.N., the world or a given country for aggravating the situation or not taking responsiblity for their actions. None are critical of the 1948 U.N. decision, but all are unrestrained in berating the organization for its criticism of Israel.

The second line includes categories two through four with the majority of cartoons dealing with Arab leaders while a bulge is caused by the cartoonists' distortion and vilification of the Arab through stereotypes. This protrusion is present in 1948, and widens as time passes, being bloated by ever greater distortions. A recent check of cartoons shows the present trend to be toward the cartoonist ignoring fact for flamboyancy. The Arab stereotype is drawn with increased concentration on details derogatory when perceived. A typical example is the August 12, 1977 cartoon by MacNelly carried in *The Boston Globe* concerning Vance's trip to the Middle East. A bus is filled with wide-eyed, mustached Arabs in flowing garb arguing, chasing chickens, and contorting their faces while Vance sits calmly reading "Kissinger's Guide to the Middle East." This cartoon gains little strength as a statement about Vance or the Middle East situation from its dependence upon the viewer's willingness to laugh at the Arabs. Such cartoons lack the thrust of which MacNelly is capable, as seen in a cartoon by him on August 14, 1977 captioned "I think I've Got the Two Parties Close to a Meeting." In this cartoon, Vance is sitting at a desk talking on the phone while two figures on horseback representing Israel and the PLO, with lances, are charging each other, a strong jab at the difference between Vance's perception and reality.

The third profile deals with categories five through seven. What few cartoons there are deal with Israeli leadership in the mildest of terms, considering the caustic abilities of the cartoonists. Although there are some Orthodox Jews in Israel, just as there are some nomads in the Arab world, this Israeli stereotype only appears once in a positive situation. Predominantly the images associated with Israel are presented in Western clothes with Western features looking much the same as an American would. The sympathetic reaction of a reader is apparent.

The paucity of cartoons in these last categories is reflective of the newspapers' editorial stand on the Middle East during the wars. With the exception of the *Monitor*, a balanced viewpoint is absent. Even the *Monitor*'s cartoonists have refrained from a direct attack upon Zionism for its repressive, racist and Western philosophies. The fear of being labeled anti-Semitic lies heavily over members of the media, and those cartoonists who are strong enough only go so far as to show an occasional leadership foible. Of all the Israeli leaders, Begin is the first that cartoonists feel safe to criticize without suffering the wrath of the pro-Israeli constituency. Even the *Globe* published two cartoons which showed that there was a rift between Carter and Begin. More refreshing is the work of Le Pelley, who on August 16, 1977, shows Carter and Kissinger meeting for lunch. Begin, acting as a waiter, pours the luncheon labeled "Mideast Progress" all over Carter's head as Carter is saying to Kissinger, "See what happens! And I ordered the same lunch."

As part of the editorial page of a newspaper, the cartoon, with few exceptions, is an extension of the opinion of that page. Years of effective development by the pro-Israeli groups in America have indirectly thwarted any assault on the essence of Israeli structure, normally the task of a good cartoonist.

One concludes that cartoonists feel the freedom to use the Arab stereotype at a time when there is a noticeable absence of this practice with other ethnic or national groups. This situation signifies the weakness of the Arab-American community's willingness to challenge that image as it appears in newspapers or in other equally pervasive forms, as movies, comic books, television and textbooks. Among media forms, the cartoon is the least likely to be responsive to pressure or change as its practitioners claim to be fierce in their freedom to be negative. The posture of the editorial page of a newspaper is the only vehicle for indirect influence on the cartoon, as most are propagandistic in nature. If the Arab stereotype is to be mollified, a concerted effort must be made to demand that the written editorials deal with the "essence" of the problem in the Middle East—the Palestinians—and offer a balanced position on Arab-Israeli, Arab-U.S. problems.

PART II: 1979-82

15

A RENEWED LOOK AT AMERICAN COVERAGE OF THE ARABS: TOWARD A BETTER UNDERSTANDING?

Edmund Ghareeb

I

Since *Split Vision* first appeared, considerable changes have occurred in the Middle East: The Camp David accords have recast the shape of Egyptian-Israeli and Egyptian-Arab relations, the revolution in Iran has overturned the political and social structures of that country with important implications for the rest of the region, Iran and Iraq have been at war for over two years, and foreign forces continue to occupy much of Lebanon. These developments and others have generated a plethora of information on the region, including news coverage, documentaries, films, scholarly works and novels.

Increased information has in some cases resulted in a more balanced approach to the region, less prone to distortion and bias. Many of the worst excesses associated with the portrayal of Arabs have been corrected. Such evil characters as Akbar the Wrestler, "who likes to hear the cracking of bones," and Abdullah the Butcher, a wrestler infamous for his lack of mercy, have largely disappeared from the popular culture. As a result of management sensitivity and public pressure, certain advertisements depicting Arabs as greedy, materialistic and villainous have been rejected for broadcasting or taken off the air despite initial acceptance. A television spot for Frigidaire showing an Arab sheikh who casually requested 150 refrigerators for his 75 wives, because "they get very thirsty," was taken off the air on CBS, after initial approval by all three commercial networks, when it was brought to the attention of Van Gordon Sauter, former Vice-President of Program Practices. A nutritional spot for "Captain Kangaroo," the children's television program, produced by the J. Walter Thompson Advertising Agency, featured a devilish animated Arab to illustrate tooth decay. Donn O'Brien, Vice-President for Program Practices at CBS-TV, rejected the film.

However, for every advertisement or television program which has cut out a particularly ugly representation of an Arab or Arabs, another has appeared in uncensored bad taste. For example, carrying out the theme of "getting back at the Arabs" for the energy problem, a Massachusetts company launched an advertising campaign for a new lighter fluid called Sheeks, inciting consumers to "Save oil and other high cost fuels . . . Burn Sheeks." A picture of an Arab engulfed in flames illustrated the advertisement. The Ken McGillivray Buick dealership of Flint, Michigan also exploited the energy crisis to its own advantage with an advertisement published in the *Flint Journal* on May 4, 1980. Equating McGillivray pricing policies with the "fight" against the Arab OPEC nations, the ad was boxed in by a thick red line and prominently displayed an American flag, which covered almost half the page. The text addressed the consumer in aggressive language, proclaiming, "Maybe it doesn't bother you, but we've had it with the Arabs and the rest of the world. We're sick of being criticized by the same nations that always have their hands out. We're tired of having the Arabs gouge us to death with their oil prices and then lecture us to death about the inflation that their oil price gouging is causing . . . . We're going to fight back. From now on every action we take at Ken McGillivray will have one objective—to beat the Arabs at their own game."

Television has been equally guilty of perpetuating a negative image of the Arabs. Jack Shaheen, who has written extensively on the portrayal of Arabs in television, noted in 1980 that, "Nearly every other week for the past five years an entertainment show projecting an anti-Arab image has appeared in prime time." The programs involved include the entire spectrum of entertainment offerings, from adventure and detective dramas such as "Charlie's Angels," "McCloud," "Hawaii Five-O," "Cannon" and "Wonder Woman," to comedies, syndicated programs and children's shows. One example of the way in which entertainment television functions as a perpetuator of stereotypes and misconceptions concerns the television program "Card Sharks." Devised to explore social myths and cliches, the program printed a questionnaire for distribution to men and

158

women in the Middle East, including such items for men as "Do you have a pet camel?", "Would you respect a girl who let you peek under her veil on the first date?", "Do you ride to work on a camel?", "Was your wedding night the first time you saw your wife without a veil?" and for women, "Can a woman who shows her face in public ever be a good wife?", "Do veils make it easier for homely women to get husbands?", "Do you sleep in your veil?" and "Have you ever disobeyed your husband?"

News programs and documentaries have also taken a biased approach to handling Middle East issues. In 1977 Public Broadcasting System station KETC in St. Louis aired a documentary entitled, "Dateline Israel with Arnold Foster," produced by the Anti-Defamation League, an organization which supports the policies of the Israeli government. However, the station did not, as is normally the policy of public television stations, list the names of the organizations which provided the operating funds allowing the program to be telecast. The film included a statement by the Israeli Ambassador to the United Nations, but gave no coverage to the views of an Arab spokesman. The station's program guide, TV Guide and the local press listed the show under the heading of "Documentary Theatre" with the subtitle "Palestinians and PLO." From the titles and descriptions some viewers were led to assume the program would be balanced because of the documentary nature of the program.

In the press, cartoons, editorials, analytical pieces and news stories alike have often expressed an anti-Arab or pro-Israeli bias. Cartoons, which by definition convey a strong statement with very few words, have projected a very negative image of the Arabs. During the 1981 AWACS debate, a major subject of discussion was the question of how the planes would be used. MacNelly, a prominent political cartoonist, provided his own answer to the question with a drawing of an AWACS with an Arab at the controls (identifiable by the kaffiyeh), to whom an American is explaining, "Your Highness will be excited to learn that with this AWACS we're selling you, you guys will be able to keep an eye on the Russians." Meanwhile, another Arab (also identifiable by the kaffiyeh) is painting the words "the Jew Hunter" on the outside of the plane, with a Star of David underneath.

Following the emergence of OPEC as a major economic power and the rise of oil prices during the 1970s, many cartoonists popularized the image of the greedy, grasping, crooked Arab, intent on undermining the American economy. This portrayal updates the traditional image of the Arab sheikh à la Rudolph Valentino with its focus on the Arab's purported appetite for material goods and ostentatious living by changing the setting. Cadillacs and oil rigs have supplanted the camels, palm trees

159

and harems of the past. One cartoon illustrating this theme encouraged readers to "Fight high oil prices! Mug an Arab today!" In the same vein, a cartoon that appeared in the *Chicago Tribune* during the summer of 1981 depicted an Arab wearing dark glasses and a nasty grin seated behind a large desk with the sign "OPEC" in front of him and a number of oil rigs visible through a window. A second sign on the desk read, "Buy American," only the "n" had been scratched out, giving graphic expression to the highly publicized stories of Arabs using their oil wealth to take control of the American economy by buying American firms and real estate.

News stories have also indicated a negative attitude toward Arabs in other ways. The notion of American dependence on the Arab oil exporters has received considerable attention. An article on the energy situation that appeared in *The Christian Science Monitor* several years ago offered readers a mixed report. The headline read, "The good news is that Americans are buying a lot less oil this year—the bad news is that the United States must keep buying oil from OPEC anyway." Even prominent politicians have found the Arabs to be an attractive scapegoat for America's ills. In a television interview during which he was asked to reflect on the state of America's economy, Michigan Governor William Milliken said, "If you're looking for a scapegoat, I point to those damn Arabs."

In his excellent book, *Covering Islam*, Edward Said cites the many methods of hyperbole, euphemism, incriminating suggestion, wild and baseless accusations, guilt by association and extrapolation from the weakest evidence that are used to discredit the Arabs, Islam and the Palestinian cause. Said shows how the Iranian revolution accelerated the already-existing trend of associating the "rise of Islam" with a threat to American interests abroad. He points to the constant confusion of Iranians and Arabs, and implies that there was an unconscious but active tendency to discredit and malign Muslims and Arabs.

The media have continued to foster stereotypes by lumping Muslims and Arabs together and by making use of scholarly and pseudo-scholarly discussions about the "sham culture of the Arabs" and the Arab mind. John Laffin's book, *The Arab Mind Considered*, which has been cited by others writing on the Middle East, provides an excellent example of this problem. In his book Laffin asserts that:

1. To the Arab there may be several truths about the one situation, depending on the type of language he is using.

2. Language is not used to reason but to persuade.

3. The Arab means what he says at the moment he is saying it. He is neither a vicious nor, usually, a calculating liar but a natural one.

4. The value of words is often assessed by quantity.

5. Words can rationalize or justify anything.

Raphael Patai's book, *The Arab Mind*, has received even wider attention than Laffin's work. Patai explains a number of Arab characteristics as a function of child-rearing practices, such as prolonged breast-feeding, and the cognitive elements of Arabic. Patai concludes that as a result the Arab personality is characterized by fantasy, extremism, preoccupation with honor, disregard for time, irrationality, fatalism, aggression and a lack of creativity. Both of these books draw conclusions and generalizations that are not, by and large, borne out by the data provided.

Patai elaborated on his themes in an article published in the *Chicago Tribune* on December 6, 1981, entitled, "Violence, the Islamic Curse." The article was accompanied by a cartoon showing four bearded figures wearing robes and stabbing each other in the back with daggers. Similar cartoons have appeared in other newspapers. The latest of these served as an illustration for an article by syndicated columnist George Will entitled, "Discord in Araby" in *The Baltimore Sun*. Patai's article uses a distorted interpretation of jihad to argue that violence is an inherent characteristic of Muslim-Arab society. By grouping the Muslim and Arab personalities together indiscriminately, Patai does an injustice to both. Not all Muslims are Arabs and not all Arabs are Muslims. The Arabs do not number more than 12 percent of the world's Muslims. Patai argues that the Arab propensity to commit violence is rooted in "the pre-Islamic heritage of belligerence." If this were the case, why speak of violence as the Islamic, and not the Arab, curse? One may also ask if all the negative characteristics mentioned by Patai can be traced to pre-Islamic Arab society. Another unsubstantiated conclusion reached by the author is that "the Arab proclivity toward conflict was exported into the territories that became Arabized or at least Islamicized, and it became a common feature of all Islamic peoples." Such statements lead one to wonder if violence is limited only to Arab and Islamic societies, or if the pre-Arabized, pre-Islamicized societies were free of violence prior to the arrival of the Arab-Muslims. Such generalizations and stereotypes based on superficial knowledge of other peoples and societies and the inability or unwillingness to understand the complexity of a different culture are no substitute for serious journalistic or academic work.

The stereotyping of Arabs as greedy, rapacious oil merchants has undoubtedly influenced many average Americans. This is suggested by an article published in the *The Washington Post* on September 18, 1982 on the subject of improvements in solar hot water heater systems and the rise in their sales. The paper quotes one home-owner in Lynnfield, Massachusetts as saying that, in addition to his desire to save money, one of his main reasons for buying the heater was that, "For every gallon of oil I save, I figure I am taking money away from the Arabs."

Other evidence of the extent to which unfortunate stereotypes have produced a mental image associating Arabs or Muslims with violence includes the attempted assassination of Pope John Paul II. Syndicated columnist Joseph Kraft also highlighted the Muslim connection in an article entitled, "The Dark Side of Islam." Kraft explained Agca's act as symptomatic of the nature of Islam. Following the attempt on the Pope's life, many reporters stressed the "Arab" or "Middle Eastern" appearance of the assassin. The use of such descriptions is all the more revealing since the incident occurred in Italy, a Mediterranean country outside the Middle East, and there was no immediate reason to believe that the accused assassin was from outside the country. Even after Mehmet Ali Agca was identified as a Turk, a radio station announcer continued to describe him as an "Arab from Turkey."

II

The coverage of the events surrounding the Iranian Revolution and the hostage crisis are not part of the focus of this article except in as much as they may relate to the coverage of issues concerning the Arab world. Professor Edward Said's *Covering Islam* provides an excellent study of the media's coverage of the Iranian revolution.

But one of the prominent features in the coverage was the fear of regional instability. American newspapers and television gripped their audience with reports of "Islamic masses" marching in the streets and "America held hostage." A *Washington Post* article of November 27, 1979, featured the banner headline, "US Sets Evacuations From Islamic Nations," noting that evacuation of non-essential US diplomatic personnel and their dependents from 11 Islamic nations would take place before "a series of Islamic holy days that officials fear will inflame passions already running high against Americans in parts of the Islamic world." Suddenly, passions here were inflamed by various reports in the media of "the increasingly restive Moslem world," "the Islamic-inspired turmoil in Iran," and phrases such as the "arc of crisis," "Islamic processions," "the Islamic wave," and by the "fact," which must be startling to most

162

Americans, that "a lot of people throughout Islam are ready, willing, and often eager to think the worst of the United States, of its policies and of its people." These phrases and assertions became statements of fact despite evidence, also presented by the papers, to dispute the interpretation that Islam was linked to anti-American sentiment or that the demonstrations were inspired by anti-American feeling. The same *Washington Post* story cited above mentioned that "Islamic scholars here have said they doubt that a wave of anti-Americanism is sweeping the Islamic world. Rather, they said, fanaticism in Iran has emboldened groups of like-minded Moslems elsewhere to test their strength." The press made anti-Americanism a tenet of Islam, and because Islam has a following of some 800 million people, scattered throughout the Middle East and Asia, any turmoil in that part of the world at the time was interpreted as a sign of sweeping hostility to the United States. An article in *The Christian Science Monitor* on November 30, 1979 under the headline, "IRAN CRISIS SHAKES FRAGILE WORLD ORDER," carried this theme even further. The story noted that President Carter, during a news conference held on November 28, had pointed out "the virtually unanimous support" for the United States' demand that the hostages be freed. It also quoted one "high level international civil servant" who remarked on the "unprecedented moral and political unity among all members of the Security Council" on the hostage issue. However, the author chose to draw attention to another aspect of the crisis: what he called, "the latent groundswell in the Muslim world that could break out like a torrent, sweeping governments along with it, if the United States made a wrong move in third world, and particularly Muslim, eyes." The author added that in U.N. Secretary General Kurt Waldheim's estimation the hostage crisis jeopardized "the entire modus vivendi and respect for law . . . between the industrialized West and the Third World, between the haves and have-nots."

These articles reveal the anxiety aroused in and by the press, often unsubstantiated by evidence included in the same stories, over any change or conflict in the Third World, and especially in the Middle East. Other stories which provide ample evidence that the logic of the Middle East differs from that of the West, or that events there defy rational understanding, figure in the coverage of the Iranian revolution as well. In one example, a *Wall Street Journal* article (November 27, 1979) on village life in Iran made a link between the villagers' way of life and "the grip on Iran held by" Ayatollah Khomeini. Lending authority to the argument, the author quoted a West European diplomat in Tehran who said,

"Iranians have deep roots in their religion and culture, a conviction that sins should be dealt with harshly and a fierce resentment against foreign interference, real or imagined. . . . It is a mistake to evaluate them with Western logic." Such "explanations" have the consequence of cutting off immediate developments from their historical and social context, and of establishing in the mind of the Western audience the idea that the Middle East is a hostile, chaotic place, similar to a pot on the stove that is constantly on the verge of boiling over. What these statements neglect, too, are the similarities among people around the world. By saying that it is a mistake to apply Western logic to Iranians obscures the fact that everything the diplomat said does, in fact, apply to Americans. The Monroe Doctrine, upheld to this day, is evidence of Americans' resentment of foreign interference in their own affairs, and the notion that sins should be dealt with harshly evokes America's Puritan heritage.

III

The 1982 War in Lebanon offers an excellent example of the superficial and distorted coverage that the media have given Middle East issues. With few exceptions, the coverage has been shallow and limited at best. The television networks, *The Washington Post*, *The New York Times*, and even some Middle East "experts" have persisted in describing the conflict in Lebanon as a "civil war" between "right-wing Christians" and "left-wing Muslims." This portrayal of the war as a conflict pitting Christians against Muslims was first used by the Israelis and was later picked up by the U.S. media. Casting the antagonisms that characterize Lebanese society in such simplistic terms is not only inaccurate but raises the specter of Medieval holy wars. By appearing to set themselves on the side of the "Christians," Menachem Begin and his government have contributed to fanning the flames of sectarian strife in Lebanon. However, scant media coverage was given to a rally by "Christians" in support of then President-elect Bashir Gemayel in the town of Sidon. The rally was banned by the Israelis because the demonstrators refused to accede to demands by the Israeli authorities that "Christian" speakers thank the Israel invaders for driving Palestinian guerrillas out of Sidon and call for a peace treaty. *The Baltimore Sun*, however, quoting Israeli television, reported the story on September 8, 1982. The article contained excerpts from an interview by Israeli television with one of the Phalangist leaders organizing the rally, who said "Peace is not something that can be forced on the Lebanese people."

The lines dividing the protagonists in the Lebanon conflict are not nearly as neat as the distinction between Christians and Muslims. While many Christians may identify with the Lebanese Front, there are many others who are neutral or opposed to it. In fact, many Christians played leading roles in the National Movement, and many Muslims were neutral or opposed to the National Movement. Moreover, the Lebanese "civil war" was only one component of the overall conflict in Lebanon, which, in its broadest lines, became a projection of external forces, each with its own stake in the outcome.

The elite press and the television networks have persisted in using the Israeli government's description of the militia forces of former Lebanese Army Major Saad Haddad as "Christian militiamen," when it is well known, or ought to be, that these "Christians" do not constitute the majority of the rank and file of Saad Haddad's forces. An example of this problem was demonstrated on the Fall 1982 ABC News *Night Line* program devoted to the Sabra and Shatila massacres. Interviews were conducted with survivors of the massacres to elicit their views as to who was responsible. The interviewers speaking in Arabic blamed the Kataeb (Phalangists), Saad Haddad's forces and the Israelis, but the English narration placed the blame on "Christian militiamen."

The fact that many Christians and Muslims have been fighting on the same side is usually ignored. The media has also failed to discuss the circumstances that led to the emergence of Saad Haddad and the role of Israel in supporting him. In addition, the media offered very little in-depth information about the composition, goals and personalities of the major Lebanese forces involved in the conflict. The fact that the "rightist Christians" had conservative as well as liberal, moderate as well as radical elements in their midst was rarely covered. The misconceptions and outright inaccuracies were not limited to the "Christians." Little was said about the fact that groups and members belonging to the "Muslim-leftist" side included communists, Arab nationalists, Syrian nationalists, religious fundamentalists as well as other forces. They also had their progressives and their reactionaries. During the eight years of the Lebanon crisis it was a rare occasion when representatives of the various Lebanese sides appeared on television, and consequently little was known about them. This lack of information was manifested in a program aired by The MacNeil-Lehrer Report, one of the more balanced and informative TV news programs, on the election of Bashir Gemayel. The report showed a film on the election but inaccurately identified Amin Gemayel as Bashir Gemayel, the president-elect. And while the film was supplied by the BBC, the fact that the reporters, anchormen, and some of the expert panelists were unable to catch the error until one of the panelists pointed it out, reveals how little was known about one of the most powerful leaders in the country other than through the simplistic identifications which were used to characterize him in the press. On CNTV when the name of Amin Gemayel, the new Lebanese President, was mentioned, the photo of his late brother Bashir was shown.

During the same seven years of the "Lebanon crisis," which led to the unbelievable death of about three percent of the population and in which hundreds of thousands were maimed or became refugees in their own land, the media and many Middle East "experts" have tended to look at events in Lebanon solely in light of the conflict between Israel and the Palestinians. The coverage of the tragedy in Lebanon was rarely looked upon as a story in its own right; the untold horrors and violence inflicted on the innocent civilian population in East and West Beirut, Tripoli, Zahle, Sidon and other areas did not receive the attention or coverage the story deserved. Events in Lebanon only made the headlines when the Israelis became involved, or when the casualties reached very high levels. Otherwise, the story of Lebanon was, if covered at all, reported in cliches and buried in brief paragraphs in the inside pages.

In much of the media's coverage, Lebanon was written off as a country artificially created by the French to serve their interests and those of the Christians. According to the *New Republic*, "Lebanon was invented in Paris almost sixty years ago." Even if one is to accept this statement as fact, Lebanon would be older than most states in the area—certainly older than Israel. Few Lebanese spokesmen have been interviewed on developments in the country. This has often been left to others. For example, two ABC "Night Line" programs that focused on the crisis in Lebanon, the first of which was aired during the initial days of the Israeli invasion and the second after the cease-fire was reached, invited the Syrian and the Israeli Ambassadors to appear on the program, but no Lebanese representative appeared. The performance of other networks was not very different.

Such coverage has engendered the notion that Lebanon ought to be used to pay reparations to other parties in the Middle East conflict, and that Lebanon can be considered as a dispensable country. Many have spoken of making necessary adjustments in the borders or even of the outright dismemberment of Lebanon. Christians and Muslims have been portrayed as implacably hostile to one another, with the Christians trying to preserve their "domination over the Muslims," and Muslims fighting to establish their "domination" for an "Arab Lebanon." In this scenario the Christians have been chacterized as natural allies of the Israelis and the Muslims as allies of the Palestinians. According to this analysis, Lebanon was not a country but only a group of sects fighting each other for power. The fact that the Lebanese combatants in the "civil war" constituted only a small percentage of the forces warring on Lebanese territory was rarely covered.

This trend continued even after the June 1982 Israeli invasion. *Washington Post* correspondent Loren Jenkins, in an article that appeared on October 10, 1982 entitled, "Lebanon Simply Does Not Exist Anymore," stated, "Just in our century, as Lebanon has passed from Turkish to French to independent rule in 1943, it is the explosive contentiousness of its people that has characterized the land. Clan has fought clan, village has warred against neighboring village, and 17-odd religions—divided almost equally between Christian and Moslem sects—have kept back conflicts that go back to the Crusades and beyond." Jenkins ignored the peaceful coexistence of various sects in Lebanon since independence and long before, emphasizing that interconfessional strife and massacres were not social aberrations, but "aspects of a dark national norm." The educational, cultural and commercial role that Lebanon played in the region for more than a century has also been overlooked, or mentioned only rarely.

A far worse example of the distorted and inaccurate coverage devoted to the Lebanon conflict was published in *The Wall Street Journal*, whose editorials and op-ed pieces have consistently supported pro-Israeli positions. In a July 26, 1982 article under the headline, "A Massacre Over a Partridge," the author depicted the backwardness and apparent eccentricity of Lebanese society in a discussion of the hostility between two villages in the Shouf area outside Beirut. According to the author, "The legacy of tribal warfare here is suggested by one local example. In 1841, a Maronite from the Beit Eddine area wandered over the hills and shot a partridge on Druze land in Baakline. A bitter quarrel developed, and by the end of the day, angry Christians had killed 17 Druze . . . . By late 1841, the Christian-Moslem violence that had started in these hills with a quarrel over a partridge had spread throughout most of Lebanon." If this is not enough to convince the reader that the conflicts in Lebanon are beyond hope of solution, the article also mentions the "tradition of taqiyya" that reigns in the "secretive Druze villages of the Shouf," allowing villagers "to tell lies to outsiders to protect the community." Finally, it says that living in the Shouf has produced some unusual social mores, such as the tradition that a young man who wants to marry "must acquire one sacred possession: a rifle."

To say that intersectarian fighting in 1841 was a "massacre over a partridge" is, as Frederick Huxley has suggested, "like saying that the American Revolution was over a bunch of rowdies throwing tea in Boston harbor." A complex interaction of internal and external factors led to the fighting in Lebanon during the last century. The situation would have been more accurately explained in the context of the Eastern Question and the manipulation of the British, French and Ottomans, by the withdrawal of the Egyptian forces led by Ibrahim Pasha and the fall of his Lebanese ally, Bashir II, and later on to the uprising of Maronite peasants against their Maronite and Druze feudal landlords, rather than by reference to "tribal warfare." Neither the Druze nor the Maronites are a tribe. Furthermore, it is misleading to attempt to view whole sects, religions, regions or countries in terms of two villages. As Huxley points out, "perhaps the major problem . . . is the focus on conflict, as though the current calamity could be reduced to primordial antagonisms." Huxley, who did field research in the area during the years 1973-75, says that he "learned of much cooperation across sectarian lines in business, politics and social life."

In this sense, the media focused only on the internal dimension of the conflict without pointing out that the internal conflict was only one component of the overall problem, and that it was greatly exacerbated by the projection of regional and international conflicts onto the fragile social structure of Lebanese society. Serious students of Lebanese history and politics who recognize the inherent weakness in Lebanese society question whether the conflict would have exploded at the time with such violent intensity if it were not for the decision of various external forces to exploit the country's internal weaknesses and make a vulnerable and open Lebanese society an arena for their battles.

The media have provided the American public with a one-dimensional view of the causes and roots of this tragic conflict. They have failed completely to discuss the war as it really was, a termination of years of suffering, war, revolution and manipulation by external interests. A balanced and in-depth analysis of the situation in Lebanon would require, in addition to discussion of the internal Lebanese, inter-Arab and international factors, an examination of the role played by Israel in the bombing of the Beirut Airport in 1969 and the bombing of south Lebanon in the early 1970s, following the arrival of PLO forces expelled from Jordan in 1970, which fostered a confrontational attitude between the "Lebanese Front" and its allies and the PLO and its allies. The struggle against Israel ended up by becoming a battle for control of certain areas of Lebanon, and ultimately led to the collapse of the Lebanese state.

IV

The extensive coverage of Israel's invasion of Lebanon and the bombing and occupation of West Beirut in summer 1982 provides substantial evidence of a trend toward greater balance in the media's handling of Middle East issues, against a backdrop of continued support for Israel's policy goals. The rapidity with which the media shifted from its initial tone of pride in the swiftness and success of Israel's attack and in the superiority of the American weaponry, as film footage and news dispatches bore graphic witness to the extent of the devastation wrought by those same weapons, led many media critics, backed by the Israelis, to issue strong accusations against what *The Boston Globe's* editorial-page editor Martin Nolan called "general angst about the media's coverage of Israel." Yet a detailed examination of reporting by the elite press and commercial television networks does not support the charges leveled against the media. On the contrary, it reveals many deliberate efforts to report events in Lebanon professionally and fairly. Moveover, by their editorial acceptance of Israel's goals in launching the invasion and the unanimity with which they documented the Israeli justification of opening up opportunities for peace and reconstruction in the Middle East through the destruction and occupation of a large portion of Lebanese territory, the media showed the extent to which pro-Israeli assumptions color American attitudes toward the Middle East.

Ironically, the evidence of the media's efforts at balance in reporting the war lies in the coverage most frequently cited by critics as anti-Israeli. The subject that aroused the greatest controversy was the level of civilian casualties, refugees and the destruction of non-military targets. Yet close analysis of the stories printed and filmed throughout the summer of 1982 indicates that the media were, on the whole, very careful to note the uncertainty surrounding the statistics they published, as well as any discrepancy in the various sources.

More often than not, television tried to assess general trends in casualty figures rather than reporting precise numbers. Peter Jennings, reporting for ABC on June 8, spoke of "mounting casualties" suffered by both sides, noting that they were "particularly heavy among Palestinians and Lebanese." In the battle for the city of Tyre, NBC correspondent Vic Aicken provided "no figures" on the number of dead. On CBS, Bob Faw told viewers on June 7 that "casualty lists climbed." When television reports did include figures they were often very vague, as in the case of NBC's story of a charge by Lebanon's president that the number of Lebanese killed or wounded "is in the thousands."

In contrast to television's lack of precision, the press did attempt to provide its readership with exact numbers of the dead and wounded, although they too resorted to such caveats as "there was no independent confirmation of casualty totals," (*Washington Post*, June 14) or phrases like the "uncounted dead" of Sidon (Jonathan Randal, *Washington Post*). Headlines such as "Disagreements Flare Over Casualty Toll in Lebanon" (David Ottaway, *Washington Post*, June 25) bore witness to the press's conscientious efforts to report the issue fully. Criticism of the media for offering "contradictory" and exaggerated casualty figures contributed to the overall charge of "lack of balance," and anti-Israel publicity. But as Cable News Network correspondent Peter Arnett stated on an ABC News special program to discuss "TV War Coverage," the statistics were "just a small part of what reporting war is all about. . .bombs explode without any political distinctions. . .it seemed to me after coming home [from Beirut] and seeing the reaction to our reportage that it was less statistics than the fact of damage that the people in the United States reacted to."

Figures on the extent of the casualties caused by the war proved only somewhat more explosive an issue than coverage of the siege and bombing of West Beirut. However, despite the mounting horror aroused by Israel's unrelenting attack, evidence suggests that the media made every effort to cover the most important and lengthy news story fairly and dispassionately. Films and descriptions of Israeli bombardments of civilian neighborhoods, and living conditions after the Israelis cut off supplies of basic necessities including electricity, food and water, were consciously balanced by reminders that the Israeli "onslaught" was brought on by the "organized and continuing" resistance of the PLO and the need to complete the task of destroying the "remaining Palestinian guerrilla strongholds" (Ottaway, *Washington Post*). Although *The New York Times* diverged from *The Washington Post* by emphasizing the political and diplomatic aspects of the war as opposed to the human suffering wrought by the siege, *Times* correspondent James Farrell brought the story into a context New Yorkers could understand in an article that compared "a graceful park in Beirut" to Gramercy Park. As a result of the war the park had become "a sunlit horror of dazed people, angry guerrillas, armed 14-year olds without a wisp of facial hair, dirty children playing in muddy puddles, women trying to do laundry in small plastic tubs and old people sitting in stunned silence." (June 30).

However, the *Times'* reluctance to print the full story of Israel's terror bombing was revealed in a telex sent over the Reuters wire by Beirut bureau chief Thomas L. Friedman. The *Times* recorded that the first week in August produced the "fiercest shelling" of the "Israeli onslaught," yet the editors clearly decided their correspondent had gone too far in an August 5 lead that described the previous day's bombardment of the city as "indiscriminate." In response to their deletion of the key adjective, Friedman cabled the editors that he had always been careful "to note in previous stories that the Israelis were hitting Palestinian positions and if they were hitting residential areas to at least raise the possibility that the Palestinians had a gun there at one time or another." He defended his choice of the word "indiscriminate" to describe Israel's bombing of the previous day by saying that a hazardous tour of the city led him to conclude that "what happened yesterday was something fundamentally different from what has happened on the previous 63 days." His disillusionment over the paper's handling of the story was written in his "profound sadness" over the failure of the "newspaper of record" to tell "its readers and future historians" of Israel's actions.

The decision of *The New York Times* editors to delete "indiscriminate" from Friedman's lead mirrored the general shock that events in Lebanon brought to supporters of Israel. Israel's attack on the Iraqi nuclear reactor, the bombing of Beirut in July 1981, its invasion of Lebanon, the massacre of large numbers of Palestinian and Lebanese civilians through bombings and the assault on the Sabra and Shatila camps have called into question the image of Israel as a beleaguered underdog fighting for survival among its hostile and powerful neighbors. The undisputed pride with which many in the media initially reported the swiftness and success of Israel's attack, and the superiority of the American weaponry that made it possible, soon changed to disgust as film footage and news dispatches began to show the impact of using those same weapons against the civilian population. The war forced many people to reexamine their assumptions about the morality of Israel's policies and the exercise of power in the Middle East. Much of this critical examination took place in and through the media. Pulitzer Prize winning journalist Richard Ben Cramer's stories in *The Philadelphia Inquirer* have publicized in horrible yet somber detail the suffering caused by the war. *Washington Post* columnist Richard Cohen, a traditional supporter of Israel, wrote in his June 27 column that "the moral standing of Israel has been eroded not only by its actions but also by its words." Columnist Georgie Anne Geyer, in her *Washington Times* column of June 14, described Menachem Begin as an "old terrorist" and Israeli defense Minister Ariel Sharon as a "fanatic Israeli expansionist." Alexander Cockburn was one of the few journalists to point to the media's willingness to swallow Israeli propaganda on the invasion at the cost of neglecting to report the very real and tremendous tragedy of the war for the Lebanese people. According to Cockburn, "You do not have to be overly familiar with Lebanon to get a clearer idea of what is happening there than is available in most commentaries here. Southern Lebanon does not become 'a Palestinian stronghold' just on the say-so of Israeli spokesmen. The city of Sidon has, or had, a population of 300,000 and when Sidon or Tyre are 'pounded' by Israeli ships, aircraft and land artillery, a large number of Lebanese as well as Palestinians—refugees as well as fighters—are dying. Geo-politicians can say that Lebanon does not 'exist' as a nation. But there are still a lot of Lebanese around" (*The Wall Street Journal*, June 10, 1982).

The media frequently provided the forum for the critical reappraisal of Israel's policies. For example, well-known pro-Israel writers such as William Buckley began to question the impact of Israel's policies on U.S. interests in the Middle East and to support the right of the Palestinians to a homeland. Buckley advised Secretary of State George Shultz on July 9 to suspend U.S. commitments to Israel's arsenal "until" it reaffirms its willingness to cede the territories in the West Bank and Gaza to demilitarized Palestinian rule. Another well-known supporter of Israel, columnist Mary McGrory, who proclaimed in a column during the 1967 war that "we are all Israelis," devoted her June 27 column to Prime Minister Begin's visit to the United States. Entitled, "Begin, Go Home," the column accused Begin of coming to Washington "with blood on your hands," and asked if Israeli security had to be achieved "by the slaughter of innocents." In an emotional broadcast from Beirut, NBC anchorman John Chancellor criticized on August 2, 1982, the "savage" Israeli attack on Beirut, "one of the world's largest cities." He went on to point to the "stench of terror all across the city." He compared the bombing to the bombing of Madrid during the Spanish Civil War and wondered aloud "what in the world is going on" and pointed out that Israel's security problem was "fifty miles to the south." He asked, "What's an Israeli army doing here in Beirut?"

The Israeli siege of Beirut and the enormous loss of life and devastation led to an ongoing debate among American Jews as well as Israelis. Some of the most sensitive articles written in the American press that dealt with the plight of Lebanese and Palestinian civilians and raised questions about Begin-Sharon policies were written by Jewish-American journalists, commentators and intellectuals such as Nat Hentoff, Anthony Lewis, I.F. Stone, Jonathan Randal, Richard Cohen, Milton Viorst and Stanley Karnow. In a forceful essay Viorst said, "These are not my people. This is not our Israel." Lawrence Meyer wrote in *The Washington Post* "you can say goodbye to the Israel and the Middle East you used to know." Writing in *The Village Voice,* prominent writer Nat Hentoff told of his revulsion as a Zionist over the reports of bodies dumped in a bulldozed pit in Sidon. Even well-known art critic and intellectual Irving Howe, who traditionally has supported Israel's policies, wrote on September 23 in *The New York Times* that American Jews must not "waffle" or hesitate before going public with their criticism: "It is the bad policies and misconduct of Begin-Sharon that provide the most substantial help to enemies of Israel. Not those who express shame over the Israeli share of responsibility for Beirut, but those who would cover it up, give comfort to our enemies, so this is where some of us stand: warm friends of Israel, open critics of Begin-Sharon, we will probably make mistakes—but if there are mistakes of speech, there are also mistakes of silence. After Beirut, silence is impossible." And while some might question whether the terms "bad policies" and "misconduct" accurately describe the policies of the Israel of Menachem Begin, or whether they were the consequences of the policies adopted by Israeli leaders long before the invasion of Lebanon, it must be admitted that it takes a great deal of moral courage and soul-searching for those Americans, Jews and Gentiles alike, who have long had a special commitment to Israel, to publicly question Israeli policies.

During the early days of the invasion many showed pride in Israel's "victories" and helped to justify its actions. This bias appeared in initial reporting of the Israeli drive north during the weekend of June 4-6. Both television and the press virtually echoed each other in emphasizing the "retaliatory" character of the Israeli bombing attacks on the Beirut stadium and on the assault of PLO "strongholds" in southern Lebanon. Adopting the Israeli code name for the invasion, Peace for Galilee, the media noted that the invasion had been "triggered" by PLO attacks and that its "declared objective" (Claiborne, *The Washington Post*) was to "clear out" the terrorists (NBC) and "eliminate" their bases (ABC).

The use of Israeli terms was prevalent during the early days of the invasion, which was described as a "stunning victory," a "cleanup" operation, or a redrawing of the "military and political map." An editorial in *The Washington Times* of June 25, 1982 included several phrases frequently used by Israeli leaders to justify their invasion of Lebanon: "If and when the Israelis finish their cleanup of Beirut PLO strongholds, Yassir Arafat's role as the wellspring of terrorism promoting the Soviet cause from Ireland to Libya may be finished for good," wrote the paper's editors. Almost all the media used the term "25-mile buffer zone." The media used terms that many of their members had criticized during the Vietnam War. It was argued then that the widespread acceptance of such terminology obfuscated the political and human ramifications of such acts and led to the dehumanization of opponents.

In the early part of the summer, the media supplied its audience with evidence in support of Israel's case against the PLO. The initial coverage of these events by the networks and the major papers, particularly until the latter part of June and the resignation of Haig, revealed that the United States continued to accept without much scrutiny the Israeli justification for the invasion. The attempted assassination of Israel's Ambassador Shlomo Argov in London, the Israeli bombing of Beirut and the rocket attack on northern Israel were the sequence of events that brought the media's attention to the unfolding tragedy in Lebanon. Up until then and despite the earlier predictions of an Israeli invasion, the crisis was overshadowed in the media by events in Poland and Afghanistan.

Television correspondents Bill Seamans of ABC and Steve Mallory and Art Kent of NBC reported on the PLO's use of Beaufort Castle to shell northern Israel. NBC also showed file footage of guerrilla exercises at the Beirut stadium which stressed the PLO's use of the facility as an ammunition dump and training site. John Chancellor chronicled the background to the invasion for NBC, mentioning Israel's attempts to subdue the PLO in 1978 when the Palestinians "got away—only to start a serious buildup again." His assessment of the origins of the invasion noted that it was "probably useless today to say just who started the fighting." The media also showed their acceptance of Israel's war aims in Lebanon even as Israeli forces exceeded the bounds of the 25-mile corridor that the leadership originally had declared to be its sole objective. *The New York Times'* correspondents judged Israel's aims to include destruction of the PLO and a "restructuring of Lebanon." The *Post* described the goal as freedom from "the threat of terrorism."

Other major themes during the first few weeks stressed the chaos into which Lebanon had fallen during the years prior to the invasion, the lawlessness of PLO occupation and the welcome "smiles and flowers" with which Israeli troops were received. The stories that would have offset this picture of Israel as a liberating force received relatively little attention, however. These included the role of internal and external forces in exacerbating Lebanon's "civil war" and the significance of the invasion to Israel's continued occupation of the West Bank. The questions about bias in the media were almost totally reported from the Israeli frame of reference, and the historical background to the invasion, which involved considerable advance preparation by Israel, received little attention. All these issues would have fleshed out the full story of Israel's interests in Lebanon and given the American audience a broader conception of the media's treatment.

One can reasonably ask whether the advances made in reporting the Middle East fairly are likely to be sustained. The fact that Congress was willing to give Israel more aid in the form of direct grants than the Administration intended, despite Israel's blatant slap in the face to American Middle East policy by expanding its settlements on the West Bank, suggests that those advances are transitory. Other evidence for this argument lies in the course of the media's coverage of the invasion itself. The initial U.S. Government response to the invasion clearly supported Israel's goals of crushing the PLO and rebuilding Lebanese-Israeli relations on the basis of a political reorganization in Lebanon. The press faithfully represented this point of view in its early reports. But as the summer wore on and Secretary Haig was replaced by Secretary Shultz, who from the outset took a more balanced view of the regional situation, so, too, did the press. Although the military defeat of the PLO in Beirut was not bemoaned, the human suffering produced by the war and the new commitment by the U.S. Administration to upholding the right of the Palestinians to a homeland received greater attention in the media.

V

The Iran-Iraq War has also been given shallow, distorted and inadequate media coverage. Despite the serious nature of the war and its possible ramifications, it has not received the attention it deserves. Many journalists admit the inadequacies of coverage. They point to the difficulties they face in gaining access to the countries involved except when one side or the other is winning, and to the unreliability of the reports published by the two sides. While some justification may exist for these charges, they do not explain the insufficient coverage.

The war's complex origins, as well as the ideologies and personalities of Iranian and Iraqi leaders, may have contributed to the problem of coverage. This war has, in fact, surprised both journalists and experts by contradicting many of the predictions about its outbreak, development and impact. The analysis of the underlying causes of the war and the position of the two sides has been sharply distorted. Understanding Iran's position has been complicated by the Iranian revolution and by the hostage crisis and the reaction to it in the United States. Understanding Iraq's position has been equally, if not more, difficult. Iraq has been one of the more stereotyped and least understood countries in the Arab world. For years, Iraq's actions were portrayed as manifestations of a secretive, xenophobic and violent society. Media emphasis on Iraq's past instability and violent upheavals, its tough stance on Israel, and its reputed closeness to the Soviet Union and hostility to the West has helped color Western attitudes toward the country.

Before the war broke out, many in the media inaccurately portrayed Iran as an Arab country. Despite the fact Iran borders the Arab countries and is a Muslim country, it is not Arab. This trend lessened somewhat after the war began, but did not disappear completely. A fall 1982 article in a Colorado daily included Iran in a grouping of Arab countries. It stated that, "Iran, Iraq and the six Gulf Cooperation Council members are all included in another group (aside from OPEC) few Americans recognize as OAPEC—the Organization of Arab Petroleum Exporting Countries." Even *The Christian Science Monitor,* which is noted for its objectivity and balance, has committed this error. In the fall of 1980 it published a short article on the deadlock in discussions at the OPEC conference in Vienna, which it claimed was the result of "negative votes from three hard-line Arab states, Iran, Libya, Algeria."

During the first days of the war, there was a tendency to portray the conflict inaccurately as a Sunni-Shia dispute, or as a battle between troublesome Arabs and/or Muslims. One prominent commentator and journalist who was asked for his assessment of the war's causes revealed bias and/or ignorance when he observed, "Those damn Arabs are at it again."

Coverage of the war also underscored the propensity of the American press to dramatize conflict in the Middle East as anti-American. Initial reports played up the "Middle East as tinderbox" approach, highlighted by a *U.S. News and World Report* story of October 13, 1980 entitled, "Mideast Cauldron." The article described "the dramatic shift in the balance of power flowing out of the War," a conflict in which "[v]irtually every facet of American interest in the Mideast" purportedly lay in the balance, regardless of the outcome. Iraq was portrayed as the undisputed aggressor due to its bombing of Mehrabad Airport, an action that "presented Moscow with its long-sought chance to recover waning Soviet influence in the Mideast and endangered the West's supply of Persian Gulf oil." In the midst of Iraq's incursion into Iran, the anti-Iranian rhetoric engendered by the hostage crisis dissolved as some in the media began to stress that Iraq was "long a foe of America" and had an alliance with Moscow. Despite the fact that Iraq's status as the aggressor in the conflict may be challenged by evidence suggesting that hostilities between the two countries pre-dated the September 22 bombing of Mehrabad Airport by weeks, depending on one's point of reference, as acknowledged in a *New York Times* article that marked the first anniversary of the war, the press did not alter its original judgment. The press also ignored the war's roots, which grew out of territorial, ideological, strategic and personal differences. The perception of Iraq as the instigator of the hostilities, and by extension, the potential leader of "a united and militant Arab world" in case of victory changed little. On the issue of Iraq's alliance with the Soviet Union, a number of journalists, including Georgie Anne Geyer and Helena Cobban, presented convincing evidence that Iraqi President Saddam Hussein had adopted a more independent stance vis-a-vis Moscow in the months prior to September 22, but this information also failed to dispel the image of Iraq as the keystone of Soviet influence in the region, despite the fact that Iraq was never a Soviet satellite and that the deterioration in relations with Moscow long preceded the war.

Thus, instead of being covered as a regional conflict of well-established yet complex origin, the hostilities between Iran and Iraq took on the dimensions of hostile, aggressive Arab anti-Americanism, rendered even more menacing by the possibility of Soviet intervention. This scenario has yet to develop. The Arab world has been seriously divided by the Gulf War, and the Soviet Union has restricted its intervention in that conflict to limited arms shipments. Yet these were the possibilities said to be confronting President Carter and his Administration. They also match up well with the forecast devised by the Israelis, as it was presented in a *Christian Science Monitor* article of October 14, 1980 entitled, 'The Gulf War: Another Surprise," and in an article by Chaim Herzog, Israel's former Ambassador to the United Nations, which appeared in *The Wall Street Journal* of the same day. The *Monitor* story forecast an "eventual 'Pax Sovietica'" growing out of Moscow's ties with both Iraq and Iran and the recently signed treaty between the Soviet Union and Syria. The Herzog essay castigated the West for its "obsession" with the Israel-Arab conflict, which, Herzog claimed, diverted the attention of Western governments and the media from "the other major issues which threaten the peace of the world in the Middle East." According to Herzog, the Iran-Iraq conflict reflects "the inherent instability in the Arab world and in the Middle East."

While it is important to note that the press carries numerous essays reflecting both Israeli and Arab points of view on Middle East issues, and sounds out officials throughout the Middle East for their predictions on the course of events in the region, on this particular issue, in which the Israelis were not directly involved as protagonists, the manner in which the Israeli point of view was publicized emphasized an interpretation of the conflict that cast the Arabs in a negative light and reinforced the aforementioned stereotypes. A story that appeared in *The Christian Science Monitor* on October 28, 1980 underscored this point by concluding that the Israelis, who "invoke the Iran-Iraq war against the argument heard in Europe and North America that Israel is the main source of Mideast instability" make the point that "Israel remains the one rock of stability in the Middle East and that the Gulf war shows just how unstable any toehold in the Arab world can be." A recent article by syndicated columnist Jack Anderson, published on October 19, 1982 in the *The Washington Post*, repeated some of these themes. Anderson, who quotes well-known pro-Israel analyst Joseph Churba to support his views, asserts that Iran's strategic position "far transcends that of Iraq, to say nothing of Lebanon's." While Iran may, at present, hold more importance to the United States than Iraq, it is not more important than Iraq, Jordan, Saudi Arabia and the other Arab Gulf states. The Soviet Union, which may have an interest in developing a foothold in the area, may prefer to see a dominant anti-Western Iran imposing its hegemony over the area, and in the process threatening the stability of the entire region. It may also be, as many in the region believe, that the two superpowers are interested in seeing the two most powerful countries in the area exhaust themselves, thus making it easier for the superpowers to impose their influence on the region and to reap financial gains from the dependence of Iran and Iraq on the outside world for arms, spare parts and other commodities.

Anderson's article goes on to emphasize the Soviet link with Iraq. He states that "when the war began two years ago, 70 percent of Iraq's equipment was Soviet made. Last year, the Russians sent Iraq 400 T58 tanks from Poland and 250 T72s." This theme is reinforced by the report, attributed to "intelligence sources," that there are 8,000 Soviet advisers in Iraq. The Anderson article and much of the media have provided little background information on the ideology and leadership of the Iraqi Ba'th Party, except in the most superficial terms. There has been little discussion of the nature or history of the badly strained Iraqi-Soviet relationship, or of the failure of Moscow to supply the arms Iraq needed to prosecute the war. On the other hand, Anderson described Israel's arms supplies to the Iranian regime, which humiliated the United States by holding American diplomats hostage for more than a year, as a "shrewd move." Scant attention was paid to the fact that these arms were sent by Israel at a time when U.S. diplomats were still being held hostage in Iran. Israel's action is justified as an attempt to cultivate "close ties" with the Iranian army, which the reader is told is the most likely successor to Khomeini. Anderson portrays this development as a favor to the United States from Israel. He notes that the United States "has been beholden to Israel for most of the intelligence information out of post-Shah Iran, so we may have to go begging to Israel for introduction to some new post-Khomeini Iranian military regime."

In some articles on the war mention was made of a difference between Middle East logic and that of the West. Often this message is conveyed in stories with a matter-of-fact tone. *The Christian Science Monitor* took up this theme in an article that discussed the seemingly high cost of the war relative to potential gains. The author noted that American defense analysts said that "if anything like Western logic prevailed, both sides would be ready for a cease-fire agreement." The superficial explanation that events in the Middle East defy rational understanding tends to obfuscate the issues, widen the cultural gap between the West and the Arab and Muslim worlds, and present the problems as though they could never be solved.

VI

The move toward greater objectivity and balance in the coverage of the Arab-Israeli conflict and particularly the Palestinian issue was clearly manifested during the Israeli siege of Beirut. Undoubtedly this coverage contributed to the change in American public opinion toward Israel's leadership and policies, since Israel's action in the words of syndicated columnist Nick Thimmesch "shocked Americans into a painful reassessment of the character and elevated moral standards of Israel."

New sources of information and discussion on Israel's invasion of Lebanon contributed to the greater awareness of Americans. The Arab League, Arab embassies, the PLO information office, the American-Arab Affairs Council, the National Association of Arab-Americans, the American-Arab Anti-Discrimination Committee and other Arab-American and American groups became more active. Most of the American and Arab-American organizations have in recent years concentrated on combatting stereotyping of the Arab world and Arab-Americans and on improving relations between the United States and the Arab world. As a result they already had lobbying and informational activities under way that increased during the invasion. The Arab Women's Council, headed by the wives of the Saudi, Syrian and Arab League ambassadors to the United States as well as the wives of other Arab diplomats and Arab-American women, emerged after the invasion and played a large role in alerting the media to the developments in Lebanon. A delegation led by Nouha al-Hegelan, wife of the Saudi ambassador, went on a two-week tour of 21 American cities to present the Arab point of view and "to make up for the vacuum in press coverage at the beginning of the war." Arab Women's Council members also staged a hunger strike across from the White House to get press attention and to focus on the suffering in Lebanon. Because of the increased activity, television networks, newspapers and radio stations featured interviews with academics, concerned individuals and humanitarian groups which allowed diversity in the presentation of news and features on the war. Television, radio and newspaper advertisements emphasizing Israel's aggressiveness and the great loss of life and destruction inflicted on Lebanese and Palestinian civilians began to appear. However, these efforts reportedly suffered from the lack of adequate financial resources, from the reactive and short-term nature of much of these activities, from a lack of coordination and long-range planning, in addition to the lack of accurate and up-to-date information on the nature of the destruction and the number of casualties.

Other reasons for the change in the quantity and the quality of the coverage of Arab issues may be attributed in part to the impact of the October War, the oil embargo, the increase in economic and cultural interaction between Americans and Arabs, the change of Israel's image from "little David" to "Goliath" particularly after the 1967 and the 1973 wars, and to the ramifications of these developments on American perceptions and attitudes.

During the last few years several developments have helped to improve the coverage of Arab issues and raise questions about Israel's policies. President Anwar al-Sadat's visit to Jerusalem and his peace initiative, which culminated in the conclusion of the Camp David accords, are seen as key turning points. Professor William Adams, editor of the book *Television Coverage in the Middle East*, stated in a *Public Opinion* article that as a result of Sadat's actions Americans ceased to view Arabs as a "monolithic foe" and Israel as "thoroughly virtuous." Nick Thimmesch has written that Sadat's popularity soared following his visit to Jerusalem, which was accompanied by "enormous and emotional media coverage" because "Americans traditionally like the underdog and make heroes of the peacemakers." He adds: "As Sadat went up in the esteem of Americans, he pulled Arab nations and Arab causes with him." Egypt soon surpassed Israel in public opinion testing about which Middle East country "is a close ally or friendly to the U.S." Six of the ten Americans came to regard Saudi Arabia in these terms and five in ten felt this way about Jordan.

There is almost a consensus among media and public opinion watchers about the significance of Sadat's action, which helped transform the American public's view of Sadat, Egypt and to a lesser extent the Arabs as a whole. Nevertheless, controversy continues to surround the Sadat initiative and its results in the Arab world. Sadat is viewed by many as the leader who undermined Arab rights, deepened Arab rifts, damaged the chances for a just and comprehensive peace settlement between Israel and the Arabs, and made concessions to Begin without getting any substantial Israeli concessions in return.

Another contributing factor was the increased sensitivity on the part of some Palestinians and Arab governments to the need to provide access and substantative and accurate information to journalists. The PLO's information offices and leaders appeared to have learned the benefits of cultivating the media. The Lebanese and the Palestinians were more than happy to allow Western correspondents to cover the story.

Even Yasser Arafat, whose image was generally perceived and portrayed in negative terms in the media and ultimately in public opinion, began to be viewed in positive terms as a wise and dedicated leader. According to Thimmesch, Arafat "became the media good guy" and Begin and Sharon the "bad guys during the siege of Beirut." Arafat's improved skills as a communicator were highlighted when he told an NBC interviewer on January 11, 1983 that even "E.T." wanted to return to his home and kept repeating "Home, home, home."

For their part, the Israelis also contributed to this trend. There is little doubt that Israel's actions in the occupied territories, the annexation of the Syrian Golan Heights and, more important, its invasion of Lebanon, particularly the siege of Beirut, changed American perceptions and attitudes toward the Arab-Israeli conflict. Newsmen were present and able to provide the American public with an unusual insight of the suffering "little Israel" is capable of inflicting with U.S. arms. The television cameras were able to show what Sharon wanted to conceal: that the Israelis were an invading occupation army; that most of the "PLO positions" were in fact refugee camps or tall apartment buildings; and that the "terrorists" were young and old men and women, fighting for their right to exist and to determine their own destiny. Television also showed pitiful scenes of innocent Lebanese and Palestinians suffering from the horrendous wounds of cluster and phosphorus bombs. There was the photograph of the five year old covered with flies and starving to death in a home for the invalid and retarded. *The Washington Post* quoted an attendant saying that a hospital located in West Beirut was hit several times and "no fewer than fifty" died. This coverage was in contradiction with the traditional image of Israel.

Through the process of personalizing and humanizing the victims of war the media coverage of the invasion of Lebanon did, despite its limitations, temporarily halt if not begin to reverse the process of stereotyping and dehumanizing the Arabs. Arab casualties and suffering were portrayed in the same way the media portrayed in the past, and continues to portray today, Israeli casualties. They were being shown as human beings, not as statistics, but as individuals who have grieving families and relatives and friends, as husbands, wives, sons, daughters or sweethearts. Basically the media showed the suffering resulting from the bombing. In a column entitled "In Defense of Casualty Pictures on TV," syndicated columnist Ellen Goodman focused on these aspects of TV coverage:

> But in the news, it's different. In the news, wars go on and on. In the news, we see less glory and more gore. In the news, the sides are not divided into good guys and bad guys, but aggressors and victims.

She articulately pointed to the dangerous implications of depersonalizing war:

> In our war-sophisticated world, we have learned that before we can kill people, we have to dehumanize them. They are no longer human beings but gooks or kikes or animals. The Japanese who experimented on human guinea pigs in World War II called them "maruta": log of wood.
> It is even easier when we lob missiles from an invisible distance or drop bombs from 15,000 feet at "targets." It's more like an Atari game than a murder. Conversely, the more we humanize people, the more we personalize war, the harder it is to commit.

The Israelis and their supporters began to loudly complain about the bias in the American media. These actions impelled the media to take the unusual step of inviting pro-Israeli representatives of American Jewish organizations to air comments and complaints about the coverage.

During a special ABC news program on the controversy surrounding war coverage by the media held on October 19, 1982 the only non-journalist invited to participate was a representative of the Anti-Defamation League who was presented as a media critic while no representatives of pro-Arab groups were invited. *The Washington Post* invited a representative of the Jewish Community Council to spend several days at the *Post* observing its coverage of issues related to the Arab-Israeli conflicts. *Washington Post* executive editor Benjamin Bradlee explained his invitation to Michael Berenbaum, the executive director of the Jewish Community Council of greater Washington, to observe the foreign desk's news operation for a week as a result of criticisms aimed at the *Post's* coverage by saying: "In my conversations with Jewish leaders in an effort to bank the fires, it occurred to me they didn't know anything about how this newspaper is conceived and produced every day." No similar invitations were issued to pro-Arab groups or individuals. NBC took the unusual step of showing on August 3, 1982 excerpts of three letters critical of Chancellor's comments on Israel's invasion of Lebanon despite the fact that they were clearly introduced as editorial commentary. The network only showed the critical letters despite an announcement by anchorman Tom Brokaw that the reaction to the commentary had been "very heavy" and "about evenly divided." The Israeli Embassy also was waging a media blitz that paralleled the invasion. General Sharon made a U.S. tour during which he passed out a pamphlet called "National Security Issues" before the invasion. It contained an elaborate explanation on the threats from the PLO and the Syrian Army in Lebanon. Israeli Ambassador Arens conducted an effective and almost round the clock public relations campaign during and after the war. The Israelis distributed thousands of photos of Soviet equipment taken from the PLO and released stacks of captured documents aimed at linking the PLO with the Soviet Union. It also distributed a black-covered booklet called "PLO Atrocities in Lebanon."

Nevertheless, the behavior and words of Israeli leaders contributed to the negative images. The remoteness, stiffness, intransigence and bellicosity of Begin, Sharon and Shamir left their impact on public opinion as more and more reporters began to refer to the "terrorist" background of these leaders. Begin's defiance of the reasonable and temperate requests of President Reagan, a well-known champion of Israeli causes, for Israeli moderation left their impact on many, both in and out of the government.

Other contributing factors included the ever-changing proclamations about Israel's intention behind the Lebanon invasion, from an operation to secure "Peace for Gallilee," to the 25-mile *cordon sanitaire* aimed at preventing the PLO from infiltrating or shelling Israeli villages, to the need for an international force to guarantee that the PLO would not return to the buffer zone, to the destruction of the PLO and its expulsion from Lebanon, to the expulsion of the Syrians, and ultimately to the establishment of a free independent Lebanon and normalized relations with it. The Israeli government's protestations of limited goals in its invasion of Lebanon, which were belied by its push to Beirut and its escalation of demands, led satirical columnist Arthur Hoppe to write on September 20, 1982 in *The San Francisco Chronicle,* under a dateline of September 20, 1984, "Prime Minister Menachem Begin today called the capture of New Delhi by Israeli forces a limited and precautionary move" designed to "prevent fighting and secure order." Hoppe explained how the Begin government had invaded and occupied Syria, Iraq, Iran and Pakistan in self-defense and that "Begin said Israel was forced to invade India in order to establish a 25-mile demilitarized zone in southern Lebanon which would protect Israeli settlements in the Galilee from PLO rocket attacks."

The Israeli government's mishandling of the press, including heavy-handed attempts by its censors to influence coverage, contributed to the growing doubts about the wisdom or humaneness of Israel's actions. When the Israeli government's aggressive and brutal tactics in the Golan Heights and on the West Bank led to increased questioning of these tactics, the government responded by trying to place greater restrictions on reporters aimed at keeping them as long as possible in the dark. Begin is reported to have even threatened to cut the budget of Israeli television because of his disappointment with coverage. Even before Lebanon, Israel began to act in a manner not dissimilar to some Arab governments. Thimmesch has reported that Moshe Yegar, the Foreign Ministry's information chief, once proposed denying visas to foreign journalists with "hostile intentions." After the first week of the war, there were complaints from Western and even from some Israeli journalists about the lack of frankness and the infrequency of briefings by Israeli officials about the conduct of the war.

The underestimated, inaccurate and contradictory Israeli figures on the number of civilian casualties in the south of Lebanon led some journalists to question the accuracy of Israeli government information, not only on casualties but on other matters as well. The Israeli attempts to censor the coverage forced reporters to find other means to transmit information. They were able to send films through Cyprus or Damascus or to send them by satellite from Beirut. CBS and NBC employed special graphics to indicate that one of their reports had been censored. On June 24 the CBS screen went dark for a few minutes and then words appeared: 22 seconds deleted by the Israeli censors. The report then showed a weeping Lebanese woman begging the United States to act to end the fighting.

In a report on Lebanese civilian casualties, NBC called attention to the Israeli censor's deletion of a portion on children injured by Israeli attacks. The increasingly strict Israeli censors were at times counterproductive despite their success at limiting photographic coverage. On July 12, 1982, *Time* magazine reported that Israeli censors refused shots of shattered residential areas and of wounded and dead civilians on the grounds that some scenes constituted "propaganda."

Tom Brokaw reported that Israeli authorities would not allow NBC to send a story about devastation in a Lebanese neighborhood: "They didn't have or didn't give any reason for censoring that story, which had nothing to do with national security." *The New York Times* published an article on Israeli censorship on June 29, 1981 and the way in which it was carried out. Other newspapers soon began to follow suit.

According to a July 7, *Baltimore Sun* editorial, Israeli officials, despite "astute planning," "seemed to have overlooked one key factor: the impact of a televised war in the American living room. . . . There is little doubt that the Israeli image in this country is suffering as never before." Israeli officials revealed their awareness of the emotional impact of photographic coverage by increasing strict censorship.

Another contributing factor to the shift in coverage may have been the change in political stands on the part of the U.S. Government. Secretary Haig and U.N. Ambassador Jeane Kirkpatrick portrayed the invasion of Lebanon as a major victory for the United States and a humiliating defeat for the Soviets and their clients. Mrs. Kirkpatrick was reported by a former U.S. ambassador to have told a group of Japanese businessmen that their oil supplies had been secured by Israel's actions, which should have taken place long ago. The media coverage reflected the political stands adopted by high U.S. officials, who saw the invasion as a means of strengthening U.S. interests in the area. Statements made by Secretary Haig before his resignation undoubtedly left their impact on governmental and media stands. Secretary Haig described before TV cameras the number of Israeli planes shot down in one dogfight with Syrian planes by saying "we" lost one F-16. And as a former Deputy Under Secretary of

State recently stated, "it was perhaps not just a Freudian slip when recently a senior U.S. official during the early days of the invasion referred to the Israeli forces as our side." While the full extent of the involvement of Haig and other high officials with the Israeli invasion may never be known, it is obvious that after Haig's surprise resignation a noticeable change occurred in Administration statements and actions. This was paralleled by changes in media focus on Palestinian and Arab news and concerns as the new Secretary of State George Shultz and others in the government criticized Israeli actions and spoke of Palestinian rights. And while it is difficult to prove the extent of this impact, it is obvious that the influence on the media of State Department and White House statements dealing with foreign affairs cannot be underestimated.

VII

The problem goes beyond the ability of the Arabs to present their case effectively to the West and beyond their capacity to control the distortions of their image. It transcends the question of technique and public relations campaigns. It is more complex than that. What is published in the United States and what is shown on television and listened to on the radio is a reflection of two distinct and yet interrelated realities. The first is that the portrayal of Arabs in the U.S. media reflects the residual cultural gap between the Arabs and the West as well as new political, economic and social interests. A number of Arab as well as Western journalists have expressed genuine concern about the impact of certain "presentations of the Arabs in Western media" that indicate the West may be preparing for military aggression against the Arab countries. Several prominent Western political leaders as well as some well-known intellectuals have pointed to the possibility and perhaps the advisability of occupying Arab oil fields. Edward Mortimer of *The London Times* dealt with this issue at a 1979 conference in London. He stated:

> *I can think of nothing more tragic or disastrous than that we should get ourselves collectively into the frame of mind where we see our economy being arbitrarily sabotaged by a group of 'wicked Oriental despots,' and therefore feel the right solution to our economic problems is to send a task force to occupy oil fields in the Arab Gulf. I really think it is as bad a nightmare as one can have, and I wish I could think it is a complete fantasy. But I really am worried when I look at the kind of cartoons on these themes, some of which I am sorry to say originate here in Britain, even printed in magazines and newspapers that might have a reputation for intelligent and liberal analysis of international affairs.*

186

Mortimer goes on to say that the problem is not a "technical" one, but that it stems from

> . . .our complete failure to understand the issue confronting us. It is therefore a problem of failure on our part as communicators who are supposed to understand the Middle East to get the problem across. We can talk to each other and explain to each other satisfactorily that OPEC is a highly rational, extremely moderate organization, that oil price is simply a reflection of market forces, that what matters is not price but supply, that supply is not infinite whatever policies governments and oil companies decide to pursue. All these things we are quite good at explaining to each other at conferences or seminars. But what good are we at actually getting these points over to the public? It is easy to draw a picture of a sheikh holding the world at ransom. I am not sure that we give enough thought to how to draw a picture of the stupidity of Western consumption policies and Western economic models or how to show, graphically enough, the kind of image that somebody like the shah of Iran presented to his own people as someone willing to spend enormous sums on arms of no earthly use to the Iranian people. I think these are things that we need to be thinking about much more seriously.

An aspect of the problem worth considering is that of understanding that the Arab image, despite obvious distortions, reflects the Arab reality. Spending more money on public relations, hiring the most competent media specialists, and even having more sensitive Western journalists who understand Arabic and have a better understanding of Arab history, politics, culture and aspirations will not greatly improve the image. As Mohammad Hassanein Heikal has aptly put it, the question is not one of "cosmetics" or "bureaucratic setups—offices, employees, cars," or of buying "advertising space in newspapers or on television" or "stridently claiming a right, legitimate though it may be." Information, he argues, cannot create new facts or "miraculously transform an ugly picture into a beautiful one." And while Heikal believes that "intensive action" could lead to a "breakthrough" in this area, he argues that the ability of the Arabs to "correct the distortions in their image is restricted, a priori, to a mere ten percent of that image." He further warns that "random and amateurish" information campaigns "often do more harm than good."

The past five years have witnessed an increase in the level of awareness on the part of many Arabs, in and out of government, about the problems facing them in the information arena and about their shortcomings in the field of mass communication. Some have come to realize that something must be done by the Arabs to correct distortion in their image. Arab information ministers have met to discuss the need for a unified Arab information campaign in the West, but nothing has happened. New newspaper and magazine articles have been published in the Arab media about the problems facing Arab information efforts, especially in the West. In 1979 a two-day seminar on "the Arab image in the Western media" was organized by Morris International in London to provide a forum in which journalists and television and radio commentators from the Arab world and the West could discuss how communication between the two sides could be improved. More than 150 delegates from Europe, the Middle East and the United States participated. In addition to prominent journalists and academicians from Europe, the Arab world and the United States, prominent Arab officials attended as well. The holding of the event was in itself an indication of this growing awareness. During the seminar Mohammad Heikal, the editor of *al-Ahram* and former Egyptian Minister of Information, related how he was given a unique opportunity in 1975 to prepare a study on mass communication for Arab information ministers. The study was supposed to serve as the basis for an ambitious Arab information campaign aimed at projecting a more favorable Arab image in the West. But Heikal went on to add that the picture that emerged from his conversations and study was "most disheartening" and that the project never got off the ground. Heikal also complained that the Arabs' awareness of their shortcomings in this area has led them to resort to "western confidence men who, passing themselves off as public relations experts, have managed to extort huge sums of money for their services. In return, they have come up with publicity campaigns that were as unconvincing as they were costly."

Some Arab journalists, academicians and even political leaders have expressed the view that the Arabs must use their substantial financial wealth in an effort aimed at mind-changing and policy changing. But despite the fact that the Arabs are often accused of using their "vast financial wealth" to alter Western policies and public opinion, very little if anything is in fact being done. "Lack of funds" is one of three major problems besetting the Arab information effort, according to a prominent Western journalist and publisher who has monitored Arab efforts closely in this area. "It is an extraordinary thing to say of countries which are the richest in the world, but if they allocate $100,000, $85,000 of that money, will go, quite sincerely perhaps, to bureaucrats in the home country and less than 20 percent will go to the offices in London, Paris, Washington or wherever." The other factors contributing to the failure of the Arab information effort that he identified were Arab apathy and the lack of trained personnel. He adds that "out of a selection of five, six or seven countries in the information machinery of the Arab world, there are only perhaps one or two men who really are capable in the first instance of assessing the problem and the doing the job. That doesn't surprise me because I know that often some of the Western countries put out a lot of people who are not really geared up to present the information. They are not information people. In the Arab world you find only a few who have practical experience." The problem remains, even if knowledgeable and competent professionals are employed. As this publisher points out, "In most Arab countries concerned, there is no backup. The man in charge of information will be working without adequate backup and even secretarial work. He has to deal with everything himself. Naturally apathy sets in."

Yet one constantly hears references to the all-powerful oil lobby and its influence on America's Middle East policy or of the massive Arab "propaganda campaigns" or lobbying effort in the United States. But as James Akins, former U.S. Ambassador to Saudi Arabia, pointed out in a recent speech: "The oil lobby may have been effective through the domestic companies in getting such lucrative government arrangements as oil quotas and depletion allowances, but as far as having any influence on American policy in the Middle East, it accomplished nothing. There is very little evidence of any company's ever having tried to inform the United States of prospective problems in the Middle East." Akins indicates that the attempts by some oil companies to point out to U.S. officials what would happen if Middle East oil is interrupted were unsuccessful because they did not make their case strongly and were never understood. Akins goes on to say: "The allegedly great lobbying effort by the Arabs in the U.S. are pitiable compared with that of the vast, organized pro-Israeli groups. The American Israeli Public Affairs Committee is superbly organized, highly effective and well-financed. There were at least twenty political action committees organized around the country this year with pro-Israel views. What did the Arabs do? What is the basis of all these references to the well-financed lobbying efforts of the Arabs? If they exist, they are remarkably silent and totally ineffective. The fact is that they exist only in the minds of those who believe that Arabs—with their wealth— must be doing something." Some Arabs, Arab-Americans and American friends of the Arabs believe that one of the major problems facing Arab efforts to influence public and governmental opinion is the failure by some Arabs to use their economic resources to that end. A prominent Arab-American academic said in a private conversation recently: "Every once in a while there has to be some retribution from the Arab world for American deeds, or the lack of them. You can't just do things and then in

189

the Arab world there is no punishment. America hasn't been made to pay any price for most of its deeds over the last 10 years."

A similar theme was echoed by a former American diplomat who pointed out that the Arabs gave the Americans no reason whatsoever to change their Middle East policies because what the United States wanted from the Arabs it was able to get, such as "high oil production, downward pressure on oil prices, protection of the dollar through most Arab holdings in dollar investments at a time when interest on them was substantially less than the inflation rate; we even got some promises of bases." At the same time Arab trade with the United States increased tremendously, with the Arabs purchasing billions of dollars of U.S. products, which created hundreds of thousands of jobs in the United States.

Following on a similar theme, many sincere friends of the Arab world have voiced bitter complaints about the way the Arabs chose to do business in the West. They accuse them of ignoring trusted and true friends while embracing con-men, fair-weather friends and sycophants and at times well-known opponents of the Arabs. A former American ambassador known for his sympathetic views of the Arabs recently was incredulous over the lavish treatment given to the head of a major bank, who would boast in the United States about how much more he was doing for Israel than any other bank. Similar stories were told by one officer of an American-Arab organization who was rebuffed in his attempt to get the president of a major U.S. corporation with large business interests in the Arab world to contact his Senators on an issue related to U.S.-Middle East policy. This company president related that he was a businessman and not a politician and furthermore he had already gone out of his way to write to his Senators in support of the sale of the AWACS to Saudi Arabia. The organization official stated that "the Arabs could have a role in influencing U.S. policies and attitudes toward the Arab world if they would start following stronger, more consistent and principled policies as well as rewarding genuine friends and ignoring opponents."

The Arab information effort continues to suffer from many of the same problems cited in the first section of the book. Some high-ranking Arab leaders continue to see little or no need for an information effort in the West. An American businessman asked a prominent Arab foreign minister recently: "Why don't you go out and try to explain what you stand for instead of letting your opponents do it for you?" His response was, "That's the job of your government. Your political leaders should be telling the country what our position is." The businessman replied that the Arab issues have to be explained not only to the White House or State and

Defense Departments and to some leading Senators and Congressmen but must be explained to the American people. To reach those who make policy it is necessary to go to the press and television as well as to prominent individuals and public organizations. Because even if a policy-maker or legislator is convinced of a certain position, he is unlikely to act on his conviction, especially if he may have to pay a political price for holding "unpopular" positions, unless he hears the message from his constituents.

A consensus exists among most observers of Arab information activity that Arabs do not appreciate the need to present their case and to present it in an effective way. Many American and Western journalists constantly complain about the enormous difficulties they encounter in trying to report on the views of Arab governments. A few years ago, two journalists toured several Arab countries to report on matters related to the energy story. In one country, they tried to arrange for appointments with officials at the ministries of oil and foreign affairs without any success. After three days they left the country without seeing even one responsible official in that country.

Western journalists and to a lesser extent Western scholars complain about the long time it takes to gain access to Arab officials and the lack of accurate information. Many Arab governments fail to compile accurate statistics or to send their embassies basic statistical information that the journalists need. Western journalists are then forced to turn to other sources, which have the information but may also have certain political axes to grind.

Arab suspicion of American journalists continues to exist. Many Arabs are very suspicious of the American media because of the prevailing perception that the media are distorting the Arab image and trying to harm their interests. This problem is beginning to disappear as a result of the growing contact between Western journalists and Arab officials. But the problem remains and may have serious repercussions on coverage if both sides continue to view each other with suspicion. An American journalist recently told this writer that the first officials she met at the border of an Arab country and later on at her hotel were from one of the country's intelligence services. Another often-heard complaint is that Arab countries send abroad diplomats and information officials who lack any sense of perspective about the values and the culture of the country in which they are serving and who are not serious about their work. But this problem is also changing; Arab officials are becoming more aware of this problem and more capable and energetic people are being sought to fill positions in the information area at home and abroad. But the problem of the lack of authority and lack of funds continues to plague many Arab embassies and even ministries of information and to hamper their efforts. As a result there continues to be a need for an adequate supply of qualified people to answer questions, give judgments and background information and analysis. Because of the nature of Arab bureaucracies, many Arab countries continue to give positions of press responsibility in their ministries to lower or middle ranking officials who cannot make judgments when they realize that they must be responsible to higher officials. In addition many people who are dealing with information do not understand or appreciate the problems facing Western journalists and at times they do not understand what they want and why they need quick answers to their questions. Many journalists complain that after calling or meeting certain officials to ask them some questions they are told to "call me tomorrow" or "you'll have to wait until the minister returns from his visit."

These problems reflect the nature of the cultural gap that exists between Arabs and Westerners. The Arabs do try to correct their stereotyped image as a people who are a threat to civilization or who have gained tremendous wealth without working for it by presenting an image of admirable cultural values and concern for the welfare of their own people as well as other less fortunate countries. But they are also plagued by a lack of knowledge about and misunderstanding of the role of the media. As Ghassan Tueni, publisher of *Al-Nahar* and former Lebanese Ambassador to the United Nations, has stated, "public relations is a concern and a craft that is alien to Arab culture." Tueni goes on to add that the Arabs "commit the mistake of wanting to change Americans, instead of changing their image of what Americans are. Many of us want to address ourselves to change the American media to what we think it should be, or we get involved in movements that are marginal. So either we want to change the United States because it is not doing us justice, or we are talking of the idealistic America we knew in the 19th century and early 20th century— an America of ideas and principles that are not reflected in the current pragmatic U.S. foreign policy. As Arabs, we must admit to these two realities in some historical auto-critique before we can really engage in an effort of understanding."

Similar views concerning the nature of the problem of communication have been echoed by former Under Secretary of State David Newsom, who said that the problem of the Arabs and U.S. public opinion is too complicated to be simply blamed on the media and that "it lies in how

192

Americans, in general, look at Israel and at the world, the nature of the Arabs and the Arab world." He warned Arabs not to "underestimate the depth of admiration and support for Israel within the United States." He added that support for Israel is "not confined to one ethnic group or kept alive solely because of unique pressures of that group" but that U.S. Congressmen of both parties continue to provide Israel each year with the largest share of U.S. military and economic aid, because the politicians recognize a "strong constituent support for their actions, and that national polls even after Lebanon continue to show that." He went on to add that "Americans identify with Israel's form of government; its land, its people and its institutions are accessible—even though its excesses may be criticized, there is admiration for Israel's military prowess." But while one cannot exclude the role of the media in helping to shape and fortify these views, Mr. Newsom argues effectively that Americans, for cultural reasons, identify more easily with the Israelis than with the Arabs. Newsom urges the Arabs to do the following if they expect to be listened to: don't criticize your adversaries; meet with non-friends (don't preach to the converted); be accessible—and candid; emphasize credibly the positive aspects of your world; concentrate on the here and now; and present constructive and realistic policy alternatives.

In reality Arab weaknesses and divisions reflect themselves in the coverage by the media. If the Arabs are weak their weakness will be reflected in the coverage; conversely their strength will also be reflected. If the Arab regimes deal humanely and justly with their own people, this will also be represented in the coverage. Concern for human rights in the Arab world will be reflected in the coverage as well as repression, brutality and violence. If the Arabs can work together and coordinate among themselves, this will also be reflected in the coverage. The Arab world, like most of the Third World, is attempting to modernize rapidly. The cost of short cuts to development has often been accompanied by violent upheavals, inter-Arab conflicts, and the absence of constitutional institutions that guarantee political participation and human rights. This negative phenomenon has undoubtedly influenced the coverage of Arabs.

This does not mean that the Arabs should give up trying to improve their image in the West. More contacts between Arab and American officials, journalists, educators, businessmen and students is essential, as are the attempts by the Arabs to try to correct the distortions in their image. But the way the Arabs behave at home and the way they deal with their own peoples and the outside world will play a major role in the coverage of the Arab world and its issues.

193

It is also obvious that while no one has a monopoly on the responsibility for the distorted image, Westerners as well as Arabs have to do more to correct this image.

Due to recent advances in communications technology, priority has been placed by the Western media on instant crisis reporting, without sufficient attention to the need for a complete background picture of events. By providing information of this nature, the media cannot necessarily guarantee a higher level of communication, since the flow of news is only one part of the process of communication between nations. Account must also be taken of the social, economic, cultural and historical dimensions of developments as they arise. Moreover, there is a need for the media to ensure a degree of accountability and accessibility by developing new feedback systems. In this manner, stereotyping of other peoples can be reduced, if not eliminated altogether, and the barriers to heightened understanding between nations can be removed.

American media coverage of the Arab world has undergone a perceptible change. This change, however, has been both limited and slow, despite growing calls from many within and outside the media community for a more balanced coverage of the region and its peoples and their concerns. The call for an end to stereotyping is made not only for reasons of justice and fairness, but also for the purpose of establishing friendlier and mutually beneficial ties between the United States and the Arab countries.

16

Interview with ANTHONY LEWIS

Mr. Lewis is a columnist with The New York Times.

Ghareeb: There are many who believe that the U.S. media are playing a quasi-governmental role in American affairs today. Some media critics have said that some anchormen are more powerful than some of the top leaders in Congress. Some have even gone as far as to say that the media are playing the role of the opposition. From your experience, how important do you think the role of the media is in helping shape decisions that affect national and international affairs?

Lewis: I recognize everything you have said, but I am a skeptic about this media power. I think that a delusion of grandeur arose during Watergate, and it wasn't even correct about Watergate. I mean, it was often said that Woodward and Bernstein had overthrown President Nixon and all that; it wasn't true. They performed an important function, which was the function envisaged for the press by those who framed the Constitution, namely to alert the body politic to a problem and alert the constitutional institutions. But in the end, those who did the work were Congress and the courts, the other two branches of government, which is the way it's meant to work. So I never believed it as to Watergate and I am skeptical about the statement that the press has become the opposition or is performing a quasi-governmental role. I'm skeptical of that in general.

Ghareeb: What role do you see the press playing? There is no doubt that the press is helping shape public opinion at least, and to some extent they have gone beyond this; they have gone to the point of not only disseminating information, and gathering news, but of helping make decisions. If you go back to Sadat's visit to Jerusalem, there were some American journalists, mostly television people, who played the role of the negotiators rather more than they played the role of news gatherers and disseminators.

195

Lewis: Well, you had Walter Cronkite acting as a sort of mechanical facilitator. I wouldn't say that he ever got into any substantive questions when Sadat went to Jerusalem. Of course, there is this sense of the pervasiveness of the American press, and it may be equally true that American public opinion may be moved very deeply by what it reads and sees, particularly by what it sees. A concrete example of this is the situation in Lebanon. In my opinion that is not so much a function of individual journalists performing a political role as it is simply a function of the medium. If you have a medium, television, which shows wounded and dying people, that reality is brought home very graphically to the citizens who help to form policy in this country. That was true in Vietnam, and it's going to be true in Lebanon. In that sense the statement is correct.

Ghareeb: So, the medium becomes the message and helps shape it. But do you believe unbalanced and biased news reporting, editorializing, or even cartoons encourage people of one country to support political hostility against another group? Here I am talking about the impact of media on foreign policy decision making.

Lewis: Yes, I don't have any doubt that it has a strong impact. However, I'm not so sure that this is conscious, semi-conspiratorial or biased. I think most of us are simply captives of our cultural assumptions. That is as true for journalists as for other people. It's hard to unlearn those. In my own case, it was only over a period of years that I came to see the Middle East question in a somewhat different framework, by meeting other people and seeing other points of view than those I had been familiar with and most Americans are familiar with, namely, Israel's point of view.

Ghareeb: Many Arabs, as well as some Americans, believe that the U.S. media have been guilty of stereotyping the Arabs. Some say it has changed recently, but historically this has been the case. Do you feel that this is true, that this is a reflection of the situation as it was and to a certain extent remains today?

Lewis: I think it is true. I think it is unquestionably true that the press (I prefer that word to "media" because it is less newfangled), not for its own reasons, but as part of a general cultural assumption, has been very unfair in stereotyping Arabs. Cartoonists portray Arabs, no matter what the reality is, as people wearing funny costumes and carrying guns. I don't need to spell out the stereotype for you.

196

Ghareeb: You have touched on the issue of stereotyping and you said that the cultural aspect is very important. Some other people have attributed it to ignorance, to bias sometimes, to a think-alike attitude that permeates the media. I wonder if you could go into that. What do you think are the most important factors influencing what appears either on television or in the press?

Lewis: Let me step back a moment and give you an example of how the press in the United States tends to get swept up in the assumption of the moment. I will take it very far away from the Middle East, so that we can do it in a detached sense, and that is to China. During the long period when the United States had no relations with the People's Republic of China and there was a great "red scare" in this country, a lot of academics and foreign service officers who had to do with China were persecuted. The press, on the whole, was very anti-People's Republic and carried out the general assumptions. Then suddenly, President Nixon went to China and we went into a phase of gushing admiration. The journalists who went to China with Nixon all wrote that everything was wonderful; the politicians, the diplomats they met in China were the most brilliant, sophisticated, profound people they had ever met, the country was running like clockwork and everything was marvelous. Really, the most amazing, naive things. And, of course, they discovered that during that very period there were an awful lot of people being persecuted and killed, and conditions were not so good. We are in a slightly more realistic phase now, but there is a tendency to ride along with the craze of the moment. In the Middle East, Arab culture is such a general term. It is very different from the American way of life, and it's hard to take it in a casual way. Those American journalists I know who have dealt intensely with the Arab governments and people have come to admire and understand that culture, and they have a very different view of it, but it is strange to most Americans, including journalists.

Ghareeb: What do you think has been the impact of this negative portrayal? How important has it been in influencing public opinion in general and governmental policies and decisions?

Lewis: It's a hard question. I think it's there, underneath. Yet, in the end, and I'm only guessing now, I still think that the main levers that have affected American government policy in the Middle East for the last forty years are otherwise. First of all, there has been a genuine, moral, historical commitment to Israel, to the creation of a Jewish state and to the survival

197

of that state, which showed very much in the Truman period. I think that is a fact quite independent of bias or stereotyping in the press. It's been reinforced very much by the great skill of Israel and its supporters in mobilizing American opinion to maintain that attitude, there's no doubt of that, but I want to emphasize that the attitude was there anyway.

Ghareeb: A point that some media critics raise is that in general one of the problems with American correspondents, editorial writers, editors, etc., is that they have, at least in the past, equated the Israeli position with the right position, the just position, and the Arab one with the wrong one, so the Israelis became the good guys and the Arabs became the bad guys. How important do you think this is, and to what extent do activities of the pro-Israeli lobby in the United States contribute to this stand?

Lewis: Very much, I think. We all know they are very articulate and very skillful. They have worked on individual Congressmen in the way that lobbying works in this country. Let me use the dreaded word, oil, but not in the Middle East sense, in the American sense. The other day there was a proposal to roll back some of the very large tax benefits that were given to the oil companies a year ago. Even though the Senate was passing this vast package of tax increases, including a rollback of many business tax benefits, nothing happened to the oil benefits, because the oil states have a very powerful lobbying system. They immediately got hold of their Congressmen and said, "Now listen, fellas, none of this is going to pass, right?" And it didn't. Something like that happens in the other area. Not totally. We all know that the Israeli lobby was not able to stop the AWACS proposal, for example, but it is a very well connected, very skillful lobby which has demonstrated its clout politically on individual Congressmen, and that's what matters.

Ghareeb: Some people say that coverage of the Arabs and their negative portrayal has been influenced by the Arab-Israeli conflict. Others attribute it to ignorance of Islam and Islamic culture, and the Arabs' culture and history. How much influence do you think the Arab-Israeli conflict has had? Before 1948, there was, if not a positive, not a hostile portrayal of Arabs. They were seen as romantic desert nomads.

Lewis: That is a very shrewd question, and I think it has to be answered with care. First of all, you took the words out of my mouth when you said the "romantic desert" character. I think that was always and still is more of an English than an American image. There is a good deal more Arab romance in England. There was some here. I think the great failure is the

198

failure to understand that the picture of the lonely Arab in his tent in the desert is a totally, grotesquely out-of-date picture, and that it is a product of two things: ignorance and the Arab-Israeli conflict. The typical American does not understand that today the characteristic Arab is likely to be an accountant or a clerk, or someone not really so different from us. I am thinking especially of the Palestinians. I'm not thinking of the peasants in Egypt, who in population terms are a very large number of people. But I don't think Americans on the whole are aware of the extent to which that lonely Bedouin figure is grotesquely out-of-date and inaccurate. So I think sheer ignorance is part of it, and part of it is, as you suggested, the Arab-Israeli conflict.

Ghareeb: Some reporters say that the Arabs have failed to present their case effectively to U.S. media and to U.S. public in general. Do you agree that this is the case? Have you found access to news sources and newsmakers in the Arab world to be more of a problem than in Israel and do you think that this contributes to the problem that we are talking about?

Lewis: I don't want you to think I think that ineptitude at news management or lobbying is the main cause. I don't think that, although it could be improved. I personally have not had such great difficulty in meeting those figures in the Arab world that I have wanted to meet. I've had good success, partly, I suppose, because I take a relatively sympathetic view. I have met the people I want to meet in Jordan, Saudi Arabia and Egypt, and among Palestinians right up to Chairman Arafat. So I can't complain. But here we come again to the cultural difference. For the typical American journalist who is making a quick visit to the Middle East, Israel is a country in which you can see anybody and everybody. The man on the street will argue with you. It is just a warm bath for journalists. It's almost as easy as Washington, D.C., and that's not true for cultural reasons in most Arab countries, as I need hardly say. It's different. I don't happen to think it's very important. I wouldn't worry about it; it's a fact of life. I think the most important thing is to try not to mislead, but to inform Americans about the reality of the change from that romantic image which isn't what the Arab world is really like. I'll make a concrete observation and a rather harsh one. If you were thinking in terms of Western opinion and how best to approach it, and you were the media adviser to Chairman Arafat, you would say "Mr. Chairman, my advice to you is to buy a smart London suit, trim up your beard and go in there with a nice snappy tie on looking like Mr. Business." That would make a difference.

I hope you understand the reason I'm saying that. I don't happen to think that the way you look is very important, but it is a reality. And when Mr. Arafat goes on an American television program, he comes through as a mixture of that romantic desert Arab you spoke of, but without the romance.

Ghareeb: Some think he is a bloodthirsty terrorist.

Lewis: But you know, he does look a bit bloodthirsty.

Ghareeb: Let's go beyond the Arab-Israeli conflict to the picture of the Arab in general, especially since the 1973 War and the Arab oil embargo. There has been a great deal of emphasis on the greedy Arabs, oil-rich sheikhs who control or threaten the Western jugular. The issue has been raised that this is far more serious and insidious than just the image of the Arabs; it helps create and shape the environment that might lead the United States to use its troops to seize the oil fields, for example. How serious a problem do you think this is?

Lewis: We are really much deeper than image here, as you suggest. I think it is serious. It is a fact of history that a small number of thinly populated countries in or near the Gulf control a very large amount of oil. That is bound, in reality, to make people resent them, especially after 1973, when they used that position to jack up the price of oil by a factor of 10 or 20. There is no getting around it. People aren't going to like it.

Ghareeb: Some people say that Israel's invasion of Lebanon has produced probably more critical commentary on Israel than usually appears in the press. You, particularly, have written several pieces taking a strong stand against the invasion. Do you think this war will change American attitudes toward Israel, toward coverage in general, making Americans less willing to accept everything Israel does than in the past?

Lewis: Yes, I do, but I would not exaggerate the amount of that. The basic committment will remain of the kind I mentioned earlier. But I think it is true that what has happened until now has made people see Israel much less as the gallant underdog. I think you hear much more criticism and I think you will, especially if the situation ends as bloodily as it might; I think there will be more of the same.

Ghareeb: Prior to the invasion of Lebanon, you had several stories in your column publicizing the voices of moderation in the Middle East, especially some of the Israelis. Such voices are not often given a prominent forum in this country. American journalists sometimes complain about the difficulty of portraying the Middle East in an evenhanded way because of this problem. Do you find this to be a problem?

Lewis: You mean for me personally?

Ghareeb: Do you think that this is a problem that contributes to the failure of understanding Middle East issues? Do you think that the American media should pay more attention to those voices, for example, the Israeli "Peace Now" Movement?

Lewis: Yes, I definitely do. I think that the American press in Israel has been too dominated by the government. I don't want to be misleading here, because I am sorry to tell you that I think public opinion in Israel, on the whole, is behind the government. I think a majority is of that view, which I regard as extreme. But I still think it is very important to tell people that there are a lot of Israelis, and among them the leading people in many spheres, the most intellectual, who don't agree with these extreme policies. I think it is important, and the job has not been adequately done.

Ghareeb: The press has been criticized also for not giving enough coverage to the heavy toll of civilian casualties and civilian suffering caused by the war in Lebanon. It has been said that this means that they implicitly side with the Israelis. Do you agree with this criticism?

Lewis: I don't think I do. I think there has been a good deal of coverage, not always exactly what I would like, but the newspapers I see have given some very compelling accounts of the casualties.

Ghareeb: Your columns appear in *The New York Times*. *The New York Times* has not always included notification that its articles on the war have been cleared by Israeli military censorship. Has this happened?

Lewis: No, no, we did that for a time. I think we do do it when anything of significance is done to the article.

Ghareeb: I see. I was going to ask if you think that this reflects a difference in the policy.

Lewis: No, we are very sensitive to the censorship question, and I know our editors have been very angry at the Israelis at some points and have told them so.

Ghareeb: One of the criticisms of some Arabs has been that the American media have been angered by the censorship more than they have been angered by the toll of destruction. How do you feel about this?

Lewis: I'm afraid that there is a little something to that. You say "the media"—it would depend on who it was. If you are talking to an editor or just a reporter who is eager to get the story, that might well be true, because journalists are rather self-centered and cynical. But if you step back a bit and talk about the chief editors of the papers, the columnists or editorial writers, I don't think you would find that to be true.

Ghareeb: Concerning your story "Eyeless in Gaza," which I think appeared in May . . .

Lewis: There were two pieces, yes.

Ghareeb: You indicated that these stories, and others as well on the occupied territories, have aroused criticism within Israel and from some American Jewish leaders sympathetic to Israel.

Lewis: That is true.

Ghareeb: How often has this happened?

Lewis: The criticism? Well, my mail is highly critical whenever I write about this subject. I have many angry readers and even telephone callers. In the course of a "Meet the Press" interview with Prime Minister Begin several months ago, before Lebanon, the moderator, Bill Monroe, quoted something I had written and asked Mr. Begin about it. Instead of answering the question, Mr. Begin launched into a five-minute denunciation of me and said I was not a friend of Israel. Of course, that kind of thing is painful to me. Nobody enjoys that, but I've gotten used to it and it doesn't affect what I write. Not at all.

Ghareeb: Have groups within this country, organized groups, also protested your writing?

Lewis: I don't know that they have done so as a group, but I've had many letters and I know that the publisher of *The New York Times* and the editors have had letters from figures in different American Jewish organizations. I don't think there has been an occasion when the organization, as such, adopted a resolution criticizing me.

Ghareeb: Have any of your columns ever been rejected or has anyone tried to put pressure on you to alter your point of view?

Lewis: Within *The New York Times*?

Ghareeb: Either within *The New York Times* or outside. I'm not talking about somebody who calls and says, I don't like what you are writing, or I disagree with you. I mean actual pressure.

Lewis: No. The answer is that no column on this subject has ever been held out by the editors. No editor has ever told me what to write, and there has never been any pressure on me, personally, other than voiced disagreement or argument on the merits, which, of course, I am always glad to get. People will write me closely reasoned letters—"I disagree with you for the following reason"— which, of course, I am always glad to get. But no, I have not been subject to any improper pressure.

Ghareeb: Have you received any support?

Lewis: Oh, yes, I have, and I'm grateful for it. I've had some letters from some Arab-American groups. But apart from that, I also get quite a lot of letters from ordinary American citizens, saying they're glad. I'll give you an example. It must have been toward the end of June, the day I left on a trip to the Soviet Union. I was on the Ted Koppel program "Night Line." Ambassador Arens, the Israeli Ambassador, was on and I asked him some pretty tough questions about the Lebanese operation. Koppel was also tough. He's a very good journalist. The next morning, I went into my office in Boston where I share space with some advertising salesmen with *The New York Times*. One of the salesmen said to me, "Gee, what did you say on "Night Line" last night? I didn't watch." I said, "Oh, I don't know, the same things I write in my column, doubtful about the invasion of Lebanon." He said, "Gee, one of my advertising clients called me up this morning and asked me if you were a Nazi." So, that's the way it goes.

Ghareeb: *The New York Times* is perhaps the most influential newspaper in the United States and it extends influence beyond its real capabilities to other papers, through its editorials, for example.

Lewis: Yes, that's probably true.

Ghareeb: Some go beyond this to say that *The New York Times* is published in New York and has many readers who are Jewish and sympathetic to Israel. They say that this is unfortunate because *The New York Times* is influencing other newspapers in other parts of the United States. Beyond this, they also say that *The New York Times'* columns, news stories and analytical pieces are used by the networks, so in a sense it has an inordinate influence. How much of a problem is this?

Lewis: I think all of that is true. I think it is true that not so much the editorials as the news judgment—what we think is important in the news—does very much influence the network judgments. I guess that's just the way life is. I don't know what can be done about it. As for the columnists, every once in a while somebody on television tells me he liked what I wrote or he disagreed with what I wrote. But I don't know. You know it's a column of opinion.

Ghareeb: At what level is the matter of what is news on the Middle East determined, do you think?

Lewis: I don't have anything to do with that.

Ghareeb: But from your own reading, your own impressions, your own experienced knowledge?

Lewis: You mean within *The New York Times*?

Ghareeb: Within *The New York Times* and outside if you can extend beyond that also.

Lewis: I can just tell you mechanically what happens at *The New York Times*. There's a foreign desk and a foreign editor who will probably talk on the telephone several times a day with correspondents in Beirut, Jerusalem, Cairo, wherever. He will go into a conference in the afternoon and indicate what he thinks are the most important stories and eventually the judgment is made by the executive editor, the top news editor. I don't always agree with the decisions, but they are made, I think, in as detached a way as they can be made from the mind of a man. The executive editor is A. M. Rosenthal, who has been a correspondent himself all over the world: Poland, India, the United Nations. He knows the world and he's doing his best to decide what's important. How else do you do it? I don't know. If the earlier part of your question was to suggest that it's done with one eye on the constituency in New York, I don't actually think that's true.

Ghareeb: That was part of it. I also wanted to know at what level the decision is made: the reporters, editors, a combination, all of the management?

Lewis: It's good that you said that, because it's important to know this. The final judgment is, as I said, the judgment of the executive editor, but on any newspaper, and certainly on this one, the reporter is crucial, absolutely crucial. If you have confidence in the reporter, and most reporters are not out there unless there is confidence in them, the judgment of the reporter is given heavy weight. There is no escaping that. Reporters are very important.

Ghareeb: The second thing that I want to discuss is the question of American coverage of foreign affairs as crisis journalism, meaning that the papers and television skip from crisis to crisis without giving readers and viewers long-term, in-depth analyses or insights of the way other countries and societies operate. I know that in your columns and in similar columns people try to go into depth. They give an analysis; they give some historical background into an issue. But this is a problem that generally affects coverage of the Third World, in particular of the Arab world. Is this, do you think, related to the general characteristic of foreign affairs? What do you think could be done about it? Can anything be done?

Lewis: My answer is to plead guilty. It has been and it is. It is less than it was. We try, in Third World journalism, to get away from crisis. I'll give you an example. We now have two first-class reporters, foreign correspondents, in Africa: Allan Carroll and Joseph Lilyville. They spend at least half their time, and maybe as much as three-quarters, doing stories that are not on the top of the news at all, just designed to show how societies work. But the trouble is that you have a very limited staff, and when there are crises you have to deal with them. There's no escaping them. If you are in the middle of a situation like Lebanon, you can't go out and write a story about how they grow peach trees. You have to cover the news. So events force you into that.

Ghareeb: One of the problems I'd like to get at is the use of certain words coined by the Israelis. For example, the West Bank is often referred to as "Judea," and the Lebanon war is often portrayed as a civil war, when it's far more complex than that. They also say Christian versus Muslim or the Right versus the Left, and again it's much more complex than that. What's your reading on that? Is it just shorthand?

Lewis: It's just inadequate journalism. Our business, like any other business, has levels of competence in it. When I read things about the Muslim-Christian fighting or disagreements in Lebanon I just groan, because, like you, I know it's much more complicated. And the better people, whether it's our people, the several correspondents we've had in Beirut, or others, don't write that because they know better. It takes a certain experience and wit, intelligence to do it, and not everybody's good enough.

Ghareeb: Some people tell me, "We need a shorthand. We have to say things easily, simply and quickly. Therefore we cannot avoid this." But you think that this could be corrected?

Lewis: I do, but I don't know about television. It's so hard to do because the time is limited. You have a minute and twenty seconds to tell about a complicated situation in Beirut. You don't want to take five or ten seconds even to tell your viewers that it isn't just Muslim-Christian, it's Maronite, and even between the Maronites, it's X and Y, Frangia and Gemayel. You haven't got the time.

Ghareeb: Although there is still a great deal of stereotyping or negative portrayal, some people say that there has been a change in Middle East coverage. Others disagree. Some people go back to the 1967 War and say Israel is no longer perceived as a David. It became a Goliath because of that victory. Others say it goes back to the 1973 War and the oil embargo. Still others say it is more recent—the image of Begin, the transition of the Israelis, especially under Begin and Sharon. Do you believe that there has been a change in the coverage in recent times and if so, when did this change start and what are the causes of it?

Lewis: I think there has been a change, and I think it reflects reality. I don't think it goes back to the '67 War, because the victory was so startling and relatively painless. I don't think too many questions were asked.

Ghareeb: By the way some people say that Sadat. . .

Lewis: Oh, absolutely, we'll come to that. I think it's certainly true. But let's take it in turn. The big change has been Begin and the policies on the West Bank and Gaza and the Sharon brutality, Lebanon and the bombing. I think that events have just forced people, however pro-Israeli they were, to confront a different reality, and the reality *is* different.

As for Sadat, there you have an example not so much of the input of the individual journalist as the effect of the mechanical medium. Sadat learned brilliantly the lesson that I suggested I would try to force on Chairman Arafat if I were his media adviser. Sadat understood that the most important thing he had to do was to get the United States on his side, that it could be very helpful to him to have American opinion favorable to him, and the way to do that was through television. He understood all that brilliantly. He did it very well; he was the picture of reason and moderation. He puffed on his pipe, he looked sage, kind and reasonable. I'm not saying that this is not reality. I'm not being a bit critical. I'm just saying that he did it brilliantly and I think it made a real difference.

Ghareeb: Critics of Sadat in the Arab world say that after the '73 War, Sadat was being portrayed as a devious and sneaky conspirator, but after '78 he became a hero of peace, and the reason for the change in American public opinion was the change in his policy on Israel and nothing really changed. Does this make any sense to you at all?

Lewis: I don't think I agree with that. If you read Kissinger's memoirs about Sadat and the post-'73 period, you will see Kissinger's judgment, or what he says was his judgment at the time. Of course, he may have reshaped it when he wrote the book in light of subsequent events. I don't know. But he says that in his judgment Sadat was a very serious politician, a man who did have in mind the possibility of making peace, and that he dealt with him as such. What we saw after 1978 was simply the public disclosure of that aspect of Sadat, his decision to play that on a public stage rather than in a diplomatic, private way with Kissinger and company.

Ghareeb: So, you don't see, at least in the media, that attachment to Israel has gotten in the way of a more balanced view of the Arab world?

Lewis: I don't think so, no. I honestly think that today the American press, or at least the reporters, are far more balanced toward the Middle East situation than American politicians.

Ghareeb: How has this improvement manifested itself?

Lewis: Because I think one gets more realistic and sympathetic—not in the biased sense but simply in the understanding sense—coverage of the Arab world. Certainly within the context of the Arab-Israeli conflict one hears the Arab side of it much more. One reads it, one sees it.

Ghareeb: But how has it manifested itself? Can you give me any examples?

Lewis: Oh boy, I don't know if I'm enough of an expert to answer that. I just have the feeling that one reads more sympathetic, understanding pieces and sees more sympathetic, understanding television about individual Arabs, victims of this or that Israeli policy, landowners, businessmen, mayors.

Ghareeb: That is the type of thing I wanted to get at, the human rights issue, and you've raised this.

Lewis: Oh yes, I think very much so.

Ghareeb: The other thing is that while there has been some improvement, and I think a noticeable improvement, on this issue of Arab-Israel, in other areas of the Arab world, the Gulf, North Africa, there has been no change. For example, the Iraq-Iran War.

Lewis: I agree, very little change.

Ghareeb: Why do you think this is so? Many are still saying the Iraq-Iran war is a war between the Shi'a and the Sunni.

Lewis: Yes. I don't know. I think probably just because there have been other, more urgent things to worry about and we haven't educated ourselves or taken the trouble to do it. I'm pretty ignorant myself. I know nothing whatever about the Iran-Iraq War. I've never been to North Africa. My mind has been gripped by other matters.

Ghareeb: What are the responsibilities of the media in this area? Do they have a special responsibility, do you think, to their public, to their audiences and perhaps to the people that they are covering? And what should it be?

Lewis: Oh, my, my. I don't think I can frame that. What does one ever feel as a responsiblity in this business? I always feel that it is a responsibility to the truth. I don't think you owe any individual something. But all of us as journalists come in with certain premises, what Justice Holmes called "can't helps," inarticulate premises. I have a premise about human rights and decencies that I bring to the subject and I write with that in mind. I don't think I can philosophize about that.

17

Interview with JOHN COOLEY

Mr. Cooley is a correspondent with ABC-TV News in London.

Ghareeb: Many people have been concerned about the role of the U.S. press in general. They are saying that the press and the media have come to play a quasi-governmental role; some even say that commentators are more influential than top leaders of Congress. What is your assessment of the role of the media, in general, in shaping the nation's policy? How do they affect the conduct of foreign policy and the attitude of the United States toward other peoples and cultures?

Cooley: I would say that over the last generation, in particular over the last ten years, the American media have perhaps almost unconsciously or unawares assumed a role which certainly they had never intended to assume, and many of the founding fathers of the great American newspapers and of the broadcasting networks would not have dreamed of. *The New York Times, The Washington Post*, some of the other leading American newspapers, are suggesting foreign policy direction or acting as critics and watchdogs over American policy as well as over Congressional operations in an almost unprecedented way. This is not to say that they have not done this in past generations; they did, in fact, as far back as the Civil War, if not earlier. But not on the scale of today. Added to this is the growing role of broadcasting, especially television. We saw it in spectacular ways, in Soviet-U.S. relations, but even more in the Middle East, where President Sadat negotiated with the United States and Israel through the intermediary of television commentators such as Walter Cronkite and Barbara Walters. It has continued in use, although perhaps not on the scale of the period after the last Middle East war, but it has advanced in ten years, and I believe it's growing.

Ghareeb: Some are saying that the role of the press is no longer restricted to news gathering, to the dissemination of news or even to molding public opinion, but has moved, as you just mentioned, into the realm of newsmaking as well. Do you feel that this is true? Can you give me any specific examples of this situation in the Middle East area?

Cooley: Well, I should say that my own present employer, ABC News, has a strict and firm policy to prohibit efforts to make news, to generate artificial news by setup situations for television cameras or radio microphones. I think this a proper prohibition. I can recall my own experience in Beirut during the Lebanese Civil War; when one or more of the factions saw television cameras approaching, the fighting would often begin. We saw it on a spectacular scale, for a while, in Iran, when night after night, mobs in the streets performed for the American television cameras. This was a most unfortunate situation, and finally it was very difficult for those working there. Their job was to cover the crisis, the mobs were part of the crisis, and they couldn't expect to be there with the cameras and tell them or the students not to demonstrate or shout political slogans. There is something about television, something innate in it, which does lead to generating such situations. The serious practitioners of television news do all in their power to avoid this.

Ghareeb: What is your assessment of the U.S. media's portrayal of the Arabs? Many believe that the coverage has been inadequate, unbalanced, even outright biased, and has contributed to the perpetuation of stereotyped and negative images of the Arabs. Do you think this is an accurate assessment? How are Arabs being portrayed in the media today?

Cooley: The stereotyping of Arabs, and of other ethnic groups, goes back many, many generations in America in political cartoons, literature, popular literature and comics. It has been projected into film in our own day. It was always present in television and radio news coverage. More recently, certainly Arabs have been unfairly portrayed. There is no doubt about it. I see it as one who is a working journalist speaking from the inside rather than the outside, and therefore I am perhaps not an objective or scientific observer of this. But my impression is that the situation has improved somewhat over the past few years, particularly since the 1973 Arab-Israeli War.

Ghareeb: To what extent are editors or journalists feeding preconceived notions and stereotyped images to their readers and viewers?

Cooley: Well, let me again speak firstly as a former print journalist. I haven't stopped being a print journalist, although at present I am primarily in broadcasting. But I worked for 15 years as a staff correspondent for *The Christian Science Monitor*. Perhaps it's a special case, but the *Monitor* has seriously sought to avoid any stereotypes or prejudicial images of anybody, including Arabs. I think mainly they tried very hard, where others have not tried hard until recently. I would say that the image of ugly Arabs still exists in political cartoons, by leading cartoonists who are well known. And I would repeat what I wrote over a year ago: that Arabs are probably still the only group in the U.S. that anyone dares to portray in pejorative terms. This kind of thing would never be tolerated by other ethnic groups in the United States—Italians, Jews, Blacks, Irishmen, whatever. Arabs themselves don't appreciate it, and bodies such as the American-Arab Anti-Discrimination Committee now direct their efforts to fight it. It is still an uphill fight, because basic stereotypes go back very far in American literature, go back long before the Arab-Israel conflict. In books by writers like Mark Twain and magazines in the 19th century, there is something almost subconscious or subliminal about some of the images. It's very difficult to eliminate this totally, but I do believe there has been progress. Arabs are now given mention, serious mention as an important American ethnic group. Their lobbies are listened to. Arab-American Congressmen and Congresswomen are now recognized as having the same basic rights for their issues as are others. And I think that's progress.

Ghareeb: Some have been saying that the negative image of the Arabs is not only harmful to the Arab image, and their own self-esteem, but even more dangerous or more insidious in that it contributes to the creation of a certain atmosphere which may allow the use of force against Arab societies. Most specifically, I am talking about the image of the Arab oil sheikh with the black headband and the cape full of money who is controlling or threatening the Western world's jugular vein. To what extent do these images affect public opinion, which in turn affects opinion makers and decision makers?

Cooley: They certainly affected public opinion, more particularly in 1974, and again in lesser oil crises. They were strongly recalled in 1978. I think that with a change in the world oil situation in particular the ugly Arab image has subsided, but it does still exist. It still crops up now and then, mainly in political cartoons and in film. I think the worst of that may be over. Undoubtedly it did leave an impression and could possibly have had a negative effect on policy making, although I think the impact on public opinion was greater at a much earlier period.

Ghareeb: Some say that part of the problem in journalism and foreign affairs coverage stems from the nature of American journalism itself, especially television journalism. I'm talking about crisis journalism, which means that the journalist would skip and jump from one crisis to another, covering developments abroad, emphasizing the sensational without giving the readers and the viewers long-term, in-depth insight and background coverage on the causes of a crisis and perhaps the way other societies operate. This, I'd say, probably applies to Third World countries, and perhaps more particularly to Arab countries. How true is this, and what are the causes of it?

Cooley: Yes, I think crisis journalism, as you put it, or as it is called in the fraternity, fire-brigade coverage (that is, the coverage of crisis situations or violence by so-called "firemen" or non-specialist journalists who are sent from crisis to crisis around the world, not because they have any background in the area they are covering but they are able to describe the situation in sensational terms) is a problem here. Yet I do believe that major American television networks are making real efforts to get away from this. I have had to work in such situations. I think that all of those journalists, including the partisans, need much more language training and area knowledge, especially of the Arab world. We ought not to send them the first time to Saudi Arabia, Lebanon, Iran or Pakistan, unless they speak one of the local languages, or have knowledge of the culture or the social structure. Some of the major media are making efforts by on-the-job training and by language training. All of this is in the right direction. However, I think as long as drama is emphasized in journalism, there will be sensational media still indulging in what I would call crisis journalism or fire-brigade coverage.

Ghareeb: What you are saying, at least about the way it seems to be in the United States, and especially with television journalism, is that there is a limited interest in foreign affairs anyway by the average reader. Even the sophisticated ones. Some editors and journalists I've talked to say that what the readers want or the viewers want is a simple capsulized form, and only the specialist wants extensive coverage. They say, "That person can get it anyway, without us. He doesn't need us." How would you compare this with the Europeans? You have had a unique experience. You are one of the few whom I would call a specialist, an expert on the area that you covered, and you covered it for a long period of time. How would you respond to these people? They are saying, in a sense, that a journalist does

212

not need a serious background. You can send one on a rotating basis, and he learns.

Cooley: I personally disagree with that theory and the people I have worked for and worked with would mostly disagree with it too. I realize that is still a view which pervades our wire services to some extent, and probably also some branches of broadcasting, but I do believe that serious efforts are being made by some people to overcome it. In Britain one sees the results of mass tabloid journalism and how they affect public and popular tastes. You simply could not sell a newspaper on a commercial basis here that does not provide its readers with large doses of news about the British royal family, of sex, of violence. I think it's more blatant in Britain than it is in the United States, and certainly as regards the Middle East. They'll make a page one story or at least a page two story, even in one of the serious London dailies, about the murder, or presumed murder, or possible accident of a British girl at a party in Saudi Arabia three years ago. It's more difficult to find a serious report about British or American foreign policy in the Middle East, for example, Iran and Iraq, in some papers. That is a fact of popular journalism, unfortunately.

Ghareeb: What I was getting to was the example of recent developments in the invasion of Lebanon. Some journalists have only been repeating what some officials have been saying about the "new opportunities" that are going to be created by this invasion. Of course, some of these people recognize the humanitarian and moral dimension of this tragedy. Perhaps the optimism may prove to be true, perhaps there are more opportunities, but at the same time I think the sophisticated reporter would want to mention or emphasize that the crisis could also lead to reassessment in the Arab world, to new challenges, to instability, and not simply to opportunities.

Cooley: Yes, well, certainly the basic problem in Lebanon has been coverage. From the Middle East again are images of war and oppression day after day, night after night on television, and looking at it from the viewpoint of one inside who is working in this coverage, I see the same problems but in greater volume. I have seen many journalists who might have never been suspected of sympathy for the Arabs, who cover from a news-daily point of view, really questioning for the first time. I would suppose news magazines and some television reporters have asked questions for the first time about what we really are doing, partly because of questions coming from society itself. Inside Israel, whether there will be

213

an opening and questions in other directions, whether we will see coverage of rapprochement of Israelis, Lebanese and Palestinians, is doubtful, though we hope that exploiting the, as you say, terrible tragedy will be constructive and help to heal the wounds. That's what we'll be working for.

Ghareeb: Sometimes American correspondents appear to use the Israeli descriptions and terms for events or places. For example, you're aware the June War becomes the Six Days War, Haram Sharif becomes the Temple Mount, the rebels become terrorists, Israeli soldiers become commandos. But what I'm interested in is your assessment of the war in Lebanon specifically. A lot of people have been describing this either as a civil war, when it's much more complex than that, or as a Christian versus Muslim conflict. They refer to Saad Haddad's Christian militia, when the majority of Haddad's militia happen to be non-Christian. How serious is this problem, and what do you think could be done to change this? It seems to be a hopeless case.

Cooley: I am one who reported the '75-'76 civil war in Lebanon, part or much of it, and I'm shortly on my way back to Beirut. I would say that it's very difficult to characterize the Lebanese conflicts. I quite agree, putting it in social terms, that terms like "Christian right" and "Muslim left" have badly misled people. All terms have their uses, but most of the time it's very difficult to find a general term to describe what is happening, what has happened in Lebanon. When I write about it, to identify exact factions, when I'm speaking of the Phalangists, I try to identify the parties by saying what it is: a political, paramilitary movement composed of some of the Maronite Christians. But I try to avoid characterizing opposing sides in sectarian terms. There is no satisfactory way of describing "Muslim leftists." In reporting the conflict in Lebanon, one must avoid the stereotyped words. One must describe more exactly the factions that oppose each other, and the reasons for which they oppose each other, because otherwise we come out with meaningless generalities which do not describe what is happening.

The situation in Lebanon, the conflict which has torn Lebanon apart since 1975, is so complicated, and operates on so many layers, that labels for the different factions are more likely to mislead than they are to inform. In order to inform people, one must find as exact labels and descriptions as possible. For example, in dealing with the Phalangist party, one may call it a right-wing party, which it is, but it is wrong to say that it is a Christian party, because it does not include all of Lebanon's Christians or even all of Lebanon's Maronites. It is correct to refer to it as a *predominantly* Maronite party, but in writing a short dispatch for a wire service, or a television program or a radio news spot, there isn't time, in many cases, to use long phrases and many words, and this is why we so often fall back on these facile generalizations, which we should be trying to avoid.

Ghareeb: What is your perception of the way Islam has been covered? To what extent has coverage of Muslim societies been affected by the Arab-Israeli conflict? What I am referring to, specifically, is that at the height of the Iranian hostage crisis, Muslims in general were perceived or viewed in higher esteem than Arabs. I was wondering about the reasons for this.

Cooley: I don't understand your question. You're saying that at the time of the Iranian crisis Muslims were held in higher esteem than Arabs?

Ghareeb: That's right. Even at a time when the Iranian revolution was identified with Israel. Muslims, in general, have been stereotyped, but even Arabs were held in lower esteem, or looked at in a more negative way, at a time when even the hostage crisis was taking place. Do you think this has something to do with the Arab-Israeli conflict?

Cooley: I'm not sure I agree with your major premise. I was in the United States during the Iranian hostage crisis, most of it in any case, and I was not active covering much of it then, except some of the Washington aspects. But it didn't seem to me that Arabs were getting any worse shake then than the Iranians. The Iranian Muslims, and Shi'a Muslims specifically, were being lumped together as rather dangerous terrorists, and it seems to me that some of the heat came off on the Arabs at the time. Now that's just my personal impression.

Ghareeb: This is a result of a poll that was taken. I don't know how accurate the poll is, but that is what the results of that poll were at that time. What about coverage of Islam in general in the media? What's your assessment of it?

Cooley: Again, I think there's been an improvement. I think that there have been many sincere efforts made to explain what is, for a Western speaker, a very different social, political, economic system, a total system and society. I don't think that the term Muslim is as pejorative a word in America, but I think we still have a long way to go, because of mutual ignorance of the West and Islam about each other, which as we know is an old story, going all the way back to the Middle Ages. But again, I have to

215

say that simple, decent essays in the major news magazines, *Time* and *Newsweek*, in the past two years have made a real attempt to explain what Islam is. We must avoid identifying extremist groups within Islam with the whole body of Muslim believers. Islam is a huge faith that has many hundreds of millions of followers. Many Americans read tabloid papers and watch some of the poorer programs on television. They still have strong images about Islam and Muslims, particularly about the role of women, and this is cause for great controversy in Islam itself, but I do see improvement here also.

Ghareeb: Partly what I am talking about is the conflict between Iraq and Iran. A lot of people in the media are explaining it in terms of Shi'a versus Sunni, and at times even as an inter-Arab quarrel. Some have continued to describe Iran as an Arab country.

Cooley: This is just simply ignorance. I can't imagine a major American newspaper or network making a mistake like that, although I suppose it still does happen.

Ghareeb: Some people we have talked to have discussed the reasons for this. You said that part of it was ignorance. Another reason is cultural insensitivity. How much of it is also the think-alike atmosphere in the American media, the influence of the major media—the impact media, *The New York Times*, the networks, for example—on the rest of the media?

Cooley: I would only say that the reasons for ignorance are not entirely cultural. If a person has gone to school and studied, or thinks that he has studied, geography and history, but has not learned the difference between Persia and an Arab country in school, he may still be ignorant of some of the basic aspects of the history Arabs have made since the early Middle Ages. If that person then becomes the news director of a television news program, or the editor of a news magazine, then his readership may be in trouble, and I cannot expect that ignorant opinion leaders overcome ignorance of their readers, television viewers or radio listeners. The fault lies in education; the basic fault lies in education. I cannot believe that this is very widespread. We must have some progress!

Ghareeb: You are someone who has worked in the printed press, for radio and now for television. What are the differences and what determines coverage for television, radio or the printed press, if any?

Cooley: Each of the three has its advantages and its drawbacks. The most satisfying thing that I have found is about radio; those of us who live in a city and tend to get our news from newspapers and television forget that there is a nomad population driving cars, trucks, on the road day and night, who listen to the radio constantly. Radio plays a role in rural parts and reaches many people. The thing I find frustrating about radio is that you are required to be so short; a news spot a decade ago was perhaps 50-60 seconds and has shrunken now to 35 because of commercial interests. Therefore, one is very hard put to define a complex situation in 35 seconds. I have found that true in trying, for example, to describe what was happening in Tripoli, Libya when the Organization of African Unity met and tried to get a quorum on the Western Sahara issue; why the existence of the OAU is threatened if this quorum is not found and a summit doesn't take place.

Television probably has the most impact, the most ability to strike a responsive chord. More often newscasters tend to show every night only violence, fighting, and bloodshed. No explanation of who's fighting, what it's about or why the various countries concerned, like Israel, Lebanon, Iran and Iraq, were objecting to this war, as well as about those who consider it a patriotic war. They would be doing their viewers a great service if they could give television more depth. The executives of major American networks are aware of this but they haven't fully met it. Depth in broadcasting is a big problem. Broadcasting is different from print. I personally find it kind of satisfying. I'd prefer to sit down and write a book about a given problem, but may not have the time to do it, and perhaps I can't find somebody to publish the book. But, barring that, the daily newspaper story has more survival value than television. A paper is printed, rolled up and carried out to the garbage next day, but it still will have been read and clipped, and so preserved. I particularly look back on my own reporting in Algeria during the revolution there as one of the happiest, most productive parts of my journalistic life. Some of those reports still read pretty well. Sometimes we give our readers reason to believe we've given them something worth preserving.

Ghareeb: At what level is the matter of what is news on the Middle East determined? This is a technical question. Is it at the level of the reporter or the editor, what you journalists call the gatekeepers?

Cooley: In the Middle East, I think, probably especially in conflict situations like we have now, it's determined on the spot in the snap judgment of the reporter working—what he's going to record, film or write

217

about. In the act of selection, he is making the decision that this is news. Now, this can be overridden and changed at a higher level by his editor, but the editor only has so much raw material to select from, and what he selects and what he discards is a crucial decision. But it's a decision already limited by the raw material he's given by reporters, especially if they are working on the scene. How about the question of determining how many reporters, for example, cover a story and where they are located? The decisions are taken almost entirely in the home office, certainly of the broadcasting networks, by large organizations like ABC News, CBS, or NBC, and at the newspapers by the foreign editor and the editors, who are moved around to some extent. The decision is made at the sub-administrative centers such as London, and this is sometimes done without referring to New York. ABC camera crews are sometimes ordered to give saturation coverage; everybody available is sent to a story. This happened in the kidnapping of Colonel Dozier in Italy. That can be taken by the very top of the network. I think this is somewhat less true in the Middle East. There's a little more delegation of authority to local bureau chiefs.

Ghareeb: One of the criticisms against the American media is that there is a great deal of coverage or emphasis placed on Israeli news and not as much on the Arab world. In the past, you used to have one correspondent in Beirut and perhaps a full bureau in Jerusalem and Tel Aviv, covering Israel. If there was a bureau in Beirut, it was covering the whole Arab world.

Cooley: Yes, this was certainly true in the '60s and '70s and it probably produced some lopsided coverage weighted towards the Israeli side. I don't think it is true anymore, because the whole nature of the Middle East has changed. The Arab world view is now polycentric. There is no satisfactory single base to cover the Arab world, just as there is no satisfactory single base to cover Latin America inside Latin America. *The Christian Science Monitor*'s Latin American correspondent lives in Boston and commutes to the Latin American countries, rather than live in Latin America. The same is true in the Arab world. In Cairo, one can cover Egypt; one can perhaps get an insight into the affairs of the Sudan, or maybe even the Horn of Africa or Libya from Cairo, but one cannot cover or try to cover the whole Arab world from Cairo, as many of us did in the late '50s or early '60s. Beirut is now destroyed as a news-gathering center, except for the situation, which is being covered by hundreds there. Whether Beirut turns back into a listening post and to a news-making and -gathering center for the Third World as it was in the '50s, '60s and '70s, depends on what kind of Lebanon emerges from the ashes of what is now being destroyed. So now, to cover the Arab world, one must travel to Baghdad, to Muscat, to Yemen, to Saudi Arabia, to write about those countries. One cannot sit at home and pontificate about them. Israel has the advantage of being a small country and covering it is still generally covering only Israel. People covering Israel generally stay there, with some exceptions. Therefore, they have that logistical advantage over people covering the Arab countries.

Ghareeb: You covered the Middle East for a long time for the *Monitor*, and the *Monitor* happens to be a unique newspaper. It's perceived as the most balanced newspaper in covering Middle East affairs. To what do you attribute this? Is it a matter of policy? Is it the quality of the correspondent? What makes it different from other newspapers? Is this impression an accurate one?

Cooley: I don't think that the *Monitor* is very different in its basic structure, or in the way it is run, from others. But it is run with a scrupulous attention to honest, balanced reporting and analysis. The *Monitor* will lean over backwards to try to be fair in a situation. There was an example I read about in another newspaper the other day, telling me the *Monitor* was the only paper that questioned the origin of an advertisement, a pro-Arab advertisement about the situation in Lebanon, and it was signed by a number of groups called Save the Children Fund, OXFAM and others, perfectly respectable and highly respected organizations. Unfortunately, it turned out that the signatures were false and *The Washington Post* and some other papers published the ad without knowing exactly who had placed it and without knowing the signatures were false. The *Monitor* apparently had the good sense to investigate and cover that. It could not authenticate who was placing the ad, they refused the check for the ad and they didn't carry it. They certainly would have much need, or more need for the revenue from that or any other ad than many much bigger, fatter and more prosperous newspapers. The *Monitor* is a very, very ethical paper. Being fair to the Arabs by the *Monitor* was a tradition which began very early, at least in the '50s, long before I came to the *Monitor*. I don't think it was a special attempt to be fair to the Arabs, I think it was simply part of their global policy of trying to be fair to everybody and not to be affected by bias or by prejudice.

Ghareeb: To what extent does the pro-Israel lobby contribute to the unbalanced and biased coverage in the media?

Cooley: I think probably less than before. I noticed a Washington newsletter recently, which first appeared several months ago, dealing with this problem. Apparently the newsletter has been printing stories and they, not liked by some, have been threatened by phone calls, solely because they were presenting favorable pictures of the Arabs. I don't know the details of this, but this would be unheard of five or ten years ago, certainly ten and probably five, that anyone would admit in print to having been threatened by what might be called the Israeli lobby. Apparently nothing's come of it and I gather the newsletter's circulation increased, so I would say that this is a step forward, certainly. The lobby does, through its organization, bring pressure to bear and what influence it can use is still considerable, but I think that influence is still stronger on Capitol Hill and in Congress than in our media. And I think that Arabs are doing rather well with some of their own lobbies, but it's very late. They are learning to lobby. I don't think they'll ever be as good at it as the others are, because the others are better organized. Greek Americans also have had a very effective lobby and have had for some time. Arabs are learning. But in a society where much of what happens, most legislation, is the result of information obtained or asked from lobbies, everyone has to play the game, and whoever plays it most efficiently and cleverly will get the best hearing for his side.

Ghareeb: Let me get back to one question I don't think we got into. How does coverage affect foreign policy decision making, specifically concerning the Middle East?

Cooley: It affects this profoundly. It has always affected it, to have this frequent direct contact between leading policy makers, even presidents, and certain journalists. Washington offers many examples. Again, I don't want to go into personalities, but there's one editor of a leading news magazine who has had constant contact with U.S. presidents and U.S. secretaries of state, private contacts. I only admire him for that and his editorials and news are read with great interest and attention. One would assume that there is probably a symbiosis between him and his informants. He reports their views, but they also read his views when he is writing an editorial very attentively. They take them seriously and they listen to them. So do Congressmen. This is where the impact on policy comes in. I think the impact is more from an elite group of columnists, editorialists and commentators than it is from general run-of-the-mill reporting, but it certainly exists and it's great, and my impression is that it is becoming greater. But it would be difficult to prove that.

Ghareeb: Some critics place the blame on the Arabs for failing to understand the nature of American journalism and to communicate effectively with U.S. correspondents. Others say that U.S. correspondents go and expect to get immediate access to top officials and they want to get sensational stories. Can you give me an assessment of the problems that face foreign correspondents in the Arab world, what the situation is? What kinds of experiences have you had?

Cooley: I've had all kinds of experiences in all kinds of countries, and it's hard to generalize, but I'll try. I would say that as a rule, access to top people in Arab countries such as Saudi Arabia, which is a friendly state, is still very, very difficult and one has to have the patience to observe local courtesy. This is as it should be, but just access to the country itself is difficult. It's very difficult for some people, seemingly impossible, to get a visa for Saudi Arabia. One waits for weeks and weeks, and when one has the recommendation of a minister it still doesn't come sometimes, and when it does come finally, another common problem arises. Received and escorted around the kingdom, with great courtesy, one receives and follows an official program. Saudi Arabia is easiest to work in when you know what you came for. On the other hand, it's almost impossible to do investigative work or work on your own without official supervision or escort. I'm not condemning it, I'm just describing it and this is one of the problems that exists to some degree in all Arab countries. There are other Arab countries where the regime or policy is hostile to American policy, and sometimes, paradoxically, it's easier to get access there because you find yourself confronted with an information minister always willing to deliver a stock anti-American lecture to the reporter, and perhaps help him too. You have access. But, generally, I would say access, censorship, these are problems, but they have also improved somewhat, though there is still room for great improvement.

Ghareeb: How would you compare access to Israeli newsmakers, Israeli officials? How would you compare the coverage? I know it's difficult, as the situation in all Arab countries is not the same. But how would you compare it in general to Israel, and do you think that this contributes significantly to the problem of balanced and fair coverage?

Cooley: Yes, I would have to say that, over time, access to Israel has always been good, because Israel is, whatever else it may be, a basically open society with many different views and opinions. One can walk there except in certain reserved areas. The occupation of the West Bank and

221

Gaza has tended more and more to become one of those reserved areas where it's difficult to get information, where people are afraid to talk, Arab people, that is. But in dealing with Israeli politics, Israeli society, it's a different ball game. Almost anyone can get access to the top people. True, Prime Minister Begin has refused to see certain journalists he regards as hostile or whom his press people regard as hostile. But this is rather unusual. The Israeli tradition has been to see everybody, talk to everybody, and this not only makes work easier there, but it also adds to the impression that many Western correspondents get of a frank and open society, which you do not get in Arab countries.

Ghareeb: Several times you have stressed improvement in coverage. To what do you attribute it? I know that some people say that it started with the '67 War, when the image of David became Goliath, and some say it's now the '73 War, and the Arab oil embargo, which forced the West to begin to reassess, to rethink its relationship with the Arab world. Others say it was Sadat. Others still say it's Begin, Sharon and their intransigence and arrogance. What is your assessment of all of these factors and what do you think is the most important fact in that change?

Cooley: It's very difficult to answer that question; it's a subjective question and the answer will be different depending on who you ask. My own answer would be that it has resulted in all of the things that you mentioned and many others as well—an amalgam of factors. The average American has been unaware of or indifferent until recently to opinions held about the State of Israel by other parts of the world, including Europeans, perhaps more inclined to accept the old myths and not particularly interested in what other people think or what seems to be reality outside the United States. But again, I think that probably the Lebanon War is helping to change this, and the fact that there are deep rifts and differences in American Jewish opinion about policies of the present Israeli government, much more than about any past Israeli government. All of these facts, I think, open the coverage up and improve it from the Arab point of view, but it would be difficult or impossible to pinpoint one of those factors that is more responsible.

Ghareeb: Have you ever been subjected to pressure or attempts to change your coverage by anyone?

Cooley: I've had a lot of expressions of opinion, both favorable and unfavorable from all kinds of people—Arabs, Israelis, Iranians, Turks, Greeks, Cypriots, Americans—but I can say that I have never been pressured, threatened, or blackmailed or anything that even approaches that, to write anything or report anything differently than I have done. Even if I saw such a thing coming, I would ignore it, because I refuse to admit that these factors can affect a serious person working in the free journalistic tradition that we work in; we are lucky to work in it, lucky to have it.

Ghareeb: How about support?

Cooley: The answer is no.

Ghareeb: How about support? Letters?

Cooley: Certainly, that's the other side of the coin. As any working journalist has in his life, I've had thousands from all kinds of people, and a great many of those have been highly favorable, and one always appreciates that and feels that one is doing the right thing. I had a series of letters from listeners on the West Coast in response to a ten-minute perspective commentary I did on the PLO recently, and the letters that were sent to me by ABC were all favorable. There must have been some unfavorable ones but I haven't seen them.

Ghareeb: Do you think that the American media have a special responsibility in this area to correct the negative image, to present a more balanced, fairer coverage of the Arabs? What could be done?

Cooley: Yes, they do have the responsibility to correct the unfair coverage of the Arabs, coverage that has been more unfair than that given any other group of people on the face of the earth.

Ghareeb: What can be done?

Cooley: Better training, orientation and briefing of people who are sent to cover the Arab world including, where possible, language study. There has to be understanding inside Arab governments, the information ministries, of the way Western and American journalists work and what they want, and more help in giving them what they want. There should be more people interested in doing a good job. Good will on both sides, on the side of the media themselves and on the side of the countries where they have to work, is needed. Probably a bit of divine help is needed by all sides, because it's a very difficult problem.

18

Interview with JIM HOAGLAND

Mr. Hoagland is Assistant Managing Editor of The Washington Post.

Ghareeb: Benjamin Bradlee, executive editor of *The Washington Post*, has suggested that the leaders of journalism, rather than the leaders of government, set the agenda for the topics that Americans take to be substantive issues of the day. Do you agree with that view?

Hoagland: No, I don't. I'm not familiar with that statement. My own feeling is that the media is distressingly captive of the national government, the federal government in particular. In agenda-setting, the attention that an Administration pays to a particular foreign policy subject is one of the major determining factors in the amount of coverage. The attention former Secretary of State Alexander Haig paid to Central America would be a primary example of that. So I guess I don't agree with that view.

I suppose the media does play an agenda-setting role in the sense that it forces the timing of discussion of certain issues in a way that makes Administrations react. One of the most interesting things about the Reagan Administration is that we do much less of that than with the Carter Administration.

Ghareeb: Why is that?

Hoagland: They are much less responsive to public discussion of their policies. They are much more closed; they don't have as much substantive discussion of their policies. There was a tremendous range of discussion within the Carter Administration and people seemed to have ways of getting their viewpoint—dissenting viewpoints—to the President, or at least to the National Security Council, and he would then make up his mind. We get the sense with this Administration that they make up their minds before there is much substantive discussion.

Ghareeb: Do you feel that this is the case more with national affairs or international affairs?

Hoagland: More with international affairs. Foreign policy is more susceptible to government agenda-setting than are national affairs, where there are a variety of forums for expressing viewpoints. With international affairs it is pretty much a Washington business; it's a company town. And it is very difficult to sustain interest in a foreign policy issue if the White House and the State Department and the Executive Branch and even Congress are not interested, or are trying to downplay that particular issue. You do have a kind of an objective ally, in such a situation, in the Congress, and usually in the party out of power. They are looking for foreign policy issues and therefore they can pick up articles and themes that appear in the press and make them an issue. But without that kind of follow-through by some part of the government, the press itself is very weak in trying to set or sustain an agenda. You can do it for a day, or maybe for three days, but at the end of the third or fourth day, if there's no echo, there is very little you can do to create that issue. Watergate would never have really happened if it hadn't been for Judge Sirica and Sam Ervin. It wasn't the newspapers.

Ghareeb: Many people, whether rightly or wrongly, believe that because the *Post* and other papers treated that issue day in and day out, pressure was placed on the government, on Sirica and others, to act in the manner they did.

Hoagland: It certainly helped focus the issue. But if Sirica had decided he wasn't going to play, that he wasn't interested, or if you had had another judge who took a different view of it, the media attention would not have led to the kind of pressure that led John Dean to crack and the whole case to change.

Ghareeb: Some assert that the role of the media, not only in domestic affairs but especially in international affairs, is no longer limited to reporting news but is helping to create it. Many journalists believe to a certain extent that this is true. Some point to the Sadat visit, for example, while others point to the hostage crisis in Iran. Do you think this is true and what are some examples?

Hoagland: The changes brought about by television are intertwining news-gatherers and news-makers in what is potentially a very unhealthy way. The Sadat trip to Jerusalem was very much a television extravaganza. And I believe that he undertook that trip in large part for the impact that it would have on television to influence American public opinion in the United States. So Sadat used the media as part of his strategy. It was not

226

the result of the media going to Sadat and provoking something that would not have happened anyway. But the immediacy of television causes a natural confusion in the mind of the audience as to what the news is— what the message and medium are. So I don't think that we journalists ought to be newsmakers or be in charge of making news. That's a perversion of our role.

Ghareeb: Isn't it sometimes a thin line?

Hoagland: Yes, particularly with television. It is much easier for newspapers to draw the line and keep inside it.

Ghareeb: You've covered the Middle East for a long time. What is your assessment of the media's portrayal of the Arabs in general? Many people, especially in the Arab world, feel that they have been depicted by the media in a very stereotyped, biased and outright distorted fashion. Do you feel that this has been the case? Is this the case today?

Hoagland: One of the first articles I wrote for *The Washington Post* out of Beirut was in May of 1972 and grew out of a conference that I attended on that very question. It became very clear to me that in Western writing in general—not just newspapers, but in books and certainly in cartoons— there was quite a distorted image of what we thought of as the Arab or the Arabs. In that piece I quoted somebody else using a line about Arabs sneaking about with knives in their teeth. And that has come from centuries of stereotyping of Arabs in the same way we stereotype Africans. I don't think it's particularly worse. I know there's a theory that because of the threat that Islam supposedly has played to Christianity, Arabs are stereotyped much more than other races or other peoples. I don't think that is particularly true. I worked in Africa for a while and Americans have very strong stereotypes about Africans as well. For that matter there is hardly a stronger stereotype than the American stereotype of Frenchmen—another country that I worked in. It's a different stereotype and maybe people would find it a little more acceptable, but it is still a stereotype.

Ghareeb: To what do you attribute the cause of this stereotype? Is it the concern about Islam here? Is it cultural ignorance? Is it a cultural gap between Arabs and Americans? Is it outright bias? Is it the Arab-Israeli conflict?

Hoagland: It's older than the Arab-Israeli conflict. Recently that conflict has had a role in shaping parts of the stereotype, but I think it's an accumulation of several centuries of received images of Arabs. Like all stereotypes, they grow out of a cultural gap, and certainly Islam played a role in that.

It's changed incredibly since 1972. Ten years after I wrote that article there is a much better understanding of the Arab world and the diversity of Arabs.

Ghareeb: How did this come about? I know that there are several theories. Some people even go as far back as the 1967 War, when they saw that Israel for the first time was no longer a little David.

Hoagland: I don't think it was the 1967 War. Because I don't think images change very much as a result. . .

Ghareeb: Some people say the 1973 War, some say Sadat, others say OPEC.

Hoagland: Maybe it's because I dealt with 1973. I suppose I went to the Arab world carrying a lot of the same stereotypes that all Americans have. As I lived and worked among Arabs those changed dramatically, and I like to think that there was a similar change going on in the West in general but most specifically in the United States. I'm not sure it's changed that much, for example, in a country like France where their stereotype of Arabs is based on Algeria more than anything else. But I think it was the 1973 War, with Sadat, the opening of the Suez Canal, the way Sadat played the peace talks and the disengagement talks, the way Kissinger and Sadat played, and it was OPEC and it was oil and it was the stories about the incredible amount of money that there was there. People began to get interested in a place where they had some financial reward and some potential financial gain, and they began to read about it.

There has begun to be a market for people who could write intelligently about the Arab world, who wrote from the inside—the John Cooleys of this world. There was much more of an interest in what they were writing and saying. There were new people coming into the Arab world. There was a historical moment there where Vietnam was in effect closing down for journalists, in a sense. In the early 1970s people were no longer making Vietnam their next stop. If you were interested in a foreign assignment, the Middle East was good. In fact people were coming from Indochina into Beirut. So you began to get the best of the profession working in the Middle East and becoming increasingly familiar with the Arab case. These are articulate and honest people who were determined to write the stories as they saw them.

Ghareeb: Some people have attributed the problems of foreign affairs coverage in the American press to the technique of crisis journalism or fire brigade coverage—jumping from one crisis to the next without giving the readers any background or long-range view. This applies not only to the Middle East but to all Third World countries. Do you agree that this is a problem? What are its causes, and how can it be remedied?

Hoagland: Yes, it is a problem. Part of the way to remedy it is in fact some of the things that we're doing. Better preparation of foreign correspondents. We have a young man now who's off at Stanford University spending an academic year studying Africa. He will be able to go out to Africa next July and write, I think, quite knowledgeably within a very short period of time. I did the same thing before I went to Africa. The other way you do it is to use very experienced people. We recently had a story by Loren Jenkins that described how he had witnessed Black September in 1970. He was also the man who witnessed the Shatila and Sabra massacres and the evacuation. In other words, he has been observing the Middle East for more than 10 years. Jon Randal has been observing the Lebanon War for more than seven years, since 1975. You use people with experience. You try to prepare younger people better, and you keep your people in a position to be able to use them. I think our coverage of Lebanon this summer was very good, in large part because we had very experienced people.

Ghareeb: One of the criticisms of the *Post* and the media in general is that some of the issues are dealt with in a simplistic way. For example, the Lebanon War. I realize that sometimes you need to use quick definitions, as when you talk about "right-wing" Christians, and "left-wing" Muslims. But you know as well as I do that the problem in Lebanon goes far beyond that. Why is it that you talk about Muslim West Beirut and Christian East Beirut, and you talk about the Christian militias of Saad Haddad, when the majority of Saad Haddad's militias are not Christian. Can't you find a better way to define the issues?

Hoagland: I personally don't know that the majority of Saad Haddad's militias are not Christian. I don't know that. Yes, I recognize the problem you're raising. It is caused in part simply by having to do it 365 times a year. That's one thing you've got to keep in mind. We will fail on any given day, just as any human endeavor will meet with failure on any given day. You've got to look at our coverage over an extended period of time, and whether we build in corrective balances and try to give an occasional

229

interpretive piece that will explain, "No, they're not all right-wing Christians, some of them are left-wing fanatics," or whatever. We probably don't do enough of that, simply by the nature of our business. We are crisis-oriented; we have to be. We have to do it within 24 hours; we have to do it in a certain amount of space; we have to do it for a readership that is not as sophisticated as you are, doesn't have your background, and wants a quick description that is somehow comprehensible to them in their terms.

The argument you ought to be making, and one with which I would agree, is that we ought to have more of the other kinds of stories as well. I don't know if you read the four-part series we ran on the Palestinians recently. That's an example of the thing we ought to do more of, and we probably should have done that a little earlier, but it's simply a question of manpower. We only have 17 correspondents overseas.

Ghareeb: That is an excellent example, especially because it linked what happened in Lebanon to what's going on in the West Bank: the impact of one issue on another. I don't think enough has been done on this, but this series that you did tried at least to deal with this issue in a very effective way.

Hoagland: It's very hard in the Middle East, I might say. We've been more successful at doing that, say, in Eastern Europe, where Poland has been the other big story. We've had three big stories over the last two years; Central America has been one, Poland has been the second, and of course the Middle East. We have an exceptionally bright young man in Warsaw named Michael Dobbs, who has a background in economics. The pace of the Polish story was such that it enabled Michael to sit down once every two weeks, or once every three weeks, and write a summing-up piece. The Middle East rarely gives you that opportunity because you are being run ragged every day with some new event. It's incredible.

Ghareeb: We were talking about this problem of crisis journalism. Is it linked, in a sense, to the function of journalism in a capitalist society as a whole? Is it related to what the reading public wants to read? Is it a buy-and-sell type of idea?

Hoagland: Not in our case. I'll answer only for *The Washington Post* . We are a capitalist outfit. We operate in a capitalist environment, and we are happy to say that we are financially healthy and make a profit and want to make more profits. I would say to you that none of our profit—zero—comes from covering foreign news. I think there's a school of thought that it costs us a lot of money. Because we have a readership that is vitally interested in foreign affairs, we really feel that it's a public service that we're doing. It is also the definition of our newspaper, the definition of our community, and we feel a heavy responsibility to do it. But if we were looking at it as solely a capitalist enterprise, we wouldn't have a single foreign bureau.

Ghareeb: Another criticism that is aimed at the American media in general, and to a certain extent at the *Post*, is that while you do cover important developments, you ignore, especially when it comes to the Arab world, the general human interest stories: the stories of development, of cultural interest, of social change. Do you think this problem is a result of the nature of American journalism as such, or is it broader than this?

Hoagland: Yes, I think you're right. It is hard to get people interested in those kinds of stories. Your readership for that kind of story would be relatively small. We did one recently on Kenya. A reporter who had lived there as a Peace Corps volunteer went back after 10 years and described the effects of change. Most of it was fairly good news; they'd built some schools, they'd done that sort of thing. I'd like to see more of that. But because the readership is usually relatively small, it requires a lot of investment for a reporter to do that. It takes time. And particularly in Arab countries it's often difficult to do that kind of story.

Ghareeb: You see more of these types of stories about Israel than you see about the Arab countries.

Hoagland: The greatest single complaint I have on the Middle East is precisely that you don't see those kinds of stories about Israel in *The Washington Post*. Not that you don't see enough, but you don't see any. I would say that's a justified criticism on both sides. But I would say if there's an imbalance in *The Washington Post*, it's probably in the Arab's favor.

Ghareeb: How do you decide on what is news? What gets front page play? What are the issues? I'm sure that you as an editor expect a story to develop, or you want a certain story, long before it appears on the front page. What are the factors that are involved?

Hoagland: I would say that 60-70 percent of the stories that appear on the front page are automatic choices. We have very little control over it. This week is an unusual period; it's so quiet, very little is happening. But when they declare martial law in Poland, that's a front page story. When Cuomo wins the governorship in New York, that's a front page story for the *New*

York Times. When Marion Barry is reelected here, that's a front page story for us. A lot of it is predictable, routine, almost automatic. There is a lot of fighting in Tripoli, Lebanon, today. On most days I'm not sure that would be a front page story. It's the heaviest fighting in seven weeks, our correspondent says. That kind of line will make that story a front page candidate, probably. Today, it's a very slow day, and that story will probably get on page one tomorrow. But the fact that it's the heaviest fighting, that it indicates problems persist in Lebanon that have little to do with the negotiations that are going on between the Israelis and the Lebanese, as far as we can see, all of that makes it a candidate for page one. It isn't dramatic, primarily. It is the unusual. News is change. The basic definition of news is change—what has changed in the world today and what has changed significantly. We also try to look for thoughtful stories that give the reader an insight; like the Palestinians series, which was based not on very much startling new information, but on insights that the reporter had developed. And occasionally you'll see stories on the front page that are there solely on the strength of the writing. Once in a while you have a piece that is written in such a way that you feel it is compelling.

Ghareeb: A recent study of the media coverage on the Israeli invasion of Lebanon showed that there was a close parallel between government policy statements and media treatment of crucial issues. It stated that while Alexander Haig was Secretary of State, the media tended to discount the magnitude of the Israeli invasion. When the Reagan Administration began to criticize Israel and talk about Palestinian rights, the media increased coverage and analysis of the Palestinian and Arab viewpoint. Other analyses of the elite press found a similar and close parallel between government policies and editorial opinions. To what extent does the press mirror the government's point of view on the Middle East or in other aspects of foreign affairs?

Hoagland: As my answer to your very first question about the agenda-setting would indicate, I probably don't disagree with your conclusion. I disagree with one point in the analysis, though. Haig's statements did indeed help condition the media to report that the Israeli invasion seemed to have limited goals, as did the Israeli statements at the time. It was the fourth, fifth and sixth days, if you go back and look at the coverage, when the Israelis were clearly going beyond what Haig was saying. That was what did it. It wasn't Shultz coming up. By the time Shultz came into it, the issue was dead. But I agree with you about Haig's statements—after

232

all, the man was Secretary of State, and said, "I've been told this by the Israelis." The media is loath to call somebody a liar the first or even the second day. It takes four, five or six days. And Haig got away with it. I think every indication, by the way, is that he also misled the President— that his statements to the President were pretty much the same statements that he was making publicly. And that may have had a role in his demise.

Ghareeb: Doesn't this raise a question about the role of the media? Shouldn't experienced watchers such as yourself at least have raised questions about, for example, Israeli intentions?

Hoagland: Yes. I would have to go back and look at the coverage and see at what point we did that. I think everybody expected—beyond Haig's statements—that they were going to go up to the Litani, that it was going to be an efficient version of what happened in 1978. I don't think that there was that much expectation either by us or by Haig or by the Lebanese government that they were going to go into Beirut.

Ghareeb: There were a few reports, but they were very few and sketchy, that said they might go to the outskirts of Beirut.

Hoagland: I just don't recall at what point we started questioning statements.

Ghareeb: I think it was about the latter part of June. How does this relate to other aspects of Middle East coverage?

Hoagland: You're talking now from a news standpoint. I can't really answer on editorials. It conditions what you are looking at. It conditions the way you look at a situation. I think in some cases some of our correspondents have a very high degree of scepticism about this government's statements on the Middle East. That's encouraged by what they hear from American diplomats in the field about the policy here in Washington. And you will find frequently that there is a gap. It has always been my experience that the American Ambassador in an Arab capital, when he knows you, will describe privately for you quite a different view of the problem than the one that is publicly stated in Washington. And correspondents hear that and I think they probably tend by and large to believe the man on the scene more than the public pronouncements from Washington. That's a very important factor in shaping the thinking of correspondents—news reporting—about the Middle East. They view the public pronouncement as one element, and frequently as one of the less reliable elements of the situation. They also go around and talk to the

American Ambassador, to the French Ambassador, to the Lebanese President or whoever they can talk to to get other perspectives on it. I don't think, if I understand the problem you are raising, that that's the problem.

Ghareeb: How many correspondents do you have at the State Department?

Hoagland: Three.

Ghareeb: How does that work out? Do you get independent and completely different points of view? Are they coordinated in any way?

Hoagland: They are generally coordinated. I will go back and talk to them and we will try to come up with something. And you will see from time to time a foreign story, a Beirut story and a Washington story. It used to happen on Iran a lot. That was the clearest example that I can think of. We would have stories from Iran saying that there was no way the hostages were going to be freed, running beside stories out of Washington saying the hostages were going to be freed. And we would run both stories and in fact put the reader in the position of having to make up his mind, because in those cases we couldn't coordinate. We couldn't come to an agreement. Our man in Iran was convinced he was right. The State Department man was convinced he was right.

Ghareeb: A survey by Professor Robert Lichter of what he calls the "National News Media Elite" indicated that 72 percent of the group believed that the United States is morally obliged to defend Israel militarily, while the general public support for this regime never exceeded 34 percent. How do such views on the part of journalists affect the media's coverage and editorial opinion on Middle East issues?

Hoagland: I'm not familiar with that survey, and I wouldn't want to accept that as a fact. I am not aware of any such question being put to our reporters. One of the things you have to understand about *The Washington Post*, and my last answer suggested it, is that it's very much a reporter's newspaper. We rely on our reporters. We have faith in them. When the point comes when we don't have faith in them any more we take them out. But we don't change their copy very much. We don't change the facts very much, so it is up to the reporter; we have "individuals" working for this newspaper.

Ghareeb: Recently you appeared on a television program in which an analyst spoke of a "gap" between the public and the media. To what extent do you feel this is true, especially as applied to international affairs or Middle East affairs?

Hoagland: I don't feel that so keenly. A recent poll by William Schneider showed that a majority of the people that he talked to think that the media's greatest problem is that it lacks credibility in the sense that it's the government's handmaiden. I think that came as quite a surprise to us. I talked to Bill Greider about this when he was still here. We were talking about Central America in fact, where we had come under incredible criticism from the Administration for not telling the truth, backing the guerrillas, being lefties, and all that stuff. I was talking to Greider about it, and he said, "You know, they are right. The people don't believe in it. The public doesn't believe us. They believe that we are lying on behalf of the Government." And I think that's something that we tend to forget, that the skepticism holds that the government and media are in bed together. It's the same kind of distrust they have about the government.

I don't feel any great sense from our general readership of distrust of our coverage of foreign affairs. On the contrary, most of the response I get, with the exception of the Middle East and largely with the exception of the Jewish community in Washington, which has been quite critical of our coverage as you know, is laudatory, reinforcing and positive.

Ghareeb: Much of the criticism about the coverage of the crisis in Lebanon is that while you sometimes appear to overplay the internal problems inside Lebanon, you seem to downplay the external sources which manipulated the internal Lebanese situation from 1969 onward.

Hoagland: Nothing that I ran in my section had any sentiments like that. If you look back at our four-part series on southern Lebanon in 1979, that was a very good example of looking at Lebanon and some of the external pressures on Lebanon, specifically the Israeli pressure and intentions in southern Lebanon. We have done some of that. We probably didn't do as good a job looking at Syrian intentions in Lebanon. We did so early on, when the Syrians first came in; we had a lot of stories. It is that problem of being current. You say it and you write it. You write it five times in two months, and then you move on to something else. And the situation remains, as the Syrians are still there even today.

Ghareeb: An Israeli professor recently said not to blame all of what happened in Lebanon on Sharon and Begin. According to him, Israeli policy toward Lebanon started as early as the 1950s and 1960s. He said he could give you specific dates in 1969 when Israel bombed the Beirut airport, and they bombed the south and forced the southern refugees to go to Beirut, putting pressure on the government to fight the Palestinians. Actually I thought that was a fascinating point of view and yet it didn't come clear in the media.

Hoagland: I agree. I can remember writing stories in 1972 in Lebanon on that very point. Let me just say we have not yet gone back and looked at that. I am aware of what he's talking about. I'm aware of some of the things that Sharett has written in his diaries, for example, about Lebanon.

Ghareeb: Some critics of the American media say that the Arabs should themselves be blamed, that they are responsible to a certain extent because they don't understand all the problems that they face in the American media because they don't acknowledge the nature of American journalism. I would like to get your opinion on this. How have you dealt with the Arabs in the past? Have you had any problems of access? Do you feel that some of your correspondents face the same problems today?

Hoagland: Much less. I'm always a little suspicious of the argument, whether it's put forward by the individual persons involved or put forward on their behalf by somebody else, that it's all a public relations problem, and if only they were better at public relations, everybody would understand their wonderful cause. I think in relationship to the West, and the West's perception of the Middle East, many Arabs thought for a long time they couldn't make their case, so they felt they might as well not even try, and then blamed the public relations apparatus rather than having to get into a serious discussion about the case. I think there was some of that. I think there was a huge cultural gap for a long time, but it has narrowed a great deal. Certainly, television has probably had a good effect in that sense, as it has made people around the world much more aware of the opportunity, and the advantage of putting your case to the American people.

So I think there has been a significant improvement in access for American journalists. Not universally; I'm not sure Saudi Arabia is terribly different today than it was ten years ago when I started working here. Or South Yemen. We've only had one correspondent get into South Yemen ever, since the existence of South Yemen. Egypt has changed a lot. I went to Egypt when the Soviets were still there. Clearly, it's a very different game. Even up until the 1973 War. The 1973 War was the real breakthrough. Sadat's October 16th press conference was the real breathrough, when he said in effect, I've gone to war to make peace. That one day changed the way reporters looked at him, and the way he was reported on. I think that it is really a significant date in the change of public attitudes toward Egypt. The Arabs are doing much better. The Palestinians have changed; they're much more adroit in this war in granting access, in getting reporters and aiding reporters to report what was going on. That always gives you some collateral gains.

Ghareeb: Some of the critics say that while there has been improvement in the coverage of the Palestinian issue, that is still not true when it comes to other Middle East issues: the Iraq-Iran war, for example, or the conflict between Somalia and Ethiopia.

Hoagland: I would agree with that. But again, if you're in Iran or Iraq, and you don't have diplomatic relations with the American government, you don't have an arms supply arrangement, you're not *getting* anything, you're really facing an American government that is treating this with benign neglect as a deliberate strategy. Why are you even concerned about American public opinion? You are probably just as well off from your own narrow standpoint. You perceive yourself to be losing nothing by keeping Western reporters out, because you are not going to get anything from the American government anyway. That's a case where there's no policy gain to be had from letting the media in, so therefore it doesn't happen. The Israelis have understood from day one the importance of public opinion in the U.S., particularly in a country where your major metropolitan center, New York, has a heavy Jewish population. You can influence public attitudes greatly.

Ghareeb: There are some people who feel that this broad and dramatic coverage of the crisis in Lebanon, for example, inhibits diplomacy. Do you feel that this is true?

Hoagland: I don't think so. I'm sure that it inhibits diplomacy somewhat, but I probably have a less exhaustive view of diplomacy than I should have, having seen it used so often as a shield or a cover. The essential questions are often resolved by public opinion, which becomes the policy that the diplomats then implement. The situation in Beirut is a good example. The changes that were caused by public opinion are still being felt and will still be felt a year or two years or three years from now. They weren't felt in that early period when Phil Habib was negotiating a cease-fire. The impact was marginal. If there was an impact on diplomacy, it stopped Sharon from the total destruction of West Beirut. It caused the Palestinians, the PLO, to hang on longer than they might have otherwise, but not significantly longer. I don't think it affected the Syrian role in any way.

Ghareeb: What kind of pressure have you come under? Have there been attempts by other people to influence you—specifically by the pro-Israeli lobby or the pro-Arab lobby?

Hoagland: The *Post* is a newspaper that is proud of the independence that it gives to its reporters and its editors. The only pressures that I have ever felt from the top of this organization have been to cover a story and cover it well. And that's it. There is no, "Do you think we are being too hard on x or y?" They pay me to make the judgments about the coverage. We have received a lot of letters, a lot of phone calls. We have engaged in a lot of discussion about our Middle East coverage, a lot of it with the Jewish community. And I think a lot of it has been very healthy. There are some extreme cases. There are some very shrill voices that are not at all interested in coverage or objective journalism, but rather they are interested in an emotional cause. We tend to disregard those voices. We listen to more reasonable, more reasoned discussion and criticism of our coverage and see if we can identify the things that we feel we are doing wrong. On the whole and almost without exception we've come to the conclusion that we've done a good job. We feel very proud of our coverage, so proud that we intend to nominate our Lebanon coverage group for the Pulitzer Prize. That's what we think of our coverage.

Ghareeb: Some people have raised questions concerning the *Post's* decision to have a representative of the Jewish Community Council observe its procedures. I believe his name was Berenbaum. How did that work out? Have you ever had anybody from the Arab-American associations or . . . ?

Hoagland: Yes, Michael Berenbaum. Berenbaum came in from the Washington Jewish Community Council. That came about after several discussions, particularly last summer, with Berenbaum and one or two others from the council. They requested a meeting; they wanted to come in and discuss our coverage. During the course of the conversation, Bradlee invited Berenbaum—he said in effect, 'If you don't believe me, I'm telling you that we're not biased, that we're not against Jews, we're not anti-Semitic, it's not a plot. If you don't believe me, why don't you come down and sit here for a week and take a look at it.' Berenbaum accepted the invitation and he came down and he went around the newsroom for a week. He was told, and he agreed, that he would not attempt to change anything—that he was here solely to observe the way we put together stories, how we do our job. And he did that; he asked a lot of questions. We had a lot of discussions. I was perfectly satisfied at the end of the week that he went away understanding the pressures of deadlines, the pressures of space and the normal human failings, and I think that if you asked him, he would tell you that he went away understanding that it's not a conspiracy, that it's not a plot and that in fact it's more chaotic down here than anything else. It's a miracle that we put out a daily newspaper at all. But it is really very decentralized; that is the point.

The week before Berenbaum came, I had invited Mr. Madani, Director General of *Okaz* newspapers in Saudi Arabia, to stay as my guest for as long as he wanted. He spent part of the day here.

We do it, we invite people to come in and sit in our news conference and do what Berenbaum did. Normally it is not a result of a complaint. Normally it is not a party that feels aggrieved. But we are quite open to having people come in and watch what we do. I guess your question to me is—if a representative of an Arab-American group were to call or write Bradlee and make a serious case, what would Bradlee say? I think I know what he would say but I'd rather have you ask him. I know what I would want him to say.

Ghareeb: Has anyone from the Arab-American community tried to reach him?

Hoagland: We're always willing to talk to anybody who's got a good case to make. Nobody has made the case yet on the Arab side, as far as I know. But there's certainly nothing in our constitution that says we'd only do it for Jews and wouldn't do it for Arabs.

Ghareeb: Do the people who call complain about specific articles?

Hoagland: A lot of them go to the Ombudsman, and he tries to deal with them. Some come in to our desk and I usually get little notes about them from the people who take the calls. We have some regular callers who basically want to harass us. I tend to ignore those. I don't return the calls of three or four people because I think they are for harassment. If any serious call comes in—like we got one the other day about a map. . .

Ghareeb: Why is it that the *Post* has published a map that shows East Jerusalem and the several hundred square miles annexed by Israel in 1967 as part of Israel?

Hoagland: No, no, not always.

Ghareeb: You have other maps, true. But the one in question, you ran recently—two or three days ago?

Hoagland: I wasn't here; we got a note on it. We sent another note to the map department. It's a mechanical problem. We get a base map that shows that and nobody thinks to do it differently. We sent another memorandum saying we want to indicate that the status of Jerusalem is in dispute.

Ghareeb: Sometimes the *Post* has a story that says one thing and its headline says something else. How do you try to deal with this type of problem?

Hoagland: We have a review system of headlines that doesn't always work. Occasionally we get a bad headline.

Ghareeb: The article you carried about Abu Nidal was headlined on the inside page, "PLO Terrorist," while the thrust of the article was that he is against the PLO. This type of article continues to stereotype the PLO.

Hoagland: Yeah, we had two headlines on that story. The front page one was a good headline, no problem with that one. When I looked at the one inside, I saw that it was a bad head, so I put a note out to everybody saying this is a bad headline for several reasons. Headline writing is a very difficult art. I did it for two years and it is extremely difficult. And we just have to get better at it.

Ghareeb: There was one *Post* story during the Lebanon invasion in which you had two pictures. One showed Israelis praying for war dead; the other showed the Palestinians shooting rockets.

Hoagland: That is also something that we could do better. I won't comment on that specific incident, because I don't remember it.

Ghareeb: Do you ever get any calls from the U.S. Government about certain stories? What kind of a relationship do you have with the State Department or the White House concerning foreign relations?

Hoagland: With this White House, very little. I'm not sure they care. I'm not sure they're reading them. I get very little in the way of formal complaints from the State Department. Once in a great while—maybe once every six months—they might call and say we've got something wrong. It's very rare. I know a lot of people from my own time out in the field, and I engage in occasional conversations with them. If they think we did something wrong, then I briefly hear about it in a friendly or joking way. But they are reluctant to do that. I can't think of one example. Recently I had lunch with an old friend of mine for social purposes. He works in the European bureau and we had run a couple of stories that had angered a particular desk officer, and the guy had some good points. The stories weren't that good and he had picked up on a lack of understanding; he had given it to my friend since he knew he was having lunch with me, and my friend showed me the stuff. But that's the only time in the last six months I can think of that that kind of thing has happened.

Ghareeb: Sometimes the press is used by people within the government for their own purposes, to leak a certain story.

Hoagland: One of my great concerns is that we tend to be used much too much by people who leak us stories for specific and often unhealthy reasons. We have an obligation to examine the motivation of our sources and, taking that into consideration, make our decision about publishing. I suppose I have a more puritanical view of that than most of my colleagues here. I am much more concerned about the question of malice of sources than the newsroom as a whole.

The basic thing I am arguing is that we should tell the reader what we know about the motivation. I want some indication in there that this leak comes as the secretary of state is leaving on this trip and comes from a source who has a vested interest.

Ghareeb: In a recent television interview you said that the American media were more or less following in the footsteps of the Israeli media in raising issues about the invasion. Why should the American media become inhibited in its criticism of Israel?

Hoagland: I think this is true. Following in the footsteps is not in fact exactly what I said. I think we were pursuing parallel tracks. It's a better way to put it.

Ghareeb: I think it makes a difference whether you are following them. Are the media inhibited about posing some of these questions? I know you have done some of this recently regarding human rights violations. The question of settlements, for example, the massacre at Sabra and Shatila seems to be portrayed as an error of judgment on the part of the Israelis.

241

Hoagland: Part of it is an expectation on the part of many Americans, most Americans who deal with these issues, that the Israelis basically play by the rules of the democratic game. There is that expectation. When you run into a situation like the one you are referring to, it is a lapse, not a systematic policy. I don't think most Americans believe that Israelis conduct torture on a systematic basis. So there is the question of expectation. There is also the question of a double standard.

Ghareeb: Had it been a country other than Israel. . .?

Hoagland: But the argument is the other way around because Israel is an open society and Israel permits people to go to the West Bank and reporters are there. When one Arab boy was shot during a rock-throwing melee, *The Washington Post* put that story on the front page.

Ghareeb: Don't you think that the treatment would have been a little bit different. . .?

Hoagland: I think so. The answer is a simple one in a way because of the peculiar history of Israel, which you could say about any country— because of the peculiar history of Ireland, we cover Ireland a certain way. But, yeah, I think because there is such an underlying pre-disposition by most Americans to assume the best about Israel, it probably is given more of the benefit of the doubt than most countries would be.

19

Interview with HODDING CARTER

Mr. Carter hosts Inside Story, *a talk show about the U.S. media televised on the Public Broadcasting Service. He was a State Department spokesman during the Carter Administration.*

Peterson: Some suggest that the media play a quasi-governmental role in American politics. What is your assessment of the role of media in shaping U.S. foreign policy?

Carter: It is not particularly meaningful if you mean that the media is an active player which, of its own volition, suggests policy and carries through in a public debate to get that policy implemented. It is not a policy player like, let us say, an advocate of a certain position. It is far too diffuse for that. As far as its editorial voice is concerned, it is much too ineffective to be a particularly meaningful player even if it wanted to be. You can put that part of it aside.

The press, however, is a vital player in the policy process, in that it provides a number of functions and services to those who are primary players. It is often the first and almost as often the most accurate conveyer of information necessary to the policy process. It is the conduit for the views of almost all the players almost all the time, directly through quotation and indirectly through leak and non-attributable quotations. But always it is a vital mirror through which all the players can get at least some kind of view of what the others are thinking and doing. It is not a fun house mirror, but obviously distorts, nonetheless, for any number of reasons, not the least of them being that it has neither the space nor time for full representation of the views of all the parties. Because of its limitations of space and time, the press is an important player in the policy process, because it edits out so much while including so much. It does not set the agenda, and it is always a mistake to say that the press does. But once an agenda is set by the major players, the press will then decide which items are really important and which items are not. And as hard as a government may try, it cannot get the press to be simultaneously interested in and concerned about the large number of items the government is concerned about.

Peterson: How does the government use briefings, and how does the press handle them? Can it extract statements from the government or change the tone of policy?

Carter: For the government, a briefing is simply what it hopes is the most controlled way to present its formal position on issues to other governments, to the public at large and to the political players in the country. It is a media trumpet to the world, in effect, of its very carefully modified and articulated views and positions. It has one desire, which is to hold what it is saying within the direct outlines of its current public posture, whatever that may be, without regard even for whether the public posture is altogether in line with the private one. The press, of course, is trying to push the government spokesman to go beyond the careful public posture, and to try to get him to state with more definition what the real policy is, private and public.

Peterson: Are they ever successful?

Carter: Sometimes. They really don't have the ability to force anything out of a spokesman. They can, however, in the heat of the moment, sometimes develop through a line of questioning some reality—such as when the government is in the process of shifting a position. It often publicly does it in little steps, trying to soften the blow, trying to present it not as a reversal, a drastic reversion or revision, but simply as the logical progression of policy. The press will push like hell and often can put a spokesman at least against the wall, so that the contradiction in his trying to say, "It's business as usual," while in fact things are changing, becomes apparent. No good spokesman can be forced to say what he doesn't want to say.

Peterson: Does the press "lobby" by trying to direct you through a series of questions?

Carter: Of course, they do. Almost every kind of grouping in the nation and in the world plays that game in the briefings. You can see it happening when suddenly a certain subject will arise. And it will be hammered. The Middle East is always a good case in point. It is probably the most closely examined area of the briefing in which the reporters represent various concerns, Israelis in the largest numbers. But any number are constantly examining and pushing on policy to see whether there has been any deviation from what is by now almost the bible of policy positions, which are so intricate that the change of a comma or a word has a great significance. I remember for the first six months that I was the briefer I refused to discuss Jerusalem because I simply didn't understand enough about exactly what the policy was supposed to be. I'd just say, "Boys, you'll take your guns from old guns, and wait until the briefer gets up to snuff on this one." I knew there was no winning that until I understood precisely what the nuances were of the current people involved.

Peterson: When you were playing that role, what were the real pushes by the press with regard to the Middle East?

Carter: There was always the 1975 Kissinger secret agreement of no negotiation, no recognition, no direct negotiation with the PLO until such time as U.N. Resolution 242 and the PLO Charter were changed. It was a push that was constantly being tested essentially by those immediately concerned, particularly Israeli reporters or those who reflected Israeli views. And then simply by smart reporters who did not reflect anybody's views but kept wondering when we would change that crazy policy.

Peterson: How were briefings prepared? Could you predict questions and prepare for them?

Carter: Yes, it was in fact the rare briefing that you would be caught flatfooted by a question that you hadn't anticipated and the way you anticipate them is severalfold. First, the staff and the various other agencies of government are looking 24 hours a day at all the press and broadcast reports, and trying to anticipate what, on the basis of the public record, might arise in the way of questions. You also are prepared for things which weren't on the public record but you knew might soon become public, and which were inevitably going to become public. And then you put forward that handful of material which you wished to volunteer, simply as a statement of government policy to set a new tone, to state a new policy or new departure, or to restate emphatically something which seems necessary to restate. You also knew what they were going to ask, not because they would call up and say, "We're going to ask you this and that," though occasionally that would happen. You would be prepared because in the course of each day, the assistant briefer, the spokesmen and various people around the building would get phone calls from reporters working on their own stories, which fed back into the spokesmen's office. Now, that still doesn't mean that every day, all the time, you know what they're going to ask. It does mean you are usually prepared for far more questions then are asked because the press generally settles down on a couple of topics for the day and strangely seem to ignore or just can't digest a lot of stuff and don't really go after much. I was always surprised at how few things they really went after. There are always, as I started to say, some questions that do arise that you didn't expect, a leak that catches you right in the eye. People have their own ideological hobbyhorses which are just simply off-the-wall questions as far as what a spokesman ought to be dealing with, but which are legitimate. You just can't anticipate them.

Peterson: How would you compare the questions posed by U.S. correspondents to those posed by the Israeli press and by the Arab press?

Carter: The main difference is that, logically enough, those who care about the immediate concerns of the Middle East whether from the Israeli or from an Arab perspective are much more single track. They don't really tend to give a damn about what the current position is on nuclear nonproliferation or something. On the area itself—now let me be careful here because there were some standard American reporters who would develop, without any particular axe to grind, the questioning about as exhaustively as somebody from the region—but basically the difference is the thoroughness and intensity with which reporters from the region will try to develop the subject. Also, those speaking from the perspective of the region are more likely to have been fed the information that they are bringing to the briefing from an embassy or an official other than an American, while the Americans, though often fed obviously by the Israeli and other embassies, are more likely to bring a perspective which has been fed from somewhere inside the building.

Peterson: Of the Arabs and the Israelis, is one group more effective than the other?

Carter: I don't think there's any question about who's the most vigorous on a regular basis. The Israelis are more vigorous on a regular basis and they go at it more tenaciously. However, there were a couple of "Arab journalists" representing any number of different kinds of outlets who were as persistent and about as well informed as the Israeli correspondents. I always had the sense, even though it wasn't even necessarily true, that there were more coming at it from a perspective which can loosely be called interested in Israel then from a perspective that could loosely be called interested in the Arab side.

Peterson: Do you see a shift?

Carter: When I left almost two years ago, I understood from those who had been there longer than I that there were more and better Arab reporters than there had been in the past. I simply don't know about the last two years.

Peterson: What do you think about the portrayal of the Arab in the American media?

Carter: You've got to start with something that Americans never liked to admit or say, which is that the portrayal of virtually all folk outside the Western industrial nations usually amounts to a fairly crude caricature.

Peterson: Is that true for the Israelis?

Carter: No, the Israelis from the media perspective since day one and from the American perspective have been portrayed and seen as an extension of the Western world—the European style of democracy in the Middle East, that sort of thing. Third World people, to use a loose characterization, are almost always caricatured simply because they are less known and there is less inclination to pay a lot of attention to them.

Peterson: Do you perceive a maliciousness in some of the stereotypes that you see on popular television now, or in the press, particularly toward the Arabs?

Carter: There's a particular subgroup which is made up of Arabs within the larger reality that there's a fairly crude caricature of Third World folk. The Arab portrayal has been almost totally wrapped up in either the notion of the totally dissimilar flowing robes, desert life, a different and strange religion, the unknown other out there, or the known and disliked other out there who had in the last ten years his hand on your throat with oil, or the unknown other out there seen as the murderer of children and women, and responsible for terrorist raids on Israel. One of the extraordinary (meaning out of the ordinary) results of the last two months has been, for the first time, a regular portrayal of weeping mothers and shattered children, and those mothers and children have not been Israelis, but Arabs. Unless it's in a war of Arab against Arab, that's almost unheard of.

Peterson: As far as the representation of the Arabs in the United States is concerned, do you think part of that problem is due to the lack of accessability of Arab cultures to American jounalists? How important is that?

Carter: Of course, I think it's very important. A reporter is only as good as his own understanding of a place, of a culture, of a people, and most reporters just automatically coming out of the West, out of the United States, out of a certain set of traditions and values, are running up against a great unknown. Even if academically known, there is a great emotional and psychological distance between his own perceptions of reality and those of other cultures, whether Arab or otherwise. Americans, for heaven's sake, suffer from culture shock when they go to Western Europe. God knows they do when they go out into North Africa, sub-Saharan Africa or Asia.

Peterson: But why don't those correspondents focus more on some of these cultural aspects?

Carter: There's no market for them. To be absolutely candid about it, that kind of journalistic focus really doesn't make it into the 30, actually 22-minute broadcast and into most stories because in fact the reporter only gets copy out of most of the Third World in the event of confrontation, conflict, chaos, change or catastrophe, when it's considered to be of interest and therefore journalistically worth the expenditure of time and space.

Peterson: So we continue with crisis reporting?

Carter: That's the name of the game. We are committed in the business to the idea, based on audience and reader surveys, that most Americans most of the time are interested in foreign news. So, a lot of our news coverage is almost considered in the category of public service. I happen to believe all those surveys are wrong, in that they only reflect the diet that people are given. A more intelligent and more consistant approach would change the perception of people's needs. But at any rate, if you consider foreign news to be a drug on the market, then you go for the foreign news which seems to have some kind of handle that people can grab hold of, and that's almost always conflict and catastrophe.

Peterson: Does the State Department only use the elite press in order to articulate its policies or make leaks?

Carter: It is the usual technique to do that. We basically use what you're calling the elite press as the vehicle of choice for leaks. And leaks are of course not something for the most part that come out of the hands of little moles in the subterranean bowels of these buildings. They tend to come from the sixth and seventh floors. And all this nonsense that comes out of every White House about the horror of all these disloyal second-echelon people shoveling out the information is just that, nonsense. Most leaks are the calculated placing of information by major players trying to effect policy before it is enunciated, trying to change it after it is enunciated, trying to get it accepted or trying to send messages. I used to always say at the staff meetings that I'd agree when word would come back from over across town that leaks have got to stop. I would confess that certainly I had been a player in the game. But I'd say that you cannot demand from the top what the bottom sees the top doing all the time. You've got to stop it there first, and let discipline be seen to be the name of the game at that level. But of course no president, president's staff, or secretary of state's staff would ever agree to that in the present climate. The game has become too inbred. You will occasionally see leaks planted with non-American papers for various reasons. But only occasionally.

Peterson: And with regard to the Middle East?

Carter: On the Middle East, almost invariably the leak goes straight to an Israeli bait. There are some other reasons for that, and in a number of the countries it is pointless to go that route simply because the connection between press and government is so close. You might as well just go straight to the government with whatever you want. You're not really having to deal with integers that are separate from each other in a meaningful way that you can see.

Peterson: Do any important examples of circumstances under which things were leaked to the Israeli press come to mind?

Carter: Frankly, specifics don't come into my mind. But you would often see stories identifying the players in various controversies within an administration and rather clearly setting forth where all of them stood on issues making it into the Israeli press. Decisions on certain matters of policy affecting Israel are much more likely to suddenly appear in the Israeli press than they would in almost any other. That is to say, I cannot imagine the number of leaks that vouch top policy debates and positions, even those affecting European countries, that you see appearing in the Israeli press about American decisions affecting Israel. It's really extraordinary, but that's the way it is.

249

20

Interview with JIM LEHRER

Mr. Lehrer is the co-host of The MacNeil-Lehrer Report *televised by the Public Broadcasting Service.*

Ghareeb: What are some of the key factors that determine what type of people you choose for your program, especially when it comes to discussing foreign affairs?

Lehrer: There are many things. The first criterion is the story, the development that we're going to report on. The next factor is the people; who would the best people be to come on and talk about it. Then, we find out who's available and who will come. We have what we call the Brezhnev-Carter rule. If we do a story about problems between the Soviet Union and the United States, ideally, we would like to get the president of the United States and the president of the Soviet Union to get on and debate it. That's the ultimate; that's where you always start. But you don't always get there.

Ghareeb: Is there a subjective point of view that leads you to determine who the best person is? Is the best person the most knowledgeable, the expert, or the person who can communicate his point of view better on television than somebody else? Is he from a certain geographical area? One of the points that I often notice not only on *MacNeil-Lehrer* but on some of the other programs is that they usually bring people only from Washington or New York. Are these the only people available? Isn't there a certain milieu that influences all of these people and moves them to think in a certain direction?

Lehrer: If you've got a Middle East question, for example, and there's a development that involves a very clear difference of opinion, you want somebody to represent the Arab position and somebody to represent the Israeli position. You've got two problems. You've got the problem of finding the person who has the credentials and holds the position that you decide editorially you want to represent. But because we're doing a live

251

program, you've got another criterion—the question of whether that person can articulate his position. It's a cop out to say, "We had an Arab. The fact that the Arab couldn't get his words out is his problem. The Israeli was ten times more articulate and won the argument, but this Arab was the most qualified guy." That won't work, and that is just one of the problems that you have got when you do our kind of television program. Not many times, but occasionally, one of our reporters or producers will come and say, "Sammy Sue Smith is the most knowledgeable person in a particular area, but he talks with such a heavy accent that our audience would never understand him. So we're going to have to go with the second best, who is Billy Bob Dunn." That's just the way it is. If you could sit down and talk to him and distill it like a newspaper man does, or as you do for a book, that's a different matter.

Ghareeb: It appears that your program is spontaneous, but is it?

Lehrer: It's done live. We plan, obviously, because the way we do it you have to plan. If somebody is supposed to be on there presenting a particular position, that person better represent that position or we've ended up with an unfair show. That happens to us occasionally. Somebody comes on and doesn't articulate quite as well. We plan the order that we're going to introduce and interview the guests. We certainly work out our questions in advance. However, a lot of times I'll interview my guest and never look at my questions, just because of what the guest says, and carry it on. That sort of thing.

Ghareeb: When you raise questions is there an image, a stereotype, a perception that you want these people to get out, or do you want them to focus on what you're asking them?

Lehrer: Oh, yes, absolutely. In most cases the people we interview are invited on for a specific reason, because they hold a particular opinion. My job is to help them get that opinion across so the audience understands it. I don't care what that opinion is, as long as it fits the way we're trying to structure the program. I'm not there to beat up on anybody. I'm there to help them, and to test them a little bit. Ninety-nine times out of 100 there's somebody sitting next to them who disagrees, so you can test them with the other guest. I don't have to browbeat people or play devil's advocate.

Ghareeb: How do you decide on what questions to ask? Do you usually meet as a group or. . .?

Lehrer: There's a series of things the producer and the reporter on the story work out, and then they give us a list of recommended questions. After we have read and distilled everything, MacNeil and I then write our own questions. He and I talk about it between us, and then we write them. Right before the program, which is at 7 p.m., the reporter on the story, the producer on the story, and Robin and I get on the telephone and go through every question. At that time people—anybody willing—are open to say, "I don't think that's the right question," and the reporter would say, "You ought to be prepared for this, if you ask that," and so on. So nobody's going to get surprised, at least in terms of our staff. We get surprised when we get out of the studio sometimes.

Ghareeb: How many of the people who appear on your program do you know personally, and how much time do you talk to them? Does that affect the type of questions that you raise?

Lehrer: I would estimate that I know personally less than one percent of the guests. A lot of these people have been on before, so I've met them, but of the people with whom I socialize in my private life, less than one percent appear on the show.

Ghareeb: When you're going to be discussing a certain topic, do you call and talk to people?

Lehrer: Our reporters do, our staff does, but I don't do that. The only time I talk to them is when they're in the studio. They come in about ten minutes before air time, and I go over with them in a general way what we're going to talk about. There are no secrets. I interview them and they leave.

Ghareeb: How much coverage have you devoted to the Middle East? Have you brought any new insights into the area? How would you compare your own program to other similar programs?

Lehrer: First, we have devoted a lot of time to the Middle East in the seven years we've been on the air, because the Middle East has been in the news a lot. Have we brought any new insights to it? I think over a long period of time we have. If somebody had watched us for seven years covering the Middle East, he would have a better understanding of the Arab position than if he had watched another television program over the same period. I very seldom get to see the nightly news programs, and I don't watch other television news that much because of my schedule, so I'm not in a position to give you an authoritative comparison. But that's my perception.

Ghareeb: When it comes to the Middle East, I would say that your focus, and this is not a scientific study, is first on Israel and then on Egypt or Iran. There has been almost nothing on Saudi Arabia, for example, or on the other issues in the area. Why does it happen this way and why is it that you do not focus on some of the other issues in-depth, say the Iraq-Iran War. It seems to be oriented toward the great deal of interest about Israel, and unless there's a crisis in the area, there is no focus on other developments in the area.

Lehrer: We've done a few programs on the Iran-Iraq War. It is very difficult to get information on it and to get people to come on and talk about it. The last program we did on it was excellent because we had the foreign minister of Iran and one of the Iraqi diplomats. They really got into it. But there is no independent information about the Iran-Iraq War. These two men sat one in one studio and one in the other, and you'd never have known they were talking about the same thing. Iran had crossed over into Iraq and said, "We're going all the way, we're going to throw Saddam Hussein out." The Iranian said, "Yes, we've captured this and that, the Iraqis are throwing down their arms, and the war is over." The Iraqi said that the Iranians had been stopped at the border; the war was over, and the Iraqis had won. There was no way to turn, no way to grab some independent force that could bring any kind of order or understanding to the issue. The fact is when you deal with Iran and Iraq and some of the other Mideast countries, the diplomats don't tell the truth. They tell the lie, and they do it in such a way that it is impossible to cut your way through. I had a long talk with a representative from the PLO about this. He comes on our program every once in a while, and will look one straight in the eye and say something that I know, and he knows, is not the truth. He says, "That's our thing." We do the story because we feel that we have to once in a while. But to the average American watching that stuff, it's awful.

But that didn't answer your question. That's no reason not to do the story; it just makes it very difficult for us when we do it. Why haven't we done anything on Saudi Arabia? Why have we done more on Israel? Because Israel is more involved in the news. You can argue with the definition of news, but it is a fact that the United States is the major ally of Israel, and that one-fourth of all U.S. foreign aid goes to Israel. They're using our weapons, they're using our training, etc. We are doing a program for the United States. Our program does not go all over the world. As for

254

the Saudis, you picked a bad example there. We did many, many stories on the Saudis. During the oil. . .

Ghareeb: There was something on OPEC, but on Saudi Arabia alone. . .

Lehrer: But that's where the Saudis most affect the average American for whom we're doing our program. The Saudis will never come on television to discuss foreign policy. We have invited them, but they have yet to send a representative. Not only won't they send a representative, they won't send a substitute and they won't help us find anybody. Their position has never been represented on our program because they won't play. So, when we have a Saudi Arabian story, as a Saudi Arabian angle we get a former U.S. Ambassador to Saudi Arabia or an American who is a lawyer for Saudi Arabia or a Member of Congress. The Saudis will never come on and explain themselves on our program, and I've never seen a Saudi on anybody else's television program.

Ghareeb: There have been a few.

Lehrer: There have been a few, but damn few.

Ghareeb: I think one time you had Sheikh Yamani on.

Lehrer: Sheikh Yamani is in a separate category. I'm talking about foreign policy people. For instance, the Jordanians will come. We've interviewed King Hussein several times, and we interviewed his brother once.

Ghareeb: This touches on two things that I'd be very interested in hearing you elaborate on. It seems that your program is trying to inform the American people, and ultimately, it creates a certain perception of the world. Specifically, I'm talking about the Middle East. Any reporter has preconceived ideas about people and their culture. For example, you mentioned that diplomats from Muslim countries lie. I'm sure that some diplomats lie. Maybe some lie better than others. But this could certainly be perceived as a stereotyped idea, as a distorted and biased view of people from Muslim nations or diplomats from Muslim nations.

Lehrer: I didn't mean it that way—that came out wrong. What I meant is that in most of the Middle East countries, this applies to the Israelis as much as it does to the Arabs, government officials don't come on to give you information. They come on to give you a party line. And it is black and white. But, based on seven years of doing our program, Israeli officials are much more forthcoming than Arab officials. That may be for a variety of reasons. They may be more comfortable here, and more comfortable in the language. Most of the Israeli officials they send over here have lived in this country for a long time. They are much more at ease with the media, and there may be a lot of reasons for that. But that has been my experience, and it doesn't have anything at all to do with what they say or what their positions are. An Israeli is more apt to concede your point and explain it, but an Arab is more apt to deny the point and not explain it. I'm talking about technique; it doesn't have anything at all to do with culture or religion. We had an Iranian on the program a few months ago who was a super guest in television terms. He was forceful, saying things that you might think are outrageous. But he whipped up on the Iraqi because the Iraqi wouldn't concede anything. Here again, it doesn't have anything to do with the points of view. When the program was over that night I remember telling the producer, "The people who watched that got no information at all, but they did get a feel for the people who are involved in the dispute." And there is something to be said for that.

Ghareeb: This is why I was saying that sometimes you might not be able to get accurate information about the military situation, for example. But it is also important to give people an idea about the dimensions of the problem.

Lehrer: It is also so important in those situations to give people at least the perspective of how the Iranian or the Iraqi or the Saudi or the Jordanian is looking at the thing, even though it may sound outlandish. At least you understand; you've heard it from their own lips. As I said, our problem with the Arab countries is that most of their officials won't come on.

Ghareeb: Your program was among the first to recognize what the story in Iran was all about. You had people like Khomeini interviewed. You also had people like Rouhani and Yazdi, and did a superb job with it. Why is it that you got onto the story before other networks or the newspapers?

Lehrer: Because our contacts are different. One of the strengths of our program is that our reporters don't talk just to government officials, but to people at the universities. They talk to all kinds of people. I'm always stunned when we do a program on Iran, for example, and we invite one of the leading foreign affairs reporters and an expert on Iran, and they've never met before because that person is not in the government. He's at the Georgetown Center for Strategic and International Studies, or at the Johns Hopkins School of Advanced International Studies. Reporters tend to go to government officials to get their information, you see. On Iran our reporters didn't. They were talking to other people who were saying, "I don't know what they're telling you over at the State Department, but the

Islamic revolution is real. You ought to talk to Rouhani at Columbia or a guy named Yazdi out at so and so. There's something going on here." They would never have gotten that at the State Department. They talked to him and became convinced this was real, and they did some other checking and so we went with the story. That's a judgment call, as you know. But if you don't talk to the right people, you're never going to get the right information.

Ghareeb: On Iran, I found it a bit strange to see journalists interviewing other journalists about an issue on which they probably had no more expertise. How do you explain this, and do you feel that this is a useful means of trying to get information?

Lehrer: We do it only when we have to, when we can't get the information. We're dependent on having people come on our program. If we cannot get somebody to come on who is a non-reporter, then we'll ask a reporter to come on. I agree with you basically, but it is something that we sometimes have to do in order to get things on the record. For instance, if the State Department won't come on to talk on a sensitive issue, sometimes it fits our purposes to have a State Department reporter come on and reflect on what those people are thinking and talking about.

Ghareeb: To go back to Iran, you mentioned Rouhani and Yazdi, but why is it that you did not focus on other people in the same way, such as the spokesmen or leaders of the Mujahidin Khalq or the Fedayeen Khalq, who were certainly an important part of the revolution? Why is it that you did not focus on these other diverse groups?

Lehrer: It was contact. But also, I think you would concede, the revolution centered on Khomeini. Without Khomeini there would never have been an Islamic revolution, at least not right then. There's no question that there were other elements, and at one time or another all those groups were represented on the program. There's no question that we had more of the Rouhani-Yazdi types, but over the long haul we've had all those groups represented.

Ghareeb: How much do you rely on press coverage for your information? I am referring specifically to *The New York Times*, *The Washington Post* and the weekly magazines.

Lehrer: Sure, we're like everybody else, we read all those things.

Ghareeb: Why is it that you spend so little time trying to get the people to understand the background to the problems in the area? As I said, you do a better job than others but you still wait until a crisis emerges and then focus on a story. How do you expect people to understand an issue without giving some background information beforehand, so that anybody who's not following the area closely would know that there are potential problems there?

Lehrer: We're not in the education business; we're in the news business. If you say "Good evening, there's nothing going on in Saudi Arabia but we're going to talk to you for thirty minutes about Saudi Arabia," nobody's going to watch it. What's the point?

Ghareeb: This raises two questions. First, how much of the news or the material you give is information and how much is entertainment? And secondly, do you create the news or are you responsive to events?

Lehrer: We're in the reporting business. When there are developments we try to find out what happened, report it, and explain why it happened. That's not saying we always do it well or we always do it the right way, but that's what we're here to do.

Ghareeb: I have a question on the Lebanon story. People have often referred to the Lebanese conflict as a Christian-Muslim war, as a conflict between rightist Christians and left-wing Muslims, or as a civil war. There are constant references to Saad Haddad's Christian militia. But these terms are not accurate; they are simplifications, generalizations. Why are they constantly used?

Lehrer: We have done three or four programs in the last three or four years in which we explained in detail all the various factions in Lebanon. There are certain identifications that arise. In American politics, it's like calling a certain Congressman a liberal. How do you define a liberal? These are terms that have grown up over the past several years to identify these various forces. Certainly there are subtleties, but we have explained it time and time again, and then we continue to use what we think are the words that people understand to distinguish these groups from one another.

Ghareeb: But even when they are not accurate?

Lehrer: Obviously they are accurate; we think they are accurate.

Ghareeb: Take Saad Haddad's "Christian militia," for example. The overwhelming majority of Haddad's people are not Christian.

Lehrer: But he calls it a Christian militia.

Ghareeb: No, he never has.

Lehrer: Well, that's what it's called.

Ghareeb: Another question on the issue of Lebanon. You had three or four people on the program after Bashir Gemayel's assassination. One of the people who appeared on the program was referred to as a Christian Lebanese or perhaps as a Maronite Lebanese, while the others—there was a Palestinian Christian, an American Jew and an American Protestant—were not identified on the basis of religion.

Lehrer: I don't know. On all our programs, we ask people how they want to be identified. That was worked out between the reporter and the guest. I don't remember any question that arose about that.

Ghareeb: After the massacres at Sabra and Shatila, you had an American, an Israeli, a Jewish American, Senator Dodd and somebody from the Israeli "Peace Now" Movement.

Lehrer: That's right.

Ghareeb: How do you select people like that? Why was there not someone from either the Phalangists, who were being accused of committing the massacres, or a Palestinian to represent the victims?

Lehrer: I don't remember what the decision making was on that. It was just on that particular night it had seemed the appropriate thing to do. I don't remember exactly why we did this or that. I know in that particular case there were two guests who backed out on us, one an hour before air time. We were supposed to have four guests on that program and we ended up with two. I don't remember what happened on that.

Ghareeb: Arabs, in general, believe that the American media has portrayed them in a stereotyped, caricatured fashion. Do you agree with that belief?

Lehrer: I think they have a legitimate complaint, no question about that. There's not a simple answer as to why that's happened. Arabs have to take some of the blame themselves for it. But there is no question that their image is stereotyped.

259

Ghareeb: Do you think something could be done to change that image? You put the blame on the Arabs but don't you think that part of the problem is the fact that journalists here do not know the area well?

Lehrer: Edward Said is a Palestinian who is very critical of the American press for the way it has handled the Arabs. In a recent *New York Times* article he made the point that some 300 Palestinians were massacred in Lebanon. And where are the demonstrations about that? In Israel. Not in any Arab country. Life goes on in Lebanon; there's no crisis as a result of that. Nor is there a crisis in the Arab world. But in Israel the people got so upset about it that they forced the government to take some action. His point was that until the Arabs start reacting to massacres the same way the Israeli people do, they're always going to have problems. This has not been lost on the average non-Jewish American. The United States is very upset with Israel but the Israeli people rose up and said, "Hey, government, we want to know what happened." Nobody in the Arab world even issued press releases. As Edward Said said, this feeds the stereotype that many Americans have of Arabs as bloody people who just go out killing each other all the time. That's an awful thing, and it must be awful for an Arab to see this. I can't think of a more recent example of where the problem is. This is not a public relations image problem, it's a reality problem. The most articulate Arab spokesman who is going to come on and be as straight as an arrow cannot get around that fact.

Ghareeb: Are you saying that the image is a reflection of reality?

Lehrer: I don't know. But those kinds of things contribute to a negative image, if there is one. It's much better now than it has ever been, but those kinds of things contribute to any negative feeling about some of the Arab world.

Ghareeb: To what do you attribute the improvement that has taken place in coverage of the Arab issues in recent years?

Lehrer: I think it's an increased awareness on the part of the Arab nations that if American public opinion is important, than you have to deal with it. You have to be willing to come on television programs to explain yourself. If you want the people in Kansas to understand what your position is, you have got to talk to the people in Kansas. The Israelis do that. The Israelis have always understood the need for that. If you are engaged in a battle with the Israelis for the hearts and minds of the American people, you've got to do it too, particularly when you're dealing with Israel's traditionally close ties to the United States. Israel is a democracy, and its way of life is kindred to the American way. The Arab world does not have those things going for it in the first place, so you have a double burden. In fact, you could argue that the Arabs ought to be more willing, just from a public relations standpoint, to explain the Arab perspective.

But that's not what has happened. When the Arabs were asked to talk about the massacre, with the exception of Edward Said, they ranted and raved about the Israelis. The whole thing backfired because the Israeli people really did do something. Then the Arabs were left holding the bag. For instance, what is Arafat doing? He's talking about revenge against Israel. There is no way to excuse that quest and desire for revenge, but at least somebody should go to the trouble to explain it. It's a very difficult thing to explain, there's no question about it, especially in a Lebanese context, where there's been all this bloodshed since 1975. It's unbelievable how many people have died over there, and it has created a stereotype that life is cheap in the Arab world. These kinds of incidents feed that. But it's got to be dealt with both ways. As long as the reality is staring you in the face and some incident erupts, you've got to deal with it. But at the same time there's got to be a willingness to sit down and say, "Now wait a minute, you don't understand." The Middle East didn't begin in 1948. You've got to understand cultures; things have to be explained. You say it's the American news media's responsibility to explain that. I will concede that, if you're willing to concede that without the cooperation of the Arab world there's no way we can explain it. We have tried, but we haven't been that successful. It is a very difficult thing and you've come a long way. There's no question about it.

Ghareeb: The recognition that there is a problem and how to deal with it is very important. Can you compare the problems you have had trying to get Arabs or Israeli spokesmen on your program? Have you often had problems trying to get certain spokesmen?

Lehrer: We never have trouble getting Israeli spokesmen; they will always come. We always have trouble getting representatives of Arab governments. Most of the people in Washington who represent the Arab governments will not do anything unless authorized by their home country. My feeling is that there are many Arab diplomats in this country who would love to come on our program and talk. I know a couple of them personally. The problem is by the time it goes through the bureaucracy back home the story is gone, and they've missed the opportunity. They are as upset and frustrated as anybody, but without the authorization of their government they can't come on. Their hands are tied but it's not their fault. They are very open for the most part.

Ghareeb: Have you ever tried to get foreign ministers, ministers of petroleum or prime ministers either when they are here or when they are there?

Lehrer: They usually end up not coming.

Ghareeb: They tell you they are going to come and they end up not coming?

Lehrer: They're always very nice about it. They always say they want to come, but it just doesn't come off. The exceptions to that are the Egyptians, who will play usually. The new Egyptian foreign minister has been on the program once. Usually we can get the Jordanians.

But there's a difference, a subtle difference. The Israelis will come on. It's a very interesting public relations question. When the news is the worst for the Israelis, that's when they will always come on because they feel that's when they need to be there to explain. When some news develops that is negative, or appears to be negative, you'll never get an Arab spokesman to come on. It's not his fault, it really isn't. I think it's a lack of understanding. If you want American public opinion on your side, the people in Amman and Cairo have to tell the people in Washington and at the United Nations, "Do what you think is right. If that means debating Yehudah Bloom on prime time American television, do it, whatever you think. If that means addressing the Kiwanas Club in Witchita, Kansas, do it." That's where the problem is. Am I wrong?

Ghareeb: Absolutely right, I think. This is one of the many problems, although there are others.

Lehrer: I have not met one Arab diplomat in the seven years I've been doing this program in Washington or New York, of the highest or the lowest level, who wouldn't relish the opportunity to come on. When we call an Arab embassy and say we're going to do a program, we always get a great reception because they want to do it. They know the need.

Ghareeb: Do you receive any calls or attempts by people to influence you about the type of program you do or who you put on?

Lehrer: I don't, no.

FOUR BOOKS

By Henry Ford, Sr.

THAT SHOOK

THE WORLD

THE INTERNATIONAL JEW THE WORLD'S FOREMOST PROBLEM

Being a Reprint of a Series of Articles Appearing in the *Dearborn Independent* from May 2 to October 2, 1920

Published by
THE
DEARBORN PUBLISHING CO.
Dearborn, Michigan
November, 1920

JEWISH ACTIVITIES IN THE UNITED STATES

Volume II
of
THE INTERNATIONAL JEW
The World's Foremost Problem

A Second Series of Reprints from
The Dearborn Independent

Published by
THE
DEARBORN PUBLISHING CO.
Dearborn, Michigan
April, 1921

JEWISH INFLUENCES IN AMERICAN LIFE

Volume III
of
THE INTERNATIONAL JEW
The World's Foremost Problem

A Third Series of Reprints from
The Dearborn Independent

Published by
THE
DEARBORN PUBLISHING CO.
Dearborn, Michigan
November, 1921

ASPECTS OF JEWISH POWER IN THE UNITED STATES

Volume IV
of
THE INTERNATIONAL JEW
The World's Foremost Problem

A Fourth Series of Reprints from
The Dearborn Independent

Published by
THE
DEARBORN PUBLISHING CO.
Dearborn, Michigan
May, 1922

FOUR BOOKS THAT SHOOK THE WORLD

At the zenith of his business career, Henry Ford, Sr., America's famous native son and industrial genius, sensed that a terrific effort was being made to rob him of his business, and to manipulate it into the hands of money-changers. Mr. Ford had the distinct impression that these manipulators were being advised by powerful Jewish financiers.

Henry Ford called to his office the most brilliant and intelligent research men of his time. He commissioned them to make a complete and thorough study of the International Jew. Their findings were published in *The Dearborn Independent* which, at that time, was the official organ of the Ford Motor Company. No expense was spared and it is estimated that several million dollars were spent by Mr. Ford on this project. The original articles were carried in serial form in *The Dearborn Independent* and later were published in book form. Made up into four volumes, a complete set of these books was given to each purchaser of a Ford automobile.

Perhaps the most astonishing part of Henry Ford's trail-blazing work is the fact that as early as 1920 Mr. Ford had in his posse ion a copy of *The Protocols of the Learned Elders of Zion*, and every chapter of is ooks carried a preface with a text from these *Protocols* or some published stateme f prominent Jews.

The *Protocols* had been smuggled out oi erial Russia. The Russian Intelligence Service had obtained them at the turn the century during a Zionist Congress held in Basel, Switzerland. Since that tin Jews and many of their most powerful and influential friends and fellow-travelers around the world have mounted a desperate effort to discredit the content of the *Protocols* and even to deny the existence of the document. Over half a century has elapsed and there can be absolutely no doubt that the horrifying contents of the *Protocols* have been and still are being fulfilled.

A great howl went up from the Jews as soon as *The International Jew* (as the books were now called) hit the scene. Every device in the plentiful and vengeful arsenal of the Jews was used against Henry Ford, from abuse to smear, character assassination, ridicule, physical threat, and boycott. The pressure was constant, consistent, and heavy, always with the one aim, to stop the printing of *The International Jew.*

Demands escalated and pressure increased to recall the books and to recant. An apology was demanded of Henry Ford. Incredible as it seems, publication was stopped and all available copies were destroyed. An apology was actually extracted from Mr. Ford, but it appeared over the forg d signature of one of Mr. Ford's lieutenants — Harry Bennett — and Henry Ford himself denied to the day of his death ever having signed such an apology.

Following this, Jews and their allies went into the bookstores and bought and destroyed all copies which could be found. Sneak thieves were hired to visit libraries and comb bookshelves to steal and destroy all copies. This made the book so rare that it became an instant "antique" item. It has remained a collector's item, often bringing hundreds of dollars per set.

In the meantime, volumes were sent as gifts to leading figures all over the world. It is thought that Mr. Ford's long-time private secretary, Ernest Liebold, a man of German background, may have been responsible for introducing the books and their invaluable content to leading business and political figures.

No one knows how, through whom, or when the first volume fell into the circle of men around a new name in German politics — Adolf Hitler. He himself was unable to read English, and so he was given translated excerpts. Hitler was so impressed, he started quoting from the material in his own speeches, and soon a publisher was found for a German edition. Thus, little known to the world, a great American genius became the teacher and mentor of Germany's new leader.

With his thirst for truth whetted, Hitler conducted a similar study into Jewry's involvement in German and European affairs. In this way, a great axis of understanding was forged between America and Europe. Henry Ford, Sr., the American of immense wealth, was brought to his knees and failed to awaken his people; Adolf Hitler, the political leader went on to power in Germany.

The dangers of Jewish influence to German society so well outlined by Ford in the American context, was checked by National Socialist Germany, Jews were removed from business, cultural posts, teaching positions, from the press and the armed forces.

Hitler, too, suffered defeat militarily at the hands of an unholy alliance consisting so unfortunately of his own racial brothers who had been incited into this worldwide war by the same Jewish money-lenders who had been exposed by Henry Ford, Sr.

Now, 42 years after Germany's defeat, and Henry Ford's death, this new edition is offered to you in an unabridged, *complete as the original*, version. These books belong in every White home, school, church, university, and library. To ignore the vital lessons they teach will mean race suicide and disaster for America and the world.

Today, the Jews have their own state — Israel. Let them go there, live there, work there, and create any kind of society that they desire. God only knows there has been enough blood-letting, misery, cheating, lying, and wholesale murder to bring forth that State of Israel; so after just compensation to the Arabs for the loss of their homeland, the Jews should now be forced to live in the *unholy* state they have created, for they do not belong among us culturally, spiritually, nor much less racially.

BUY THESE BOOKS NOW!

The International Jew,
4 volumes, pb. , approx. 1,000 pages — Order No.: 09004 $26.00

ALSO READ THESE EYE-OPENERS:

Ghareeb: Does the government ever try to steer you into the direction of a story or away from it?

Lehrer: The U.S. Government? Not in any way. They talk to our reporters but there's never been any overt attempt to influence our program.

Ghareeb: How about from either Israeli or pro-Israel or pro-Arab groups? Do you ever get calls from these people?

Lehrer: No calls but a lot of mail. Every time we do a story on the Middle East we always get a lot of mail.

Ghareeb: Does the response or the reaction that you get from people influence your judgment in any way?

Lehrer: It doesn't influence us, but we read it very carefully.

Ghareeb: What do you look for?

Lehrer: We read it just to see what people have to say. If, after having done a program, I feel uneasy that we may not have treated the Arab position very fairly—for whatever reason—or that the Israelis got a bad rap, the mail will usually reflect that. A new development is that Arab-Americans or people interested in the Arab cause now write letters. The Israelis and the American Jews have always done that. Before, you'd never hear from an Arab, but now we're hearing from them. It is fantastic, it really is. Whether they're right or wrong, it's just good to hear about the perceptions that people have.

Ghareeb: Does a squeaking wheel get more attention?

Lehrer: Sure it does. If I get five letters from five Arabs who say, "Hey, you know you really took some cheap shots at us last night" or "Where the hell was the Palestinian on that program last night?", it causes me to explain it. I have to sit down and write an answer and explain it. I believe that if you can't explain something, then you probably shouldn't have done it. It is a good test. If I feel that somebody has got a legitimate complaint, I'll tell them, "You're right, we made a mistake." But it's hard to explain to people, whether they're Israelis or Arabs, why on particular things we only had Israelis on. You can't fight the Middle East fight every time you do a story on the Middle East. If you're doing a story about the revolt of the people in Israel, what's the point of having a Palestinian talking about that just because it's a Middle East story. And every time we've done a few stories with just Arabs on, the Israelis have complained because the Arabs

263

are knocking the hell out of the Israelis. We always have to explain that the story we're doing is part of the Middle East story.

Ghareeb: This is true, but when there is a massacre such as Sabra and Shatila, wouldn't it have been worthwhile and valuable to get either a representative of those who had been accused of committing the act, or someone to represent the victims?

Lehrer: On the nights that we did those programs it was our judgment that what was happening in Israel was the story, and there was no outcry. One statement from the Phalangists said, "We didn't do it," and then another statement said, "Yes, we did." The American correspondent saw the Phalangist soldiers there.

Ghareeb: They saw people in Phalange uniforms, but not necessarily Phalangists. Some reporters said that there were even people who looked like Haddad's people, and I'm sure Haddad's people would never have made it there without Israeli knowledge and approval.

Lehrer: Absolutely.

Ghareeb: The reason why I'm raising this issue is because the opinion in the Arab press is that the American media have been following the Israeli media by trying to whitewash the Israeli role and their involvement. They are going to have a commission now, since a lot of pressure was applied, and we will see what it produces. The American media are also following the Israeli lead in putting the blame solely on the Phalangists.

Lehrer: That certainly is not true. Anti-Israeli stories have appeared in the American news media. The uproar in the United States over this was absolutely incredible, and it was all anti-Israeli; not anti-Phalange, not anti-Lebanese, not anti-Arab, but anti-Israeli. Americans expected Israel not to do that. The fact that the Phalange went in there and killed those 300, that's what you have to combat. And then when the Arabs don't act like it's a big deal, it feeds on that way of thinking. The Israelis are the ones who are indignant, and the Americans are indignant at the Israelis.

It was clear, or at least it appeared clear, that the Israelis were culpable by letting those folks go in there. Then when the government stonewalled it, they were culpable. It had absolutely nothing to do with anybody's preconceived ideas about Israel or the Arab world. It's just the facts. Again, all American columnists, particularly pro-Israeli columnists, have been condemning Begin and Sharon, and saying that you can't have it both ways. The Israelis are held to a different standard because they have asked to be held to that standard. They have said that they are different. We judge then by their rules, rules that they have violated. What hurts the Arabs and the Arab cause vis-a-vis American public opinion is that the Arabs have not done something comparable. By their silence they have said essentially that it is no big deal. But it is a big deal under Israeli standards. In the American press, the fact that the Israeli people held their government to these high standards was a hell of a story, and the story was reported. The American press has been derelict in not reporting the lack of Arab reaction and in really coming down on the Arab world.

Ghareeb: There has been condemnation from the Arab world, a very strong condemnation. In this case it happens that the Arabs were the victims and not the aggressors.

Lehrer: In this case they were both. They were both the aggressor and the victim; they were Arabs killing Arabs.

21

Interview with TRUDY RUBIN

Ms. Rubin is a special correspondent of The Christian Science Monitor.

Ghareeb: I know that you've been covering the Middle East for at least eight years now. What's your assessment of the American media's portrayal of the Arabs? How do you see the coverage?

Rubin: Do you mean the coverage of specific countries? Or across the board?

Ghareeb: In general, are the Arabs being stereotyped? Has the coverage been fair and balanced; has it presented an accurate picture to the American reader of what the Arabs are all about, what are their problems, what are their issues?

Rubin: I think that you have to differentiate between wire service coverage, which is what goes into most American newspapers, and the coverage of the better newspapers who keep their own correspondents out there. If we are talking about the better newspapers, I think the standards are fairly reasonable. If there is a weakness in American coverage of the Arab world, I think that that's a part of the globe where it's really helpful to have serious background knowledge, to have knowledge of the culture, of the history, and especially to have knowledge of the language, which I don't. The risky part of American coverage is that people are sent to the Middle East on a rotating basis, say every two or three years, and arrive without exposure to any of these factors: culture, language, history. It takes a while to understand what is going on. There are layers, undercurrents and crosscurrents, and it takes a sophisticated viewer to sort them out. British coverage, for example, is usually provided by people who stay in the area for much longer and often are Arabists. This also presents a risk because sometimes British and French correspondents become a creature of the area they cover. They stay there for 20 years and become so close that, perhaps, they lose the distance they need to assess more correctly. On the other hand they have the advantage of being immersed in the culture, so the pieces they write are more sophisticated and give a much more serious sense of what's going on.

Ghareeb: How does this problem, the fact that American correspondents who work in the Middle East do not know the language, and do not know the culture, affect what they are writing about the Middle East? And how does that influence public opinion?

Rubin: It's a problem that affects not only the Middle East. What it means is that the American reader might lack a deeper perspective of what things mean in the long range. In the short run I think the coverage is probably pretty reasonable. But, in the case of the Israeli invasion of Lebanon, somebody who is more familiar with the Middle East could convey to the reader an understanding of why what on the surface seems to be a situation which, as the Israelis would put it or as the Americans seem to be putting it, would offer "new opportunities" in Lebanon or for restructuring the Middle East, could instead cause cataclysms in the Middle East: why it could cause a deep sense of shame in the Middle East; why it could cause reassessments and challenges of current governments. A correspondent who had some knowledge of Islam and some knowledge of religious trends could give a much better portrayal of how the Lebanon crisis might affect currents of fundamentalism in the Middle East, whereas somebody who had just been out there for six months and didn't have too much knowledge might simply be assessing it in terms of the superficialities, i.e., that the Israelis were in the ascendency, that Lebanon could be controlled and that the PLO was busted, and might not see the long-range implications.

Ghareeb: So, we are getting an inaccurate, and to a certain extent, distorted picture.

Rubin: I'm not saying that. I'm saying that that's the risk. Having been in the Middle East from '77 to '81, I think that in the major newspapers you had some pretty good coverage. Most of the major papers manage to produce intelligent reports, and I think an intelligent reporter who has an interest in the beat is going to try to immerse himself. The difficulty is that in the initial period when they are there, when they are just learning, they won't know as much and then they won't stay as long, so somebody else will go through the same initiation period three years down the line. But in the middle I think you get a fairly good cross section. *The New York Times* has just sent down a young correspondent, Tom Friedman, who speaks Arabic, and who, I understand, has a graduate degree in Middle East studies. That is an exception. But, most of the correspondents that I've known from the *Times*, from the *The Washington Post*, from *The Los Angeles Times*, have been hard-working and have tried to get a grasp on it, and to some extent have succeeded pretty well. On the other hand, too, the American audience often isn't interested in reading in-depth analysis. I think probably a lot of the readers of papers that belong to chains, a lot of the readers in Middle America, just want the UPI type of coverage. But, to address your question specifically, I think it is true that if somebody sophisticated enough to know what they really want waits to find out what's going on in the Middle East, they probably would read *Le Monde*, or they would look to *The London Times*. They would know that they get pretty good coverage, say, in *The New York Times*. But to get the analysis of someone who one knows is an Arabist, who one knows has been going to the Middle East for years, knows the key parties, is getting as close an approximation to reality as is possible to get in the Middle East, I probably would prefer to read Eric Rouleau in *Le Monde*.

Ghareeb: What would you say to those people who are saying that one part of the problem with American journalism in general is that the American press does not go into the issues in-depth? For example, whenever there is a crisis, somebody is sent, they cover it, sometimes it is sensationalized. But it's often without a true and a genuine understanding of the issues, which is what you were hinting at a minute ago. This is one problem. What other types of problems do you see in the coverage, not only as a correspondent but also as a reader, of the American press? Since you went to the Middle East, you have gained some experience. You have a different perspective on things. What kinds of problems do you see?

Rubin: I think I have to step back a bit before I can answer that question. As with many things in a capitalist society, the product often fits the needs and desires of the consumer. In the United States, I think there is a limited readership for really in-depth coverage of probably any area, on the whole. And even an intelligent reader wants to get a grasp of foreign affairs but is probably concerned with the elements, the essence; Americans like to condense things and to get it in nuggets. I think it's probably the exceptional reader, somebody who has a special interest in the area, who wants really extensive coverage. Things are different, say, in England and France, especially regarding the Middle East. In European countries there are often special linkages with certain parts of the world. The British obviously have had long links with the Middle East. They consider themselves involved there and that creates a certain readership that's more intense, that wants some more in-depth background. Similarly, the French also have newspapers that cater to intellectuals, like *Le Monde*. The whole concept is to give an amount of material which probably very few American readers would be interested in digesting, and in an analytical way, which *The New York Times* could sustain. The purpose served is different. The French prefer to deal in ideas and the Americans prefer to deal in facts. Which is not to say *The New York Times* doesn't do analysis, but it's a different concept of the way you present news. I think that has to be stated to begin with. It isn't necessarily a problem or a fault of the coverage. It's simply that American journalism is oriented toward presenting information in a certain way. Maybe that's a weakness here and maybe it isn't. I think you can be well informed on the Middle East. I think the *Monitor* has traditionally done a good job, and as I said, I think the *Post* and the *Times* do commendable jobs.

Concerning problems in coverage, I think that there are serious problems in the Arab world in getting to the stories that one wants to cover. I certainly think it has improved, and I think that the American coverage in the Middle East has been probably much better in the past ten years, since the Arab world has changed so much in that time. First of all the Arab world has produced a generation now of age that is sophisticated and educated. American correspondents going in to cover the Gulf states 20 years ago would have had an exotic adventure story. Now they are going in talking to sophisticated, educated people with degrees from American and European universities, speaking excellent English, analyzing in terms that an American correspondent can understand. There is much more give and take. In that sense, I think the coverage of the Middle East has become much easier, much more accessible. On the other hand, you have a war like the Iran-Iraq War which is a major story, but which has not been covered well. Why is a war like that not covered well? I'm speaking from second-hand knowledge because I have never been to Iran or Iraq, and I didn't cover that. Although, having been based in Jerusalem for four years, an awful lot of my colleagues were going off to Iran regularly and to Iraq, so I certainly had plenty of feedback on what the problems were. First of all, it is a war for which Americans have very little affinity. It seems very far away. Americans don't appreciate its relevance to them, even though the U.S. has been very involved in Iran. But I think now there is a hostility toward Iran, and antipathy. People think, why should they read about this horror of war. Americans have enough just to deal with occasionally seeing Khomeini's picture in the paper. They really don't want to know any more. That's a story they'd rather forget about.

The war was not accessible, it was difficult to get to. One certainly couldn't go in from the Iranian side unless the Iranians were in a period when they wanted to show off. One could go in from the Iraqi side but in a very organized fashion from what I understand and in a very supervised fashion. And one couldn't get accurate statistics. There was no way of wandering off and encountering troops oneself, or assessing damage.

Ghareeb: Doesn't that happen in any war? In the current war in Lebanon?

Rubin: No, it's extremely different from the current war. In the current war you can go to Jerusalem, you can get in your rented car. The Israelis give you an escort and you drive up. The problem is that what you see may be censored or that you might not be able to get to some areas that you want to get to. But, basically, the American television cameras are now sitting inside. All they have to do is turn around and they can film the story.

Ghareeb: But can't they do this from the Iran-Iraq front as well?

Rubin: Yes, but from what people told me, just getting to the battle front in Iraq was such an ordeal. The Iraqis were not shipping you over in their good buses so that you could neatly cover the battle front. It was an extremely different kind of situation. Furthermore, I think that communication with the combatants in Iran and Iraq was far more difficult.

Ghareeb: This might pose a problem for covering the war, the casualties, the battle; but what about the analysis of the causes of the war? Many journalists and so-called major, prominent newspapers were explaining it as a Shi'a-Sunni conflict. Some were even saying it was an inter-Arab conflict.

Rubin: Here, again, you're getting into two factors. First of all, speaking of the journalists, and watching what goes on in my newspaper, which is the same as any newspaper, everyone's fighting for limited space. And these days advertising footage is going down which means there's less space for news copy. So, the editor, even in a high-grade newspaper, wants a story that the readership is going to read. And let me tell you, if you had a list of stories, starting with the Prince and Princess of Wales, even in a high-class newspaper, and then moving on to the Lebanese War and to the Falklands War and then you got to the Iran-Iraq War, I can tell you what would be on the bottom of the list. It is not a story which seems of relevance to the American readership. You might say, "Can't the correspondent show the reader why it's of relevance?" Well, you could, but that takes a sales job.

271

You could make an argument that a good newspaper has a responsibility to show the reader. Then you come to point two. Point two is that—as I said before—certain countries have areas where there's a natural inclination, both of the country and the reader, to want to know what is going on. For a long time I don't think Americans cared about anything in the Middle East except perhaps Israel, because there was a large group, an interest group, in America. A Jewish community which reads newspapers, reads books. So, there was an interest in copy. There has always been a disproportionate amount of news space given to Israel, compared to say what would be given to Greece or to Ireland, other areas where there would be minority segments of the population which you would think would have an interest here. But, Iran-Iraq? Now that interest has expanded in the Middle East, suddenly Americans have become interested in Saudi Arabia. So you can sell a story on Saudi Arabia and you are beginning to get expertise on Saudi Arabia because the readership wants to know and the correspondent has to learn. Iran-Iraq I don't think has reached this. I think it's the rare correspondent who has any grasp of the politics of Iraq, certainly. A lot of correspondents were in Iran because of the revolution, but that didn't mean they had a grasp. I think even the experts have difficulty totally grasping what's going on. A lot of people were supposed experts in Iran—it took them a long time to figure out that the Iranians were really going to win this thing. Everyone started out analyzing that the Iranian Army was going to fall apart, that it had been decimated, that it didn't have the spare parts, and then suddenly it picked itself up, put itself together and it took a long time even for the experts to catch up with the analysis. You don't have the expertise and so people don't know what they are doing.

Ghareeb: This is true, but let's go into something else you were saying earlier, which is that the American press just caters to the interests of the consumer. I would tend to think that it is the other way around—that the American media help shape the demand. They create the demand instead of responding to it. In the case of the Iran-Iraq War, I would tend to think that if the American media were responsible media this would be one of the most important issues in the Middle East. It's as important as any other issue and as explosive and, from the point of view of American national interests, it should have been covered in-depth, even though they could not go in there given the problems of covering the Iranian side or the Iraqi side. And yet this was not done.

Rubin: That may be true, but you can't lightly dismiss the problems of getting in there. We could say, for example, that maybe more analysis should be written back home about Iran-Iraq, but frankly speaking there have been long periods in the last couple of years when no Americans were even allowed in, at all, to Iran, whereas Europeans often could get in. That's one thing. In Iraq it has been very difficult to get a visa—except during periods when the Iraqis decided that they wanted to bring people to the front when things were going well. When one got there one often was forced to go back. I have heard great stories of difficulties and horror stories of trying to get to the front and trying to get an assessment. It is very difficult in Baghdad to get anyone to talk in an honest way, in a frank way. Even in Israel where there is censorship, there are so many divergent opinions. Right now, you have people telling you too much. You can't even print it all. Certainly in Lebanon there's no end of sources which you have to weed through, but there's a surplus of information and within that you can find some pattern of what's going on. In Iraq—much more difficult there. The Iraqis were not either accustomed to, or necessarily interested in, dealing with the foreign press except where they could see that it was to their advantage. Now that they're losing the war it's not to their advantage.

Ghareeb: But even now they have a lot of journalists going in.

Rubin: I know a lot of journalists who have applied for visas and haven't gotten them. Or it takes weeks and weeks, and by the time they get them, they're off somewhere else. The other thing is that the Iran-Iraq War has been competing with other stories in the Middle East that are more immediate to an American audience and more easily comprehensible. This isn't to excuse it. I agree that it's a very important story which has been underplayed. But I think that the difficulties really are a legitimate partial excuse. I think that the best that could have been done, and perhaps should have been done, is that more analysis should have been done from a distance. I think there's plenty of scope to do that since there are plenty of experts on Iraq-Iran.

Ghareeb: How do you think the Arabs have been portrayed in the American media and perceived by the public? Do you see any change in the Arab image since you started covering the area eight years ago?

Rubin: Yes, I see some change. I think one important change is Anwar Sadat. I think that Anwar Sadat legitimized the image of the good Arab. He became such a culture hero. Whatever his politics, he was perceived in the United States as someone like us—a good guy—and he somehow

273

crossed that barrier from the foreigner, the native, into the acceptable panoply of American hero figures. I think because of that, suddenly there was a different perception, certainly of Egyptians. I think that opened the way to a different kind of image.

Ghareeb: How much of this change in the image of Sadat and the Egyptians had to do with the fact that Sadat went to Israel? As a result, friends of Israel within the media who perceived Israel sympathetically began to portray Sadat and the Egyptians differently. Why did Sadat become a hero in 1977 and was not a hero in 1973?

Rubin: It is because he went to Israel. But I don't think that Israel is the key word. I think "peace" is the key word. I think that the image of the Arabs up until then was simply of warmongers, of people who say "No" to peace. And I think that what Sadat did was to create the image of the Arab who wants peace as much as Israel does. Because I think that for a long time the Israelis were perceived as wanting a peace settlement and the Arabs were perceived as being against peace—with a lot of the negative images that went with it. Now, there are a lot of contradictory sounds that come out of the Arab world. It's a big place; there are a lot of countries with different politics. Israel is one country, with a leadership that speaks in a way that Americans can understand and usually has leaders that speak clear and eloquent English. Arab leaders as individuals were not well known in the United States—I suppose Nasser was fairly well known, but to people who were interested in the Middle East, or maybe beyond that. But, he was not a figure who would be common currency among the American public. Sadat became a known figure, a person with a name, a person who was seen as possessing all kinds of good characteristics—a peace lover, an international figure. He was a charmer, too. This obviously was a factor as well. Perhaps he was more charming to the Americans than he was to the Egyptians, but it didn't hurt him.

Ghareeb: A lot of people have been saying that Sadat did help. Of course, other factors contributed to this changed perception, too. But there has been some agreement among the people interviewed that a stereotyped image of the Arab has prevailed, either of the oil sheikh controlling the jugular vein of the United States or of the Palestinian terrorist.

Rubin: Sometimes I get impatient with this. I think that there is a lot of unfairness in cartoons and so forth that always portray the Arab as some kind of bad sheikh or as a greasy bandit—this is unfair. However, who are the Arab leaders that Americans are familiar with? Let's get right down to it. Yasser Arafat is probably the most publicized Arab leader next to the late Sadat and behind him come the anonymous oil sheikhs. I don't think the American public really knows one from another. They don't know Crown Prince Fahd from King Khalid. The idea is flowing robes, black headbands and suitcases full of money. So, we have the stereotypes. I ask you, and I don't say this facetiously, why doesn't Yasser Arafat shave? Yasser Arafat portrays a certain image. He has almost flaunted that image. Public relations has never been his bag. On the one hand the PLO is among the most media conscious of Arab groups; on the other hand, it has never really been interested in concentrating on presenting an image that would be comprehensible to the American public. Yasser Arafat says one thing one day, Abu Ayad says another thing the next day. Arafat projects—he choses to project—that image.

Ghareeb: Don't you think that part of what we were talking about is the media's failure to cover the issues and, instead, to synthesize certain aspects. Maybe Arafat does not shave, but why focus just on that? Why not focus on the issues? Castro never shaved. And yet he was portrayed in certain segments of the American media, including the elite press, as a hero. Ho Chi Minh had a beard, also, and a number of other revolutionaries in other parts of the world were portrayed in a more evenhanded, more balanced way. At least the media tried to present the issues, the reasons why they were fighting.

Rubin: I think there are two issues here. First of all, if you're talking about image in general these days, a lot is portrayed by the television camera and we all know that television gets a disproportionate portion of the news. Here visuals count. Secondly, the causes of Castro and Ho Chi Minh were more easily comprehensible because they were seen as a zero-sum game. Castro was fighting against an ugly dictatorship on an island in which he was a Cuban. It was clear to Americans that he was trying to push out another Cuban who was corrupt. Ho Chi Minh, the same thing—it depended on who you thought were the good guys. Since the south seemed corrupt and so forth a lot of people felt Ho Chi Minh was the good guy, so they sympathized, or even if they didn't sympathize, at least what he was doing seemed legitimate. I think that it was a long time before the Palestinian situation could be seen here as anything but a zero-sum game. For a long time, the way it was presented by the Palestinians to the media was if we win they lose, if they win we lose. I think once the Palestinians started changing that line, you know, by saying there's a possibility for both sides to win, then they started getting more favorable press coverage.

But they keep undermining that line. Every time they would say there's a possibility for both sides to win then the next day someone would say, but of course it's just the first stage and then the second stage is we win. But I think that since 1974 the Palestinians have gotten tremendous press coverage. Anyone who says that people have been ignoring the PLO, the Palestinians, has not been observant. Ever since the cover stories when Arafat came to the U.N. in '74, there has been a great deal of coverage of the Palestinians, endless stories not just about the PLO but about the Palestinians in camps, the Palestinians in Jordan, the Palestinians here, there and everywhere. I've been involved in covering this issue since 1974 and there were reams of coverage, and I think a lot of it very sympathetic, so I don't think that the problem is that the issue isn't covered.

Ghareeb: But isn't it true that the press has always emphasized that they were Palestinian "terrorists"?

Rubin: If you look at the coverage in *The New York Times, The Washington Post, The Christian Science Monitor, The Los Angeles Times*, I think that the only time that the Palestinians are referred to as terrorists is when they place bombs inside Israel and they kill civilians, or where they come in on raids and kill civilians. Then they're called terrorists. Or, on the West Bank, in incidents where people are killed, as in Hebron. But, when articles are written about Palestinians in camps in Lebanon, as you will frequently find in *Time, Newsweek, The New York Times*, nobody refers to them as terrorists. They're referred to as guerrillas.

Ghareeb: This is just in the last few years rather than. . .

Rubin: Right, but that's what we're talking about. What I'm saying is that the Palestinians started getting better coverage when they started putting out a better class act, when they started talking in language the West could understand. Sometimes it's done very cynically and reporters aren't stupid. When you sit in an office and you know people well enough that they tell you, "We put this guy in Paris as our representative because he knows how to talk to the Western audience," reporters take it in. But at the same time I think that the press covering the Palestinians were willing to take seriously and did take seriously the coverage of changing Palestinian political views and the coverage of attitudes toward a West Bank state. Arafat is always referred to, frequently referred to, in the media as a moderate, although the Israelis challenge this. Well, those reporters who call him a moderate are those reporters who have made an assessment of the relative moderation of various Palestinian groups and consider him a moderate because he's willing to accept the mini-state. Well, I think that's fair coverage. The Israelis consider it biased coverage. Regarding the use of the word "terrorist," sometimes I think wire services filing from inside Israel refer to all the Palestinians north of the border as terrorists, using the Israeli characterization. But I think basically the reporters who are covering out of Lebanon use the standard definition, which is, if you take a gun and you kill a civilian who's not involved in combat, political purposes, to publicize a political cause, then you are a terrorist. But if you're a guerrilla in Lebanon you're a guerrilla, and I think that's the word that's usually used.

Ghareeb: While I agree with you there has been a shift, I think at the same time some of that is still there in some of the newspapers and some of the television network coverage.

Rubin: Well, I think that I'm speaking from a perspective before the Israeli invasion of Lebanon. I think that the PLO is comprehensible to an American audience and to American reporters who are not experts in the area when it sounds reasonable. A reporter who has just come out doesn't know the code words and terminology the PLO uses. So I mean PLO officials who talk in reasonable terms are more likely to get fair coverage, I think, generally, when the PLO presents its aims in terms that don't indicate the demise of Israel. I think for the past several years it's been getting a pretty fair hearing. After the Israeli invasion of Lebanon I don't know how things will change because the whole image has changed now. Before this invasion the question was does the PLO want the destruction of Israel. I think if a reporter unsophisticated about the area came in and found the PLO were reasonable men, he would give their cause a hearing, be willing to write stories about the camps and so forth. Now we have a whole new situation where the question is, does Israel want the destruction of the PLO and the Palestinians, and there's no question of the PLO destroying Israel, so it will be interesting now to see how this affects press coverage. Just tonight on ABC Richard Threkeld referred to Israel as the bully, so it may be that we're entering a whole new area of imagery. It seems to me that when the PLO was uniformly labeled terrorist it was another era where the PLO didn't explain itself in a way that the Western media comprehended and therefore got stuck with a label.

Ghareeb: You've covered the Middle East both from the Israeli side and the Arab side. Do you see any difference in the way you are dealt with, the way you are treated, the problems and the advantages that you have in each place? Let's start first with the Israelis. How do you find coverage from Israel of the Middle East?

Rubin: Let me just say one thing about both sides and then I'll get to the Israelis. I think the Middle East is a place where on both sides there is somehow an assumption that if you're not 100 percent for us then you're an enemy. So, neutral coverage or objective coverage is something that's not regarded as a virtue. This is something I think that gets on reporters' nerves in covering the Middle East.

On the Israeli side, there are some distinct advantages over covering the Arab world. First of all, it's very easy to get information, there's almost a surplus of information, you drown in information. The Israelis have a very efficient government press office. They translate the Israeli press into English for you. There's a very good English language news service, there's good television. Not only that but the press is very varied so it's amazing the stuff that you can pick up in your box. You have a box if you're a journalist registered there. You could come in in the morning, at least until the time I left, and you could get an article laying out all the awful things that Israel was doing in the West Bank by a regular Israeli West Bank correspondent who was very liberal. You could maybe even get two in your box, you could get an article by a defense correspondent questioning whether Israeli aspirations in Lebanon made any sense. You get all this stuff that's extremely critical and it's sitting right there in translation. Even after the change to the Begin government, while there was a little bit less of this stuff translated, there was still quite a substantial amount. So that makes things very easy. Then, Israel is a fairly safe place to get around. You're not confronted on street corners with armed gangs or you don't have some of the problems of Beirut before the invasion, let alone after the invasion. There's mobility. There are plenty of people that talk the language, which is a real asset. Of course you have that in Lebanon as well. But you also have in Israel something which you had in Lebanon before the civil war. In Lebanon before, you had all kinds of views and people were able to express them freely. That disappeared. In Israel you still have it, you have thoughtful people who will sit there and criticize the government. It's very nice for a correspondent to come in and be able to get all kinds of views and be able to get people who'll say them. Those are the pluses, and I think they're very serious pluses. The minuses are censorship. Before the invasion it wasn't such a critical problem. It was a pain sometimes, but it rarely caused difficulties. For example, when the Iraqi bombing story broke, the wire service knew about it several hours before they could break it and they just weren't allowed to. Their machines would have been stopped, cut. So, there are some times when it becomes an obstacle. Until this invasion, it was becoming more of an obstacle in the West Bank but that happened basically after I left. The second problem in Israel, which is also a problem in the Arab world, is that if you're not with us you're against us. I think this has become more and more of a problem in covering the West Bank. A lot of the correspondents who cover the West Bank are considered not to be friends of Israel. Now that doesn't mean you don't get appointments. It can mean Begin just won't see you. It can be uncomfortable. The Israelis are very diligent about clipping articles by correspondents. There are files on all the old-time registered correspondents and their clippings, along with letters from the Israeli consuls in the United States if there's anything they want to draw to the attention of the government press office. It's a very organized system, and, for example, if you're considered not friendly and, say, Defense Minister Sharon is going on a tour of West Bank settlements and all the correspondents sign up, you might find somehow your name has been dropped from the list and you're told the bus is full, even though you were the third person on the sign-up list. It's not insurmountable; you just go and get your friends to complain, and usually you can overcome it. It's just annoying and it's also anger-creating, since correspondents don't feel it's justified. That's a problem but it doesn't necessarily impede coverage. After I left, I was told that there were some limitations on the West Bank, but again I think when pressure is applied they usually lift them. I would say that the main obstacle in Israel to coverage is censorship; the potential of censorship, not always the practice. You write about the West Bank, but you're not stopped generally, except on certain occasions. There was an attempt to restrict the movement of correspondents in the West Bank. Supposedly, when there would be demonstrations, you were going to have to go in only with a military escort. I never saw that actually put into operation. I think it probably happened occasionally after I left.

Ghareeb: Did you have any problems?

Rubin: I had a problem along with *Time* magazine in 1978 once. There was an incident in Beitjalah where tear gas was thrown into a school and kids jumped out the window and there were a lot of very badly broken bones. I happened to go out there by chance with a *Time* magazine correspondent. We met up while we were both interviewing the same person on the West Bank. He had a car and I didn't so I joined him. We had no knowledge of the stories each of us wrote but they were about this

279

incident which we investigated very thoroughly. The Israelis then denied that it had happened, totally. Now, not only had the two of us written it, as well as *The Washington Post* and *The Baltimore Sun*, but they focused on *Time* magazine and they claimed that the story had been a lie and a fabrication. I was also subjected to some unpleasant pressures and rumors that the story had been manufactured. It happened that two days after the story, I had talked to a military government official whom I knew, and he had told me that the officer who had been in charge of it had already been disciplined. There was no question that it was true. They said that tear gas canisters had never been thrown, but we had collected fragments, and the place reeked of the tear gas. It was CS gas, American made. There was no question that the story was true. Anyhow, the upshot was that the military government of the West Bank was dismissed, fired, so the whole thing was vindicated, but there were a lot of repercussions. Rumors were deliberately spread about me and things that aren't true were said, and also about the *Time* magazine correspondent. Ultimately, it blew over.

Ghareeb: *The Christian Science Monitor* is seen as one of the most balanced, most objective newspapers in the United States in its coverage of the Middle East. How do you see the difference between the *Monitor* and some of the other newspapers?

Rubin: This is a tricky question. I think the *Monitor* has always had very strong coverage of the Arab world, there's no question about it. They had John Cooley for all those years and he was really an expert. Like a lot of British correspondents, he had been in the area for years and years and had a really thorough familiarity, spoke the language, was there from the time of the Algerian revolution up through the Lebanese civil war. That's a pretty long expanse for anyone, enough to drive you crazy. So, I think for that reason he was familiar to the Arab world and they were very happy with his coverage, which also sometimes dismayed the Israelis. But it was a knowledgeable coverage, a well-informed coverage.

Ghareeb: You said that part of the problem in covering the Middle East is that the Arabs have not managed to present their case effectively. What are the main problems on the Arab side? We've touched on some of the problems on the Arab side, but overall, what are some of the pluses and minuses you could cite, as you did with the Israelis, and how do you think they can present their case in a way which would allow American journalists to see things as they really are and to present a fairer and more accurate picture of the Arab world?

Rubin: I think there are several levels. For starters, on a general point, I think that the American public is much more amenable to an Arab approach which says we accept the existence of Israel, but we also want to exist, so let's co-exist on a fair basis, with neither side trying to dominate the other. As the Arabs have come closer to that position I think there's been more acceptance of them on the American side. Frankly speaking, the American public accepts the State of Israel, always has, and I think will never accept a policy that stands for the destruction of Israel. Once that was abandoned, as after '67 and moving on after '73, once that was no longer perceived as the official Arab position, especially with moderate Arab states, then I think there was a greater receptivity. That's stage one and I think that holds true both for correspondents and for the audience that they were reporting to. I think that a favorable presentation of the Arab world also depends on the politics of the Arab world. This is not to say that radical Arab states don't have a right to have their politics and their social change reported fairly and accurately, but there's an easier time to be had by states that have a moderate position.

Take a country like Jordan, for example. There are a lot of stories to be written about Jordan which probably don't get covered. There are very interesting things going on with development, problems that relate to the political situation, which deserve to be covered. What makes the difference between when those things get covered or they don't get covered? I think part of it involves the presentation. The Israelis are extremely effective at helping journalists. Journalists come into Israel, they register at the government press office, they are given every service. One of the ways journalists find out about all the stories to be had in Israel is that the Israeli press is so good. It covers its own society in such depth that foreign correspondents have an easy job of finding all kinds of stories. In the days before there was a crisis every week in Israel they used to have all kinds of economic and social stories favorable to Israel because they were available. You could easily find out about them from the Israeli media. If you wanted to follow them up, the government press office was tremendously effective. They would send you a translator, they'd help you get a car or they would give you a car. They were anxious to promote their own stories and they helped the correspondent. I'm not saying that correspondents have to be fed, but obviously ready access makes it easier. A country like Jordan has a lot of talented people and they have become more effective.

281

22

IN THE MIDDLE IN THE MIDDLE EAST: THE MEDIA AND U.S. FOREIGN POLICY

Patricia A. Karl

Ms. Karl has taught international politics at the State University of Kansas and Vassar College and is also Associate Producer of "Coming of Age in Armageddon," a documentary film on children in the Middle East.

Since the December 1979 Soviet invasion of Afghanistan, President Ronald Reagan has publicly condemned the invasion and has had members of his International Communications Agency (ICA) produce a television spectacular, "Let Poland be Poland," in a "show" of solidarity with Polish workers. On June 6, 1982, Israel invaded Lebanon and Washington was silent. Instead of a production, "Let Lebanon be Lebanon," the White House invited Israeli Prime Minister Menachem Begin to Washington for talks and afforded Mr. Begin access to the American public through the American media. *The New York Times'* front page headline of June 22 states: "Reagan and Begin Appear in Accord on Lebanon Steps." If the headline did not make the point, the picture did. The photo shows President Reagan and Prime Minister Begin leaving the White House. In the foreground of the picture is a White House guard holding a large Israeli flag. It was not until July 12 that Yasser Arafat, speaking from Israeli-bombed Beirut, commented on a CBS evening newscast: "I don't know what he [Reagan] wants and he doesn't know what I need." Mr. Reagan and Mr. Arafat may not be talking to each other, but they are talking at each other, through the media.

Everywhere, the media are part of the action—manipulating, manipulated, participating, building and destroying images, and acting as the bullhorn for the once-upon-a-time whispers of diplomacy. Nowhere is this more obvious and more dangerous than in Middle East diplomacy. Government's manipulation of the American media and media participation in foreign policy have conditioned situations where events are often shaped to fit policies or foreign policy programming becomes a substitute for policy. Part of the danger of all of this lies in the fact that journalists are not diplomats. They usually have different objectives, and the immediacy of "prime-time" diplomacy creates effects that cannot always be reversed. Giving a new meaning to "diplomatic channels" has its defenders, but because politics is both theater and education to the media and their audiences, media coverage may exaggerate, sensationalize and manipulate the images and issues with little regard or sense of responsibility for the consequences. From Washington to Tehran to Cairo, government and media manipulations have created false images of and disinformation about the Middle East in the United States. This, in turn, has made it more difficult for the U.S. Government and public to understand the complexity of Middle East politics and the need to create a U.S. Middle East policy compatible with those political realities. Recent examples abound in which the interdependence of the media and government in foreign policy and the use or misuse of the media have created a gap in perceptions about the Middle East. There are three dangers inherent in this marriage of the media and diplomacy in Middle East foreign policy—fractured foreign policy tales, false images and information, and the increasing vulnerability of the press.

Fractured Foreign Policy Tales

Middle East media diplomacy might be dated from Egyptian President Sadat's historic 1977 visit to Jerusalem. The three American commercial networks fought over the honor of fostering President Sadat's first visit to Israel. (Mr. Sadat credited *The Jerusalem Post*'s Washington correspondent, Wolf Blitzer, with the idea.) The Egyptian leader's initiative and the happy acquiescence in it of Israeli Prime Minister Begin were intended to head off Washington's and Moscow's announced intention of reviving the Geneva Conference for a comprehensive Middle East settlement. Given the increase of Israeli settlements in the occupied territories since the Camp David accords, the Israeli annexation of the Golan Heights, the Israeli invasion of Lebanon on June 6, 1982, the Israeli clamp-down on Palestinian nationalism in the occupied West Bank, and the dismissal of seven mayors from the occupied West Bank and Gaza, historians may well decide that then U.S. President Carter and Soviet First Secretary Brezhnev had a better idea than Walter Cronkite, Barbara Walters and Mr. Blitzer. When asked about President Sadat's televised journey to Jerusalem, the late Israeli Prime Minister Golda Meir remarked: "I don't know about the Nobel Prize, but I think they both [Mr. Sadat and Mr. Begin] ought to get Oscars."

The Egyptian President was an adept manipulator of the American media, always hungry for the "Big Story." Mr. Sadat, anxious to impress the U.S. Congress with his need to rebuild military forces, envenomed his politically useful conflict with Libya by calling President Khadafi a "raving lunatic." (He also had called King Hussein of Jordan a "dwarf.") What was downplayed by Mr. Sadat and the American media and therefore never understood by the American public was that: 1) Egypt, economically, needed peace and its people were tired of war; 2) most Arab nations viewed Sadat's initiatives and the U.S.-sponsored Camp David accords as a "sell-out" to the enemy because the separate Egyptian peace treaty with Israel effectively removed the likelihood of another Arab-Israeli war, since the Egyptian army had always borne the brunt of the fighting and casualties in the Middle East wars; 3) the Palestinian issue is a question of land and a homeland. American Jews and Israeli Jews, of all people, should understand this; it is one of history's cruel ironies that they understand it the least; and 4) that the Arab world, like Lebanon, has always been divided. The myth that the Arab world is a united monolith has never been dispelled in the United States, despite Mr. Sadat's media diplomacy in the West. If anything, Mr. Sadat's public diplomacy should have confirmed the divisions in the Arab world to the American public.

Another example of the manipulation of the American media in crafting Middle East policy was Ayatollah Khomeini's use of the U.S. media in Iran after the 1979 seizure of the U.S. Embassy and hostages in Tehran. What Iran consecrated was the pre-eminence of television in instant diplomacy. The media moguls met the media mullahs, and the American public was treated to one of the longest diplomatic soap sagas in network history. As Barry Jagoda, President Carter's former television adviser, suggested: "If a picture is worth a thousand words, a television show is worth millions." Nobody in Tehran would talk directly to the U.S. Government. Negotiations were through the media. If Vietnam was the living room war, Iran became the living room revolution. Khomeini, no doubt influenced by the show's title, gave Mike Wallace of CBS 60 minutes of his time; glancing perhaps at the Nielsen or Arbitron ratings, he gave ABC and NBC only 15 minutes. Having learned that the Public Broadcasting System was not the only network in America (as it is in Iran), he relegated Robert McNeil from first place to fourth, whereupon McNeil flew home.

Khomeini had earlier used touchtone dialing at Neauphle, near Paris, to record cassettes by phone in Qom and overthrow a dynasty in the name of fundamentalist Islam, borrowing the technology of the 20th century to advance the cause of the 7th. The instant replay of his sermons turned into a page one disaster for the Shah of Iran and for the United States. This time around, he staged a media show for viewers in Cleveland and Bowling Green in which Iranian mobs cried slogans in English (for one Canadian television crew, in French) and shook fists on cue. When the kleig lights were turned off, so were the demonstrations, and American crews and rent-a-riot extras fraternized over soft drinks and candied beets. The "students" holding the hostages at the U.S. Embassy were also media conscious. To ensure that the programs they produced, with U.S. network cooperation, would not be censored by their own government or the U.S. Government, they installed three cameras of their own in the embassy compound, along with a dish antenna to relay live, via satellite, straight into the American home.

In Washington, President Carter and Secretary of State Vance were talking to whoever in Tehran might be listening, not through their helpless Charge d'Affaires L. Bruce Laingen, but through spokesman Hodding Carter; in other words, through the press. The Carter Administration was further hobbled by not knowing exactly to whom it was speaking through the press and was miffed that the press had access to power sources in Tehran denied to the U.S. Government's official emissaries. Khomeini, for his own reasons, also became annoyed with the media coverage of the crisis. By August 1980, he was expelling Western journalists every week, staging demonstrations in the streets of Tehran against the Western media (while closing *Ayandegan* and other domestic voices of moderation), and intoning that "the pen in the hands of the foreign press is a pen in the hands of the enemy, something that is worse than the bayonet to the fate of mankind." The Ayatollah became so dissatisfied with American television reporting that he even ran a full page advertisement in *The New York Times* to "define his stance in respect to [the] embassy takeover."

The use of media diplomacy, especially the misuse of television, is undermining the traditional methods and practitioners of diplomacy. The traditional diplomat simply cannot compete with the electronic envoy, the radio revolutionary and "terrorvision." *Washington Post* columnist Richard Cohen complained that the television coverage of the Iranian hostage issue was unreal because we saw only the captors, not the captives. "What we have going now," wrote Cohen, "is some sort of idiotic debate between peoples." Fellow *Post* columnist Haynes Johnson asked: "When does an event stop being new, therefore news, and become merely staged propaganda, cynical theater designed to reach the widest unfiltered audience through the tube?" If the press was carried away by Iran and made "rent-a-riot" look real, perhaps the main harm came from what George Ball described as Iranian television's refusal of "equal time." The Iranian "students" holding the hostages never learned that they had lost their Tet offensive for U.S. and world opinion because their own television never told them so. However, the replay reports from Iranians in the United States did lead them to drop the "Death to Carter" show segment in favor of presenting their case against the ex-Shah. Similarly, the U.S. media, especially television, did not do as much as they should have done to counter the sickening racism triggered by the crisis against Iranians (the main victims were largely anti-Khomeini Iranians in the United States) or against Islam. If the Tehran "students" were Islamic terrorists, as some commentators and papers called them, should we call the Baader-Meinhof gang "Christian terrorists"?

More recently, the Iranians have used the U.S. media to confirm their claims of victories over Iraqi forces in the Iran-Iraq War. Reporters from the United States have been invited back into Iran to media-hype the Iranian position in the dispute. In a July 1982 Bill Moyers Special for CBS, for example, Moyers is found chatting with Iranians in combat fatigues and tennis shoes with signs in English in the background that read: "We export our revolution" and "We want to revive Islam." This program contained no counter report from Iraq. A viewer might find this program somewhat strange. While the United States has publicly tried to remain "neutral" in the conflict, Iraq and the United States have moved closer together; the United States clearly does not want Khomeini's Islamic revolution to storm across the Persian Gulf. While this broadcast did mention that the Soviet Union had been supporting both sides in this war, it neglected to tell the audience that the Israeli government has been supporting the Iranians in the dispute. Was this report a balanced presentation? If, in the television age, image is all, then access is everything. Governments who do not or will not talk to the press will never have their positions heard, let alone understood. As Henry Kissinger once remarked, "If you don't talk to the press, your enemies will."

The Iranians, it seems, are fascinated with the media. During the U.S.-Iranian crisis of 1979-80, the captors of the U.S. Embassy in Tehran evidently discovered, among other documents, a classified Central Intelligence Agency (CIA) report entitled *Israel: Foreign Intelligence and Security Services*. This 47-page document had been issued by the CIA in March 1979. Why the document was at the U.S. Embassy in Tehran is still unknown. The study indicates that not only have the Israelis spied on the United States, but that they have also "blackmailed, bugged, wiretapped and offered bribes to U.S. Government employees." The report also contained an appraisal of Israeli intelligence agencies and their top personnel. The Iranian government decided to publish this document as a paperback book and it was on sale at downtown Tehran bookstores and at the airport when William Worthy, a journalist, purchased several copies. One set of the book was placed in luggage on a Lufthansa flight to New York and the other set was apparently placed in a separate piece of luggage which accompanied the journalist upon his arrival in the United States. The first set of books was confiscated by customs agents in New York who called in Federal Bureau of Investigation (FBI) agents. However, the second set of books escaped undetected and later formed the basis for a series of articles on the subject by *The Washington Post* in February 1982. The publication of the information forced the United States and Israel to deal with the issue at that time.

Technological capabilities enabled the Iranian government to mass produce what was a classified U.S. Government document on Israeli intelligence agencies. Obviously the Iranian public and anyone else in Iran had access to this information. The U.S. Government, on the other hand, tried to restrain the publication of the information in the United States. Worthy, an American journalist funded by CBS television while he was in Iran, had to use *The Washington Post* to get the story out. The impact of the publication of the document may have resulted in several strains in U.S.-Israeli relations and raised a number of questions about the relationship between the government and the media in the United States regarding Middle East foreign policy. First of all, the Israelis surely had to revise their major intelligence operations. Second, it was an embarrassment to both the Israeli and U.S. Governments to have it publicly admitted that each country was spying on the other. Third, the Israelis might have wondered both why the report was in the U.S. Embassy in Iran, and why it was not destroyed when the embassy was seized. Fourth, did the U.S. Government have the right to confiscate the private property of an American journalist in an attempt to prevent the publication of the story in the United States when it was obvious that the Iranian public and certainly foreign intelligence agencies had already obtained the information? Fifth, clearly the technological capabilities of the Iranian government (or any government) indicate that in the future a government, if it can, will declassify the information of another government, creating foreign policy issues between governments and/or third parties which would not be issues if the information were not published. One might also suggest that the publication of the CIA study damaged the relationship between U.S. and Israeli intelligence agencies.

There are other examples where government manipulation of the media may have created Alice-in-Wonderland images of U.S. foreign policy in the Middle East. In April 1980, this writer was in Beirut when the Reuters wire service at the Commodore Hotel informed us that the U.S. Government had attempted a hostage "rescue mission" in Iran. I did not believe that cover story then, many of my colleagues in Beirut at the time did not, and I still do not accept that version of the operation entirely. One certainly did not expect to see the headline, "U.S. Military Operation in Support of Coup in Iran Ends in Disaster," but why did the media in the United States so blindly accept the U.S. Government's version of the story?

Given the pieces of the puzzle, alternative explanations of the adventure were as plausible as the government's story. The timing and extreme secrecy of the operation, for example, were curious. The takeover of the U.S. Embassy in Tehran occurred on November 4, 1979, the rescue mission did not occur until April 1980, and there was an upcoming U.S. presidential election in November 1980. The turmoil in Iran during this period left the government of Ayatollah Khomeini in control of only two areas, Qom and Tehran, which meant that to be successful the planners of a possible coup would have to take only these two cities. At the time of the mission, no one knew whether the American hostages were still in the embassy compound or whether they had been moved, and there were, at that time, approximately 200 other Americans in Iran who could have been taken hostage if the embassy personnel had been rescued. There had been a series of high level visits between U.S. military personnel and members of the Iranian military during the period between the Shah's departure from Iran, the return of Khomeini to Qom, and the creation of the interim government of Prime Minister Bazargan. *Aviation Week & Space Technology* ran a series of three articles on September 15, 22 and 29, 1980 called "Iran Rescue Mission: Group Analyzes Reasons for Failure." The secrecy in the planning of this mission was beyond belief. There was no coordination among the various military elements except at the top and there was no "trial run" or practice exercise of the mission prior to its departure for Iran. Nor were there any provisions for verbal or nonverbal communications among the rescue crew's members once the mission was airborne in Iran. Surely these considerations should have prompted a media re-evaluation of the government's version of the episode.

Another Middle East issue that was largely mismanaged by the media in the United States concerned the American sale of AWACS to Saudi Arabia. The debate on the AWACS/F-15 enhancement sale to Saudi Arabia became, in the U.S. media, essentially a horse race or beauty contest between those predominantly concerned with the security of Israel or the security of the technology, and those who were predominantly concerned with the security of America's, NATO's, and Japan's oil supply. The White House downplayed the contingency role of the Saudi AWACS as a future stratospheric command station for the U.S. Rapid Deployment Force (RDF), and the American media compliantly concentrated on the AWACS' limited, almost cosmetic, role in helping the tiny Saudi air force defend a huge country from attacks (as De Gaulle would have said, *tous azimuths*). The White House understressed the RDF role of the Saudi AWACS in order not to embarrass Riyadh or the U.S. Government, and in the main the U.S. media complied. The notion that Saudi Arabia might get the world's most sophisticated radar-control aircraft and the world's most sophisticated fighter-bomber as a "signal" of a U.S. commitment to the Saudi kingdom, i.e., that the sale was at least as political as military, was largely buried in State Department and think-tank reports. The U.S. media failed to report that Israel's objections to the sale were also more political than military, i.e., that the Israeli position might have been a question of sibling rivalry with another of America's Middle East partners, a partner more crucial than Israel to the economies (and fuel tanks) of the United States and its defense treaty allies.

Current examples of U.S. media compliance in U.S. Government-sponsored Middle East tales involve the stories surrounding the allegation by the Reagan Administration that President Khadafi of Libya sent assassination squads to the United States to kill the President and top U.S. Government officials, and that former CIA and Green Beret personnel were supplying the Libyan government with explosives and training Libyan terrorists. Depending upon the reports you read or the broadcasts you heard a few months ago, the Libyan "hit teams" were poised in Canada or Mexico ready to strike their American targets. No American intelligence agency has, so far, been able to substantiate those charges.

Several months ago, too, the front page headlines told the American public that a former CIA agent, Edwin P. Wilson, and former members of the elite Green Beret forces were training Libyan terrorists and supplying them with explosives. The U.S. Government's story is that these people were acting on their own, that many of them thought it was a legitimate CIA operation to infiltrate the Libyan guerrilla organizations, and that the U.S. Government was unaware of the mission and appalled at the whole discovery, and would investigate the matter. Mr. Wilson was, as *The Washington Post* headline told us, "lured from Libya," arrested in New York on June 15, 1982, and is now being held in a Washington, D.C. jail in lieu of (an unprecedented) $20 million bail, at the U.S. Government's request. Should the American public believe their government's story, accepted and duly reported by an unquestioning press, that President Khadafi of Libya is public enemy number one, and that Edwin P. Wilson, Frank Terpil, Douglas M. Schlacter, and Mr. Khadafi are the Four Horsemen of the Apocalypse? Perhaps the operation *was* a CIA plan. Or is it simply that small enemies like Libya or Cuba are easier targets to select, to prove American strength, than, let us say, the Soviet Union? Hyping a threat to American security helps the defense budget process and the demand for more covert action by the CIA, and so on, although if the U.S. Government's stories are true and if CIA and Green Beret alumni were in Mr. Khadafi's service, it would surely make any prudent person raise the question of the source of the eventual flight of covert technologies. Another issue might be raised. A July 4, 1982 *New York Times Magazine* article, "The Secret World of a Green Beret," by Philip Taubman, supports the notion that some of the Green Berets (like Luke Thompson, the subject of the article) may have, indeed, thought that the operation was a legitimate CIA mission. The story tells us about Mr. Thompson's earlier life in the army. According to the article, "Thompson was eventually brought up before [an Army] court martial hearing in 1956 and given a dishonorable discharge as well as a year at Fort Leavenworth Prison in Kansas." One might have questioned what Mr. Thompson was doing in the Green Berets. Surely the American media should have been more skeptical about the government's story regarding the Edwin P. Wilson/Libya connection.

False Images and False Information

"News, if unreported, has no impact. It might well have not happened at all," says Gay Talese, historiographer of *The New York Times*. The media, in short, may deform or delay issues, actions or perceptions of

291

foreign policy matters. Selective media transmissions, like selective diplomatic omissions, may lead to foreign policy distortions and false images and false information.

According to the State Department, for example, Moscow's *aktivnyye meropriyatiya* operation in 1979 placed a report in the Indian weekly *Blitz* claiming that "the Americans" had engineered the seizure of the Great Mosque in Mecca. As a result of this false report, the U.S. Embassy in Islamabad, Pakistan was burned down. We simply live in an age when more Reichstag fires, Dunkirks, Tets and other false reports and falsely slanted stories are more possible than ever before.

Government and media use of language and negative images has also contributed to American misperceptions about the Middle East. The FBI's choice of fictitious Arab sheikhs for its "Abscam" operation was clearly a blatant form of racism that projected a negative and false image of Arabs in the United States. There has been no evidence of any Arab involvement in attempts to bribe U.S. Congressmen or officials. Can you imagine the outcry in the United States if, for example, the operation had been called instead Jewscam, Paddyscam, Afroscam or Greekscam? Another example of slanted coverage of the Arab world was the airing of the program "Death of a Princess," which projected a negative (even barbaric) image of Saudi Arabian society. This, in turn, encouraged a less than mild media melee between the governments of the United States and Saudi Arabia. Why was there no counter program to balance the images projected in this film? Nor was there a counter program to the recently aired "A Woman Called Golda" about the late Israeli Prime Minister. This show was media-hyped by Oriana Fallaci, the famous and controversial Italian journalist, in the April 24-30 issue of *TV Guide*.

Language may also be used to obscure or to create a positive impression of a government's policies. For example, at the time of the debate over the AWACS sale to Saudi Arabia the United States announced a new "strategic relationship" with Israel. While it might have sounded good in Israel and was undoubtedly intended to settle ruffled feathers with the Israeli government in light of the proposed sale of AWACS to Saudi Arabia, we are still waiting for an explanation as to what this "strategic relationship" means in U.S.-Israeli foreign policy. The U.S. Government also selected very positive terminology to describe its military maneuvers with Egypt and other Middle East countries. "Bright Star" and "Gallant Eagle" perhaps projected an image of military capability which may or may not exist for the United States in the Middle East. When President Reagan stated that he accepted "in principle" a military role for U.S.

292

troops in Lebanon as a result of the Israeli invasion of Lebanon and the PLO plight in West Beirut as a result of that invasion, members of Congress and the U.S. public balked. (It is interesting to note that the Israelis, who have always tried to encourage a U.S. military presence in the Middle East, leaked President Reagan's statement on Israeli radio before the announcement was made from Washington and before the President had discussed it with members of Congress.) The Israelis, too, chose to label their invasion of Lebanon with positive language, "Peace for Galilee." Only a George Orwell or a Lewis Carroll could appreciate the irony of it all.

An October 1981 series in *TV Guide*, "Blind Spot in the Middle East: Why you don't see more Palestinians on TV," traces the imbalances in network coverage of the Middle East, although the author of this series, John Weisman, at times perpetuates many of these past imbalances in his own articles. For ten months *TV Guide* reviewed nightly newscasts (from July 1980 through April 1981). These were the findings:

> There were 38 reports of raids and retaliations by both sides. 24 of the 38 were Israeli raids on Palestinian targets in southern Lebanon. Only three of these reports—for a total of one minute, ten seconds—showed pictures of the effects of the Israeli attacks. None showed any Palestinian victims. On the other hand, of the 14 reports of Palestinian raids and attacks on Israel during the period, 11 included pictures of Israeli victims, and the filmed reports totaled some 17 minutes.

While the author clearly demonstrates a pro-Israeli slant in the networks' coverage, Weisman's own account contains a not-so-subtle slant of its own. Notice that, according to his account, the Israelis attacked Palestinian "targets," implying, of course, that they were military targets. The Palestinians, according to this account, attacked the state of Israel, implying a civilian population. Why was this distinction made by an author reporting on television's "Blind Spot in the Middle East"? Nor did these articles contain any pictures of Palestinian victims; they did contain a picture of two Palestinians with weapons.

Israel has used the U.S. press for years to make Palestinian nationalism a dirty word. It was able to persuade American correspondents in the early 1970s to refer to Israel's three wars and to omit the fact that in 1956 and 1967 Israel had been the aggressor. Israel today does not admit that the June 6, 1982 invasion of Lebanon was an invasion. For months the Israeli government has been blatantly manipulating the American media.

In April 1982 Prime Minister Begin wrote a letter to President Reagan reassuring him that Israel would not attack positions in southern Lebanon unless it was provoked. The timing of this front page attention did occur at an interesting time, a few weeks before the scheduled Israeli departure from Sinai on April 25, 1982, and days after extensive media reports of violence and Israeli censorship of the Arab press on the West Bank. However, what is not reported may be as important as what is. Surely two Middle East governments would have appreciated a public Israeli confirmation of Israel's intentions of bombing Beirut and attacking the Iraqi nuclear power plant in the summer of 1981. As it was, the Israeli government used the attempted assassination of its ambassador in London to rationalize its invasion of Lebanon. Where there's a will, there's a pretext.

Both the U.S. government and the Israeli government have manipulated the U.S. press in the current Lebanese crisis. Begin's assurances to Reagan in April were projecting a false image of Israeli intentions. Many reporters in Washington who cover Middle East affairs, for example, have privately suggested that had Alan Harry Goodman not attacked the Islamic Dome of the Rock and killed two people in mid April (a media event in itself), and diverted public attention, the Israelis would have invaded Lebanon then. During April, the U.S. Government was also using media diplomacy in its Middle East foreign policy. The headlines in U.S. papers in mid April indicate that the U.S. Government continually kept the issue of an Israeli invasion of Lebanon in the public's mind, which served two purposes. This was an attempt to create a climate of public opinion in the United States against a possible Israeli invasion that, it was hoped, would make the Israelis think twice about an invasion at that time. The United States was afraid that if the Israelis invaded Lebanon prior to the return of the Sinai to Egypt on April 25, 1982, the return itself would be jeopardized and Egyptian President Mubarak would move closer to what in the United States has been called the "radical" Arab position and further damage, if not destroy, the American-engineered Camp David framework. The press reports also served to prepare the U.S. public for an invasion if it came, and provided the U.S. Government with "proof" that it had tried to prevent the action.

The Israeli government has been very selective in the use of the media to manipulate public opinion. The Israeli news blackout at the end of April regarding the Sinai evictions of Jewish settlers, for example, was described by Eli Nissan, a television reporter who heads the Israeli journalists' union, as "an unprecedented act" in Israel. "The (Israeli) Government is taking upon itself authority that no elected government has: to decide what is permissible to know and when." This manipulation of the media by Israel, in light of Israel's actions in Lebanon, has created a new public relations problem for the Israeli government. As Richard Cohen of *The Washington Post* noted in a recent article: "It is Israel, in short, that has a major credibility problem. It has repeatedly lied both to its own citizens and to the rest of the world." Cohen explains why:

> It was Israel, after all, that said it would go only 25 miles into Lebanon in order to secure a safe border for itself. It went to Beirut instead.
>
> It was Israel that said it was responding to the attempted assassination of its ambassador to Britain but was really using that as a pretext to administer a punishing blow to the PLO. It bombed civilian sectors of Beirut.
>
> It is Israel, in the person of Menachem Begin, who keeps denying what the world can plainly see. He rejected the use of the word 'invasion,' saying 'Israel did not invade any country.' But if a rose by another name is still a rose, then what Israel did in Lebanon is an invasion.

Anthony Lewis of *The New York Times* also questioned the public Israeli justifications for the invasion:

> For nine months not a single rocket or shell was fired by PLO gunners into Israel. When Israeli planes bombed Lebanon on April 21 for the first time since the truce started, the PLO did not respond. When there was another bombing on May 9, there was a limited response; about 100 rockets that Israel said caused no damage or casualties. Then, after massive Israeli bombing last week, the PLO responded with full-scale barrages.
>
> In short, the cease-fire kept the Galilee safe until Israel bombed Lebanon. The argument that aggressive new military action was needed to keep the rockets out turns reality upside-down.

The gap between Israel's media diplomacy and its military actions in Lebanon has further divided Israeli public opinion and raised questions about U.S. military support of Israel in the United States. The only country in which there was a demonstration against the Israeli invasion of Lebanon was Israel, although the coalition government of Prime Minister Begin is stronger now than it was before the invasion. Israeli use of American weapons in the invasion, especially the use of American-made cluster bombs, has also drawn public criticism in the United States, as have Mr. Begin's twisted statements that these weapons were used for "defensive" purposes. Whether this negative publicity will alter U.S. foreign policy in the Middle East or toward Israel is uncertain; it has damaged the credibility of both the U.S. Government and the Israeli government not only in the Middle East but in Western Europe and the Third World. Presumably fewer countries will feel constrained to keep commitments regarding the use of weapons they purchase in the United States.

Public diplomacy also damaged the efforts to resolve the problem of West Beirut. While U.S. special negotiator Philip Habib was negotiating with the Lebanese government and the Israeli government and through the Lebanese government with the PLO, it became public that the negotiations concerned the removal of PLO fighters to Syria. The problem was, according to the Syrians, they had never been consulted prior to the publication of this information.

Increasing Vulnerability of the Press

The current crisis in Lebanon demonstrates how increasingly vulnerable the media are to manipulation, to censorship and to disinformation on the part of governments. Since the Israeli invasion of Lebanon, all of the reports and broadcasts coming out of Israel have been censored by the Israeli military authorities and criticism is gradually appearing in the American press and in Israel. In a July 6, 1982 article in *The New York Times* by David K. Shipler, Hannah Semer, editor of the Hebrew-language daily *Davar*, explains that there are three kinds of censorship in Israel:

> *Censorship at the source: You're not given correct news, or you know half of the truth, but the other half may be much more important.*
> *Military censorship, to which all domestic and foreign dispatches on military matters are subject. This is aimed mainly at specific security-related information, and has been relaxed considerably since a strict period during the first week of the war, when the censors would not allow even United Nations observers' reports on the fighting to be transmitted to foreign newspapers.*
> *Voluntary censorship: In the first week you didn't see any criticism in the newspapers, and no unpleasant questions were asked.*

As Shipler notes, these forms of censorship have resulted in situations where the Israeli public is largely unaware of the civilian Palestinian suffering, no political remarks may be made on camera by anyone in uniform, reserve officers from the army's spokesman's office are stationed in the (television) studios, and, as Hirsh Goodman notes, "Israeli troops were relying entirely on Lebanese radio for their information on the war, and they found these reports more accurate than their own army's announcements." Goodman, who is a correspondent for the English-language *Jerusalem Post*, also notes that "a combination of heavy censorship and misinformation by the army spokesman had allowed the war to expand without the country's realizing it." He also charged that "the untruths dispensed by the army undermined the commanders' credibility among the troops."

296

A *Time* magazine article of June 21, 1981 described the problems of foreign correspondents covering the Israeli invasion of Lebanon from Israel. During transmissions of stories, telephone lines have been cut and film has been confiscated at the Tel Aviv airport. David K. Shipler, *The New York Times'* bureau chief in Jerusalem, complained of military censorship. "It's pretty frustrating," he said. "We can go in and ask the [military] spokesman what's going on, but we won't get very much." While it was clamping down on the Arab press in the occupied territories, the domestic Israeli press and foreign journalists, the Israeli government was pursuing a public relations campaign in the United States with full access to the American media. On June 6, 1982, for example, the day of the Israeli invasion of Lebanon, the Israeli Ambassador to the United States, Moshe Arens, appeared on the ABC News program, "This Week," and stated that Israel's sole objective was to "push Palestinian Liberation Organization forces out of artillery and rocket range of northern Israeli settlements." This theme was echoed by Mr. Begin on the front page of *The New York Times* on June 7. It was a deceptive tactic to buy time with the American public. Mr. Begin, in his mid-June visit to the United States, also took advantage of the media to present the Israeli position to the public in New York and Washington. Edward Cody of *The Washington Post*, who is based in Jerusalem, noted in a June 15 story that:

> To boost Israel's image in the face of criticism abroad, the foreign minister has dispatched two reserve lieutenant generals and the head of the Israeli broadcast authority to the United States for a round of meetings with editors, television talk shows, and speaking appearances. Deputy Foreign Minister Yehuda Ben Meir has traveled to London on a similar mission, a ministry spokesman said.

In the United States there also appears to be some censorship with a pro-Israeli bias in the current Lebanese crisis. James Whelan, editor and publisher of the new Washington newspaper, *The Washington Times*, evidently took Russell Warren Howe off of the Arab-Israeli stories after the Israeli invasion. Another reporter covering the Middle East for *The Washington Times* was evidently told by Israeli authorities that he "would get no assistance from them" and that he was "on his own."

Censorship? Manipulation? Vulnerability of the Press? In this country? While increasing public propaganda campaigns abroad and at home, President Reagan has also been attacking the press on different levels in the United States. Look, for example, at the President's proposed New Executive Order on National Security, which will restrict the public's and media access to government information now protected by the Freedom of

Information Act. Similarly, a directive to U.S. Cabinet officials not to grant major interviews with the print or electronic media without prior White House approval may further reduce public access to government information.

Anyone who has been a part of a media project in the Middle East knows that there are problems of a technical, political, military and physical nature in most countries. Communications facilities are difficult and one needs a permit to film most political events. The Arab world has not had a good press in this country for a variety of reasons, including a lack of access for Western reporters in their countries and a news bias in the United States. In ancient times, kings and princes conducted their relations with personal emissaries and messengers, and it was not uncommon for a messenger bearing bad news to be killed by the offended recipient. Today the situation is often the reverse; we are living in an age of the shooting messenger. Many political battles today are often won or lost first in the press. This continues to be true of U.S. media coverage of the Middle East, U.S. foreign policy in the Middle East, and the American public's perceptions of the politics of the Middle East.

23

MEDIA MYTHS OF THE MIDDLE EAST: THE U.S. PRESS ON THE WAR IN LEBANON

Mary C. McDavid

Ms. McDavid is a Washington, D.C.-based writer and public affairs consultant specializing in the Middle East. She wrote the following in July 1982.

At a human toll of some 14,000 dead, 60,000 wounded, another 10,000 imprisoned and still another 600,000 left homeless, the majority of whom are Lebanese and Palestinian civilians, the 1982 war in Lebanon led to four changes in the U.S. political landscape.

1. After a painfully slow start and badly skewed coverage of the war in Lebanon, the American public had, for the first time, at least an opportunity to read and see—if only for a comparatively brief period—a slice of the aggression that the Israeli government, aided by U.S. tax dollars and weaponry, undertook in Lebanon.

2. The U.S. media, both broadcast and print, went beyond reporting the official Israeli version of the 1982 war in Lebanon. While only in a halting manner, it moved toward objectivity and truth in partially reporting Israel's role as aggressor in the latter stages of reportage in July 1982.

3. Some American Jewish leaders, including both religious and opinion leaders, who looked hard at Israel's role in the latest Middle East imbroglio, did not like what they saw and dared to say so publicly.

4. For the first time since the creation of Israel, Americans of conscience and courage, both members of the media and opinion leaders, in some significant and vocal manner, joined a widening public debate on the

question of whether Israel deserves to hold a lock on America's hearts, minds and purse strings while it wages war against the peoples of the Arab world.

By the time Israel had invaded Lebanon and killed some 10,000 people in its first forays, individual journalists and daring camera crews began to step outside of the confines of Israel's "disinformation" perspective, away from what Israeli military censors called a "mopping up" or "flushing out" operation. They stopped short of suggesting what sort of destruction the Israeli "cordon sanitaire" may have wrought for civilians in Beirut and southern Lebanon. Reporters never fully opened their lenses, but offered, in occasional asides, a partial view of the other (i.e., Arab) side of the story. Still grossly uneven, still relaying messages of Israel's need for "security" from the television vantage point of weeping widows, the U.S. coverage of this latest episode of war did show the beginnings of balance.

Therefore, gains made by certain of the major broadcast networks and by major metropolitan dailies in pursuing the news should be recognized and encouraged as a first step toward objectivity in uncovering the realities of the Middle East.

After the first two weeks of the war, a modest public debate began, aided by a series of thought-provoking newspaper and radio advertisements using photographs or sobering casualty figures to tell what the American media had not reported. These ads were placed by organizations including the American Arab Anti-Discrimination Committee, the Arab Women's Council and American Near East Refugee Aid, which adopted a public relations tactic to take the case to the people. Later, through the American Federation of Ramallah, Palestinians added their voice, declaring, ". . . our tears are as tender as those of an Israeli . . ." and "no army can defeat an idea whose time has come." By offering a sharp counterpoint to the portrait presented by daily news organs, this pro-Arab education campaign helped stir the conscience of large numbers of the American public and probably the press. "I've never seen [such] objectivity by the U.S. media. And I've given talks before. We're [the Arab Women's Council] really working at a time when I think there will be a change in American public opinion," remarked Hala Maksoud, wife of the Arab League's ambassador to the United Nations, to *The Washington Post* on July 8. "I sense a turning point in the way we think about Israel, and it is a turn for the better, the more normal," agreed Meg Greenfield, *Newsweek* columnist, that same week.

Nevertheless, questions on objectivity must be raised. Is it fair for news coverage to be governed by whichever side generates more conveniently provided press releases and more battle "tours," interviews or photo opportunities? Does the easy availability of pre-packaged "information" dispel an obligation on the part of the press to seek other sources? Any reputable journalist would say no. Yet the number of those who continue to rely on Israel's image machine, both in the United States and in the Middle East, have crippled this incipient objectivity of reporting and the emergence of realistic portraits of the people and events in the Arab world. Individual reporters, editors and producers in radio, television and print are indeed responsible when the filters of Israeli perspective are not removed from the cameras.

American journalists eager to see the war marched around in cadence with Israeli censors in Tel Aviv, Jerusalem and Beirut. "Oh, to Be in Beirut When the Bullets Bloom," alliterated Thomas Lippman of *The Washington Post*, who thought Beirut was a city where "the only requirement" was "to watch the war and stay alive." Had he been there, his instructions for reporting the dimensions of destruction of this war would have come from Israeli officials who decided which footage or paragraphs had to be excised because of "military secrets."

While print journalists had a relatively easy time escaping this control, some remained subject to scissors, as were camera crews and TV correspondents. For the most part, reporters, editors and producers accepted the censorship with little fuss or complaint, although it meant the U.S. public saw only one side of the conflict. Israeli censorship, extended to cover "neutral" U.N. statements as well, merited only three paragraphs in *The New York Times* on June 6.

In "Lebanon: the (censored) price of war," Trudy Rubin wrote in *The Christian Science Monitor*, June 16, of "astonishingly little mention of Lebanese civilian casualties by either American media or the U.S. government." Television lenses focused on clashing airplanes and rolling Israeli tanks. Columnists talked of Israel dictating "the 'restructuring of Lebanon' minus the PLO."

Television news didn't touch on the civilian casualties until June 10, when ABC aired a report from Sidon. When Ambassador Shlomo Argov was said by Israel to have been shot by the PLO, somehow the massive killings in Lebanon were made to seem justifiable to American audiences, whose attention was kept on the Israeli version of events. Voices such as that of Sir Anthony Parsons, Permanent Representative of the United Kingdom to the United Nations, were not heard in the United States. His eloquent plea that "this assassination attempt, however despicable, does not in any way justify the massive attacks on Lebanese towns and villages by the Israeli Air Force, attacks which have already inflicted major loss of life, casualties and damage to property . . . " was not matched by a forceful U.S. condemnation and was thus remaindered in the Security Council.

Reportage in the crucial first week of the war originated from Israeli headquarters. There, Israeli "public information" officials dealt out daily doses of government-sanctioned news pegs and paragraphs, while offering Lebanese Christian testimonials on the need to rout the PLO. No single reporter tackled Begin, Sharon or official spokesmen on camera or in print for Israel's refusal to allow reporters into Tyre, Sidon and other southern Lebanese cities and villages after they had been bombed. None deemed newsworthy or remarkable Israel's refusal to allow emergency medical relief to reach civilians in those areas, even when it continued throughout the war, with much official protest to the contrary.

Not until almost three weeks into the war did the media begin to ask the relevant questions. Only in its July 12 edition, five weeks after the first fire, did *Time* magazine discuss "A Double Standard for Israel?" It turned out the double standard was applying a harsher standard to Israel than to other, less "democratic" states. "I think we are picking on them," opined Reuven Frank, president of NBC News.

Earlier in June, according to *Time*, "The Israelis scissored a report by NBC Correspondent Steve Mallory on civilian casualties in Beirut, taking out shots of an old woman and three girls but leaving in a wounded Palestinian guerrilla. Complains Mallory: 'The Israelis have tried to dismiss the existence of a civilian population. Every time we tried to show it, they tried to hide it.'"

In the same article, CBS News President Van Gordon Sauter commented, "There have been some compelling word pieces about the devastation in Beirut, but the Israelis know that words, however eloquent, lack the emotional impact of pictures of people grabbing at stones and clearing rubble to find a human leg." ABC, for its part, defied Tel Aviv's ban only to find its use of satellite transmission facilities cut by Israel. ABC's use was restored two days after it had formally expressed its "regret" in a letter to the Israeli government.

"Leave West Beirut!" a headline in that issue of *Time's* "World" section instructed the PLO, aptly illustrating the several problems of the American media's development of the war story. Nowhere in the article were any civilian casualties mentioned, nor were there any figures given on the hundreds of thousands ordered by Begin to leave. While figures were cited repeatedly for the comparatively smaller number (6,000) of PLO fighters in Beirut, the ordinary people were referred to in an impersonal manner as "the civilian population."

Photographs, too, in that magazine, as in others, reinforce the image of the Israeli presence as benevolent. Israeli soldiers in a placid scene "gaze in silence" at Beirut while on the opposite page a lone "Palestinian soldier, his rifle slung across his shoulder," is pictured walking on a "rubble strewn Beirut street that was hit by an Israeli raid." In fact, an entire building was shown collapsed in a heap, caused by furious aerial bombardment—action somewhat stronger than a "raid."

Meanwhile, a story on cluster bombs featured an illustration that greatly downplayed their harm to civilians. Earlier eyewitness accounts had contradicted Israel's official contention that these "anti-personnel" bombs were "never" used in civilian areas. Richard Ben Cramer, writing in *The Philadelphia Inquirer*, fully detailed on June 30 how "the Israelis have used cluster bombs, made in America, to get the maximum kill per hit." (On July 7, an American nurse just back from rescue work in Beirut told a National Press Club gathering about a young boy she had treated. He asked where she was from and when told he said, "This American, too," pointing to the numerous wounds from metal fragments that had been embedded in his limbs from cluster bombs.) Yet *Time* referred to "possibly illegal use," a frequent allowance for Israeli claims made by the U.S. press.

In the early days of the war, while Lebanese, Palestinian and international agency medical personnel sought to cope with the upheaval and losses throughout the south of Lebanon, Israeli authorities continued to refuse to allow an International Red Cross shipment of 750 tons of relief supplies to sail from Cyprus. After a week's talks, Israel still did not relent and claimed mines off the coast made such a proposition too risky for the agency. No front-page story resulted; instead, only parenthetical mentions were squeezed in on the back pages (e.g., *The New York Times*, June 20). Although the United Nations and individual countries decried this questionable delay, none of the major dailies investigated the Israeli government on its policy of espousing concern for civilians while in reality acting altogether unconcerned. Were it true that the area off-shore was mined, and that the expressed concern for the civilians was genuine, surely a team of Israeli naval experts could have removed them. Instead, this controversy was nonexistent in the body of public knowledge about the war in Lebanon.

Knowledgeable international medical authorities and other observers believe that Israel first wanted to properly "clean" the streets of Sidon and Tyre of the bodies that were "littering" them before allowing in any non-

Israeli officials who might not have fully appreciated actions that resulted in bulldozers digging mass graves for civilians killed while the PLO was being "flushed out." Despite Israeli declarations to the contrary, the first Red Cross and U.N. relief aid was not allowed to leave for Sidon and Tyre until June 17. "First Convoys of Relief Supplies Reach Some Lebanese Civilians," read the headline in *The Washington Post*, with no mention of Palestinian civilians or whether they were being reached. Nor was it mentioned that the International Red Cross Center in Sidon had been destroyed by Israeli bombing on June 7. Instead, this back-page story referred to Red Cross plans to launch "a test by sea, to see if the Israelis stop us." At the same time, Red Cross air shipments were being delayed, too, with little press notice given and Israeli excuses readily accepted.

Norman Kempster of *The Los Angeles Times* wrote in sophomoric terms about a convoy dispatched to southern Lebanon "to help relieve suffering caused by war." His page A-11, June 18 account did not mention what Rep. Lee Hamilton (D-IN) had called the day before "a carnage of enormous proportion," or who had hit how many people and how badly they were suffering. Israel had barred U.N. teams and food from Tyre, where there was "an urgent need for basic foodstuffs, water and, especially, baby food," according to a U.N. bulletin noting that 10,000 people there had sought emergency aid. Meanwhile, the scandal of the blockage of aid continued to receive low-key, intermittent background coverage, if any at all, in newspaper accounts and none on television.

Despite "A Crisis of Conscience Over Lebanon," David Shipler wrote in *The New York Times* on June 18, 'Unmentioned [on Israeli TV] was a United Nations bulletin that the [Israeli] army had left civilians on beaches for two days without food and water and had later barred the U.N. peacekeeping force from continuing relief convoys."

In *The Baltimore Sun*, Douglas Watson wrote of life in southern Lebanon, fully three weeks after Israel had devastated the region. It was "beginning to return to normal for many Lebanese but conditions are much more severe for about 200,000 Palestinian noncombatants—largely cut off from emergency relief supplies."

Still the Israelis banned reporters and U.N. relief officials from visiting the three Palestinian camps hardest hit by Israeli bombs, even in the final days of June. "There also appeared to be considerable Israeli reluctance to let the world see the extent of the destruction of the Palestinian camps, which were the bases for Palestinian armed forces but also had large civilian populations," he wrote.

Watson reported on June 28 that the United Nations Relief and Works Agency (UNRWA), according to its top official, had "only managed to get three or four small truck convoys of aid—not very much—to the Palestinians." Watson was an exceptional reporter because he sought answers from Israeli sources and dug into the question of Israeli treatment of Palestinian prisoners, an issue still not addressed with any vigor by reporters in the United States, who presumably would have been outraged had the players been different.

"Israel Does Not Consider Palestinians POWs," in *The Washington Post* on June 13, revealed that the PLO "Guerrillas clearly have not conducted their operation in accordance with law and customs of war." No comparison was made to Israeli war conduct to gauge its symmetry with law and customs. Nor was the question of what would happen to the PLO soldiers addressed thoroughly. Ultimately, U.S. press coverage of the prisoners' fate was either restrained or nonexistent.

The Toronto Star, on the other hand, gave full rein to a strongly corroborated eyewitness account of Israeli military officials who "beat civilian prisoners to death with their fists, clubs and whips" (June 27). *The Village Voice*, too, reported: "As for prisoners taken by the Israeli forces: captives, including children, have been blindfolded and taken away in trucks. The Red Cross was refused permission to see them. . .no one knows where they are, what has or will happen to them" (Cockburn and Ridgeway, June 22).

French TV viewers saw Israeli soldiers mark the forearms of men with black chalk to indicate if they were Lebanese. American viewers, who saw none of this, could not note the obvious similarities to Nazi treatment of Jews.

Instead, Americans saw the Israeli victor as humanitarian and friend. The picture came through loudly, clearly and repeatedly in two types of TV broadcasts and was reinforced in print accounts. One showed Lebanese civilians from the south, identified as Christians, hailing the conquering soldiers, even proffering flowers. While U.S. news consumers obediently digested this, even cynical correspondents did not pause in their reportage to question whether the humility of defeat, fear of reprisal or even the process of selection itself might not have played a key role in the performance.

The second type, broadcast on all three major news networks, identified "Lebanese Christians" running eagerly to an Israeli truck distributing bread for the hungry in Sidon. One Lebanese woman "was overjoyed until she saw that accompanying the truck was an Israeli camera crew, filming the scene for home consumption. The bread truck, she says, hasn't been back in her neighborhood." (*The Wall Street Journal*, June 22.) No correction was broadcast later; significant discrepancy between appearance and reality remains in the minds of American viewers.

With their vision still blurred by the Israeli report, members of the media faithfully funneled that view back to readers and viewers at home. It began with the skewed headlines, then shifted to justifications, Israeli rationales for the war, each accepted and repeated in turn by the press and commentators.

When Israel launched its "retaliation" for the assault on Ambassador Shlomo Argov in London, the hue and cry over this justification was quickly reinforced in the U.S. media: "Israeli Jets Bomb Guerrilla Targets in Reprisal Strike" (*The New York Times*, June 5th). No quotes were used around "reprisal" to indicate *Israel* said it was in retaliation, a subtle distinction, perhaps, but an immensely significant one. In days to come, the war as told through headlines began to avoid mentioning Israel's responsibility for bombing, striking or attacking, to say nothing of killing.

The Chicago Tribune's headline blared, "Israel retaliates as jets hit Beirut," in another front-page article: Two-thirds of the way through, in paragraph 12, came the PLO denial of responsibility for the Argov attack. *The Baltimore Sun's* front page headline that day, too, read "Israel raids Beirut in retaliation." With 49 dead in Lebanon and 400 wounded after the first day of the war, reporters and editors had forgotten that Scotland Yard had refused to link the assassination attempt to the PLO and they had all but ignored the PLO denial. Palestinian charges that the attack on Argov's life was part of a campaign to discredit them were mentioned on page A-22 once, then went unheeded. (*The Washington Post*, June 5).

The "air raid's primary target," according to the Israeli military command, was a soccer stadium purported to be a training center and arms depot for the PLO. Again, no follow-up coverage was given to the families who had been living there who were killed when two or three stories of the stadium collapsed on them, or to the medical rescue efforts.

Once any association of the PLO with the murder attempt had been dismissed by Prime Minister Margaret Thatcher and British authorities, Israeli officials introduced a second justification, one of "Arab terrorism." Although the assailants were two Jordanians, an Iraqi and a Syrian, Avi Pazner, a spokesman for Israel's Foreign Ministry, laid the blame on an all-encompassing "Arab terrorism," saying, "it made little difference which group was responsible since the Arab terrorist groups are all in Lebanon" (*The Baltimore Sun*).

Justification number three became the "war for peace" theory with a "quick war to destroy the PLO once and for all rather than a longer, less damaging, war of attrition," wrote Norman Kempster in *The Los Angeles Times*.

"The Fighting in Lebanon," (*The Washington Post*, June 7) echoed the Israeli argument. The editorial discredited the PLO for its tendency "to be selective about accepting responsibility for acts of Palestinian violence," and reaffirmed the Israeli "right to protect their people," since, after all, the British had "just gone 8,000 miles to assert the same principle."

The New York Times chose June 5, the day after Israel's "raid" on Lebanon, to condemn Syria's President Hafiz al-Assad for "The Murder of a City," although that massacre had occurred several months before and was not linked to Israel's action, except, in the paper's view, as another striking example of "Arab terrorism." Herschel Auerbach in *The Chicago Tribune* similarly denied the issue by asking, "Could it be that the Arabs have created the Palestinian problem as a weapon with which to destroy Israel, while they keep silent about the Afghanistan problem because it does not suit their interest to attack the Soviets?"

The Baltimore Sun editorialized that "the provocation is a PLO mobilization, with Syrian and perhaps Soviet help, that goads Israel into actions that more secure nations deem excessive." Elsewhere, Israeli tanks had crossed into Lebanon under cover of night while two of its gunships bombarded areas near the Rashidiyeh refugee camp, and its planes blasted 40 different PLO "targets" in southern Lebanon.

While the number of civilian deaths mounted, *The Washington Post* adhered to the Israeli line of reasoning, that even "the Lebanese are coming to the position that the undigested and undisciplined Palestinian presence is the root cause of Lebanon's agony."

Although showing greater comprehension of the Israeli motives in a sarcastic editorial entitled, "Ever Greater Israel," *The New York Times* on June 7 still deferred to Israel's need for "secure boundaries" as excusing its pursuit of "a chimeric security in an ever wider arc of territory, buying time and breathing space by means that inflict new wounds of Arab grievance." It did strike at the heart of the matter by noting that "the foul attack on Israel's Ambassador to Britain was only a pretext for a long-planned strike into Lebanon." But its balancing act resumed with a poke at the "hostile populations" of the West Bank and Gaza and the lament that "it was never reasonable to expect Israel to leave the Galilee hostage to an unfettered PLO army within rocket range," without mentioning that that range was only six miles. The *Post* explained that an 18 to 25 mile zone would put Israeli settlements "out of the range of the 130-mm artillery used by Palestinians."

Up popped Israel's coding of its attack as "Operation Peace for Galilee," with a "clear-cut single mission: pushing the PLO out of the artillery range of northern Israel," according to Moshe Arens, Israel's Ambassador to the United States. Anthony Lewis of *The New York Times*, who earned either the animosity or respect of readers with eloquent, disturbingly accurate assessments of the Israeli incursion, noted, "For nine months not a single rocket or shell was fired by PLO gunners into Israel. . .in short, the cease-fire kept the Galilee safe until Israel bombed Lebanon." This fact was discarded by most of the media.

Douglas Watson, too, noticed the discrepancy (*The Baltimore Sun*, June 7): "However, what Israeli officials did not say yesterday is that before June 4, Palestinian forces in southern Lebanon had fired into northern Israel on only one occasion, May 9, since the start of the ceasefire last July." That instance had occurred "only after Israeli air raids earlier that day, [just] as the PLO shelling Friday [June 4] began only after Israeli air attacks. No one was injured in the May 9 shelling, which military experts said appeared to be a deliberately limited, token counterfire."

"Reports on the invasion were limited by the refusal of Israeli authorities to provide any details on the conflict or, for many hours after the invasion had begun, even to officially acknowledge it," he further explained.

Meanwhile, only three days after the Israeli bombing of Lebanon had begun, did the *Post* decide this "raid" had become an "invasion." News reports and television coverage continued to cite Israeli officials such as Prime Minister Begin and David Kimche, spokesman for the prime minister, proclaiming, "Our sole aim is to free ourselves from the threat of terrorism," and "We are not the aggressors. We are acting in complete and total self-defense of the lives of our citizens." Without any statements from dissenters, the public was left with the impression of a totally justifiable Israeli "sanitizing" action in the face of action by Palestinian "terrorists." The facts were not stated. Again and again, the simple omission of words of attribution such as "claimed Israeli authorities," or "insisted Begin," give the weight of truth to political statements.

A U.N. Security Council vote (15-0) for Israeli withdrawal only made it to page A-10 of the *Post*. Page A-11 of that paper saw the first note of the Arab side of sorrow inserted in "Thousands Flee From Sidon Toward Beirut." The headline did not say what the thousands were fleeing from, which was "advancing Israeli invasion forces," another euphemism for a three-pronged air, land and sea assault by a highly sophisticated army.

The unquestioned repetition of the Israeli jargon—"sanitize," "flush-out," "eliminate," "purify"—directed against the PLO did not provoke comparison to a similarly racist vocabulary used by Hitler's troops. Instead, this phraseology was adopted, as in "Israel has been threatening for months to clean out Palestinian guerrillas in southern Lebanon . . ." (*The Baltimore Sun*). "Israel: Forces to Remain to Flush Out PLO," read *The Washington Post* headline of June 12. Stuck back on page A-13 of *The New York Times* was news that "Mrs. Thatcher Says 'Hit List' Included Name of PLO Aide," on June 7. Thus, Israel had to find a new justification for its attack since its original basis was proven bogus.

"Then What?" in *The Washington Post* still sympathized with Israel, seen as "relieving the sort of border threat that no nation with the choice could abide. It is doing so, regrettably, not only by striking PLO forces but also by dealing death and injury to a great many Lebanese and Palestinian civilians who found themselves in the way of war." It blamed the PLO and said, "Israel's determination to police its northern border cannot be faulted . . . ," without saying whether Beirut had now become part of that border. *The Chicago Tribune* blew no ill wind toward Begin either in "The Pious Outrage About Israel."

Joseph Kraft in "Mideast Opening," on June 8, took up the soon popular Israeli-spawned "opportunities" theory, that Israel had actually moved everyone concerned closer to peace by making war. "In sum, the Israeli attack on Lebanon opens a whole range of diplomatic opportunities." Henry Kissinger hurried to echo the theme as well.

Calling Lebanon a "Gang Rape Victim," *The Baltimore Sun* still concluded, "But it [Israel's action] ought not to be exaggerated." "Too Far," said *The Washington Post,* citing the danger that "Israel, either in cold calculation or in the heat of battle, is going too far." Yet the *Post* blamed "the Palestinian provocation," an old refrain still not true.

News accounts, with remarks including "the Israeli invasion has had a severe impact on this battered city," muted the catastrophic effect of total devastation and implied that since Lebanon was already a war-torn country, this war against civilians was no different and the people must be accustomed to evading gunfire and bombs.

Both *The Baltimore Sun* and *The Washington Post* gave first mention to reports on the details and circumstances of Israeli deaths, while relegating the Israeli estimates of Arab deaths to subsequent placement in the same stories. Nora Boustany's "Israeli Bombers Target Palestinian Coastal

Road," with its news of Arab casualties and Palestinian rescue attempts, was found on page A-31 in the *Post*. On page one, "130 said to die in New Israeli Raids on PLO," illustrates well how headlines and capsulizations of stories can subtly deter a reader from the truth. As Boustany's report details, civilian construction workers and passengers in transit eight miles from Beirut were victims of a nine-hour Israeli bombardment. Yet the words, "said to die," cast doubt upon the mortality of the victims and the source of the figures, while, again, "raids" conveys a notion of sporadic or brief and daring operations, and not of a fully orchestrated, unprovoked attack on civilian lives in a neighboring country. The "Palestinian coastal road" implies an attack on a road belonging to, rather than utilized as a route by, Palestinians, again deflecting attention from the fact it was Lebanese territory that was assaulted. Similarly, mention of "PLO" as the target is accurate only if one listens to Tel Aviv's version of events.

"Israelis hit PLO From Air and Sea As Clashes Widen," in *The Washington Post* implies an equivalent exchange on both sides, while, in fact, Palestinian forces were already outgunned and outmaneuvered as Israeli jets, gunboats and ground troops cut a swath out of its northern neighbor.

David Shipler's early dispatch to *The New York Times* from Jerusalem was "subjected to Israeli censorship." Paragraph three revealed news of the death of an 81-year-old Israeli man from a heart attack suffered while running to an air raid shelter and of the wounding of a 13-year-old girl. No parallel article or even a single paragraph detailed civilian deaths from the Arab side, although there were some 130 dead in Lebanon by then, with at least 250 others wounded.

Curious, too, was the lack of press on the question of Israel's timing in launching its invasion of Lebanon. President Reagan was settled in at the Versailles conference when Israel invaded, just as during the Ottawa, Canada summit in 1981 the President and other industrial world leaders were gathered together when Israel bombed Beirut, with a resultant death toll in the hundreds.

Israel's attack ironically coincided with, or perhaps was meant to divert attention from, the reunion of the survivors of the U.S.S. Liberty, an American electronic intelligence-gathering ship that was sunk by Israel on June 8, 1967 during the 1967 War. (While Admiral Thomas H. Moorer (Ret.), Chairman of the Joint Chiefs of Staff from 1970-74, maintains the attack "could not possibly have been a case of mistaken identity," as Israel and the United States insist, some U.S. officials remain tongue-tied. "This is one I really don't want to handle. This is a loser in every direction. You get in a crunch between the Israeli lobby and the rest of the world if you start commenting on this thing." The official, speaking to *The Christian Science Monitor*, did not want to be identified.)

When Israel assured its ally, the United States, that the number of casualties was small and that civilians had been avoided at all costs, American journalists for the most part either accepted Israeli figures, avoided reporting casualty figures at all, or gave them little play, sticking them at the back of the paper or tacking them onto the end of articles. However, three weeks into the war, Peter Goodspeed of *The Toronto Star* painted a picture that contradicted every single Israeli assurance. Yet his disturbing account was not picked up and run by U.S. newspapers, nor did it prompt radio or TV coverage. Instead, the Arab side of sorrow continued to be well hidden from public view by cooperative members of the media and by the Israeli censor. For the most part, figures on the Arab body count were far from the front page. When discussed at all, the terms employed did not link the number to faces or to families; there was no attempt to humanize or personalize the Arab losses.

An exception was a July 7 commentary by Edward Cody of the *Post*, although even it was couched in qualified terms. Another was when the Palestinian assistant to *The New York Times* lost his family in Beirut; still the headline reference was to a *New York Times'* family, not a Palestinian one, and the bereavement became a newspaper's and not a nation's.

Close-up photographs of any Arab civilians suffering were rare, as were interviews with, profiles of or comments from anyone other than Israeli-sanctioned subjects. Curiously absent, too, were political cartoons that attacked the Israeli-launched invasion and massacre with any degree of strength or sarcasm.

At the same time, network television coverage provided a full-color visual panorama of Israeli sorrow and full, personalized details of Israeli sacrifice, whether from the soldier's or civilian's point of view. Israeli censorship, on the other hand, did not provide for any personal views of Lebanese or Palestinian mothers grieving. Americans were not even allowed to see whether they did, in fact, grieve.

Also, when Arab casualty figures were mentioned, if they were mentioned at all, an authoritative Israeli disclaimer or rebuttal was immediately cited, if it had not already been reported in the top third of the story. For example, lodged in the very last sentence of a *New York Times'* story from Beirut on June 12 was the PLO assertion "that the fighting this week had left 10,000 people killed or wounded."

The slights to the Arab world verged on racism as in *The Baltimore Sun's* June 12 censored article filed from Jerusalem: "reaction from the Arab world . . . has been characteristically hostile and verbose . . . ," with Kuwait listed as the source of "some of the most extreme Arab rhetoric." American eyes were directed in print reports away from the evidence of the nature of the Israeli assault toward the Arab world's lack of a unified or vocal response.

A disturbing pattern of distortion was evident in the headlines of the war. "Why Israelis Invaded Now," explained a typical headline in *The New York Times* on June 7, with the subhead, "Heavy PLO Shelling Said to Tip the Scales." However, the article pointed to Israeli aggression which had launched a PLO defensive action. In the continuing see-saw of reportage, David Shipler said the PLO shelling was "the most severe ever directed against Israeli towns and kibbutzim by the PLO," but did not mention the relative force of the Israeli offensive attack or the comparative death toll inflicted.

Only *The Christian Science Monitor* first used a forceful verb in a headline to describe Israeli aggression, a verb that came close to being appropriate: "Israel's 'Peace for Galilee' Operation Blasts into Southern Lebanon." John Yemma was careful to note that the assault on Argov had no PLO link. He also demonstrated an early understanding of Israel's practical ulterior motives for its northward thrust: water from Lebanon's Litani River, and the secondary psychological factor, a "Biblical 'manifest destiny'" that includes Lebanon as part of Eretz Israel. Alexander Cockburn and James Ridgeway of *The Village Voice* wrote on June 28, "Israeli plans for a Christian Southern Lebanon go back two decades."

Twisted headlines confused the issue once again in "Shelling of Israel Pulled the Trigger," in *The Chicago Tribune*, although the author wrote that the PLO shelling had begun "after Israeli air strikes on Palestinian bases near Beirut."

Headlines continued to rule the interpretation of the war by the American public. Some shied away from linking Israel to offensive war action. Instead, "Hostilities Widen," with the subhead, "Attackers Advance into Palestinian-Held Area to Beirut's South," was typical. *The Baltimore Sun* did not say "Israeli" in a headline of a page A-1 story in early June, opting for "Lebanese Port of Sidon Falls, Invaders Say." The same article spoke of "Israeli jets" in contrast with "Syrian warplanes." "Battles With Syrians Reported," said the *Post* without saying who was battling with them. Predictably, paragraph nine carried a brief mention of Arab casualties in the thousands. "Planes, Ships Back Invasion," broadcast another headline with again no direct connection to Israel's role as invader.

"Syria Reports Clash with Attackers," in *The Los Angeles Times*, kept the ubiquitous Israelis' secret safe from casual newspaper readers. Again, when a series of five cease-fires were made and then broken, the lasting impression given on radio, TV and in print was not that Israel had broken them (or ignored them in the first place) —which it had—but that this constant warfare was pro forma in the Middle East. Not until mid-July when President Reagan was reported to be angry at the Israelis for their lack of cooperation in negotiations and in keeping the cease-fires was there a suggestion in the press that Israel might be at fault.

24

IMAGES OF THE MIDDLE EAST IN CONTEMPORARY FICTION

Janice J. Terry

Dr. Terry is a Professor of History at Eastern Michigan University in Ypsilanti.

Middle East themes have long captured the imagination of Western novelists. The dramatic possibilities offered by the Arab-Israeli conflict and the increased economic and strategic importance of the Arab world have proven to be fertile themes for writers of contemporary fiction. Contemporary novels dealing with the Middle East command attention, not only as literature, but for their influence in forming and reflecting attitudes held by the Western public. Popular fiction is of interest to anyone seeking to understand Western attitudes toward the Middle East.[1]

Pro-Zionist supporters quickly recognized the effectiveness of popular fiction as a vehicle to establish and reinforce sympathy for Israel. Leon Uris's novel, *Exodus*, which described the struggle to establish the state of Israel, remains an outstanding example of the power of fiction to sway public opinion. For many Westerners, *Exodus* stands as the definitive account of Israel's creation. No matter how many times the factual case is

---

[1] Parts of the following have appeared previously in "Arab Stereotypes in Popular Fiction," *Arab Perspectives*, April 1982 and in "The Arab-Israeli Conflict in Popular Literature," *American-Arab Affairs*, Fall 1982.

presented, the dramatic—albeit misleading or false—version has, in the public imagination, assumed the force of reality.

A novelist who wishes to describe the Arab world in a favorable or balanced fashion has first to dispel the body of negative stereotypes the West holds with regard to the Middle East. Because these negative images often have been assimilated unconsciously, many Westerners are unaware of the deeper causes of their latent hostility toward the Arab and Muslim worlds. It appears that most Westerners' support for Israel and hostility to the Arab world spring solely from a desire to see a people grievously wronged given some measure of retribution.

Images of Arab society and the Muslim world are remarkably similar throughout contemporary fiction. Whether they are described as backward, greedy, lustful, evil or inhumane, the Arabs and the Muslims in general are convenient scapegoats in almost all contemporary fiction that deals with Middle East themes. Racial, religious and ethnic stereotypes that are no longer acceptable when applied to Italians, Poles, Jews or Blacks are still applied to Arabs.

The views expressed by novelist Saul Bellow in his book *To Jerusalem and Back* and by historian Barbara Tuchman in a July 25, 1982 *New York Times* article clearly illustrate the common assumptions and attitudes regarding the Middle East that are held by most authors of contemporary fiction. Justifiably renowned for the literary skills and sensitivity they have brought to innumerable other topics, Bellow and Tuchman reveal a marked myopia toward the Middle East.

Both Bellow and Tuchman assume that Western civilization is superior to that of the Arab world. The tacit implication is that as a Western creation, Israel is morally superior to all other nations, particularly those of the Arab world. Although Bellow admits that the Israelis might have done more to aid the Palestinian "refugees," he argues that their creativity and moral superiority have exonerated them. Tuchman totally absolves Israel of any responsibility for the refugees. She argues that the problem of the refugees and, indeed, the entire conflict, has been caused by "Arab intransigence" and, being Arab problems, must be solved solely by the Arabs.

Having assumed the superiority of Israel's national claims, Bellow urges Arab nations to accommodate the "trifling occupancy" of Israel. Similarly, Tuchman describes Israel as a "relatively tiny intruder." That writers as sophisticated and otherwise humanistic as Bellow and Tuchman can describe Israel's "occupancy" or intrusion while simultaneously denying Palestinian or Arab claims, indicates the extent of Western prejudice

316

regarding the Middle East. Arab perceptions of Zionism, not as a higher moral force, but as an alien, imperialistic, expansionist force in the heartland of the Middle East, are rejected. The racial and cultural stereotypes of the Arab world that pervade contemporary fiction stem directly from assumptions of Western and Israeli superiority.

Assuming Western superiority, both Bellow and Tuchman also are thoroughly critical of Islam and Arab history and civilization. Both writers ignore the religious heterogeneity and historic tolerance of the Arab world. Bellow belittles its "traditional religious patriotism" and Tuchman writes about holy wars. Islam is criticized as simultaneously being backward and threatening to Western-Christian hegemony. Arab nations are also depicted as backward and quarrelsome. Completely distorting the reality of the Arab world, Tuchman rhetorically asks what Arab nations have done other than to "quarrel and fight, build skyscraper cities in the desert and ludicrously enrich their sheiks."

Bellow and Tuchman blame the Arab world and "its" Soviet ally for the mounting violence in the region. Again, both writers ignore the diversity of politics and governmental approaches in the region. Because the Arab world is perceived to be less humane than the West, Bellow, like Moshe Dayan and Abba Eban before him, warns against the Levantization or assimilation of Israel. In addition to using these anti-Arab and anti-Islamic motifs, contemporary writers caution against OPEC and Arab control of their own petroleum resources. Tuchman describes OPEC as "holding its Western customers in pitiful thrall."

The assumption of Western and Israeli superiority is basic to almost all contemporary fiction dealing with the Middle East. Bellow and Tuchman were not the first or only writers to devise or to enunciate anti-Arab, anti-Islamic and anti-OPEC sentiments. However, that writers of their intellectual abilities should accept these stereotypes without seeming to question their origins or validity indicates the pervasiveness of negative Western attitudes toward the Arab world. Thus it is not surprising that novelists of considerably less distinction and literary reputation commonly use these same negative images.

The assumptions of inferiority and negative stereotypes regarding the Arab world are deeply ingrained within Western society. Hence novelists who use Middle East themes can depend upon the "willing suspension of disbelief" by readers. Plots and characters that would seem totally outrageous in some other locale or when illustrative of other national groups are readily accepted when used to describe events or characters in the Arab world. Because the average Westerner already has a preconceived image of the area, novels dealing with the alleged mystery and intrigue of the Middle East are also highly saleable.

Novels in which Middle East themes predominate tend to fall into three categories: simple adventure stories; espionage or mystery "thrillers"; and those in which the plots revolve around international finance and Arab petroleum reserves.

In the adventure stories, the Israelis are the heroes and the Arabs are the villains. As in old style westerns, there are innumerable confrontations between the forces of "good" and "evil." *Israeli Commandos* by Andrew Sugar typifies this genre. The plot features an Israeli hero who triumphs over enormous odds. The Israelis are all noble and courageous and the Arabs are cowardly and barbaric. In *Jordan Patrol*, Iqal Lev, a native-born Israeli, writes about "reprisal raids" and "Israeli freedom fighters" from the personal perspective of one who has actually participated in hand-to-hand combat.

The Israelis in *Jordan Patrol* talk extensively of Arab enemies who are perceived as alien outside forces. Many Israeli and Western novelists depict Arabs or Palestinians as hostile, often faceless enemies. In contrast, the Israelis are portrayed as a peace-loving people. Lev refers to "the refugees," never Palestinians, who are "silent columns of human beings" fleeing because their irresponsible leaders have convinced them they will be killed if they remain. Ignoring the military and political ramifications of the Israeli occupation, Lev states that the flight of the refugees was a spontaneous one.

In a particularly revealing scene, the patrol searches the home of a poor Arab (again, never Palestinian) sheikh and his family. In an exchange of gunfire, the Israeli patrol kills a young boy who is perhaps the sheikh's son. The conflict is personalized for the first time when Lev remarks that he realized that a soldier should never see the enemy's face. In spite of the soldiers' momentary depression over the death, they demolish the sheikh's house.

For a brief moment in the narrative, the reader is permitted to pity the Arab enemy. As if to compensate for this lapse, Lev immediately turns the narrative to an Israeli soldier who remembers the 1956 Israeli invasion of the Gaza Strip. He recounts how the Arabs were groveling cowards who only attacked after their enemies had turned their backs. For the reader, the Israeli protagonists are portrayed as sensitive, humane individuals. If they respond to the suffering of their enemies, the Arabs only take advantage of their sympathy. The message is that to survive the Israelis must be strong and vigilant. The deeper implication, which is emphasized in scenes throughout the book, is that the Israeli value system is based on honor and respect for life, but that the Arabs respect neither women nor children and will stab a man in the back if given the slightest opportunity. As an adventure story aimed for the general public, *Jordan Patrol* is revealing for its characteristic portrayal of Arabs in completely negative images and for its rather more positive and three-dimensional descriptions of Israeli attitudes.

A second theme in contemporary fiction centers around the dramatic possibilities posed by espionage activities in the Middle East. Authors of these "super thrillers" create multitudinous plot variations in which Americans and Israelis are the protagonists and the Arabs and Russians are the villains. Since Middle East conflicts are often international in scope, the authors can realistically spread their plots' actions over the entire globe. Using the Arab-Israeli conflict as a basis for plots enables novelists to draw upon Western stereotypes about the Arab world, its society, people and geography.

Literally dozens of these popular novels are available wherever paperback books are sold. Many are jacketed in eye-catching covers which not infrequently depict stereotypic, evil-looking Arabs. The themes have been repeated so often in the mass media that publishers do not have to add explanations. It is assumed that readers will realize that the villainous Arab is terrorizing innocent people. For example, the cover jacket and plot summary of *The Vatican Target* by Barry Schiff and Hal Fishman give no indication that the entire novel is replete with anti-Arab images. In fact, casual references to Arab villains and Muslim fanatics have become commonplace in popular Western literature.

Jihad by Isser Harel, *The Masada Plan* by Leonard Harris, *Khamsin* by Menachem Portugali and *Saladin!* by Andrew Osmond are typical espionage novels featuring the Middle East. As former chief of Israel's secret service, Harel is particularly well qualified to write an espionage novel. Portugali is in fact a pseudonym for two Israeli writers. *Khamsin* is set in Saudi Arabia and features Russian and Arab villains. As Israelis these writers, not surprisingly, perpetuate the image of Israeli superiority and anti-Arab stereotypes. Osmond is a former member of the British foreign service and founder of *Private Eye*, a popular British journal devoted to witty, urbane exposes of scandals and undercover activities. These writers all utilize their firsthand experiences in the Middle East to lend verisimilitude to their narratives. The details in their novels are fairly accurate in contrast to the more contrived descriptions in Harris's *The Masada Plan* in which the plot is set in the United States.

Briefly, the plot in *Jihad* revolves around a Palestinian scheme to incite a full-scale Middle East war by bombing Mecca in an Israeli jet. The plan comes perilously close to succeeding, but is foiled because the hero has actually been an Israeli agent from the very beginning. Harel's characterizations are well drawn, and he uses his knowledge of the Palestinian organizations to good effect. It is, however, unthinkable in this schema that the Palestinians should be victorious. In the end all of the plotters are either dead or under Israeli detention. In the final analysis, the novel imparts the message that in spite of the alleged Arab willingness to instigate any calamitous barbarity in order to gain their ends, these schemes cannot succeed because Israel has superior military and espionage forces.

Similarly, in *The Masada Plan* the Israeli secret services emerge as victors. In a rather convoluted plot, the heroine, a worldly television newswoman, has been having a long-term affair with an urbane Israeli diplomat. Through a series of calculated "leaks" she discovers that the Israelis have atomic capabilities that they are willing to use. The title, *The Masada Plan*, suggests an Israeli determination to fight until death. In this case, the Israelis seek to demonstrate to the world, particularly the United States, their determination to survive even at the cost of nuclear holocaust. Because most of the plot's action takes place in the United States, the Middle East seems far removed and the Arabs are almost peripheral to the reactions of the West. In the conclusion there is some ambiguity as to whether the Israelis would actually have detonated their atomic bombs (which they had allegedly planted in a number of major cities around the world). However, there is absolutely no question of Israel's moral right to manipulate Western responses. Nor is there any question of Israel's right to use nuclear weapons if necessary.

Andrew Osmond's *Saladin!* presents a more accurate description of the Middle East. From Great Britain, Osmond's firsthand experiences in the Middle East are used to good effect as he describes the landscape, personalities and social mores. His protagonist, a former officer in the British Special Air Service, is engaged by Saladin, the code name for a humanistic Palestinian, to lead a sabotage operation within Israel. The motivations of the characters are generally more complex than the two-dimensional figures in the aforementioned novels. Osmond's characters operate from a variety of incentives. Some Israelis work out of commitment and hope for peace; some murderous Arabs are bent only on revenge, but there are also thoughtful, highly educated Arab characters who want to break the cycle of escalating violence. Initially, the protagonist is the willing implementor of Saladin's daring scheme to blow up the newly constructed building for Israeli intelligence (which has been ill-disguised as a post office). As the action progresses, the hero, who is caught by the Israelis, alters the plans so as to abort the original mission.

In the narrative, Osmond focuses on a pair of killers, one Israeli and one Palestinian, and on a pair of essentially ethical individuals, again one Israeli and one Palestinian. The latter are caught in a web of events from which there is no escape. Rather like tragic figures, they are ultimately destroyed by their own better impulses. Osmond, whose hero returns to the bucolic English countryside, concludes that there is no possible resolution to the conflict. The narrative concludes on a grim note:

> No moderate Palestinian leader is in sight; Arafat's star is in the ascendant, Hussein's on the decline. Israel drives a hard bargain, the Arabs have the oil.[2]

Osmond's conclusions are that both sides are culpable and that the PLO, led by Yasser Arafat, is an entirely radical force. As Westerners, Osmond and the hero in *Saladin!* have the luxury of being able to stand apart from physical and emotional involvement in the conflict. The assumption is that the Western world is a superior one. From that position of superiority, Osmond reasons that although both sides have rights and legitimate grievances, their stubbornness and tenacious determination to cling to the past have made a rational (one might even read Western) compromise impossible. Barring compromise, which seems unlikely, the conflict will drag on and more people on both sides will suffer and die. Osmond's protagonist, as with most Westerners, returns to the safety of the Western landscape and dismisses the conflict. In effect, the hero closes the narrative by saying "a plague on both your houses."

Phoenix by Eli Landau and Amos Aricha offers some provocative comparisons to the Osmond novel. Aricha's background knowledge of the Middle East is not provided in the back cover information. But Landau, a prolific writer on Israeli subjects, is knowledgeable about, and in the novel has provided information on, the Israeli government and secret services. *Phoenix* has enjoyed extensive sales and was widely distributed throughout the United States. The plot revolves around the attempted assassination of

---

[2] Andrew Osmond, *Saladin!*, (New York: Bantam, 1979; Doubleday, 1976, p. 333).

Moshe Dayan. The Arabs, with the exception of the Egyptians who are not described as belonging to the Arab world, are presented in thoroughly unfavorable terms.

All of the Arab characters in *Phoenix* are inept, venal and brutal. The assassin, hired by the Libyans, who are portrayed as having limitless financial resources, is a Westerner of uncertain national origin. Although he aims to assassinate the foreign minister of Israel, the assassin gradually comes to admire Jewish culture and Israeli professionalism. He also despises the Arabs for being bumbling, ineffectual amateurs. In other words, the cool, calculating professional cannot help admiring the technical skills and cultural richness of Israeli society. These assumptions, which are evident in all of Landau's writings, are familiar ones throughout popular fiction. For Landau and other writers, the Israelis are superior and there is little, if anything, to admire in Arab or Muslim civilization. Israelis always triumph in these popular novels because they have moral right and Western civilization on their side.

In these popular novels, Western intelligence services and governments always cooperate with Israel. Even allegedly neutral French characters, if they are portrayed in positive terms, assist Israel. Interestingly, in these novels, in perhaps a reflection of reality, Israeli intelligence services operate easily and independently within the United States. Indeed, the novelists assume that domestic U.S. intelligence services have historically cooperated with Israeli intelligence. Accepting the common Western stereotypes of the Arab world, the authors of these "thrillers" assume that readers will agree that any Israeli action, including terrorism and assassination, is acceptable in order to eradicate Arab terrorism.

The few novels that present a more balanced or sympathetic image of the Arab world generally receive limited acclaim. Thomas Roberts *The Heart of the Dog* is a rare fictionalized thriller that is sympathetic not only to the Arab world, but to the issue of Palestinian self-determination. Roberts, an expert linguist with extensive experience in the Middle East, creates a Palestinian heroine who is described as beautiful and as a caring, thoughtful human being. The Arab characters in *The Heart of the Dog* are a far cry from the usual two-dimensional stereotyped figures in most popular literature. However, Roberts' novel appeared only in hard cover form and enjoyed limited sales.

As in *Saladin!*, the hero in *The Heart of the Dog* is a Westerner who becomes thoroughly disillusioned with the Middle East. By the end of the novel, the hero believes a resolution to the conflict is impossible. As a Westerner he can only wash his hands of further involvement. In spite of its essentially cynical and negative conclusion, the novel renders a far more balanced account of the Arab world than others of its genre. In addition, *The Heart of the Dog* gives readers a rare glimpse into Palestinian and Arab motivations.

A third type of popular fiction uses Western dependency on Arab petroleum as a theme. Novels such as *On The Brink*, which is reminiscent of Paul Erdman's *The Silver Bears* and *The Billion Dollar Sure Thing*, revolve around international financial speculations and boycotts or price increases of Arab petroleum. The action in *On The Brink* by Benjamin and Herbert Stein is built around the upheaval allegedly caused by increased petroleum prices, with concomitant spiraling inflation and depleted oil reserves.

The Iranian and Arab members of OPEC are depicted as crafty oil magnates who care nothing about the economic well-being of the world. Instead, they are only interested in retribution for personal slights received in the West. The Saudi delegate, who is described as a "short, dark, clumsy, rich stranger," imagines how sweet the revenge will be.

In an unusual display of Muslim unity, the Iranians and Saudis propose an increase in petroleum prices. Excited by the proposal, the other OPEC members quickly express their support. The inference is that Muslim nations can only unify for actions that will harm Western interests. The chasm between the Muslim world and the West is subtly emphasized with the suggestion that had most of the OPEC delegates not been Muslim, prices would not have increased and "it would have been an occasion for breaking out champagne."[3] In popular fiction, as in most of the Western media, the relationship of OPEC, led by Arab/Muslim nations, and the West is always one of confrontation.

One exuberant OPEC delegate, who is presumably representative of Third World attitudes, asks, "Does this mean that the Zionist racist swine are going to be thrown into the sea?"[4] Again the assumption of the writers is that all Arab, Muslim and Third World leaders have racist attitudes toward Israel and that all are equally hostile to the Western world. In *On The Brink* the petroleum-rich Arab and Muslim nations attempt to bring about the complete collapse of the Western world. The novelists assume

---

[3] Benjamin Stein and Herbert Stein, *On The Brink*, (New York: Ballantine, 1977, p. 24.)
[4] *Ibid.*

323

that the Western reader, steeped in preconceptions about the Arab world, will readily accept the idea that Muslim nations, united under the Prophet's banner, will eagerly wage full-scale economic war against their Western/Christian enemies.

Historically, it was, of course, the Catholic nation of Venezuela that initiated the increase of petroleum prices; however, historic errors and omissions are all too common in popular novels. Thus in *On The Brink* only the Ecuadorian delegate warns that price increases will cause an inflationary spiral that would result in global suicide. As he predicts, the prices in the United States and the rest of the world rise to such an extent that a simple taxi ride costs thousands of dollars. Not surprisingly, the average American vainly strives to maintain the usual standard of living. Meanwhile, all the available gold is being bought by an unnamed purchaser. In a nightmare scenario, extreme parties on the right grow in popularity. Violence breaks out in major cities and thousands are killed. The novel implies that the entire crisis is due to Arab/Muslim greed. Finally, it is revealed that China has been the mysterious gold purchaser, but that it will resell the gold in exchange for wheat from the United States. As the United States regains its economic ascendancy, the OPEC nations are forced to lower petroleum prices.

In a final scene the Ecuadorian OPEC delegate urges the Saudi Arabian delegate never again to raise petroleum prices. However, the Saudi remains unconvinced and prefers to "keep an open mind." There is no such doubt for the reader. The conclusion is that the Arabs and Muslims were solely responsible for the disaster that was only averted by the fortuitous (if not wildly improbable) assistance of the Chinese, who emerge as heroes. In the narrative, the Arabs not only bring the world to the brink of calamity, they fail to learn from the debacle. The Arabs emerge as the enemies who should never be trusted by the Western world. Indeed, the reader is left with the impression that the petroleum-rich Arab nations should be brought firmly under the control of the industrialized West.

The novels discussed here represent only a minute proportion of the popular fiction in which anti-Arab stereotypes appear. The assumptions about, and negative images of, the Arab and Islamic worlds elucidated by Saul Bellow and Barbara Tuchman pervade all genres of popular literature that deal with Middle East themes. These negative images are reinforced and perpetuated in virtually every aspect of the media.

The presentation of the Arab world in popular fiction is riddled with anti-Arab and anti-Islamic stereotypes. Arabs as a group are consistently denigrated through the basest kinds of racial and ethnic slurs. They are portrayed as inhumane, cowardly and hostile to women and children. Likewise, Islam as a religion is presented in the most negative terms. The positive aspects and achievements of Arab and Islamic civilization are almost never mentioned. Furthermore, popular fiction also describes the relationship between the Western world and the Arab world as one of constant economic, military and political confrontation.

These stereotypes and images have been reiterated so frequently in popular fiction that they have become the reflection of reality for most Westerners. The impact of these negative stereotypes has been particularly pervasive because there are few works of popular fiction in which the Arab world is depicted in favorable terms. For all practical purposes, there are no counterweights to the continued negative stereotypic rendition of the Arab world throughout popular fiction. As a result, the average Westerner continues to perceive the Arab and Islamic worlds in terms of the distorted, racially and religiously biased images and stereotypes that are commonplace in popular fiction.

BIBLIOGRAPHY

Aricha, Amos and Eli Landau, *Phoenix*, New York: Signet, 1979.

Bellow, Saul, *To Jerusalem and Back: A Personal Account*, New York: Viking Press, 1976; Penguin, 1977.

Eisenberg, Dennis and Menachem Portugali, *Operation Uranium Ship*, London: Corgi, 1978.

Follett, Ken, *Triple*, New York: Signet, 1979.

Harel, Isser, *Jihad*, London: Corgi, 1978.

Harris, Leonard, *The Masada Plan*, New York: Popular Library, 1978.

Lev, Igal, *Jordan Patrol* , New York: Modern Library, 1970.

Osmond, Andrew, *Saladin!*, New York: Bantam, 1979; Doubleday, 1976.

Portugali, M., *Khamsin*, London: MacDonald Futura, 1981.

Roberts, Thomas A., *The Heart of the Dog*, New York: Random House, 1972.

Schiff, Barry and Hal Fishman, *The Vatican Target*, New York: Fawcett Crest, 1979.

Stein, Benjamin and Herbert Stein, *On The Brink*, New York: Ballantine, 1977.

Sugar, Andrew, *Israeli Commandos: The Alps Assignment*, New York: Manor Books, 1975.

Tuchman, Barbara, "A Task for Arabs," *The New York Times*, July 25, 1982.

25

THE ARAB IMAGE IN AMERICAN MASS MEDIA

Jack G. Shaheen

Dr. Shaheen, Professor of Mass Communications at Southern Illinois University in Edwardsville, is the author of a forthcoming book on television stereotyping of Arabs, entitled Billionaires, Bombs and Belly Dancers.

The all-pervasive Arab stereotype remains embedded in the American psyche. Ugly Arab images are found nearly everywhere—from comic books to television comedies. The Arab remains the media's favorite whipping boy. A few years ago I met with James Baerg, Director of Program Practices for CBS-TV in Washington, D.C., who told me: "I think the Arab stereotype is attractive to a number of people. It is an easy thing to do. It is the thing that is going to be most readily accepted by a large number of the audience. It is the same thing as throwing in sex and violence when an episode is slow."

Why is the stereotype so "attractive"? Why is it an "easy thing to do"? And why do most people continue to accept it? Most important, what steps should be taken to change this image?

Before responding to these questions, certain observations about Arab images need to be made. Each time I prepare a paper or a speech, I encounter the difficulty of too much material. My desk is overflowing with documentation about stereotypes. For example, one file features notes on motion pictures such as *The Formula, Cannonball Run, Paradise, Rollover, Wrong is Right,* and Cheech and Chong's current disaster, *Things are Tough All Over.* The films reveal three basic myths perpetuated about Arabs: (1) they are fabulously wealthy; (2) they are barbaric and

327

backward; (3) and they are sex maniacs with a penchant for Western women.

All three myths are not restricted to the cinema. With some embellishments—harems, nuclear bombs, and flashy Middle Eastern costumes—they appear in editorial cartoons, television shows, comic strips, comic books, college and school textbooks, novels, magazines, newspapers and in novelty merchandise. Those who doubt that stereotypes affect American public opinion are not aware of this all-encompassing image.

The Growth of Stereotypes

To illustrate the omnipresent stereotype, I will begin at the beginning—with children. Before a child learns to read or write he watches Saturday morning cartoons. He sees a host of television heroes and villains. Soon he learns to differentiate between the "good" and the "bad" guys. The heavies, who wear robes and harm innocent people, are Arabs. Children see them lurking in the shadows of the pyramids and double-crossing their American friends (the superheroes Speed Racer and Johnny Quest) in the name of Arab unity. Arabs give watches as gifts—but the watches are time bombs of terror.

Saturday morning cartoon images that the child views are reinforced by the educational television program *Electric Company* on weekdays. This series features an animated Oriental rascal called Spellbinder. Spellbinder is a culprit. Young viewers cheer when Spellbinder is humiliated by the show's hero, Letterman.

While learning to read, the child browses through books about his favorite television heroes: Woody Woodpecker, Donald Duck, and Lassie. He discovers new heroes and old villains. In a Lassie book the setting is Australia, not Arabia. The villain is an Australian criminal, not an Arab. But the author calls the criminal "the shabby sheik." Why? Because he "resembles a phony Arab."

Daily comic strips in newspapers also attract the child's attention. In November 1979 millions of children saw my favorite cartoon character Dennis the Menace ridicule Arabs. Dennis complained on Thanksgiving Day: "Dewey's family's havin' meatloaf. His dad says some Arab is eating *their* turkey." Other comic strips expose the child to oily "sheiks" with too many women and too much money. In *Broom Hilda*, several Arabs sing of *Greed* to the tune of "Mother":

G is for the gold in our closets;

R is for the rubies in our hands;

E is for the ears hurt by your cursing us;

E is for our earning power so grand;
D is for the dirty prices that we charge;
Y is for your dollar's misery;
Put them all together they spell *GREEDY*, the word that fills
our hearts with glee.

Kids and adults love comic books. While waiting for my son to have a haircut, I picked up a copy of *G.I. Combat*. Here, the brave sergeant observes a vulture hovering over a dead American soldier. He swears vengeance on Arab nomads: "This is the fifth time those desert thieves have stripped the bodies of G.I.'s. We're going to hunt down those *human hyenas*." Eventually the hero confronts the nomads. He sets a T.N.T. "booby trap." Hordes of Arabs are killed. The sergeant boasts: "The vultures are back. But this time they'll feast on human [Arab] hyenas."

The child enters his teens. He familiarizes himself with a dictionary, thesaurus, and thesaurus of synonyms and antonyms. These reference works are essential to the learning process. In them, Arab is defined to mean: "vagabond," "vagrant," "tramp" or "bum." An Oxford Children's Reference Library, *The Arab World*, asks, "What is an Arab?" The author gives several answers: "The baggy-trousered workman asleep on the corner of the pavement, and not bothered at all whether he finishes his work today, tomorrow, or never. A peasant. . .who rides a donkey, while his wife, in a long black robe, walks behind carrying the bundles." Concludes the author: "All these people are Arabs."

School textbooks teach teens that "Jerusalem is the capital of Israel," that "one out of four Arabs is a Bedouin," and that Arab teens are not expected to have fun. Says one writer, "in fact in some parts of the Arab world if a girl is thought to have behaved badly, her brother may kill her, and the neighbors will admire him for doing his duty."

While perusing Isaac Asimov's *Science Fiction Magazine*, he discovers the following ad: "THE ARABS HAVE MILLIONS TO LOAN. INVEST. $25,000-$10,000,000 Possible. FREE DETAILS! Arab-DC, 935 Main, Vidor, Texas 77632." If he responds to the ad, the young man will receive gobs of literature from a Mr. Sam Paradice, who promotes "the Arab Money Hotline." "This is where the money is to be found," writes Paradice.

Many youngsters read the nationally syndicated magazine, *The Weekly Reader*. The *Reader* is distributed to numerous schools throughout the country. Youngsters see editorial cartoons depicting the Arab as a terrorist or as a grotesque. Such cartoons are reprinted from major newspapers. *The*

329

Weekly Reader also publishes original cartoons submitted by teens. One award-winning cartoon shows Arabs ready to start *WW III*.

"Learning" about the Arab continues when teens read "fun" magazines after school. Youngsters discover innovative games to play with friends, such as *Cowboys and Arabs*. Instead of a football, an oil can is used. The goal posts are marked "Mideast" and "USA." The team that places the most cans of oil in the end zone wins. Winners (Cowboys) wear white cowboy hats. Losers (Arabs) wear headdresses.

Teens also play the "Oil Sheik" game. Like Monopoly, the players in "Oil Sheik" try to acquire real estate. Unlike Monopoly, the money is tributed in billions of dollars. The teens try to "gain control of the oil-producing nations." To make the game more "life-like," kids are advised: "Wrap a pillowcase around your head. If you are ugly put your head in the pillowcase." Each playing card features a scimitar or an oil well. Instructions are written on the back of the cards: "Arabs are ready to go to war if you cut off supply of cadillacs," and "impress Arabs with your patriotism by dating a camel."

The youth purchases "Honest Abdul's" model oil wells. Besides the phony Abdul and his well, an illustrated booklet tells him that he can live like a Middle East oil man—gamble, drink, drive at top speed, and ride fine horses. "Your job is to uphold this lifestyle," says the pamphlet. "You are now entitled to as many wives as you care to have," followed by a number of cliches, including a list of don'ts, beginning with "Don't get a job" and ending with "Don't think of yourself."

Other novelties-for-profit are more slanderous. A Massachusetts firm promoted its charcoal briquet called "Sheeks" by featuring a robed Arab with a headdress perched above a flame. "Sheeks," says the ads, "save oil" and "are so easy on the pocketbook."

At a popular shopping mall teens see, prominently displayed next to scary animal masks, a disfigured mask of an Arab. Blazing red T-shirts also attract youngsters. Emblazoned on some shirts is a gas pump designed as a slot machine. Smug faces of four bearded, chubby-cheeked Arabs appear next to the inscription: "One-arm Bandit."

Most likely, by the time a youngster is ready to graduate from high school he will not have known any Arabs. Over a period of years, however, the media image has filled the gap. CBS's *30 Minutes* (March 1981) tells him that Israel is "surrounded by hostile Arab states," and that the PLO "kills women and children." As a high school student, an editorial cartoon by Herblock teaches him that Arabs are "Jew Hunters." The motion picture *Rollover* suggests that Arabs are intent on destroying the American way of life. Automobile ads (what is more precious to a student than his first car?) also pave the way to providing clouded images. Ads encourage youths to "Beat the Sheik" and to "Drive an Arab Crazy."

When it comes to music, a youth's record collection may include two Middle Easterns: "Hava Negela" and "Ahab the Arab." He often hears "Hava Negela" on the radio or when he goes to a sporting event. When the home team is about to score the organist usually plays "Hava Negela," accompanied by the stomping feet of cheering fans. As for "Ahab the Arab, the Sheik of the Burning Sands," this song is occasionally featured on television in order to show scantily clad women in harem-dress.

The youth prepares to enter college, armed with a thorough media education. He has spent more time before a television than in the classroom. He takes a break from his studies to watch his favorite wrestlers: The Sheik, Akbar the Great, and Abdullah the Butcher. The television announcer explains that these "Arabs" wrestle for the sheer pleasure of inflicting pain on others. What the announcer does not say is that the wrestlers are Americans—not Arabs.

At a local bar, our college student may opt for a game of darts. The dartboard is covered with a poster of an Arab wearing dark glasses, his palms outstretched.

No longer interested in Walt Disney films that show Arabs taking farmland belonging to elderly American farmers, he now sees motion pictures such as *Black Sunday* that show Palestinians trying to assassinate an American president. In *Ashanti*, he watches an Arab abuse young Blacks at an open-air slave market in Saudi Arabia. He sees a rerun of a rerun on television, such as "Our Man in the Harem." Here American beauty queens are "branded" and enslaved in the Kingdom of Aramy's bordellos. Some television images do not pass into video heaven. I first saw "Harem" in the mid 1970s. Then, in November 1981, "Harem" attracted my attention on the CBS late, late show. Afterwards, I couldn't sleep. "Harem's" imagery troubled me. I had assumed that such programs were gone—for good. Such was not the case. The plot merits a brief summary. In "Harem," the Arab villain, Ramal, wants his imported women to be "beautiful, blonde, young and innocent." If they refuse to love him, they will be branded on the face and sent to the local bordello where men pay 25 cents for moments of pleasure. "Business is booming." As for Aramy's sheikh, he demands his nephew be beheaded on the day of his birth.

On occasion the youth picks up a novel—there are hundreds—that feature Arab villains. The publishing industry has profited by perpetuating offensive, false images. One novel that best sums up the Arab image in works of fiction is *The World Rapers* by Jonathan Black. Says Black: "Jemel Karami is an American Arab. . .men like Karami have been raping the world for years and pass the art down from father to son with each son improving on the old man's techniques." Karami is portrayed as a killer of innocent Israeli women and children, and as an American draft dodger who ruthlessly deceives his two friends, a Gentile and a Jew. He seduces and causes the death of one friend's wife while achieving financial gain at the expense of the other. Jemel's brother is a mentally unbalanced homosexual. His sister is a nymphomaniac. When Jemel finally meets his fate, can we fault the young reader for rejoicing?

There are hundreds of examples of Arab stereotypes in contemporary popular fiction. Yet, to date, I have not read a single novel that features heroic Arabs unless there is a host of Arab baddies nearby. The contemporary Arab villain is sometimes half-German (*Key to Rebecca*). And a familiar plot depicts this villain, complete with belly dancer as accomplice, matching wits against a British or American agent and a heroic Israeli woman. In most novels, Arabs are portrayed as oil junkies determined to crush the West and as inept assassins intent on wiping Israel off the face of the earth with nuclear weapons. (Yet Israel is the only nation in the Middle East with nuclear arms.)

When the young adult's formal education is completed, his media education continues. On television, he witnesses commericals, reruns and old movies that show Arab villains pitted against American or Israeli heroes.

On Broadway, he opts for the humor of Neil Simon. He sees *California Suite* and is told: "Mecca is a smelly place." In *They're Playing Our Song*, the protagonist says "American Independence was worth fighting for. . .and Israel is worth fighting for." In *Chapter Two*, the actor is asked: "How was London?" He grunts: "Full of Arabs."

Magazines ranging from *Playboy* (where Arabs try to buy the Grand Canyon or fail to acquire harem-maidens) to *Change* reinforce the stereotype. In *Change* (August 1981), he learns that Bir Zeit University is an "Israeli University," that the Palestinians who "live" on the *Israeli* "West Bank" are either "radicals" or "terrorists." He is unaware that the article is biased, that it contains a minimum of 12 factual errors such as: "In 1920 Jerusalem had a firm Jewish majority."

When reading both the front section and financial pages of newspapers he learns that Arabs are buying up his country. The paper does not inform him that "Arab investment is small—substantially behind the sums invested here by Europeans, Canadians or Japanese." Financial expert

Sylvia Porter tells him that Americans should beware of oil money—saying that in America "Arabs are behind practically every business deal." Where else have we heard this kind of rhetoric during this century?

While doing research, now a Congressional aide, our young adult finds no major government documents that refer to Arab stereotypes. Officially, the stereotype does not exist.

On ABC-TV's *20/20*, our researcher sees a one-hour special on Palestinians (August 1981). This top-rated news series dramatized a story wherein Palestinian terrorists hold innocent people hostage and threaten to blow up an oil tanker in New York harbor. They demand that the president establish a Palestinian state on the West Bank, or else millions of New Yorkers will perish.

Such news programs may be viewed as "the truth." Since childhood, the Congressional aide, now a Congressman, has been programmed to accept Arabs as villains and "others" as heroes. Over the years he received a host of misconceptions about Arabs. Will such perceptions influence his decisions concerning Middle East policies? Will he believe that Palestinian equals terrorist, that Arab means oil-rich, that Arab woman equals belly dancer? Conversely, will he accept the other myth that those who occupy Palestinian land are heroic "James Bond" types?

The media distortion of Arabs and the "play on words" is all encompassing. On the day of Anwar Sadat's death, correspondent Mike Wallace said, "Sadat launched," not the October 1973 war, but "the Yom Kippur War." Half-truths and fiction have a way of becoming real.

The Governor of Ohio (August 1981) complains that Californians are becoming the "Arabs of America" by withholding energy lands from production. Other politicians, a Detroit official and Boston's mayor, make racial slurs. U.S. Government bumper stickers state "Driving 75 is Sheik: Driving 55 is Chic." The FBI creates ABSCAM. Like Arab money, Arab people are labeled "unsafe at any price."

Americans and Arabs should admit there has been and continues to be a failure to address the stereotyping problem. Media images affect public opinion, which in turn affects U.S. foreign policy. The imagery about Arabs that is disseminated throughout the United States acts as a barrier to peace. Yet both Americans and Arabs have only themselves to blame. Why? Because we have not yet educated ourselves or others. The stereotype endures because of improper action and inaction.

What steps are Arab nations and Arab-American organizations taking to counter negative images with positive portrayals? Do they respond to anti-Arab images as a unified force or do they react sporadically? Will the children of the fictional Congressman view Arabs as their father does?

Michael Hudson of Georgetown University has written: "A conspiracy is not needed to maintain the vicious cycle of stereotyping—just complacency." We know that ethnic slurs are not restricted to Arabs only. It took Black Americans over 60 years before the motion picture industry began addressing the problem of Black stereotypes. Blacks and other minorities discovered that just because you are being unfairly stereotyped does not mean that those images will change.

In spite of the denigration of Arabs in the media, I am optimistic. "The openness to change is an enduring, ongoing vitality, an American tradition, and the true strength of the American experience," said Brandon Stoddard, President of ABC Motion Pictures. An increasing number of Americans want to better understand the Arab world. And recently, many publications such as *The Washington Post, The Wall Street Journal, Time, National Geographic* and *TV Guide* have featured well-balanced articles. In contrast to "entertainment" images of Arabs, television also projects evenhanded reports. At present, thoughtful articles and TV programs treat Arabs not as terrorists or "oil sheiks," but as individuals with rights and aspirations. The main objective of the reporter is, after all, to capture fragments of reality and to arrange them in an honest, meaningful manner.

Informed journalists—print and broadcast—have informed Americans about the Israeli occupation of the West Bank. ABC-TV's *20/20* program "Under the Israeli Thumb" (1982) provided American viewers with a well-documented analysis of how peace-loving Palestinians are being persecuted by a state that was established to escape persecution. The documentary humanized the lives of the Palestinians under Israeli occupation. It showed Palestinians being pushed off their lands, denied water for their crops, and being jailed and beaten.

Eight years ago, I saw CBS reporter Mike Wallace equate Palestinian with "terror." In a 1981 CBS documentary, however, Wallace equated Israeli with "oppressor." The documentary shows how Israel "expropri-ates" Arab land. The message conveyed by Wallace and the producers? Israel the oppressed has become Israel, the oppressor.

Journalists provided Americans with the tragic realities of the Israeli invasion of Lebanon in 1982. For months we saw relentless bombing raids, flickering images of destruction, the homeless, the maimed, the dead. To their credit, American journalists covered this invasion well. No one should accuse them of being pro-Arab or pro-Israeli. Pro commitment-to-truth best summarizes their coverage.

The United States is the world's leading exporter of information. Unless we begin now to seriously work against the stereotypers and distorted images of the Arab people, they will continue. Tomorrow's citizens will inherit today's imagery.

Let us not minimize the influence of the mass media. One reason the rape of Palestine took place was because journalists failed to show us the Palestinian people. We could not *feel* for those we did not *know*.

Today, Arabs are known, but not as they have been or as they really are. To date, no major picture or television program, no best seller, no Broadway play has traced the life of a humane or heroic Palestinian. Isn't it time for us to see an Arab version of "Fiddler on the Roof," "Exodus," and "Roots"?

In Los Angeles, California, the story editor of the *Trapper John, M.D.* television series told me that he would love to write a screenplay about Arabs. But, "I can't write about what I don't know," he said.

During a recent sabbatical in Jordan I saw men at prayer, devout Muslims expressing their faith. A taxi driver kept his passengers waiting as he removed a prayer rug from his car. Kneeling at the curb, he paid homage to his creator. At an office, an elderly man walked into an empty room and softly recited mid-day prayers. One day I hope to see entertainment programs portray Arabs and Islam in this manner—on a human level.

Change is occurring. Perceptions of the Middle East by today's journalists are becoming more balanced. But the ugly "Arab image" in popular culture remains. In order to eradicate such imagery, let us assist those responsible for stereotypes to see for themselves what Arabs really are. If, as Ali Ghandour, President of the Royal Jordanian airlines, says, "Arab is beautiful," then let Arab beauty be exposed. For as it is written in the Quran, if we do not have the capacity to change ourselves and our attitudes, then nothing around us will change.

Tunisian Prime Minister Mohammad Mzali has said that "the Arabs need to publicize their cause to the world." He asked an important question, one to which both cynic and optimist should adhere: "What have we, as Arabs, done in the fields of information, culture, and politics to acquaint the American people with our point of view?" The problem, said Mzali, "is that the Arabs tend mainly to criticize—not to act."

The time for talk to cease and action to begin is the present. The Arab stereotype is due not so much to malice as it is to ignorance. As Jordan's King Hussein said, "We [Americans and Arabs] belong to the same family and our hopes and aspirations are the same. All we need do is concentrate

335

on understanding each other better." Hussein's words reflect what the Prophet Mohammad said 1400 years ago: "All mankind is one family in the care of God."

THE EFFECT OF AMERICAN PERCEPTIONS OF ARABS ON MIDDLE EAST ISSUES

Michael W. Suleiman

Dr. Suleiman is a Professor of Political Science at Kansas State University.

Numerous studies have shown American partisanship in favor of Israel both in attitudes as well as in suggested policies toward the peoples and countries of the region. These same studies have also revealed a strong anti-Arab bias as reflected in the public's negative stereotypes of the Arabs, their society, culture and institutions. It can be argued that Arabs, including the Lebanese, have been so dehumanized in the American media that Americans (public officials, opinion leaders, the general public) are inured against the miseries and concerns of the Arabs or any segment of the Arab world.

It is worthwhile for us, therefore, to look carefully at American views of Arabs to see how these stereotypes have contributed to American insensitivity about the needs and concerns of the Arabs. The first and very significant finding is the absence of historical writings in America in which Arabs and/or their contributions and history are mentioned. It is as if Arabs did not exist, had no impact on America, or were completely ignored by historians and social scientists. As Leuchtenberg put it:

> *From the perspective of the American historian, the most striking aspect of the relationship between Arab and American cultures is that, to Americans, the Arabs are a people who have lived outside of history . . . For one may read any standard account of the history of America, until the most recent times,*

*and derive from it the impression either that the Arabs have had no history or
that it was only of the most inconsequential sort.*

Until this century, very few Americans came in contact with Arabs.
American views of Arabs were primarily based on their reading of
European accounts about the Middle East and its peoples. These views
represented Arabs as fanatical, ignorant and dangerous. Also, the
American image of the Arabs was influenced by the early European
colonists' encounter with Native Americans. A theory of social and
cultural superiority vis-a-vis the American Indian, referred to as an
ideology of "savagism," was apparently applied to Arabs as well. All these
negative stereotypes were not restricted to popular writings by travelers
and diplomats but often extended to the scholarly works of the
Orientalists.

The fear of Islam and Muslims is a major factor in the production of the
negative Arab image in the West, most specifically in the United States.
This is the case since, in much of the writing about Arabs, there is
confusion concerning Arabs and Muslims. Consequently, to many if not
most Americans the terms "Arabs" and "Muslims" are interchangeable.
Ignorance about, and negative images of, Islam (and there are many) are,
therefore, readily transferable to Arabs. Furthermore, one often gets the
impression that "Arabs" and the desert are almost synonymous—or at
least they belong together. While at one time, early in this century, there
developed a rather romantic image of the desert and its assumed
inhabitants, i.e., the Bedouins, the more recent view stresses the aridity
and absence of development. Rarely, if ever, do Americans get exposed to
the image of Arabs "making the deserts bloom." The usual emphasis is on
Arabs doing little, if anything, to improve their conditions or the
productivity of the land on which they live.

In the desert, where Arabs are found, one also finds oil. Although oil is
an indispensable energy source for the West (perhaps *because* it is such),
Arabs are almost always associated only with the negative aspects of oil,
i.e., oil boycotts, price increases (often referred to as "gougings,"
"robbery," etc.), and the price-fixing "oil cartel." Furthermore, there is
hardly any distinction, even by many national reporters for American
media, between the Organization of Petroleum Exporting Countries
(OPEC) and its Arab counterpart, the Organization of Arab Petroleum
Exporting Countries (OAPEC). Very frequently, OPEC translates into
"Arabs," who get blamed for its actions. In fact, cartoonists' favorite
depiction of OPEC is a barrel of oil looking like an Arab sheikh or having

338

such a sheikh holding the gasoline nozzle as if it were a gun—and pointed at the American consumer. Only rarely is Saudi Arabia, for instance, given credit for its moderate views and its attempt to keep oil prices relatively low. Indeed, even this helpful action is sometimes debunked or explained away as not really done to help the United States and the West but in the self-interest of Saudi Arabia. In other words, the Arabs find themselves in a situation "damned if they do, damned if they don't." If they raise the price of oil, they are viewed as engaging in price gougings, if they try to keep the price down, some people's attitude is that "they are not doing us any favors!"

Based on American reporting about the Middle East, the general public gets the impression that Arabs are either fabulously rich or in dire poverty—with hardly a reference to the middle class. The fabulously rich Arabs squander their wealth, we are told, on consumer products and the leisure industry, gambling, wild parties, as well as "stupid" acts of generosity, like using a Rolls Royce in London for two days and giving it to the chauffeur as they reach the airport to leave the country. As for the poverty-stricken Arabs, i.e., allegedly most of the population, these are believed to be denied the benefits of their countries' fabulous wealth by rulers who are despotic, corrupt, vicious and/or uncaring. Among the possible exceptions are those viewed as pro-Western, at least as long as they are in total agreement with the United States on foreign policy issues, especially on the Middle East.

The First World War era's romantic image of both the Arabs (Bedouins) and the desert has been changed by Hollywood to one of mean-looking, dagger-wielding individuals lurking outside someone's tent (or door of a house) ready to stab him in the back at the first opportunity. In other words, this image of the Arab presents him as a liar and a cheat, one who cannot be trusted. He is, furthermore, dirty and immoral, i.e., does not subscribe to Western codes of morality. Arab women, on the other hand, are generally viewed as either completely and violently suppressed or willing and docile "slaves" or harem to their menfolk.

At least until the 1973 War (and since then, though to a lesser extent), Arabs were viewed as united only in their opposition to Israel. Even in this case, however, they are believed to be unable to unite effectively. Furthermore, with some exceptions, Arab soldiers are seen as poor fighters and the Arab fighting machine as ineffective. To this add the view that Arab regimes are undemocratic and/or unstable and, therefore, they are undesirable and/or unreliable allies for the West and for the United States in particular.

339

Implications of Negative Stereotyping

Since it is obvious that Americans generally hold many negative stereotypes about Arabs, it is important to spell out clearly what the implications of this situation are. To begin with, it makes it difficult for reporters in any medium, whether it be radio, television, the movies or textbooks, to report objectively, honestly and adequately. They first have to overcome their own prejudices—prejudices that are broadly shared by their colleagues, superiors and the public in general. Thus, if they present views or even information different from the "accepted" ideas, they will have to fight or have conflicts with their bosses. Even if they win there, they will be reporting to readers who have strongly held preconceived ideas. Consequently, their reports will often be viewed as shallow or prejudiced and, in either case, are likely to be easily forgotten or dismissed as the exception rather than the rule. The alternative, which is the most comfortable option to choose, is for reporters to exercise a degree of prior restraint so that they refrain from reporting too favorably on Arabs or Muslims—even when the facts warrant such reports. Conversely, reporters often avoid reporting too negatively on the Zionists/Israelis—again even if the facts warrant such reporting.

Perhaps the best indication of how widespread and deep-rooted negative Arab stereotyping is in the United States would be the so-called "Abscam" operation. In this 1978 con game, an agency of the U.S. government, charged with maintaining law and deterring crime, itself resorted to the use of a reprehensible mechanism in which it both exploited *and* reinforced a popular image of Arab sheikhs as extremely wealthy individuals who are liars and cheats and who resort to bribery and corruption to get what they want illegally from American legislators. I think it is important to discuss the facts of the case and their implications in some detail. As you might recall, Abscam was an operation in which the FBI invented an Arab sheikh, named him Kambir Abdul Rahman and gave him a false business entitled "Abdul Enterprises, Ltd." FBI agents then pretended to work for Kambir and proceeded to pay hundreds of thousands of dollars to American public officials in return for influence peddling in the areas of "investments, obtaining permission for Arab businessmen to reside in the U.S., and building hotels and gaining a casino license in Atlantic City, New Jersey."

First, let us look at the caricature or the stereotype of the Arab in the mind of both the FBI agents *and* the Members of Congress involved. This fabricated Arab sheikh was not only rich and corrupt, he also had a non-Arab name, i.e. Kambir—but one which *sounds* Arab to Americans.

340

Furthermore, "Abdul," as the name of the fake business enterprise, again reflects and reinforces popular ideas of the typical Arab name. Hardly anyone on either side of this sting operation appeared to know or stopped to reflect, it seems, that, in Arabic, "Abdul" is not only nonsensical, but almost sacrilegious since it leaves out the most important part, i.e., God's name. One would think that even in English it is rather silly to have as a name "The Servant of." Furthermore, the success of this operation demonstrates most clearly Hollywood's triumph in shaping the American image of Arabs. For how else can we explain this situation in which at least one U.S. Senator and seven Congressmen were completely taken in by this clumsy attempt at playacting, Hollywood style—a situation otherwise devoid of any reality or even real Arab characters?

In an era in which ethnic jokes are frowned upon and when the U.S. government is engaged in extensive programs to protect minorities against discrimination and prejudice, it is indeed most alarming that the FBI agents who carried out the Abscam operation did not even *consider* that they were maligning anyone or any group. In other words, this negative stereotype of the Arabs is so well ingrained that it appeared to be the real thing! As has been asserted many times since then, no Jewscam or Blackscam, for instance, would have been contemplated, let alone tolerated or carried out.

In the political realm, numerous grave implications follow from negative Arab stereotyping. Thus, aspirants for political office as well as those already elected often end up not only supporting Israeli (i.e., anti-Arab) causes, but find it useful to say something nasty about Arabs or their viewpoint. As one former Congressperson confided to me: "I figured I would be hurt if I went against Israel or pro-Israeli interests and I would *not* be helped if I publicly sided with the Arab view. I had to play it safe." The lesson is learned early and is reinforced in every national election. A politician is thus hurt by "controversy" if he or she appears to be pro-Arab, even when such a stand is believed to be in the national interest. Furthermore, the politician hopes that moving in the opposing direction might well help. Aspirants to the Presidency in particular have to be careful about what they say or write and how they vote practically throughout their entire political life. Appearing to be pro-Arab is viewed as a definite handicap—and possibly politically suicidal.

It is common knowledge that during election years, and more so during national presidential elections, U.S. policy toward the Middle East is either at a standstill or is very pro-Israeli and anti-Arab in tone, primarily to please Israel's supporters. Here again the feeling is that displeasing Arab supporters may be done with impunity. Even after the election is over, the President and his Administration feel the strong pressure not to act in a manner which may be construed as pro-Arab. Under such pressure, a weak President, or one whose popularity is low or slipping, is greatly tempted to go with the easy and "popular" decision. Jimmy Carter's Presidency provides two recent examples. The first was in October 1977 when a joint American-Soviet statement about how to proceed in the Middle East peace process was abandoned by the President shortly thereafter, under much Israeli and pro-Israeli pressure. The second and even more glaring example of buckling under pressure and abandoning what was termed by the Israelis as a pro-Arab stance was the "reversal" after the fact of the U.S. vote on a U.N. Security Council resolution that condemned Israeli settlements in territories occupied in 1967.

Because of negative stereotypes, even Arab investments in the United States which bring in money and jobs and, therefore, help both the balance of payments and the employment problems, are viewed with suspicion and discouraged, if not severely restricted. Various headlines in the media illustrate this almost racial stereotyping, which is meant to raise the spectre of "Arab" takeover of the United States. Examples are: "Arabs buy up plush real estate in Hollywood"; "Arabs are taking over banks in the U.S."; and "Does Arab Cash Imperil U.S.?"

In the case of the Palestinians, negative stereotyping has practically made a non-people out of them. They have been dehumanized, and the consequence is to treat them and other Arabs generally as not having much, if any, demand on our conscience. Also, if Palestinians are a non-people, it is easy to wish them away, refuse to talk to them or their representative, the PLO, and to persist in excluding them from any formula for a proposed solution to this nagging problem. Furthermore, the language that is used to describe incidents involving the Palestinians is sanitized and almost noncommittal. Recent encounters on the Lebanese-Israeli border provide good examples of this type of reporting. While we are provided with much detail and many pictures and television coverage about the inconvenience, concern, fear, insecurity, suffering, injuries, deaths, funerals, sadness and overall rage of the Israelis after an attack by Palestinian forces, termed terrorists, we are then informed of the "retaliation" of the Israelis in which, "according to Palestinian" or "Lebanese" sources, tens or hundreds of individuals were killed or injured. The reports often merely repeat Israeli claims that "guerrilla" or "terrorist" bases were the target. Even Lebanese civilians are ignored or merely included among those counted as residents of "terrorist" camps.

The conclusion is inescapable: to the reporters or news directors, an Arab life is not equal to an Israeli life, and Arabs do not apparently suffer as much as Israelis or else their suffering is not as important or pertinent to us. While there was more of an uproar over the July 17, 1981 Israeli bombing of Beirut in which over 300 people were killed and about 800 injured, the true extent of the tragedy and the shattered lives of hundreds of civilians hardly received the attention it deserved in the United States. Their frustration and anguish were reminders, if such were needed, that, stereotypes to the contrary notwithstanding, Lebanese and Palestinians, as well as Arabs generally, are human too.

The way policy–makers view major issues greatly determines the policies followed in resolving those issues. Thus, American attitudes toward Arabs have at times caused them to make serious and very costly mistakes, leading to dangerous world situations. The 1973 War provides a good example of miscalculation on the part of American policy–makers, primarily as a result of stereotypic thinking about Arabs, Palestinians and Israelis. It should be remembered that this situation was generally admitted and widely reported in the press—after the fact. Is a similar situation developing with respect to Lebanon? American policy–makers apparently continue to operate on the assumption that their most important concern is Israel's security—and to accept Israel's definition of what "security" means and how best to bring it about. In the process, the legitimate rights, sufferings, security and other concerns of the Lebanese, Palestinians, Syrians and Arabs generally are accorded a lower priority. This is the inevitable conclusion that one reaches after reviewing American pronouncements, policies and actions concerning Israeli encroachments in Lebanon.

Thus, in the first few months of 1981, Israeli attacks on Lebanon became quite numerous and diversified and caused much damage and many civilian casualties. Instead of restraining the Israelis, high American officials put out strong signals of approval. For instance, Richard Allen, President Reagan's National Security Advisor, called such attacks justified "hot pursuit." Also, on July 24, 1982 the United States was instrumental in bringing about a ceasefire agreement between Israel and Lebanon—but not before a day of terror was visited upon innocent civilians in the Lebanese capital which resulted in over 1,000 casualties. Furthermore, the U.S. government's reaction to this act of carnage was, to say the least, rather mild. It is true that Secretary of Defense Caspar Weinberger attacked Prime Minister Menachem Begin's policies as disruptive of the peace mission of U.S. envoy Philip C. Habib and as obstructing the peace process generally. Also, Deputy Secretary of State William P. Clark, in an interview, expressed "disappointment and maybe some embarrassment" with Begin. However, White House Chief of Staff James Baker specifically rejected the notion that these officials spoke for the Administration, and asserted that they spoke for themselves.

Also, the Reagan Administration on July 20, 1981 suspended "indefinitely" F-16 deliveries to Israel. However, even though this decision came after the Israeli raid on Beirut, the Administration refused to link the suspension directly to the raid. In fact, Secretary of State Alexander Haig was very explicit in stating that the decision was "not related to any specific action of the government of Israel." Furthermore, a statement on the Middle East was issued on July 20, 1981, by leaders of the seven major industrialized democracies (including the United States) meeting at Chateau Montebello, Canada. That statement deplored "the escalation of tension and the continuing acts of violence now occurring in the region." It also referred to the destruction of Lebanon and the "heavy civilian loss of life on both sides," calling on all parties to show restraint and not engage in retaliation. The message American officials wanted to deliver was very clear: the Israeli attack, which caused a tremendous loss in innocent lives, including women and children, was *not* singled out for condemnation but treated on a par with other hit-and-run guerrilla tactics. Thus, in both word and deed, the United States showed its partisanship toward the Israelis. As was the case in previous encounters, American political leaders were displaying a strong pre-disposition to accept as the "truth" the Israeli version of events in the Middle East, even when they should have had doubts, while simultaneously being skeptical of the Arabs' account of any particular situation, no matter how sincere and objective. To the extent that such thinking continues to linger on, it hinders all attempts that seek to arrive at an acceptable and feasible settlement of the major issues in the area, including Lebanon.

27

ARAB STEREOTYPING IN CONTEMPORARY AMERICAN POLITICAL CARTOONS

G. Neal Lendenmann

Mr. Lendenmann is the Coordinator of Research and Information Programs for the National Association of Arab-Americans.

It is curious that many well-meaning individuals who vigilantly and conscientiously decry ethnic aspersions when they are directed at certain ethnic groups, fail to recognize defamation if less protected or less organized ethnic communities are victimized. Unfortunately, political cartoons depicting themes or caricatures that would be clearly unacceptable if they were made toward, say, Blacks, Orientals, Irish or Italians, are not yet perceived as inappropriate if the subject is the Arab people or their culture. Often such oversight is due to an inadvertent misunderstanding of the harm that can be caused by such stereotyping. At other times, however, the aspersions appear so deliberately malicious or derogatory that they become inexcusable.

One of the most notorious and constant media propagandists against the Arabs has been Herblock, whose anti-Arab cartoons adorn the editorial pages of *The Washington Post* with unfortunate regularity. Two major themes seem to pervade Herblock's "analysis" of events in the Middle East: 1) Arab "blackmail" of the United States, usually in order to procure arms, through their enormous oil supplies and the obverse theme that U.S. officials are willingly susceptible to such blackmail and 2) the disreputableness of the Palestinians and the PLO, usually personified by Yasser Arafat.

Herblock has remained remarkably consistent on the first theme in the past five years, having depicted both President Carter and President Reagan in unflattering subservience to the Arabs. In a cartoon published on December 19, 1978, Carter was portrayed as trading U.S. warplanes and support for Arab demands on Israel in return for oil price boosts by the Arabs. Carter, dressed in Arab garb to emphasize his obsequiousness and heighten the stereotype, was shown naively explaining to the U.S. public that "I give them something, they give me something."

President Reagan came in for even harsher criticism on November 6, 1981, when he was shown prostrating himself before an unidentified Saudi, backed by a number of oil derricks and holding a list of Saudi "requirements" of U.S. policy. "Oh, this is just an old Arab custom," Reagan explains sheepishly. It is not explained what the custom is, of course, and even superficial reflection will indicate that neither the United States nor President Reagan is prostrate before the Saudis. The longstanding friendship between the two countries is based on mutual respect.

Depicted also in the cartoon is Reagan's famous remark made when Israel was attempting to intervene in the AWACS debate to influence Capitol Hill: "It is not the business of other nations to make foreign policy." Herblock, apparently angered at what was at the time clearly a reference to Israel, wished to convince his readers that the real culprits in the Middle East resided elsewhere.

Coming at the height of passions over the AWACS debate, the obvious inference from the cartoon is that AWACS were only offered to Saudi Arabia because of their oil weapon. No such cartoons are forthcoming when Israel is to receive weapons, for obvious reasons.

Besides directly impugning the integrity of the Presidents depicted in the above cartoons, Herblock rather cleverly distorted the facts to influence his readers. To him, the world's supplies of oil and oil price levels are manipulated and controlled by greedy Arabs, despite the fact that some of the leading price moderates in OPEC (most notably Saudi Arabia) are Arab and indeed, six of the 13 OPEC nations, including several of the greatest "hawks" on oil prices, are non-Arab. In reality, of course, the interdependence of the OPEC nations and the United States is a symbiotic one without sinister connotations. If American Presidents pay careful attention to the Arab world, it is because it is in the interests of the United States to do so, not because they are being blackmailed.

Herblock's second theme, namely the villainy of the Palestinians, is most vividly expressed in a cartoon that appeared nearly one month after the beginning of Israel's invasion of Lebanon in June 1982. By the time the cartoon appeared, the carnage and destruction that had resulted from the invasion had already left thousands of Lebanese and Palestinians and hundreds of Israelis dead or wounded.

Somehow Herblock managed to ignore the war and the human suffering connected with it until July 1, 1982, when he showed a lone PLO thug standing among the rubble in Lebanon with a machine gun, holding a picture of himself relaxing in similar rubble marked "Lebanon 1981" and remarking woefully to a TV camera that, "We had made this place into such a nice home for ourselves." The implications are preposterous. Whatever responsibility the PLO must shoulder for the events of the war (and the civil war) in Lebanon, Herblock's inability to criticize Israel and the obvious implication that the Palestinians must accept the entire blame for the destruction of Lebanon, highlight Herblock's inclination for propaganda rather than objectivity or fairness.

Indeed, this tendency degenerated into the depths of distastefulness in a cartoon published on August 6, 1982, in which a PLO guerrilla is depicted holding a child with decidedly non-Arab features in front of him and firing a smoking machine gun with a broad smile on his face. A second guerrilla tells a television camera crew: "You can see he's very fond of children." It is incredible that Herblock can seriously maintain that the Palestinians enjoyed having their own children slaughtered just in order to carry on the fight with Israel. The cartoon also deflects the reader from considering Israel's responsibility for killing civilians at a time when Israel was coming under severe criticism for the siege of West Beirut.

The themes propounded by Herblock find their echoes in the works of other political cartoonists as well. The scenario of U.S. officials being under the influence of the Arabs was often repeated with the nomination of George Shultz as Secretary of State. Because Shultz, like Secretary of Defense Caspar Weinberger, was an officer in the Bechtel Corporation (which does business in the Middle East) prior to his service in the Reagan Administration, his views on the Arab-Israeli conflict came under a great deal of Senate scrutiny.

Much of the criticism directed toward Shultz concentrated on his ties with Bechtel, which began to be portrayed extensively as a sinister force directly under the influence of the Arabs. An archetypal cartoon impugning both the Secretary of State-designate and "the Arabs" in general was published by Timothy Atseff on July 14, 1982, in *The Syracuse Herald–Journal*. During questioning in the Senate, Shultz is asked if "your position at the Bechtel group may have undue Arab influence on you as Secretary of State?" Shultz, clad in Arab clothing, leans over to

347

Weinberger, who is dressed in similar garb, and says: "P-s-s-st Cap, what does he mean by "undue 'influence'?"

This cartoon, and the many variations on it, are particularly unfair insofar as they imply that anyone in business or government who has sympathetic views toward the Arabs could not have come to such opinions through judgment and reason. Rather he or she must have been bought or brainwashed.

A more equitable alternative might be that Americans, whether businessmen or government officials, who have had greater first-hand experience with the Arabs or who have studied the Arab world in depth, might have divested themselves of some of the more insidious stereotypes so often found in the press and enhanced their ability to view the situation in the Middle East more objectively. Having a deeper understanding of an issue is normally an attribute rather than a disqualification.

Herblock's concomitant theme of abject U.S. dependence on Arab oil is also pervasive in American newspapers, particularly when an arms package is being proposed for an Arab nation. Saudi Arabia, America's closest ally in the oil producing world, is often the butt of unpleasant characterizations. One cartoon that appeared in *The Washington Star* in May 1978 showed two Arabs, one labeled "Dependence on Imported Oil" leading Uncle Sam by the nose. One of the figures declares to the other: "I've trained him to sit up, beg and roll over, but he's a little stubborn about selling warplanes." If Israel were substituted for the Arab sheikhs in such a cartoon, the cartoonist would undoubtedly have been subjected to severe criticism.

A second example published by Hugh Haynie in *The Louisville Courier Journal* on April 23, 1981, showed a Saudi sheikh who looks remarkably familiar holding up a check made out to Saudi Arabia and signed by Ronald Reagan for the amount "all they want." An inane caption reads: "AWACS EXCESS. Don't leave the White House without it." Although the reason for the blank check is not mentioned, the obvious inference is that the Saudis can get all the weapons they want from the United States because of their oil power.

Cartoons such as these ignore or deny the fact that Arab oil-exporting nations, like all others, need weapons for their defense; that it is often in the interests of the United States to sell such weapons to them; that it is, after all, the Arabs and not the Americans who pay the check; and that the Saudis have been close friends of the United States and indeed the most influential proponents of price moderation within OPEC.

G. NEAL LENDENMANN

"What Are You Two Smiling About?"

AWACS EXCESS
Don't leave
the White House
without it!

Another invidious genre of political cartoons that has arisen over the past few years has been the "Abscam" cartoons, which stereotype Arabs for a scandal with which they had absolutely nothing to do. These cartoons have appeared with alarming frequency since the revelation that several Congressmen and a Senator had been caught in illegal activities by FBI agents posing as "Arabs." Even though no Arab was involved in the FBI investigation, the word "Abscam" gained popular usage and the political cartoons dealing with the affair became for the most part unwitting, but nevertheless potent vehicles for disparaging Arabs and, by unintended implication, Arab-Americans.

The iniquity of the whole Abscam affair and its attendant political cartoons was its contribution to the growth of a general perception that Arab "perfidiousness and intrigue" was insinuating itself into the very corridors of the U.S. Government even though no Arab had had anything to do with Abscam. This has been particularly damaging in the wake of such cases as the "Koreagate" scandal a few years earlier in which foreign nationals were actually caught engaging in illegal activities. As such, even where political cartoons employing figures dressed as Arabs were meant to criticize the FBI, the use of such figures merely emphasized and perpetuated anti-Arab stereotypes that would not be tolerated were other ethnic groups the victim.

A typical example of an Abscam cartoon appeared on March 7, 1982, by T. Flannery in *The Baltimore Sun,* during the Senate hearings into the case of Senator Harrison Williams. Six discouraged Senators leaving the hearings pass two figures labelled "FBI" and "Abscam," the latter, bearded and smoking a cigar, unmistakably in Arab dress. One senator asks the grinning figures what they are smiling about. Even though the *Sun* may not have meant to convey any derogatory racial connotations in the Abscam cartoon (and indeed maintained an editorial policy critical of certain FBI methods in the scandal), its cartoon and others like it perpetuate an unwarranted stereotype and encourage prejudice toward Arabs.

A cartoon by Don Wright of *The Miami News* and published in the *Post* of West Palm Beach, Florida on July 31, 1982, ingeniously bridged Herblock's two major themes by vilifying the PLO and maligning U.S. officials at the same time. Ignoring the arduous and painstaking negotiations carried on by U.S. special negotiator Philip Habib that led to the evacuation of the PLO from West Beirut, Wright chose to concentrate upon Habib's peripheral ties to Bechtel. He depicted Arafat and two henchmen walking through the rubble of Beirut. Scruffy and well armed,

Arafat says to his equally bedraggled companions: "And not only is it a way to get out of Beirut. Just think of the job security. I recommend we accept Habib's proposal!" To which one of his cronies replies, "But, Yasser, we don't want to be consultants for Bechtel!"

Wright's cartoon verged on the ludicrous in its distortion of reality. It need only to be said that Habib was later honored by President Reagan in a special ceremony for his efforts leading to the PLO evacuation and that the evacuation was carried out successfully. Any connections between the PLO and Bechtel must be considered a figment of the artist's fantasies.

Indeed, defaming the Palestinians has become so widespread in the American media that it gets in the way of changing circumstances in the Middle East itself. Many positive trends in American thinking toward the Palestinians in recent years have gone unexplored by political cartoons, which remain in most newspapers primarily vehicles for negative stereotyping rather than positive characterizations. Thus, although a great deal of attention has been paid by the U.S. Government and the press toward the necessity of addressing the legitimate needs and rights of the Palestinian people as a prerequisite for achieving a comprehensive peace in the Middle East, this attention has been virtually ignored by political cartoonists, who prefer to concentrate on and caricature the PLO.

At times, the theme of a duplicitous Arafat has even been used as a not-so-subtle means of impeding a more objective study of the overall Palestinian question. In early 1982, five Seattle clergymen went to Lebanon and met with a number of Palestinian officials, including Arafat, in order to study the views of the Palestinians on the situation in the Middle East. Upon their return, the clergymen were subjected to considerable criticism and even invective. The outcry culminated on March 7, 1982, in a particularly patronizing cartoon by David Horsey in *The Seattle Post-Intelligencer*. That cartoon depicted Arafat sitting on a rock above the five clearly brainwashed clergymen, who hang upon his every word. The caption read: "Terrorists? Destroy Israel? Surely you sophisticated Seattle clergymen can't doubt that all I want in the world is to milk goats in the desert."

By subjecting the clergymen to such gratuitous and unfair ridicule, others may subsequently be deterred from delving into the issue from a non-Israeli viewpoint, and objective study of the Arab-Israeli conflict may be discouraged. In an era when the Palestinian question has become encrusted with misinformation and encumbered by irrelevancies, cartoons that discourage dialogue and intellectual curiosity do a disservice to the American public.

A particularly odious caricature of the Palestinians and the PLO that has gained popularity since the beginning of the war in Lebanon has been their portrayal as rodents, cockroaches and other detestable animals. One such cartoon by Steve Benson appeared in newspapers throughout the country in June 1982. It depicted Arafat as a rat caught in a trap. The metal snapper that kills the rodent is shaped in the form of a Star of David. The caption, apparently designed as a clever pun, reads simply "Yasir Ararat." The Star of David, a proud symbol of one of the world's three great monotheistic religions, would seem debased by such a sickening secular use.

Benson's infatuation with the imagery of vermin was repeated in an even more disgusting cartoon that appeared in *The Syracuse Herald-Journal* on August 28, 1982. A flute-playing figure labelled "[U.S.] Marines" skips out of a burning Beirut followed by hundreds of rats carrying suitcases marked "PLO." The cartoon, playing on the theme of the Pied Piper of Hamlin, is particularly defamatory because it brands a whole people with an odious and unwarranted stereotype. This abominable cartoon and others depicting the Palestinians in a similar manner have caused indescribable outrage and resentment by Americans of Arab descent. Such irresponsible use of derogatory racial connotations in political cartoons is truly intolerable, whatever the cartoonist's political views of the PLO.

There are more than three million Americans of Arab ethnic origin in the United States, and large numbers of them have become particularly sensitized in recent years to the political prejudice that has been directed at Arabs and Arab culture through political cartoons and other stereotypes. They have also organized, like ethnic communities before them, to protest inaccurate, stereotypical or derogatory references toward their people in the press. As a result, while such negative references to Arabs still appear, and at times abound, in American newspapers throughout the country, they are far more likely to be challenged than ever before. Such challenges represent a healthy aspect of the current American political scene.

It is to be hoped that defamatory cartoons against Arabs, whether malicious in intent or not, will gradually disappear from the media. This can only happen if the general public is sensitized to the unfair stereotyping and defamation of Arabs in the American media and the pain it causes an entire ethnic group in this country. Arabs are not the first group to be unfairly scapegoated and vilified in the United States. Nor, unfortunately, will they be the last. In the long-run, however, stereotyping of one ethnic community is an affront to all.

28

THE AMERICAN IMAGE IN THE ARAB MASS MEDIA

Adnan Abu Odeh

His Excellency Adnan Abu Odeh is Minister of Information of the Hashemite Kingdom of Jordan and Vice President of the Jordan World Affairs Council.

The quality of social, economic and political cooperation among peoples and nations has always been determined, in essence, by the measure of cross-cultural understanding these peoples and nations have achieved. Today, in our age of instant communications, our understanding of other cultures is very much enhanced or diminished, our relationships with other peoples and nations often forcefully directed and shaped, by the powerful impact of the mass media.

Images, good and bad, are propagated—sometimes unwittingly and sometimes intentionally—by those media. The fast news media, particularly the daily press, radio and television, have become increasingly important in conveying these images. An international network of communications, facilitated by satellite transmission, carries the news hourly to all corners of the world, and transistor radios extend the reception of that news beyond urban centers to millions more people in remote and isolated regions.

As everywhere else, the news media in the Arab world play a major role in formulating and reflecting popular opinion and attitudes, not only socioeconomically and culturally, but also and more importantly in the political domain. In this respect, for the past 35 years the dominating political issue dealt with by the Arab news media has been the Palestinian question and the Arab-Israeli conflict and its consequences, both regional and international. And, of course, on an international level, the positions of the superpowers vis-a-vis the various aspects of this conflict have been the subject of close attention by the media and of great concern to the Arab audience.

The image-building power of the media is manifested very clearly when we examine the status of just one of those superpowers—the United States of America. As it exists today, the American image in the Arab media is made up of two conflicting aspects, one negative and the other positive, and both have developed for valid reasons.

The negative aspect unfortunately appears to be outweighing the positive one in current Arab public opinion. This negative aspect, as reflected in the Arab mass media, emanates primarily from American political behavior in the Middle East, in action and in words. Statements lacking an evenhanded position and made by American governmental leaders, whether of the executive or legislative branch, feed this image, as do the similarly partial commentaries and editorials that appear in the various media.

It is most effectively reflected, with strong visual impact and wit, in the cartoons that appear in the Arab press. It also comes through strongly in radio and television news commentaries and in press editorials.

There is the positive aspect, a most admirable one that continues to persist despite the heavy influence of the bad image. This positive aspect of the American image emanates from a cultural and technological source. It emanates from America's values, its faith in democracy and its dedication to the ideals of freedom, justice and the rights of the individual. The Arab mass media reflect this good image primarily and most effectively by American films and to a lesser extent in the press and radio. Television films, particularly within the last decade of dramatic expansion in the television capabilities of the Arab world, are important in showing qualities of the American way of life, which have a positive impact on Arab viewers. These American films are very popular and are watched by young and old in most of the homes in the Arab world.

News reports and film documentaries on America's technology, its achievements in science, medicine and industry, also add significantly to this positive image. If, for example, an American scientist makes some new discovery in the field of medicine and wins the Nobel Prize, he appears on television news programs throughout the Arab world, and thanks to satellite reception in a number of Arab countries, on the same day.

This positive image is real and penetrating. It is fed through indirect avenues and has a strong influence. One of the best indicators of this influence is that most Arab parents would like to see their children educated in America. They admire the dynamic energy of its society, and they want their children to acquire its advanced technological knowledge and to emulate the efficiency and organization of its system.

As mentioned earlier, the positive image is best conveyed in films and to a lesser degree in the printed media, such as books and magazines, and through radio and television news bulletins and documentaries. But there is also another medium which plays a noticeable role in enhancing this positive picture and that is, surprisingly, advertising. Most consumer products, from blue jeans to modern kitchens, invariably appear in Arabic advertisements as American, regardless of whether they were actually produced there or not. Housewives have long called any and every detergent Tide and to all of us in the Arab world every paper tissue is a Kleenex.

These two conflicting aspects of the American image, as spelled out generally, are symptomatic of the American-Arab relationship. One is reminded of the situation of a couple that have been married for many years. They have a family; they have raised children together and shared many experiences, good and bad. Now, they are at the threshold of divorce. Why? Because one spouse suddenly discovers that the other is in love with someone else. Life starts to become difficult for both of them; they stand at the threshold and the one spouse pleads with the other, "Please, let us not divorce. . .how can you forget our many years together? All that must still mean something to you." But the other spouse is not receptive.

Many people will agree that the Arab and American worlds are now in a position similar to this. When the Arabs talk about America, one senses this impending danger of divorce; one hears them saying, in effect: "Look, what you are doing is wrong. . .you must remember, you must reconsider and think how much we could still have together." And, of course, their mutual friends also continue to hope that the divorce will never materialize.

Before continuing with a further elaboration on the specific sources that have contributed to the negative image of the United States in the Arab mass media, we should briefly describe how the various media function. In practically all Arab countries, the media of radio and television are government sponsored; the press, meanwhile, is privately owned and operated in some countries, and in others is government sponsored. The radio and television media usually restrict their activities to transmitting the news with or without comment or analysis and to providing

357

entertainment and educational programming. They direct their programs to the wide general audience of both the educated and uneducated alike. The local daily, weekly or monthly press, on the other hand, provides its audience with the news accompanied by a full analysis and frequent commentary, and also gives a substantial part of its space to the coverage of cultural, social and economic events and developments, both domestic and foreign. It addresses itself to that educated segment of the population which is interested in reading newspapers and magazines.

Although more than 30 news agencies or wire services supply the Arab media with news in all fields, from the political to the cultural, most of them service only the region or even only the country within which they operate. For foreign and particularly non-Arab news in all fields, the Arab media depend on the five major world agencies: the American AP and UPI, the British Reuters, the French AFP and the Russian TASS, all of which disseminate news on a daily basis through their wire services.

As for media density in the Arab world, there were in 1980 approximately 20 million radio receivers, 8 million television receivers and 100 daily newspapers with a total daily circulation of 5 million. The radio and television media reach a vast audience due to group listening or viewing of about five to ten people per receiver and also because of the wide and popular use of small, inexpensive transistor sets. The Arab press, however, because of the low literacy rate in a number of countries, still reaches only a limited audience. But newspapers are looked at also by the illiterate for their pictorial content, advertisements and especially for their cartoons.

Now, to return to the core subject—the negative image of America, why and how it has developed, and what its ramifications are. There are several factual elements that have created and continue to maintain this negative image, the principal features of which are:

1) **American policy toward the Palestinian question is partial and biased**. *Evidence*: America recognizes and fully supports Israel's right to exist, while it refuses to recognize the Arab Palestinians' rights to their lands, which have been under Israeli military occupation for 16 years.

2) **America is foolhardy and unwise, because it is endangering its own interests in the whole region in favor of one small and aggressive state, Israel**. *Evidence*: In addition to its vital interests in Arab oil, America benefits economically from an export trade with the Arab world that in 1980 amounted to $13.3 billion and comprised 6.1 percent of all total U.S. exports, while its exports to Israel that same year totaled $2 billion or 0.9

percent of America's total exports, according to U.S. Department of Commerce figures and excluding major arms sales.

3) **America does not live up to the ideals of its policy in the Middle East.** It does not practice what it preaches. *Evidence*: It talks about and defends human rights of many people, but not of the Palestinians, who have been striving for their human rights for 33 years.

4) **America is impotent when it comes to Israel.** Any decision on the Middle East is made not by America, but by Israel; it's a case of the tail wagging the dog. *Evidence*: On most of the resolutions concerning conflicts in the Middle East that have been put before the U.N. Security Council, the United States has sided with Israel against the Arabs. To cite an example: Only Israel and the United States voted against the October 27, 1981 Security Council Resolution to halt the Israeli excavations which are endangering the historical, cultural and religious sites of Jerusalem.

5) **America is imperialistic in its approach to the Middle East; its only interests are hegemony and exploiting that region's resources.** *Evidence*: America reacts positively and strongly only when it feels approaching danger to its supply of Middle East oil; otherwise it reacts to events in the Middle East by voicing no more than mild concern without any effective reaction. *Evidence*: Fears of a chain nuclear reaction in the Gulf oil region after the fall of the shah brought American fighter planes on flights over Saudi Arabia; the Israeli bombing of the Iraqi nuclear reactor brought only a perfunctory American reprimand.

6) **America is losing ground before the Soviet Union in the Middle East because of its imbalanced policy.** *Evidence*: Iran and Afghanistan are two examples of radical revolutionary elements fed and supported by the Soviet Union that are becoming stronger.

As a result the Arabs find that America does not keep faith with its friends in the Middle East and is loyal to only one state there, Israel.

These elements provide the structure of America's negative image, an image that is reinforced by three individual protagonists in the image-making game. Each differs in its motivation, but all are consistent in their portrayal of this negative image. These three actors are the Arab mass media, the Soviet Union and Israel—and the latter two are very instrumental in feeding the first.

The Arab mass media consciously portray these bad features of America as a natural reaction to American policies in the region, especially its policies toward the Palestinian question and its components. These policies, after all, relate to the Arabs in a very vital way, to their lives and to their future. And since most of the time the news dealing with the

Middle East and America's role in or reaction to that news is unfavorable to the Arabs, it is reported and commented on in the media in a manner critical of America. There are countless examples, but to quote a recent one from the Arab press, the Kuwaiti daily, *Al Ra'i Al Aam*: "America commits a deadly mistake if it continues to think it can convince the Arabs of the Soviet danger. The Arabs know and feel in their hearts that the real danger is the Israeli danger, ever growing and under the very protection of America."

The second negative image maker, the Soviet Union, has a long-recognized purpose: to wrest political and strategic control of the region from the United States and the West, quite as the United States does its best to maintain its presence and influence in the area. Its job of discrediting America in Arab eyes is made very easy by the continued pro-Israeli bias in U.S. policies. The Russians are exploiting the mistakes of the Americans in the Middle East. They rarely initiate a practical political approach to the Middle East conflict, but simply react toward American actions or pronouncements. They wait to see what the Americans say, and when it is received negatively by the Arabs, they try to win over the Arabs by taking the opposite position. In this area, an analogy can be made to a gambling table: There are always losers and winners, but the croupier is always the constant winner who takes no risks—and that is the Soviet Union. A headline, which ran in *Al Sayyad*, an Arabic weekly, on June 5, 1981, sums this up sharply with a minimum of words: "Israeli America and Arab Russia."

The third negative image maker, and the most important one in contributing to America's bad image, is Israel. The role it plays in antagonizing the Arabs against the Americans is most deeply felt. Its purpose clearly is to destroy the Arab-American relationship; it is, in fact, the promoting agent in the impending divorce described earlier. Israel wants to convey the message that America will eternally be on its side against the Arabs in general and the Palestinians in particular.

Israel's most effective propaganda weapon, regarding the Arab world, is its Arabic radio service. The Israel Broadcasting Authority (IBA) transmits 18 hours daily in Arabic on three major frequencies on the medium wave with a signal power of 600 kilowatts that during optimum transmission hours can be received up to a radial distance of 2,000 kilometers, even by a small transistor set. It directs its Arabic service not only to the Palestinians living in Israel and in the occupied territories, but also to the millions of Arabs throughout the region. During its 18-hour transmission in Arabic (in comparison to the 20 hours that any Arab radio

AL RA'I   (9-15-81)

ARAB NEWS—Jeddah

361

ARAB NEWS, Jeddah   (7-4-81)

JORDAN TIMES, Amman   (10-19-81)

station operates), IBA broadcasts nine news programs and from three to five short news commentaries under various names. The remainder of its programming is devoted to music and other entertainment to attract Arab listeners, its target audience.

In serving the purposes of its Arabic transmission, IBA has two advantages over Arab radio stations, advantages that derive from the fact that its programming is not intended for its own domestic audience. First, unlike all other national radio services in the Third World, including the Arab part of it, which have to deal with the four purposes of culture and religion, news and commentary, entertainment and development, Israel's Arabic service can concentrate its programming primarily on two areas—news and commentary and entertainment.

Second, the Israeli service can transmit without the constraints the Arabs are subject to in their broadcasting. For example, if the Hashemite Jordan Broadcasting Service (HBS) is transmitting a news item about Saudi Arabia, it is always concerned that this news does not irritate or offend Saudi Arabia. Saudi Arabia is our friend, our ally, and we wish to maintain Arab solidarity. Syria, for instance, cannot transmit everything about Libya; Israel can. Kuwait cannot transmit everything on Jordan; Israel can. The Arabs are its adversaries, after all, and it uses its radio to wage pyschological warfare on them. It not only can transmit more news, in terms of quantity, but also is free to analyze, comment and point out the failures of the Arab states without any inhibitions or constraints. Because of these advantages, IBA has gained credibility in its Arabic news over the Arab mass media.

These two advantages serve Israel very efficiently in its campaign to demoralize the Arabs and condition them along the following lines:

1) To make the Arabs believe that however much they try to remain united, all their efforts are futile—they will never achieve unity or consensus.

2) To remind the Arabs constantly of Israel's military superiority over them and make them feel weak.

3) To advertise Israeli superiority in science and technology.

4) To alienate the Arabs from America and create animosity toward America.

5) To discredit and radicalize moderate Arab states in the region.

The last two objectives, to engender Arab hatred toward America and to discredit moderate Arab states, are the most important vis-a-vis their impact on the Arab audience and the Arab media. A fact that will surprise many Americans is that Israel, America's adopted child in the region, is daily engaged in reinforcing the negative image of America among the Arabs while America is seeking a strategic consensus with the Arabs. Here we have America's ally, Israel, hard at work antagonizing America's potential allies, the Arabs, against it.

To illustrate how Israel achieves its purpose of damaging America's image in Arab eyes, there are several examples of IBA's tactics which deal with the most important issues that arose in the Middle East in 1981.

First, the assumption of power by President Reagan and the policy of his Administration toward the Middle East. On May 25, 1981, IBA's Arabic service broadcast this item on one of its news programs:

> *"President Reagan stressed that the U.S. considers Israel a first-class strategic asset, an allied state whose military force constitutes a deterrent to Soviet aggression in the Middle East. President Reagan added that U.S. support to the security of Israel through military, economic and political assistance promotes U.S. strategic interests and contributes to the achievement of peace and stability in the area. "*

On May 31, 1981, Israeli radio gave us this news bulletin:

> *"In a telegraphic message of congratulations on the occasion of the People's Assembly for Zionism and Israel held two days ago in New York, President Reagan declared his full support for the Zionist movement and its objectives. In his telegram, published in the press today, President Reagan reaffirmed that Israel is a major strategic asset and ally whose military forces prevent Soviet aggression in the Middle East. He added that Zionism is considered the embodiment of the commitment to liberate the land of Israel and to establish a country with an economy and a society enjoying complete freedom in this part of the world, which is considered so very vital for the security of America. The President ended his message saying that he joins the many who declare solidarity with those who are establishing a democratic edifice in Israel, and thus pays his tribute to the Zionist movement. "*

And on September 10, 1981, IBS broadcast this item:

> *"NBC reported last night that ex-President Nixon met secretly this past June with Israeli Ambassador Evron to discuss President Reagan's position toward Israel. Nixon assured the Israeli Ambassador that President Reagan is a friend of Israel and that Israel could trust him; and he urged Israel to cooperate with the Secretary of State Haig, whom Nixon also described as a friend of Israel. "*

The message to the Arabs in such news bulletins is obvious. Israel is telling the Arabs: 'Don't entertain any hopes that America will help you; America is our friend and will always be on our side.' More specifically in the last item, Israel's intention is to convey to the Arabs that it has always had and will continue to have the support of the Republican Party, despite an Arab belief that the Republicans are less supportive to Israel than the Democrats; hence, don't look for any help from the new Administration.

Such selective news items aim to destroy Arab hopes for American support and increase Arab feelings of alienation toward America. To the Arab listener, they mean, in effect, that America continues to support the Israeli occupation of Arab lands. As perceived by the Arabs, the stability the U.S. pursues in the Middle East depends on Israel's military strength, a strength made possible by American aid, and thus a strength that the Arabs are unable to challenge to regain their lands.

On a second issue, the Israeli bombing of the Iraqi nuclear reactor, Israeli radio had this to say on June 16, 1981:

> *"President Reagan announced in Washington that Israel was justified in its worry about the Iraqi nuclear reactor that its planes destroyed. He said that Israel must have honestly believed that its attack on the Iraqi reactor was a defensive action. In his statement, made at his first press conference after the attempt on his life in March, the President added that one must confess that Israel has the right to worry, in view of Iraq's record."*

And the next day, on June 17, Israeli radio fed its Arab listeners this item:

> *"Arthur Goldberg, previous U.S. envoy to the United Nations and once a Justice of the United States Supreme Court, declared that according to international law Israel had full right to strike the Iraqi nuclear reactor."*

In utilizing this issue almost daily over a certain period of time, Israel's aim was to convince the Arabs that U.S. leaders believed in the validity of what Israel did, that it destroyed the reactor in order to protect itself. And to add credibility to the news item on Goldberg's statement, the audience is informed of his legal qualifications by intentionally mentioning that he was once a justice on America's highest court.

You can imagine the painful impact this particular event had on the Arabs and on their spirit. While in June 1967 the Arabs felt defeated, in June 1981 they felt utterly naked. The Israeli strike on the Iraqi reactor seared and stripped the Arab spirit to the core. And Israel did its best, through the selectivity of its reporting on American statements, to show the United States as its ally and a contributor to that painful blow to the Arab spirit. It was a deep disappointment to the Arabs that the United States did not respond in the way they expected it to; and there was again a sudden loss of faith in America. Although something was said about referring the matter to Congress to investigate whether Israel had violated the terms of its armaments agreement with the United States, nothing was done nor has been done to this day. On the contrary, the United States, after a short, mild reprimand, resumed its shipment of fighter planes to Israel. Of course, IBA was quick to report on this as well.

A third issue and another good example of Israel's radio campaign of psycho-warfare against the Arabs is the AWACS deal. There is no need to comment on the deal itself, whether it was necessary, whether it will prove to be good or bad for the Middle East. What is pertinent is how this deal and Israel's reporting on it has contributed to the negative image of America. It played a very critical and unprecedented role. The AWACS debate took a long time and gave the Israelis months to say over and over again, in many different ways, with many different quoted statements from American leaders: 'The Americans, even the President, cannot take a decision without great difficulty, because our friends in Congress are so powerful and so loyal to Israel.' And they could say this with confidence, despite the influence of Saudi Arabia in the Arab world as a voice of moderation and despite its cooperation with and importance to the West and to America.

Here are a few of the frequent Israeli broadcasts to Arab listeners on the AWACS issue that show the sly manner in which Israel was able to discredit not only Saudi Arabia, but also other moderate Arab states such as Jordan and Morocco:

September 2, 1981:

> "Democratic Senator Gary Hart of Colorado has requested that a written commitment be given by Saudi Arabia to the American Administration, in which it will agree to abide by the restrictions that the Americans have imposed on Saudi Arabia, particularly the restriction that would prevent its using the AWACS against Israel. When asked about America's arrangements in this context, Undersecretary of State James Buckley refused to confirm or deny whether the Saudis had given such a commitment."

September 4, 1981:

> "A diplomatic source in Washington reports that President Reagan will stress Israel's strategic role in the Middle East when he meets with Prime Minister Begin. The unidentified State Department source said that President Reagan will also review with Mr. Begin the process of the autonomy talks and will also raise the issue of the AWACS deal within the context of their discussions on a comprehensive strategy for the area."

These two items suggest to the Arab audience that Saudi Arabia, in its possible acquisition of the AWACS, could be an element in this "comprehensive strategy" and thus become an indirect ally with Israel in

366

America's strategy planning. Clearly, it is an attempt to cast suspicion on Saudi Arabia and damage its relationship with other Arab countries.

October 3, 1981:

"After a meeting in Washington with Secretary of State Haig, Senator Robert Packwood, one of the leaders of the opposition in the AWACS sale to Saudi Arabia, commented that he expected that a number of the Congressmen opposed to the sale would change their opinion due to intensive pressures on them from the Administration. Senator Packwood said that Secretary Haig has explained to him during their meeting that if Congress blocked the sale, the peace process in the Middle East would be obstructed. The Senator said he told Haig that the approval of the AWACS deal will come only when King Khalid of Saudi Arabia announces his intention to go to Jerusalem and hold peace negotiations with Israel."

To an Arab, what springs to mind here is the scenario of a Roman emperor waiting for the tribal chieftains on the outskirts of his empire to come to him submissively, to pay homage and obey his slightest command.

October 14, 1981:

"The U.S. House of Representatives this evening rejected by an overwhelming majority the Administration's proposal to sell the AWACS to Saudi Arabia. The vote was 301 against 101 for the proposal, with one abstention and 20 others who did not participate. Our Washington correspondent reports that a majority of the negative votes were cast by Democratic Party members of the House, but that there were also many other negative votes cast by Republicans."

The correct vote figure was 301 to 111, but what is reported here is exactly what IBA announced. This focus on a joint Democratic-Republican negative position toward the AWACS deal is intended to stress to the Arab audience that both American parties are firm supporters of Israel.

October 24, 1981:

"The Senate Foreign Relations Committee announced that the rejection of the AWACS arms package sale to Saudi Arabia would not prevent realization of America's objectives in the Middle East, despite any temporary negative reactions to such a decision."

The meaning here is obvious: Arab reaction is of no significance; American policy will be imposed regardless and the Arabs are helpless to do anything about it.

And, finally, on October 25, 1981, the Israeli radio program "The Morning Press" included this report on an article that had appeared that day in the Israeli Arabic daily *Al-Anba'* under the headline "Israel and Prince Fahd's Plan":

> *"The article commented on a recent meeting between President Reagan and Prince Fahd in Cancun, Mexico, and said that although the meeting was publicized as a discussion of the AWACS deal, the most important significance of the meeting undoubtedly relates to the reinforcement of American strategy in the Middle East, a strategy that aims at herding the Arab horses into one corral, with Washington as the main tamer and instructor. The article added that it is logical to assume that King Hussein's recent tour of the Gulf states, as well as the message sent by King Hassan of Morocco to Egypt's new President Husni Mubarak, are both connected with events in the Middle East during the last weeks. Also, the efforts of the Moroccan ruler have a special significance, remembering the role he played in paving the way for the Camp David accords."*

In broadcasting this press item, Israel's intention was to generate suspicion among Arabs about Prince Fahd's policies and also about King Hussein's planned visit to Washington. The special reference aimed at discrediting King Hassan of Morocco was shrewdly timed, since Morocco was to host the Arab Summit in late November.

Surely the foregoing examples are enough to prove the purpose of Israel's Arabic radio service. Selecting specific news items and quoting statements out of context, it relays positions taken by the United States that provoke Arabs to react negatively toward America. This reaction is, in turn, reflected in the Arab mass media, in the press and on radio and television, and relayed to an even wider Arab audience.

Is it any wonder, then, that the Arab media convey this bad image? Not only do America's biased and often reckless politics feed the media, but more significantly, Israel reinforces the negative impact of those policies, seriously harming America's attempts to establish a firm and mutually beneficial relationship with the Arab world.

This negative image-making process that Israel and the Soviet Union are engaged in has been described at length, and America's own responsibility for providing substance for that image has been pointed out. Through a visual medium, the result of that negative image making is best expressed in the political cartoons of the Arab press. As we all know, cartoons are a very strong conveyor of messages and are very effective as image reinforcers. One good picture speaks, as the previous cartoons illustrate, louder than a thousand words.

29

IMAGE FORMATION AND TEXTBOOKS

Ayad Al-Qazzaz

Dr. Al-Qazzaz is Associate Professor of Sociology at California State University, Sacramento.

Social images, the pictures an individual or group of people hold of another individual or group, play a vital role in influencing people's social interaction. The content of these images may determine in large part whether an individual reacts positively, negatively, or in a neutral manner to another person, particularly to someone of a different racial, cultural or religious background than his own. To the student of social behavior, a study of the sources from which people acquire or construct their social images can reveal a great deal about the nature of their interaction.

In this area of mass communication, people form their images from a multitude of sources. Yet, in the view of social and behavioral scientists, one of the most important transmitters of social information is the school system, and particularly, the experience of grades Kindergarten through 12. School attendance is one of the most nearly universal experiences of American children. It begins when the individual is at a young and impressionable age, and, in many cases, constitutes the major part of a child's waking hours. In this way, school rivals the family in its influence on a person's social and intellectual development. Studies in the field of social psychology on the socialization process indicate that information acquired in elementary and high school tends to have a lasting influence. Attitudes held by adults regarding particular groups of people can be traced in part to this training.

The foundation of formal education in this country is the textbook. For teachers at the elementary level, textbooks provide necessary background in subjects which they are expected to master but in which they may have no prior training. At the secondary level, a teacher who sees as many as 150 students a day cannot be expected to prepare a set of materials tailor-made to the needs of each student or even each class. Thus, the textbook provides the readily available, pre-packaged information he needs.

By meeting the needs of all teachers under a variety of conditions, textbooks have become the main source of knowledge in the classroom. Although this is true for all subjects, it especially applies to the humanities and social sciences. Textbooks supply students with the raw material for their study of human history and culture. Moreover, they transmit values and beliefs about the student's own society as well as other societies. In this sense, they are an indispensable part of the learning process.

The significance of the process of value transmission to the educational system of any country explains the degree of control exercised by most, if not all governments throughout the world over the institution of education. By means of textbooks and other approved teaching materials, teachers impart to their students a knowledge of their own country and of foreign nations. These materials may foster the development of positive or negative images of the countries which are discussed. By the very simple technique of admission or omission, the authors send out a message with a positive or negative connotation. A negative picture is created by omitting information that would cast the society in question in a positive light, or, on the other hand, by incorporating into the text irrelevant, incomplete, inaccurate and biased information. The implications of textbooks' messages to image formation and social relations were recognized by Luther H. Evans. He noted that,

> Textbooks and teachers can be the seed of an eventual harvest of national understanding and friendship by the presentation of facts qualitatively and quantitatively correct and in proper prospect, but they can also be the seed to a crop of misunderstanding, hate and contempt among natives and toward other ways of life by the presentation of facts of unqualified, unbalanced and inaccurate statements.

Of all topics covered in American textbooks, none has been subject to quite so much bias, misrepresentation, distortion and omission as has Islam. Many scholars, including Kenny, Griswold, Perry, Alami and Jarrar, have recognized the dimensions of the problem, and their work

370

reveals that much revision of the available material is needed in order to correct the situation.[1]

However, all previous studies on textbook coverage of Islam have dealt with books published before 1975. The current study was undertaken to determine if texts published since 1975 have improved in their representation of Islam. It employs the technique of qualitative content analysis, a method of studying the mass media developed during the 1920s and 1930s, which has since been adapted to include other materials, including personal documents, unstructured interviews, projective tests, records of patient-therapist interactions and textbooks. By analyzing chapters or pages of world history and social science high school textbooks, with special attention to pictures and maps, adjectives used to characterize Islam, inaccurate, distorted and false information, and omission of information that gives a positive picture of Islam, we will be able to discover what, if any, changes have occurred in the content and scope of Islam's coverage in these texts. If any changes have taken place, we will also discuss whether they represent a qualitative improvement over the previous presentation.

One methodological problem must be pointed out regarding the comparison between old and new textbooks. All prior studies of the image of Islam in textbooks were part of a wider analysis of the image of Arabs or the Middle East. Keeping this in mind, our comparison will be made only when it is relevant and appropriate.

The textbooks surveyed in this paper were chosen from lists of texts compiled from a high school teachers' workshop conducted by the author during 1979 and 1980 in California, Nebraska and Washington, D.C. At these workshops, teachers were asked to list the names of textbooks they used or which were recommended to them by their district or state for world history courses or an equivalent. The textbooks chosen for the study appeared on all the lists submitted by the teachers. It is also assumed that these texts are in widespread use throughout the United States. All are published by private companies whose objective was to distribute them nationwide. Neighboring states learned from one another to resolve issues and problems of common concern, including the adoption of textbooks.

---

[1] Al-Qazzaz, 1981, *passim.*

371

Finally, the author spoke with several high school teachers in the west, midwest and eastern parts of the United States about these texts. All seem to confirm the usage of them in their states.

The findings of the study will be presented under eight major headings: 1) Overall Treatment of Islam, 2) Naming the Religion, 3) Number of Muslims, 4) Portrayal of the Prophet, 5) The War Character of Islam, 6) Women in Islam, 7) The Crusades, and 8) Miscellaneous.

Overall Treatment of Islam

Generally speaking, the overall treatment of Islam in the textbooks examined does not represent a significant improvement over those included in previous studies by Alami, Kenny, Al-Qazzaz, Griswold and Perry. Although most texts explain accurately the essential elements of Islam, including the basic doctrine, the five elements of faith, the five pillars of Islam and the life of the Prophet, the discussion is very brief and vital points have been omitted. For instance, Islamic contribution to world civilization on the whole is acknowledged, but most of the time the discussion is short, over-simplified and superficial. No serious attempt is made to discuss the debt of our society to Islamic civilization in such fields as mathematics, algebra, philosophy, medicine and chemistry. Another area rarely mentioned is Islam in Spain, although for nearly 700 years scholars of all faiths—Christianity, Judaism and Islam—worked together to create and develop one of the highest civilizations of Medieval Europe.

In all other areas, the texts published since 1975 revealed the same deficiencies as those published earlier. The only major improvement noted concerned the name of the religion.

Naming the Religion

In all the textbooks surveyed, the term Islam has replaced Mohammad-ism to describe the religion of the Muslim people. Several of the texts offered an explanation for why the term Mohammadism is incorrect. One text noted that, "One of the prophets of God, according to the Koran, is Mohammad. Though he is held in high regard, Muslims don't worship him in any way. Mohammad was simply one of the chosen persons through whom God conveyed *His* word. It is more proper, therefore, to refer to the religion as Islam rather than Mohammadism."[2] In the same vein, another mentioned briefly that, "It is not correct to call them Mohammadans, for Mohammad did not put himself before his people as God."[3] Finally, a third went so far as to recommend that teachers discuss "why the people of the area don't like to be called Mohammadan."[4]

These explanations represent a clear advance over some earlier textbooks, in which the term Mohammadism appeared frequently. The Muslim people abhor and reject the term, as it elevates Mohammad to the central position in Islam, endowing him with sacred qualities that he never ascribed to himself. Mohammad never claimed to be anything more than God's messenger. Yet, Alami's study of Ohio elementary textbooks of the 1950s found the term to be in widespread use. A study of California world history and social science texts of the 1960s and 1970s found the term rarely used.[5]

Number of Muslims

The change in naming the religion stands out as the sole area of improvement in the textbooks surveyed. In other words, distortion and inaccuracies still prevail. This is true of the texts' estimates of the number of Muslims throughout the world, which tend to be inexplicably low. Three texts estimated the number of Muslims as less than 500,000,000 people. Exact figures varied between 445,000,000[6] and "nearly 500 million"[7] A fourth text noted that, "Today, more than half a billion persons, or one-eighth of the world's population are Muslims. Islam is the second largest religion in the world"[8] These figures contrast sharply with the figure of over 700 million calculated through a cursory look at the countries where Islam represents the religion of the majority of the people.[9]

---

[2] J. Norman Parmer, *People and Progress, A Global History*, Laidlaw Brothers Publishers, 1978, p. 244.

[3] Melvin Schwartz, *The New Exploring a Changing World*, New York, p. 366.

[4] M.S. Garbarino, *People and Culture*, McNally and Company, Chicago, 1975, p.167.

[5] Alami, p.74, Al-Qazzaz, p. 121; and Griswold, p. 12.

[6] D. Roselle, *A World History, A Cultural Approach*, p. 182.

[7] R.V. Strowski, et. al., p. 291.

[8] B. Linder, et. al., *A World History*, p. 149.

[9] Said, p. 28; also Weeks, p. XV.

Portrayal of the Prophet

Another popular misconception about Islam perpetuated by some textbooks concerns the pictorial representation of the Prophet Mohammad. A number of the texts surveyed incorporated pictures of the Prophet into their discussion, and used their captions to initiate discussion about Mohammad's qualities on the basis of the pictures. One text included a Persian miniature with the caption, "Mohammad and his followers. What qualities does the artist see in the religious leader?"[10] Another text has two pictures of Mohammad with the following caption, "Angry citizens of Mecca once attempted to stone Mohammed because of his religious teaching. A respected merchant of the city pleaded with the citizens and saved Mohammed's life." "Mohammed preached religious sermons to the followers of the new faith. Why do you think Mohammed is shown as faceless and surrounded by a large flame?"[11]

These texts could have informed students instead that in the eighth century, Islam prohibited all pictorial representation, including that of the Prophet. The ban is believed to have originated with the Prophet himself. Although no verse in the Koran specifically forbade Muslims to depict living figures, the injunction was voiced in a statement attributed to Mohammad's wife, Aisha. Mohammad is said to have found her making a pillow with a picture on it, whereupon he remonstrated, "Don't you know that angels refuse to enter the house in which there is a picture? On the last day, makers of the pictures will be punished for God will say to them 'Give life to that which you have created.'"[12]

The War Character of Islam

Earlier studies indicated that textbooks have placed excessive emphasis on the martial character of Islam.[13] Discussion of this issue contained many pejorative expressions, factual errors and questionable assertions and significant omissions, contributing to the perpetuation of a misconception of the true message of Islam. This study indicates that those findings apply also to texts published since 1975.

---

[10] M.S. Garbarino, et. al., p. 167.
[11] S.D. Lee, pp. 128-129.
[12] D. Stewart, *Early Islam*, New York, 1967, p. 105.
[13] Alami, p. 75; Griswold, p. 13; Al-Qazzaz, p. 122; and Perry, p. 49.

374

The texts devoted considerable attention to the concept of jihad, or holy war, and to the spread of Islam through this means. One text explains, "in contrast to the teachings of Jesus, Mohammed praised what he called the Holy War. He said, 'the sword is the key of heaven and hell; whosoever falls in battle, his sins are forgiven.' The fallen warrior was promised enticing heavenly rewards."[14] Another text states, "Arab warriors carried both a sword and an unswerving faith into battle; they believed that they were engaged in a jihad, a holy war, to spread Islam. The Koran stated that those who died on the jihad would gain a place in paradise."[15] Another text states, "The growth of Islam was rapid. Mohammed preached a holy war of jihad against those who would not believe in Islam. In 652 Mohammed died, but his followers took up his cry for a holy war. The Arabs joined hands in a Jihad that swept the Middle East and moved West."[16] Another text noted that "People other than Jews and Christians were to be converted to Islam by force, if necessary. And a holy war might be declared to spread the faith of Islam."[17] Another text informed readers that, "Arabs spread Islam by warring against their neighbors . . ." "Judaism used minimal proselytizing in its spread; Christianity spread the gospel by missionaries; Moslems often spread their religion by war and violence."[18] Another text linked Muslim military successes to religious fervor. It noted, "The Moslems were successful in their campaigns because their military tactics were intelligent and because they were stirred by a desire for the spoils of war. Most important, they were not afraid to die for their religion. Mohammed said, 'I swear to God, in whose hand is my life, that . . . to fight for religion is better than the world and everything that is in it and verify the standing of one of you in the line of battle is better than . . . prayers performed in your house for six years.'"[19] Finally, another text featured eight pictures about Islam, all of which dealt with war, and over one page of text to the concept of holy war, ending the discussion with the question, "Do you think the spirit of Jihad still exists today? Can you cite evidence to your answer?"[20]

[14] Anatole Mazour, et. al., p. 253.
[15] M. Perry et. al., *Unfinished Journey*, p. 151.
[16] G. Leinwand, p. 121.
[17] A. Kownslar, p. 279.
[18] Davis, et. al., p. 241.
[19] D. Roselle, p. 183.

This singular emphasis on war as an instrument for the spread of Islam tends to create a misleading mental image in which Islam is associated primarily with holy war and violence. Few textbooks included information which would establish a more balanced perspective. Conversion to Islam did not take place overnight but through a slow process which lasted for centuries. Islam's policy of tolerance toward "people of the Book," who were in fact protected through the ages by the Muslims, received no mention. Nor did these textbooks reveal that the Prophet and the Caliphs always advised their military leaders to be careful not to mutilate or kill a child, an old man, or a woman, not to cut palm trees, or burn them, not to cut any fruit trees that were bearing, and not to kill sheep, a cow, or a camel, except for needed food. Finally, and most significantly, no distinction is made between the religion and the state. Islam, like other religions, is a religion of justice, equality and high ideals. The Islam that conquered was not the religion but the state. The state, throughout the centuries, misused the religion and practiced many things which are not Islamic, both in form and content. It used Islam as a cover and disguise for its own purposes.

Women in Islam

The role and position of women in Islam received the same kind of treatment as Islam's martial character. The combination of misinformation and lack of balance contribute to fostering the notion that Islam puts women firmly in a second-class position.

Several texts contrasted the position of men and women in Islam in the most radical terms. One focused on the promise of an afterlife, explaining, "He (Mohammed) promised male Muslims a wonderful life after death. They shall lay back on jeweled couches . . ., there shall wait on them immortal youth with bowls and a cup of purest wine. . .They shall be served fruit of their own choice and fresh fowls that they can relish. Women, however, could not look forward to a life after death. They were believed to lack souls."[21] Another text emphasized women's unequal

---

[20] R.V. Strowski, p. 190.
[21] Lindner, et. al., pp. 139-140.

treatment in the family. It mentioned that, "Islamic law teaches that women should serve and obey their husbands and their fathers. . .Muslim law said that they could never show their faces to strange men. Even at home, they had to hide their faces when guests came. Women might cook and serve a great feast for guests. However, they could not share it. Women and girls had to eat what was left after the men and boys had eaten. Sons were taught that their mother's main duty was to serve them. Daughters were not even counted among a father's children."[22]

The authors of these textbooks have given only the most simplistic explanation for the role of women in Islam and, at the same time, have failed to establish the status of women in a historical context. They did not bother to tell their readers that the position of women in Islam has improved enormously compared to the period before the emergence of Islam. Historians tell us that women in pre-Islamic Arabia were considered by men as accessories and possessions that could be bought, sold and inherited. Islam, on the other hand, granted a woman the right to possess and dispose of property as she wished, to keep her name after marriage, and to become a guardian over minors, as well as the right to undertake a trade or profession, and to sue others in court without having to secure her husband's approval. Regarding Islamic teaching on life after death, both sexes are entitled to go to heaven, if their deeds while on earth are in conformity with the principles of Islam. Rewards and punishments are meted out not on the basis of the sex of the individual, but rather according to the degree of piety and their conformity to the principle and spirit of Islam.

The Crusades

As with earlier textbooks, most texts published since 1975 do not blame the Arab Muslims for the Crusades, but rather the Seljuk Turks who conquered the Holy Land and besieged the Christian pilgrims. One text specifically notes the difference between the Arabs and the Turks. It explains that, "In 640, the Arabs conquered Palestine. Although devout Muslims, the Arabs tolerated other religions. They allowed Christians to

---

[22] *Lands of the Middle East*, pp. 52-53.

continue making pilgrimages. . .The Seljuk Turks attacked Christian holy places, and robbed and enslaved Christian pilgrims."[23] Another text notes, "In 1071, the Seljuk Turks, a new wave of nomadic invaders only recently converted to Islam . . . began to hinder pilgrims to the holy land by asking for taxes and tolls."[24] Another text differentiated between the Muslim rulers of Palestine and the Turks. According to this text, "In the 7th century, the holy land fell into the hands of the Muslims. In general, Muslim rulers allowed Christian pilgrims to come and go as they wished. The Turks were not tolerant to Christianity. Pilgrims returning to Western Europe told stories of Christians who had been killed or tortured by the Turks. They also claimed that Christian churches were being destroyed or turned into Moslem places of worship."[25]

Miscellaneous

Several textbooks, like the earlier ones, reported other miscellaneous, inaccurate and misleading statements about Islam. One text mentioned that, "Devout Muslims pray five times a day. For six days of the week, they pray wherever they are, at home, work, school or play. But on Friday, they pray in a Mosque."[26] The author gives a somewhat misleading impression. A Muslim can pray anywhere he wants, including on Friday. The only requirement for group prayer is for male Muslims to pray at noon at the Mosque on Friday. The same author noted that, "Ramadan is the month in which Mohammed was born, received his revelation from Allah, made the Hejira from Mecca to Medina and died."[27] With the exception of the revelation, which was first received during Ramadan, the rest of the statement is totally false. Mohammed was born in Rabih-Awal and his hejira took place during Muharram, and he died during Rabih-Awal. Finally, another text reports that Mohammed was "the sixth and last" of the prophets.[28] This is also false. The Quran mentioned 22 prophets chosen by God before Mohammed.

---

[23] Lindner, et. al., p. 180.
[24] R. Ostrowski, p. 305.
[25] A. Kownslar, p. 209.
[26] Lindner, et. al., p. 41.
[27] Ibid.
[28] R. Ostrowski, p. 286.

Conclusion

This study of world history and social science textbooks published since 1975 and used throughout the United States reveals very little improvement over earlier texts in their coverage of Islam. Practically all the texts surveyed contained information on a number of aspects of Islam which was misleading. The explanations incorporated material which was incomplete, taken out of context, irrelevant or badly presented. In this manner, all texts contributed to the creation of a negative image of Islam. Moreover, the new texts reprinted, in one form or another, biased material which had been included in earlier texts, thereby perpetuating among another generation the negative stereotypes of Islam.

Without a concerted effort to correct the information disseminated in these textbooks future generations of students will grow up believing that Islam is a warlike religion in which women occupy a position of servitude. The following recommendations and suggestions are included to improve the coverage of Islam and create the conditions for an objective study of Islamic faith and civilization.

Firstly, regular studies of the image of Islam in American school texts, grades K-12, should be conducted for many years in order to provide educators with a continuous flow of data about the kind of information disseminated in textbooks and to establish a set of criteria by which a change in the information may be detected and measured. Secondly, all those concerned with the image of Islam created in the schools should organize pressure groups, urging local schools and Boards of Education to use textbooks that offer a balanced presentation of Islam and encouraging publishers to improve their material accordingly. Thirdly, seminars, symposia and conferences should be organized to sensitize teachers and others to the facts about Islam. Fourthly, additional materials should be made available to students and teachers to balance the information disseminated in textbooks. For example, a handy, easy-to-use dictionary on Islam, written in concise, readily understandable language, and including references for further study, would provide a source against which students and teachers could compare the materials published in texts. Finally, Muslim communities throughout the United States should develop outreach programs to local schools and other community groups, including a bureau of people available to speak on Islam. The bureau should consist of people who can communicate with students effectively in order to achieve the best results.

These are just a few suggestions for ways in which individuals and groups can work to change the image of Islam that has developed in the

United States. Although the task is urgent, it can be accomplished even if only some of these ideas are carried out.

30

THE TREATMENT OF ARABS IN U.S. SOCIAL STUDIES TEXTBOOKS: RESEARCH FINDINGS AND RECOMMENDATIONS

Samir Ahmad Jarrar

Dr. Jarrar has served as an educational consultant to the World Bank. He is the co-author of Education in the Arab World *(Praeger).*

The exposure of Americans to other cultures and people is derived mainly from two sources: mass media and books. The role of media in forming images and value judgments about people is duly discussed in this book. The media have been trying to do a better job of reporting through an attempt at objectivity and evenhandedness in their portrayal of other people and cultures, but in many instances reporters have fallen short of achieving these objectives. One of the causes of misrepresentation or misinterpretation of societies may be found in the images, stereotypes and value judgments that the media people form during their school years.

This chapter will examine the manner in which the Arab is represented in secondary schools' social science textbooks used in the United States. While reviewing the main studies that have been conducted in the last two decades on the representation of the Arab in textbooks, we will examine the image of the Arab presented in the materials, as well as the value judgments made about the Arabs.

Traditionally, books have been used as major tools of influence in the study of cultures. Images of other cultures which students receive from books are symbolic representations. They serve three basic functions:

1. Images serve as a means of object appraisal. The manner by which students acquire knowledge orders the physical world external to their persons.

2. Images mediate the interactions students have with others by providing a shared view of classes or persons so that each newly encountered individual is not entirely a unique experience.

3. Images provide a means of internalization since they provide a way for students to deal with inner tensions through displacement and the projection of negative feelings onto others.[1]

Books, as formal means of learning about other cultures, play a distinctive role in forming images of other cultures. If images presented are misleading or misrepresentative, then attitudes developed and actions taken toward other cultures will be faulty to the degree presented. Images contribute to an imbalanced and inaccurate picture of a people, because they are familiar indicators which are seized upon without an attempt to look further for the obscured realities.[2]

Few studies have been conducted in the United States and Canada dealing with the images of Arabs in textbooks. The first was a master's thesis entitled "Misconceptions in the Treatment of the Arab World in Selected American Textbooks for Children" (A. Alami 1957). For her study Alami sent questionnaires to 175 teachers in 20 school systems in northeastern Ohio in an attempt to determine "how important the textbook is in providing the basic information about the Arabs" (p. 115). Ninety-seven percent of the teachers stated that they used only textbooks in teaching about the Arabs. This finding supports the assumption that textbooks are one of the major resources in learning about the Arabs.

Alami then analyzed 58 textbooks that were used in the elementary and junior high schools (K-9). Her findings revealed that the textbooks studied had misconceptions about the Arabs and their culture. This was due to:

1. Inaccurate statements.
2. Misleading statements.
3. Incomplete statements which led, at times, to wrong impressions.

---

[1] E. L. Simpson, "An End to Ethnocentrism: A Bilateral Model for Training in Intercultural Studies," *Notre Dame Journal of Education*, 1972, 3, pp. 219-234.

[2] C. A. Lydon, "American Images of the Arabs." *Mid-East*, May-June 1969.

4. Omissions of important facts about the Arabs and about famous characters in Arab history.

5. Information that in many cases was not brought up-to-date in new editions of textbooks (p. 117).

Alami's study revealed that the treatment of the nomadic life of the Bedouins dominated the textual as well as photographic presentation of the Arabs. The textbooks studied overemphasized the backwardness of the city and village life, stressing the primitive conditions of farming and farm life. When describing Islam, textbooks totally neglected the main aspects of this monotheistic religion. Distortions prevailed in other presentations and discussions relevant to the Palestinian question, education, Arab nationalism and other topics.

The findings of Alami were reinforced by M. Suleiman's 1974 study, "The Middle East in American High School Curricula, a Kansas Case Study." Research conducted by Suleiman revealed that the Middle East, the homeland of the Arabs, was a "terra incognita" to 66 percent of the teachers who answered his questionnaire. Sixty-three percent of the teachers felt unqualified or inadequately prepared to teach about the area. When teachers were asked to evaluate the textbook treatment of various peoples of the Middle East, only ten percent of them felt that the textbooks provided a generally favorable treatment of Muslims, Egyptians, Palestinians, and somewhat less for Iranians, Turks and Arabs in general. The study states that the "Turks, Egyptians, and Arabs are the Middle East groups most often associated with negative characteristics!" (p. 11).

The study of the images of Arabs in textbooks reached the national scene when the Middle East Studies Association (MESA) established the "Committee on the Middle East Image in Secondary Schools." The review of the books was done by the eight members of the committee chaired by F. Ziadeh. In the 1973 annual convention of MESA a report on the results of the evaluation was presented.[3] The committee found some "well-written, thoroughly researched textbooks with few discernible faults." However, the majority of the books evaluated "erred in content, perpetuated stereotypes in political and social description, oversimplified

---

[3] W. Griswold, et. al., *The Image of Middle East in Secondary School Textbooks.* New York: Middle East Studies Association of North America, 1975.

383

complicated issues, listed outcomes while ignoring causes, and provided moral judgment on the actions of nations in the guise of factual history."[4] Summarizing the findings of the report we see that textbooks:

1. Overstressed some aspects of life and culture in the Middle East, such as nomads, often with photographs supporting a stereotype of the area.

2. Overemphasized the poverty of the tenant farmers, ignoring efforts to reclaim land and desert.

3. Ignored the similarities of Islam and other monotheistic religions that flourished in the area, namely Christianity and Judaism. Strangeness and peculiarities of certain practices were stressed.

4. The negative nature of Arab nationalism is stressed. U.S. difficulties in the area are attributed to this as well as the Arabs' hostility toward Israel. The reader rarely finds any glimpses of the Palestinians' or the Arabs' point of view, while the Israeli point of view is presented.

Two studies by members of the MESA committee were presented separately in 1974. The first was on "American Images of the Arab in Elementary and Junior High Schools' Social Science Textbooks." This study by Al-Qazzaz covered 27 books in the state of California looking at images of Arabs focusing on nomadism, Islam and the Arab-Israeli conflict with special emphasis on: pictures and maps; adjectives used to characterize the Arab; inaccurate, distorted and false information; omission of information that gives a positive view of the Arabs. The study found that the treatment of nomads was overemphasized, with coverage exceeding any other topic in or about the Arab world. As usual, the negative aspects of nomads were in the forefront.

As for Islam, aside from the basic pillars of the religion that were presented, little was mentioned about its contribution to world civilization. The presentation of the Arab-Israeli conflict was unbalanced, favoring the Israeli point of view. Matter-of-fact coverage and space given to the State of Israel in many books was more than that given to the 21 Arab countries.[5]

Al-Qazzaz with Afifi ad Shabbas conducted a second study on "Arabs in American Textbooks," that reviewed 24 textbooks in the state of

---

[4] W. Griswold, op. cit., p. 2.

[5] A. Al-Qazzaz, "Images of the Arabs in American Social Science Textbooks," in Abu-Laban, et. al., *Arabs in America*, Wilmette, IL: The Medina University Press International, 1975. pp. 113-132.

California. In this study the status of women in the Arab world, nomadism, Islam and the Arab-Israeli conflict were examined. The findings reaffirmed the regular stereotypes of the Arabs. As for women, they were portrayed as veiled objects with no rights or decision-making power, their education hampered by obstacles.[6]

The faulty images of the Arabs and their culture, as well as Islam, was not unique to their treatment in U.S. social studies textbooks. L. K. Kenny, in a study of 70 textbooks used in Canada, found that the coverage of the Middle East is "narrow, parochial, and western oriented." The study focused on history and geography textbooks. The treatment of Islam in the history texts contributed to the perpetuation of fundamental misconceptions about Islam as a religion, culture and civilization. Many factual errors, questionable assertions and omissions helped in reinforcing the negative image. Islamic contributions to world civilization are either briefly discussed or totally overlooked.

The Canadian geography textbooks reviewed by Kenny shared the same problems found in the American counterparts, namely, overstressing the nomadic aspect of life and rarely presenting urbanization and the vast advances. Kenny's study noted that authors by and large have not kept up with demographic, social and economic changes taking place in the Middle East.[7]

In 1975 two main studies used content analysis to examine textbooks in American high schools. These studies were among the most systematic approaches that dealt with the stereotyping of the Arabs and their images. The first was conducted by Perry, "Treatment of the Middle East in American High School Textbooks,"[8] and the second by Jarrar, "Images of the Arabs in the United States Secondary School Social Studies Textbooks: A Content Analysis and Unit Development."[9]

---

[6] A. Al-Qazzaz, et. al., *The Arab World: A Handbook for Teachers*, San Francisco: Tasco Press, 1978.

[7] L. K. Kenny, "The Middle East in Canadian Social Science Textbooks," in Abu-Laban, et. al., *Arabs in America*, op. cit., pp. 133-148.

[8] G. Perry, "Treatment of the Middle East in American High School Textbooks," *Journal of Palestine Studies*, vol. IV, No. 3, April 1975, pp. 46-58.

[9] S. A. Jarrar, *Images of the Arabs in the United States Secondary Schools Social Studies Textbooks: A Content Analysis and Unit Development*. Unpublished Ph.D. Dissertation, Florida State University, 1976.

Perry content-analyzed 20 textbooks used in American schools. His findings revealed the following main issues:

1. Most texts analyzed use the terms Arab and Muslim interchangeably.

2. Islam as a religion and a way of life is confused in the presentations of the authors of these texts.

3. Nomadism is highly visible in the discussions regarding the Arab world, giving the wrong impression that it is the dominant way of life in the area.

4. The Arab-Israeli conflict discussed in most of the textbooks reviewed is presented with a bias toward the Israeli point of view; in fact 11 texts were considered biased, while only five were considered as "somewhat objective."

In studying the images of the Arabs in U.S. secondary school social studies textbooks, Jarrar identified the 43 most used textbooks in four areas of the social sciences: world history, geography and world affairs, problems of American democracy and social studies. He examined the manner in which the Arab is represented. His study sought to find how dominant social studies textbooks do represent the Arab culture, what is the image of the Arab presented in the materials and what value judgments are made about the Arabs.

To evaluate the coverage of the Arab in social studies textbooks the author used the Evaluation Coefficient Analysis (ECO Analysis) developed by Pratt.[10] This instrument is designed to provide valid and reliable quantitative measurement of value judgments about minority groups in textbooks. A basic assumption here is that attitudes are communicated in textbooks to a large extent through the value judgments which are expressed. The evaluative term is the unit of analysis; these terms are words which express favorable or unfavorable value judgments. Evaluative terms are normally adjectives but could also be adverbs, nouns or verbs.

After listing the evaluative terms used to describe Arabs throughout the textbook being analyzed, a calculation was made of the percentage of the evaluative terms that were favorable as against evaluative terms that were unfavorable. A coefficient score between 0.0 (totally unfavorable) and 100.0 (totally favorable) indicated the textbook's attitudinal position about

---

[10] D. Pratt, *How to Find and Measure Bias in Textbooks*. Englewood Cliffs, New Jersey: Educational Technology Publications, 1972.

the Arab on a favorable-unfavorable continuum, with 50.0 representing a point of neutrality or ambivalence.

The ECO Analysis does not examine all the components of the textbooks, such as inaccuracies, omissions and biased illustrations. To cover this and other qualitative areas Jarrar developed an eight factor "Evaluation Criteria Checklist."[11] This checklist includes the following items: 1. Inclusion; 2. Validity; 3. Balance; 4. Comprehensiveness; 5. Concreteness; 6. Unity; 7. Realism; 8. Miscellaneous. Under miscellaneous the following aspects were checked: (a) The consistency of the information presented; (b) The clarity and lack of ambiguity of the presentation; (c) The use of the out-of-context statements; (d) Any misleading statements.

The qualitative as well as the quantitative analyses were performed by Jarrar and an independent judge, Dr. V. Pantelidis, an American professor, to insure the objectivity of the study.

The ECO Analysis revealed that more negative terms are commonly used to describe the Arabs and their culture. This could be clearly seen from the combined coefficient of 25.5 for all the reviewed textbooks. One can easily conclude that the authors' attitudinal position toward the Arabs and the Arab world was *unfavorable* on the favorable-unfavorable continuum.[12]

Among the four areas of the social sciences studied, the treatment of the Arabs was most unfavorable in the geography textbooks, with a coefficient of 17.7. World history textbooks have a coefficient of 23.7, while problems of American democracy texts had a coefficient of 31.8. The social studies textbooks with a coefficient of 32.8 were the least unfavorable, but still on the negative side of the continuum.

Using the "Evaluation Criteria Checklist," Jarrar found that deficiencies in describing Arabs and the Arab world were displayed not only in the evaluative terms used, but also in the overall material presented. Results of the study clearly demonstrate that the image of the Arab as presented in social studies textbooks is very cursory, and more negative than positive. This negative image is caused by a number of factors which include such things as omissions, stereotypes, over-generalizations, and lack of balance in presenting the materials. The Arab is portrayed as primitive, backward,

---

[11] S. A. Jarrar op. cit., p. 48.
[12] Ibid., p. 149.

desert dwelling, nomadic, war loving, terroristic and full of hatred. The Arab world is most often depicted as an area of desert and oil, lacking modernization, united in its hatred of Israel. The evaluation of the 43 most used textbooks revealed that authors have not kept up with economic, social and demographic changes that are taking place in the Arab world. This shows why what is often described is not only untruthful, but is an "unrepresentative truth." What all this leads to in the final analysis is a lack of thorough knowledge and understanding of the Arabs and their life. The materials produced were found to be loaded with half truths, unrepresentative cases and outdated information.

In 1980 the National Association of Arab-Americans (NAAA) sponsored a study of textbooks entitled "Treatment of the Arab World and Islam in Washington Metropolitan Area Junior and Senior Textbooks."[13] Eighteen textbooks were surveyed by a nine-member evaluation committee. Nine subjects were chosen for evaluation: culture, economy, political factors, religion, Arab characteristics, ancient history, women, Arab-Israeli conflict and geography. The study used a "scale in conjunction with a context analysis to measure bias, stereotype, and balance."[14] The study identified five areas to which educators should be sensitive when using the materials surveyed:

1. Arab culture and history are frequently measured (and therefore found wanting) by Western standards.

2. Information is often out-of-date or inaccurate.

3. Negative stereotyping, including value-laden language, is frequently employed to describe Arab culture and characteristics.

4. Exposition of the Arab-Israeli conflict often comes out as Arab = bad, Israeli = good.

5. Islam often fails to receive its due as one of the world's largest monotheistic religions.

The NAAA study reached the following conclusions vis-a-vis the reviewed books:

1. Fifteen percent of the material reviewed could be highly recommended. This covers one textbook and two supplemental resource units.

---

[13] NAAA, *Treatment of the Arab World and Islam in Washington Metropolitan Area Junior and Senior Textbooks,* Washington, D.C., 1980.

[14] D. Jacobs, "Teaching the Arab World, Evaluating Textbooks," *The Social Studies,* vol. 72, no. 4, July/August, 1981, p. 150.

2. Thirty percent of the books surveyed needed revisions or supplementary materials in certain areas.

3. Fifty percent of the textbooks reviewed were of such poor quality that they could not "in good conscience" be recommended for teaching about the area.[15]

The findings of the NAAA study are consistent with the previous studies of the images of the Arabs in textbooks all over the country. The problem raised, however, is multifold:

1. The image of the Arab and the Arab world presented in secondary school textbooks is negative in nature, due to many factors such as omissions, stereotypes, over–generalities and lack of balance in the presentation.

2. In spite of the movement in the 1970s to remedy the stereotypes, biases and negative value judgments in textbooks by the revisions of sexist representations and biases as well as in role models attributed to certain ethnic or minority groups, not much has changed vis-a-vis the image of the Arab.

The results of all the studies suggest, as Jarrar (1976) noted:

> ". . .all the textbooks studied were disparaging, denigrating, or condescending towards the Arabs and the Arab world. . . .the treatment of the Arabs in the reviewed textbooks was, to some extent, either 'progress-oriented,' exalting the importance of novelty and denigrating tradition, or actually 'ethnocentric,' measuring and evaluating the Arabs by western standards. In discussing traditions, authors were found to have either ignored them or juxtaposed them with modernization, leading to a belief that these concepts oppose each other. What added to the negative image presented is the rarity with which observed deficiencies and misrepresentative truths were balanced by fair presentations of recent achievements and the rich cultural heritage that the Arabs share with the rest of the world."[17]

The task of improving the common perceptions and knowledge of other people and cultures and bringing them to parity with the multicultural society of contemporary America is imperative. Attempts at producing a better presentation and understanding of the Arab and the Arab world have started. The following is a list of recommended works that could be

---

[15] NAAA, op. cit., pp. 2-3.

389

used as resources and reference texts when teaching about the Arabs in secondary schools:

1. H. S. Haddad and B. K. Nijim, *The Arab World: A Handbook*, Wilmette, Illinois: Medina University Press, 1978.

2. A. Al-Qazzaz, et. al., *The Arab World: A Handbook for Teachers*, San Francisco: Tasco Press, 1978.

3. M. A. Farah, et. al., *Teacher's Guide, Global Insights: People and Cultures*, Columbus, Ohio: Charles Merill Co., 1980.

4. J. Friedlander, ed., *The Middle East: The Image and the Reality*, Los Angeles, California: University of California, 1980.

5. J. Will Soghikian, *Lands, Peoples and Communities of the Middle East*, Middle East Gateway Series, Waverley, Massachusetts, 1980.

6. B. G. Massialas and S. A. Jarrar, eds., "The Arab World," *The Social Studies*, vol. 72, no. 4, July/August 1981.

The studies of the images of the Arabs in the U.S. social studies textbooks and the findings to which they led point to the following recommendations:

1. Very little information and coverage regarding the Arab world is found in textbooks. The need is for more information so that a balanced treatment is implemented into social studies textbooks.

2. Information presented about the Arab world should be based on reliable sources, and not on biased national interpretations.

3. Primary sources and data provided by international organizations such as the United Nations and its agencies as well as scholarly organizations such as the Middle East Institute, the Association of Arab-American University Graduates, the Middle East Studies Association and the Institute of Arab Studies should be utilized.

4. Textbook publishers and authors should use area specialists in systematically revising and evaluating existing materials or releasing new textbooks, making sure that present-day situations and contemporary developments in the Arab world are emphasized beside the historical events.

5. The treatment of the Arabs in textbooks should be directed toward the developmental strides taking place in the area, moving away from the traditional emphasis on primitive, nomadic and early agricultural life styles.

31

CANADIAN MASS MEDIA AND THE MIDDLE EAST

Thomas Naylor

Dr. Naylor is a Professor of Economics at McGill University, Montreal, Canada. He has written on Middle East affairs for numerous publications.

I t has become a truism that, with the reactivation of the Cold War and the escalation of the nuclear arms race, the 1980s will be the most dangerous decade in human history. Political flashpoints abound in the contemporary world. But of the multitude of trouble spots, actual and potential, it will not be Namibia or El Salvador and certainly not the Falkland Islands that will cause the great powers to push the nuclear button and incinerate the human race. The area that holds the greatest danger for this decade is precisely that which has held the greatest danger for the last three—the Middle East. Yet despite the evident danger to mankind's survival, and despite the massive outpouring through every conceivable medium of words ostensibly dealing with the situation in the Middle East, the level of public ignorance in North America of the true origins and actual dimensions of the problem remains appalling. Myth-information controls the public consciousness, thus precluding rational discussion and political mobilization within North America around precisely the foreign policy issue that most demands rational discussion and political mobilization. The responsibility for perpetuating this sorry and dangerous state of affairs rests with the North American mass media, whose portrayal of the region and its political problems has been nothing short of scandalous.

The task of offsetting and, eventually, reversing the damage done to the public interest by the North American mass media is enormous and urgent. It is rendered all the more difficult, but not for that reason less urgent, when the broader social and cultural factors conditioning public understanding, or misunderstanding, of the Middle East are taken into account. The central issue in the political upheavals that have torn apart Middle East societies and brought the world to the brink of superpower conflict time after time since the Second World War is the question of Palestine. But the North American public rarely perceives the moral or political necessity of a resolution of the question of Palestine. Even more rarely does it see the outrages being committed daily against the people of Palestine, and the denial of their human and national rights, as worthy objects of their concern. It is *not* just a lack of factual information, though that is bad enough. For so thoroughly is public opinion in North America conditioned, that even if the flow of hard facts through the mass media could be enhanced, the initial results would be marginal. Incidents and developments that would produce mass moral outrage if perpetrated anywhere else in the world against any other people bring a shrug of indifference in North America when directed against Palestinians. This bizarre situation exists because the question of Palestine has been caught up inextricably in the North American consciousness with a complex of three powerful attitudes that influence public opinion.

First, the most general, is that the United States and Canada are "new" societies of European settlement, with a "cowboy and Indian" opposition deeply instilled in the public mind by films, folklore, fables and history books. The result is an intrinsic propensity to sympathize with parallel situations where white settler civilization is seen as pitted against the "natives" in its struggle to tame the wilderness or make the deserts bloom.

The second, and more particular, is the historical antipathy of the Occident to the Orient, a factor often overlooked in the past decade when the global conflict paradigm was perceived more in terms of North versus South. But the conflict of Occident and Orient is even more powerful, rooted as it is in several centuries of historical experience. To understand this phenomenon, it is important not to lose sight of the degree to which the cultural and commercial advance of the West since the Renaissance was conceived in emulation of the East, and put into practice in opposition to it. Given the long history of political, economic and indeed military conflict, the West has always had its Islamic "bad guy" to color popular culture—be he Salah Ad-Din throwing the Crusaders out of Palestine, the Ottoman Sultan Suleiman, banging on the gates of Vienna, a Barbary pirate chasing English and French ships out of the Mediterranean, an "oil sheikh" brandishing the so-called "oil weapon," or, as the culmination and personification of the Western world's current prejudices and fears, the image of a Palestinian guerrilla, wrapped in his kaffiyeh, with Kalishnikov in hand, threatening to bring international civil aviation to a standstill. Thus the Palestinians are, on one level, simply the latest of a long series of victims of a process of racial and religious vilification in the West that has deep historical roots.

The third major attitude influencing North American perceptions of the Middle East is the resurgent Cold War hysteria, which has recently taken an especially insane dimension with the enunciation of the doctrine of limited nuclear war. A Cold War consciousness is a particularly powerful component of the North American mass culture. Hence the perception of the importance of the strategic alliance of the United States with Israel as an instrument for containing the spread of Soviet influence. It suffices often just to *assert* that an independent Palestinian state would be a satellite of the Soviet Union, and the principle of self-determination of nations, for which American leaders have always professed to stand, is put on the political back burner. Thus Palestine is, or at least has become, in a sense, simply another tool in the game of nations in which morality is always shunted aside when it conflicts, as it usually does, with the demands of global Realpolitik.

The result of these three conditioning influences—the latent, and often overt, racism of North American popular culture; the legacy of centuries of fear of and hostility to Islam and the Arab world; and the politics of superpower hegemony—in conjunction with a flagrantly biased media coverage is to convey to the average North American an image of "Arab Terrorism and Islamic Fanaticism," usually depicted as marching arm in arm with the International Communist Conspiracy, on a Jihad intent on destroying the moral and economic foundations of some imaginary construct called "Judeo-Christian Civilization." This is what the North American mass media would call "news."

To understand the North American attitude toward Palestinians and their struggle, it is necessary to look far beyond the question of Palestine. For the antipathy of the North American to the Palestinian is simply a variant of the general hostility toward the Arab world at large and to Islam beyond. Despite the fact that a substantial and disproportionately influential minority of Palestinians are Christians and despite the fact that the Palestinian national movement is a profoundly *secular* one, North American attitudes toward Palestinians cannot be disassociated from mass media misinterpretations of the Islamic revival. Indeed they cannot even be disassociated from attitudes toward Iran, which is taken to embody the quintessence of the Islamic resurgence and the dangers it supposedly poses to "Judeo-Christian Civilization." Hence the mass media invention of links between the Palestinian national movement and the Iranian revolution, with a view to discrediting both. To take but one example, the Canadian Television (CTV) national news picked an auspicious day on which to perpetrate the fable that the Popular and Democratic Front for the Liberation of Palestine was in some way responsible for the takeover of the American Embassy in Teheran. Citing an impeccably objective source, the CIA, it made the announcement on the very day the United Nations had declared a day of international solidarity with the Palestinian people. Needless to say, that latter piece of information was *not* reported.

The upshot is that the image of Islam as portrayed by the Canadian mass media and as perceived by the Canadian public is vital to shaping Canada's public consciousness of the question of Palestine. The image of Islam as portrayed by the Canadian mass media has three aspects: the image of the Muslim, particularly the Shi'a, as a religious fanatic; the association of Islam with violence; and the link between religious belief and an alleged desire for a return to medieval social and economic conditions. These themes have been reiterated frequently by the Canadian mass media in lieu of actual political analysis and factual reporting.

A favorite exercise of the North American mass media is the association of Islam with the dual themes of fanaticism and violence. Thus, CTV, Canada's largest private network, on its national news on October 25, 1981, following the Sadat assassination—which it imputed solely to religious fanaticism on the part of his opponents—actually described running gun battles in Cairo between police and a phenomenon it described as "underground Muslims." As to just what bizarre species of creature this would be, CTV never enlightened the audience, leaving them with the impression that it was somewhat akin to an idolatrous troglodyte. Another example of sensationalism by the media occurred when Canada's largest circulation daily newspaper, *The Toronto Star* (October 10, 1980), displayed a photograph of a military firing squad in Mauritania executing a convicted murderer, with the boldfaced caption proclaiming it as an example of "Islamic Justice." Now apart from the obvious question of whether this man's execution was decided upon in accordance with Mauritanian law, one is inclined to ask whether the *Star*, or any other North American newspaper, reporting the execution of convicted murderer Gary Gilmore, by firing squad, in Utah a few years ago, would have portrayed it as an example of "Christian Justice"?

A third theme much beloved and belabored by the mass media is the alleged desire in Islamic societies for a return to "medieval" social conditions as the intensity of religious belief grows. Yet if the authors of such caricatures had bothered to take the elementary precaution of examining the policy program of the Egyptian Muslim Brotherhood, for example, they would have discovered, among other things, a call for: the nationalization of natural resources, the elimination of control by foreign capital, redistribution of land, comprehensive social insurance, encouragement of industrial growth based on local raw materials and craft traditions, and compulsory trade unionization. One can call such a policy program a lot of things; but "medieval" is certainly not one of them.

Why then the characterization of the Islamic revival as a completely reactionary social movement? The obvious reason is that religious stereotyping is a handy substitute for the much harder job of factual reporting and careful political analysis, for these require knowledge, a scarce commodity among North American mass media pundits. Hence the reporters and producers look for quick explanations that are compatible with their own personal biases and the meager state of their own knowledge. And blaming the quaint, superstitious rites of the natives is a safe formula for guaranteeing high profile exposure without the need to actually explain the phenomena under scrutiny.

In fact the phenomenon of the Islamic revival is readily comprehensible to the Occidental mind if it is explained in terms of parallels to the West's own historical development. The notion of separation of Church and State, popularly regarded as unknown in the "medieval" East, is in fact a very recent and far from complete phenomenon in the modern West.

A similar process of racial and religious stereotyping underlies the mass media's treatment of the Arab world. Major concepts reiterated time after time in the media are the backwardness of the region, the untrustworthiness of its peoples, oil as the new Holy Sepulcher to be wrested from the control of unscrupulous Orientals, and the innate propensity of the Arab, particularly the Palestinian, to commit acts of "terrorism."

Thus on October 18, 1979, in its series of programs on the world's great cities, the Canadian Broadcasting Corporation (CBC) ran a special show on Jerusalem. It was run in prime time at a period when Canada's own foreign policy on the Jerusalem question was being subjected to serious diplomatic and political scrutiny. It was made in Israel without consultation with a single Christian or Muslim organization. It harangued the viewer incessantly about the "Jewish" character of the city, making one condescending reference to Christianity and none at all to Islam. And it punctuated the diatribe by showing Palestinians in only two guises—as street vendors or donkey riders.

Another interesting example was CTV's coverage of the death of Marshall Tito on its national news. The news commentary described Tito as the man who, along with India's Prime Minister Nehru, founded the Non-Aligned Movement. A picture of the founding conference was shown in which all *three* of the founding fathers of the Non-Aligned Movement were shown seated around the table. President Nasser was never identified by name, and few viewers would have recognized his picture.

A second concept harped on in the mass media is the Western world's supposed vulnerability to the use of the so-called oil weapon. Ask the man on the street in Canada and he will likely inform you, on the basis of what he has learned from newspapers and television, that OPEC is an organization of Arab oil sheikhs (necessarily mispronounced), the members of which divide their time between plotting gasoline price hikes and gambling away their ill-gotten gains from Western motorists in the casinos of Monte Carlo.

Take for example a feature article on the front page of the Weekly Review section of the *Gazette*, the sole English language daily in Montreal. To assure its readers of factual accuracy and knowledgeability, the *Gazette* (June 23, 1979) commissioned a special article called "The Great Oil Robbery" written by the well-known Middle East expert, Jon Kimche. The gist of this article was that the world is awash with oil and that high prices were simply a tool for diabolical foreign policy intentions by wily Orientals.

Parenthetically one might point out that the CBC and the Montreal *Gazette* make frequent use of Kimche's peculiar talents as a political commentator, parroting and publishing his most ridiculous propositions including the theory that at one point the presidents of Iraq, Libya and Algeria conspired with international terrorists to arrange the kidnapping of their own oil ministers (*As It Happens*, CBC Radio, 22 January 1976). This and numerous other fables of Kimche's authorship are printed or broadcast without any attempt to identify him as the former editor of *The Jewish Observer* or, at most, the brother of an under secretary in the Israeli government's foreign ministry, which identifications might imply to the reader or listener that perhaps this "expert" has his own political axes to grind. The situation is bad enough when Kimche is presented as an authoritative political commentator. But the situation becomes intolerable when a supposedly respectable newspaper gives Kimche front-page space to comment on the complex and technical world of oil. To put it simply, Jon Kimche is not a specialist on oil.

Underneath the multitude of mass media myth-representations on the oil question are three implicit assumptions. One is that oil, unlike any other commodity in the world in limited supply, should not rise in price in the face of general inflation of demand and prices. The second is that Middle East oil is "ours"; i.e., that it is the legitimate right of the West to plunder the non-renewable resources of the Middle East at will, and that any efforts by Middle East societies to conserve the supply of what is for the most part their only natural resource are intrinsically illegitimate and immoral. The third is that oil is the unfortunate preserve of the "Arabs," who being backward, do not need it, and being unscrupulous, should not control it. The fact that the majority of the population of the OPEC countries is not Arab would be a surprise to the average North American.

To illustrate the last point, take the caricature presented by columnist Barbara Amiel in Canada's national magazine, *MacLean's*. She actually described oil as "the stuff under the sand where the Arabs park their camels." That kind of racial stereotyping, typical too of the work of many Canadian cartoonists, would produce outrage in Canada, if not court proceedings, if it were applied to any other ethnic minority represented in the Canadian mosaic.

However, the two themes noted above (the retrograde and alien nature of Arab society and the West's vulnerability to an oil embargo) receive much less media attention and do much less harm than the media's exploitation of the third major theme in the coverage of the Arab world— the supposed propensity of Arabs, especially Palestinians, for acts of "terrorism." Indeed so often is the phrase "Arab terrorist" used on the airwaves and in the printed media that the two words comprising it have become not only inextricably linked, but virtually interchangeable in the public mind. To illustrate this process, take the example of a generally excellent anti-nuclear film by Canada's publicly owned National Film Board. In the film *No Act of God*, much stress is laid on the dangers of plutonium falling into the hands of terrorists. This is indeed a frightening possibility. Yet instead of mentioning any terrorist organization by name, the film followed up its warning about the dangers of terrorist acts by showing an Israeli soldier with gun in hand watching over a West Bank town; and the very next scene showed armed militiamen running loose through the streets of Beirut.

Apart from the obvious rebuttal—that the objective of the Palestinians is to return to their homeland, not to turn it into a radioactive cinder heap—one is entitled to ask, what became of the notion of "balance" and accuracy in the presentation of problems? There was no mention in the film of the facts that: Israel has the world's sixth largest nuclear arsenal, which lies in the control of the only formerly active terrorist to be freely elected to represent his people as head of state; the only documented case of state-sponsored theft of fissionable materials was conducted by the secret service of the same state; it is the only state in the Middle East with nuclear facilities to have refused to sign the Non-Proliferation Treaty, and; it is the only state, outside the two superpowers, to have actually and openly threatened its neighbors with nuclear incineration in order to achieve its political objectives.

To take another example, one in which some members of CBC take great pride, the Canadian publicly owned network on September 25, 1979, on its supposedly elite program of news and current affairs, *Fifth Estate*, presented an item entitled "The Russian Connection" that left informed observers of the Middle East to choose between laughter and tears. In this program, the PLO was presented as an organized network of "terrorists." There was no mention at all of the PLO's myriad of social, cultural and educational functions, of the schools and hospitals and refugee relief facilities that it operates. Furthermore, there was a patently preposterous effort to portray the PLO as an agent of Moscow—"Arab Terrorism and the International Communist Conspiracy" in league once more. And lest the final element in the holiness of mass media mythologizing about the Arab world be neglected, the program went on to portray the Lebanese Civil War (one of the most complex and multifaceted political phenomena of this century) as nothing more than a battle between "Palestinians" on the one hand, and "Christians" on the other. This, CBC afterwards protested, was merely balanced coverage.

Lest the CBC's main rival, CTV, feel discriminated against by omission, it should be noted that it too has proven itself more than equal to myth-informing the Canadian public's consciousness of the real situation. Thus, during the Eight Day War in southern Lebanon in 1978, CTV faithfully replayed an American network's coverage of Israeli mopping-up operations, culminating in an assault on a nest of "terrorists." The hiding place was surrounded by Israeli troops who called out to the "terrorists" to come out with their hands up. This was done not in Arabic, or in Hebrew, or even in French—but in English, while the obliging camera crew busied itself capturing the high drama for posterity. Out of his hiding place came one frightened-looking individual in civilian clothes—with no weapons of any sort, nor even holsters or ammunition belts—and he declared with evident fear "I'm Lebanese." Back to the CTV studio where the news commentator boldly announced the upshot of this operation, "two terrorists killed, one captured." The three "terrorists" in question turned out to be Beirut journalists, but no clarification or correction was ever forthcoming on CTV.

On one level these kinds of mistakes of fact, or deliberate lies as the case may be, are bemusing, and ample evidence of the abysmally low standards of either technical competence or professional integrity of Canadian journalists and their institutions. But on another level they are tragic and dangerous, for they contribute strongly to the general process of the dehumanization of the image of the Palestinian in the eyes of the North American public. In that way they serve to cover up for Israeli state terrorism aimed at the liquidation of the national existence, and indeed even the physical existence, of the Palestinian people. For when all is said and done, the PLO is not a *military* threat to Israel; it is a *political* threat. Hence the bulk of Israeli military action is directed against welfare facilities, administrative centers and refugee camps in an effort to destroy the PLO politically, while the mass media faithfully parrot the Israeli propaganda line that the objective of the napalm and cluster bombs is to stamp out "terrorist" activity.

Within the United States, the reasons for the perpetuation and intensification of traditional racial and religious stereotypes, and the resulting reinforcement of the public antipathy to Palestinians and lack of sympathy with their struggle to maintain and exercise their national and natural rights, are clear enough. They derive from the current conjuncture of interests between advocates of Cold War confrontation and apologists for political Zionism, working against a background of historical prejudice. Hence the happy consensus witnessed everyday among Hollywood studios, the major newspapers, the television networks and the New York literati and belletrists.

However, the reasons for the same process of racial and religious stereotyping taking place with the same intensity in Canada are not as immediately evident. Nonetheless a little reflection reveals four principal reasons for the mass media in Canada essentially hewing the same line as the American mass media. The obvious one is the presence in Canada, equally with the United States, of a very competent Israeli public relations machine, backed up by a well organized Zionist lobby—this in contrast to the uncoordinated and weakly financed nature of Arab efforts to present their point of view. But Zionism did not *invent* the biases evident in the mass media. Hence reasons for the Canadian mass media presenting such a distorted image must be sought in much deeper factors than simply the presence of an active and powerful lobby group.

One of the root causes of the Canadian conformity to the American perspective is that Canadians, pious disclaimers to the contrary notwithstanding, basically share the American "cowboy and Indian" view of the world, into which an image of Israel as the frontier of white civilization under siege by barbarian hordes neatly fits. Canada too shares the fundamental antipathy of the Occident to the Orient; for it was also a product of the European post-Renaissance efforts to break free of cultural and economic subordination to the Islamic world. Canadians equally share America's Cold War consciousness. For political consciousness ultimately derives from material circumstances, and Canadians certainly know on which side of the Iron Curtain their bread gets buttered.

Another reason for Canada's acquiescence in the American view of the world is that English-speaking Canada lacks a strong and coherent *national* culture of its own. Hence the country is extremely vulnerable to the influx of moral, political and cultural values from New York, Hollywood and the Pentagon, particularly when these three dominant ideological power centers in the United States find themselves in fundamental agreement, as they currently do with respect to the Middle East.

The fourth reason, closely related to the last two, lies in the actual organizational structure of the Canadian mass media and public information sources, which produces an enormous and direct dependence on American sources and therefore American points of view.

The French mass media in Canada are in a somewhat happier situation, not because of intrinsic merit so much as because the accidental effect of the language barrier is to divert their dependence on Agence France Presse and their reprints toward such sources as *Le Monde* which have a far better track record for fairness and accuracy than the American sources.

However, Canadian media's dependence on American sources is not absolute. The larger entities do maintain a roster of foreign news reporters and commentators of their own. But the results are scarcely encouraging. Reporters on foreign affairs assignments, reflecting the limited resources *and* limited importance attached to the job, are moved about quickly and forced to become instant experts, thus failing to build up the long-term experience and contacts necessary for accurate and intelligent reporting of various areas and diverse events. In Canada it is hard enough to find a journalist for a major English daily who speaks French, let alone Arabic, Farsi, or Urdu; and the first response of many to events such as the Soviet move into Afghanistan was likely to rush to their atlases to locate it.

Given the lack of depth of knowledge that structural constraints impose, reporting on the Middle East, if not elsewhere in the foreign arena, in the Canadian mass media reflects two influences. One is the underlying prejudice of the society as a whole, which journalists share and reflect. This manifests itself prominently in the moral hobby horse journalists love to ride in denouncing "Arab terrorism"—a direct consequence of their own fears about their own (real or imaginary) "anti-Semitism" which causes them to be constantly seeking and/or inventing, and then denouncing in others. The second major influence to which reporting is subject is commercial pressure on the mass media. For, after all is said and done, they are business enterprises, intent on maintaining or expanding their audiences in order to assure a flow of advertising revenue. That involves catering to the taste, or lack thereof, of the public. It also renders them vulnerable to economic pressures, carefully coordinated and selectively mounted. The result of all of these influences is the sensationalization and trivialization of the events and places being reported.

The situation with respect to the public consciousness of the Middle East in general, and the rights of the Palestinian people in particular, is clearly unacceptable on moral grounds alone. It is also extremely dangerous, given the distinct possibility that the next round of fighting in the Middle East, when Israel makes its move into southern Lebanon in an attempt to liquidate the Palestinian resistance and annex the territory, will degenerate into a direct superpower confrontation at a time when Cold War tensions are very much on the rise. Unfortunately in Canada attempts to force an awareness on the mass media of the harm being done and the dangers posed by their slanted coverage have been generally quite useless. That does *not* however constitute a discharge from social responsibilities. Those who *do* know what is really happening must continue to speak out in every available forum, to develop new mechanisms to bring the frightening reality to the general public, and to demand that the mass media correct the record. They must do so not merely out of a desire to assure the rights of the Palestinian people, though that is certainly reason enough, but also because everyone on earth has a stake in the outcome, which may well be no less than his or her own survival.

Dr. Edmund Ghareeb, a Ph.D. in history from Georgetown University, is a consultant for Middle Eastern and media affairs in Washington, D.C. He is a former correspondent for *Al-Ittihad* and *Emirates News of the U.A.E.* Dr. Ghareeb was a reporter and columnist for the *Beirut Daily Star* and a former assistant editor of the *Journal of Palestine Studies.* He is the author of *The Kurdish Question in Iraq,* Syracuse University Press, 1981 and co-editor and co-translator of *Enemy of the Sun: An Anthology of Arabic Poetry.* He contributed to the books *The Security of the Persian Gulf,* Croom Helm, 1981 and *The Arab Image in the Western Mass Media,* Outline Books, 1980. His articles, interviews and book reviews have appeared in Arab, American and European publications.